NORTHROP FRYE

Myth and Metaphor

Selected Essays, 1974–1988

Edited by Robert D. Denham

University Press of Virginia
Charlottesville and London

THE UNIVERSITY PRESS OF VIRGINIA
Copyright © 1990 by the Rector and Visitors
of the University of Virginia

First published 1990
Second paperback printing 1996

Library of Congress Cataloging-in-Publication Data

Frye, Northrop.
    Myth and Metaphor : selected essays, 1974–1988 / Northrop Frye ;
edited by Robert D. Denham.
        p.   cm.
    ISBN 0–8139–1261–X (cloth) ISBN 0–8139–1369–1 (paper)
    1. Literature—History and criticism.   I. Denham, Robert D.
    II. Title.
    PN45.F74   1990
    809—dc20   89–49172
                                                            CIP

Printed in the United States of America

FOR
Wayne C. Booth

Contents

Acknowledgments

✧

The provenance of each of the essays in this collection is given below, along with the publication data for the fifteen essays that have already appeared in print.

"The Koine of Myth: Myth as a Universally Intelligible Language." Originally presented as an address to the Society for Mediterranean Studies, University of Toronto, 4 October 1984. Previously unpublished.

"Literary and Linguistic Scholarship in a Postliterate World." Originally presented as an address at the annual meeting of the Modern Language Association, New York, 27 December 1983. Reprinted by permission of the Modern Language Association of America from *PMLA* 99 (Oct. 1984): 990–95.

"The Symbol as a Medium of Exchange." Originally presented as an address to the Royal Society of Canada, 26 October 1984. Published in *Symbols in Life and Art: The Royal Society of Canada Symposium in Memory of George Whalley,* ed. James A. Leith. McGill-Queen's Univ. Press, 1987. 3–16. Reprinted by permission.

"The Survival of Eros in Poetry." Originally presented as a lecture at the University of New Mexico, 16 February 1983. Reprinted from *Romanticism and Contemporary Criticism,* edited by Morris Eaves and Michael Fischer. Copyright © 1986 by Cornell University Press. Used by permission of the publisher.

"The View from Here." Originally presented as an address to the Victoria University Alumni, 12 April 1983. Previously unpublished.

"Framework and Assumption." Originally presented as a lecture at Smith College, 24 October 1985. Published in the *Northrop Frye Newsletter* 1, no. 1 (1988): 2–10. Reprinted by permission.

"The Dialectic of Belief and Vision." Originally presented as a lecture at the School of Continuing Studies, University of Toronto, 3 December 1985. Published in *Shenandoah* 39, no. 3 (1989):47–64.

"The Expanding World of Metaphor." Originally presented as an address to the annual meeting of the American Academy of Religion, Chicago, 8 December 1984. Published in the *Journal of the American Academy of Religion* 53 (Dec. 1985): 585–98. Reprinted by permission.

"The Responsibilities of the Critic." Originally presented as a lecture at Johns Hopkins University, 20 February 1976. Published in *MLN* 91 (Oct. 1976): 797–813. Reprinted by permission.

"Some Reflections on Life and Habit." Originally presented as the F. E. L. Priestley Memorial Lecture, University of Lethbridge, 17 February 1988. Published as a pamphlet by the University of Lethbridge, 1988, and reprinted in the *Northrop Frye Newsletter* 1, no 2. (Spring 1989): 1–9. Reprinted by permission.

"The Rhythms of Time." Originally presented at the Comparative Literature Colloquium on "Time and the Poetic Self" at the University of Toronto, 2 March 1974. Previously unpublished.

"Literature as a Critique of Pure Reason." Originally presented as the second of the 1982 Wiegand Lectures. Published in *Descant* 14 (Spring 1983): 7–21. Reprinted by permission.

"Literature and the Visual Arts." Originally presented as a paper at the Conference of the Associazione Internazionale per gli Studi di Lingua e Letteratura Italiana, Toronto, May 1985. This is the first English publication. Previously published in Italian as "La letteratura e la arti figurative," *Lettere Italiane* 3 (1985): 285–98. Reprinted by permission.

"The Stage Is All the World." Originally presented as a lecture at Stratford, Ontario, July 1985. Previously unpublished.

"The Journey as Metaphor." Originally presented as a lecture at the Applewood Centre, Toronto, 8 October 1985. Previously unpublished.

"The Double Mirror." Originally presented as an address at the Stated Meeting of the American Academy of Arts and Sciences, Cambridge, Mass., 9 December 1981. Published in the *Bulletin of the American Academy of Arts and Sciences* 35 (Dec. 1981): 32–41. Reprinted by permission.

"The Mythical Approach to Creation." Originally presented as a talk to the Canadian Theological Society at the meeting of the Learned Societies of Canada, Montreal, 4 June 1985. Previously unpublished.

Acknowledgments

"Crime and Sin in the Bible." Originally presented as an address to the Law Faculty, University of Toronto, 15 April 1986. Previously unpublished.

"Blake's Bible." Originally presented as an address to the St. James Piccadilly Blake Society, London, 2 June 1987. Previously unpublished.

"Natural and Revealed Communities." Originally presented as the Thomas More Lecture in the Humanities at the College of Holy Cross, Worcester, Mass., 22 April 1987. Previously unpublished.

"Castiglione's *Il Cortegiano*." Originally presented as a lecture at Aula Atti Accademici, Venice, 23 May 1979, and at the University of Urbino, 29 May 1979. Italian text published as a pamphlet by the University of Urbino. English text published in *Quaderni d'italianistica* 1, no. 1 (1980): 1–14. Reprinted by permission.

"The Meeting of Past and Future in William Morris." Published in *Studies in Romanticism* 21 (Fall 1982): 303–18. Reprinted by permission.

"The World as Music and Idea in Wagner's *Parsifal*." Originally presented as an address to the Toronto Wagner Society, 27 October 1982. Published, as part of a "Festschrift für Ernst Martin Oppenheimer," in *Carleton Germanic Papers* 12 (1984): 37–49. Reprinted by permission.

"Cycle and Apocalypse in *Finnegans Wake*." Originally presented as a lecture at the University of California, Berkeley, February 1985. Published in *Vico and Joyce,* ed. Donald Phillip Verene. Albany: State University of New York Press, 1987, pp. 3–19. Reprinted by permission.

Introduction

❖

THIS IS the eighth collection of Northrop Frye's essays. Al-most without exception the papers brought together in each of these volumes began as public lectures, and for twelve of Frye's fifteen other books the "radical of presentation" was the oral ad-dress. Few contemporary critics have been called on to lecture so frequently as Frye, the calls having come not just from his native Canada and the United States but from Italy, England, Denmark, Japan, Australia, Norway, Pakistan, Guyana, the Soviet Union, Ireland, Turkey, and Israel as well. In *Anatomy of Criticism,* Frye uses the word *epos* to describe the radical of presentation of the oral address, "radical" meaning original form. *Epos,* Frye says, includes all those structures of verse and prose that make "some attempt to preserve the convention of recitation and a listening audience."[1] The problem of capturing the ears and minds of the listening audience is, of course, familiar to all who have con-fronted a sea of faces, and they can surely understand what Frye means when he says, "I still find the public lecture a fantastically difficult genre."[2] Still, the testimony of Frye's audiences reveals his success in overcoming the difficulties. The obvious purpose in now altering the radical of presentation from the oral address to the printed page is to make conveniently available a selection of Frye's talks during the past dozen years and so to expand their original audiences.

What motivates this collection is what the essays have to say about the subjects they address, and for these it is best for the editor to remain silent, letting both the general and the local

1. *Anatomy of Criticism: Four Essays* (Princeton: Princeton Univ. Press, 1957), 248.
2. *Fools of Time: Studies in Shakespearean Tragedy* (Toronto: Univ. of Toronto Press, 1967), vii.

insights speak for themselves. The second reason for bringing these essays together is for what they tell us about Frye's own thought, and here it will perhaps be of some value to outline the major contexts in which the essays here might be placed.

For those familiar with Frye's criticism, it will be immediately obvious that the questions on which he has focused from the beginning of his career have not disappeared. This means that each of the essays is ultimately about the conventions of language, literature, and discursive thought: the myths, metaphors, cosmologies, images, symbols, and genres that form the fabric of Western writing, or, perhaps better, the loom upon which that writing has been woven. The first context for this chrestomathy, then, is the entire body of Frye's work, which has formed itself now into a grand epic. Like the body of Blake's Albion before the fall, it has taken the form of a giant in both time and space. Frye began writing for publication in the early 1930s, and the sixty intervening years have seen the number of his books, essays, reviews, editorials, sermons, interviews, and the like grow to more than 850 items. The striking thing about this body of work is its continuity. What Frye discovered about the iconography of the mythopoeic imagination in his study of William Blake, which was begun in the 1930s, he continues to affirm. *The Great Code* (1982) is built upon the insights developed in *Fearful Symmetry* (1947) and *Anatomy of Criticism* (1957).

One will discover in these essays, then, Frye's continuing attention to the fundamental issues that have occupied him all along. These include, to mention only some of the most obvious, the way that literature moves in time and arranges itself in space, the social function of both literature and criticism, the principles of unity that resolve the dialectical split between subject and object, the relation between primary and secondary mythologies, the recreative power of the imagination, the mysterious workings of radical metaphor, and the relation of literature to other literature. There is a great deal to be said for the singular, discrete, discontinuous critical insight, and such moments of illumination strike us, with the energy of the epigram, on almost every page. But there is a great deal more to be said for the plural, comprehensive, continuous vision, and this vision is what permits us to identify these essays as belonging to the Frye canon.

A second context is contemporary critical theory. It is not possible to read *Anatomy of Criticism* without feeling the presence of the old New Criticism hovering in the background, usually as a foil, and in these essays we see Frye casting an occasional glance at the new New Criticism. In "Framework and Assumption" he says that "an influence can also be an anxiety, but I should call this a special factor in a writer's struggle with his contemporary culture, rather than putting it on the socially isolated Freudian basis that Harold Bloom does." Bloom's other cameo appearance is in "The Expanding World of Metaphor," where Frye remarks that "the relation of a poet to the ideology he expounds or reflects is the genuine form of 'the anxiety of influence.'" The relationship of critic to critic is not unlike that of poet to poet, and although Frye does not seem particularly anxious about such current movements as deconstruction or Marxist criticism, the essays collected here reveal that he is clearly aware of the ballpark in which much of the critical game is now being played. Derrida is cited in a quarter of the essays, and there are references to Benjamin and Kenneth Burke, Saussure and Barthes, Heidegger and Husserl, Nietzsche and Wittgenstein.

In "The Mythical Approach to Creation" Frye refers to deconstruction as "a birdshot critical technique: it aims at a variety of targets and bags whatever it happens to hit accidentally." But Frye's attitude toward Derrida's work is not, as the reader will discover, altogether unambiguous. He calls upon Derrida's notion of *écriture* to help define the apprehension of a simultaneous pattern, as opposed to narrative structure, in both literature and cosmologies ("The Koine of Myth"). In discussing the *Phaedrus,* Frye remarks, with a glance toward *Of Grammatology,* that "for Phaedrus at the beginning and Thoth's critics at the end, writing is a vestige of a presence that has vanished" ("Literary and Linguistic Scholarship"). He observes that the Bible both constructs and deconstructs itself ("Framework and Assumption") and that "it is, as Derrida would say, an absence invoking a presence, the 'word of God' as speaking presence in history" ("The Double Mirror"). And he notes in the essay on Joyce that "it was perhaps not until Jacques Derrida and his 'deconstruction' techniques that the theory implied by *Finnegans Wake* really came into focus" ("Cycle and Apocalypse").

Although Derrida turns out to be the most frequently cited contemporary critic in the present collection, Frye does not at all engage poststructuralist thought. He will sometimes call on Derrida to confirm a local insight, but his relation to the central tenets of deconstruction is one of opposition. In *The Great Code* Frye speaks of "the metaphysic of presence" meeting "us at every turn in the Bible," and it meets us at every turn in these essays as well, for Frye continues to maintain his commitment to the center of the orders of words and to the priority of identity to difference.[3] He remains basically skeptical of deconstruction and the other -isms that make up what he calls "the wasteland" of current critical theory ("The Dialectic of Belief and Vision"). Critical theory today, he says, has too often "relapsed into a confused and claustrophobic battle of methodologies" ("Literary and Linguistic Scholarship"). And in reading the Bible, he argues, in opposition to Derrida, that "the critical principle involved is that the text is not the absence of a former presence but the place of the resurrection of the presence. . . . The Logos at the center, which is inside the reader and not hidden behind the text, continually changes place with the Logos at the circumference that encloses both" ("Literary and Linguistic Scholarship"). Frye's relationship to "currently fashionable doctrines" ("The Dialectic of Belief and Vision") is, therefore, the same as his relationship has always been to whatever the dominant critical modes happen to be at the moment: he assimilates the incidental insights, using them for his own purposes, but he rejects the fundamental hypotheses. His view of the critical path seems always to be larger and more inclusive.

Frye's relation to current versions of sociocultural criticism is also that of a disinterested spectator, not an active participant. One of his recent commentators remarks that "Frye does not often use the word 'ideology.'"[4] However true that may be of Frye's work before the 1980s, it is clear from the present collection that ideology is very much on his mind, the word itself appearing in all but one of the theoretical essays of the first two sections. A central issue for Frye throughout these essays, as throughout his entire career, has been the social function of both art and criticism, and this book provides ample testimony that those who depict Frye solely as a formalist have drawn a caricature. The social dimension of literature is in fact, for Frye, its ultimate dimension. The focus of literature, he argues, is the

---

3. *The Great Code: The Bible and Literature* (New York: Harcourt Brace Jovanovich, 1982), 213.
4. Ian Balfour, *Northrop Frye* (New York: Twayne, 1988), 121.

community. Literature gives us the freedom to see and understand the world. It creates visions of what life can become when
freed from the ego, and it provides, therefore, models for social
change. All of these themes form a frequent refrain in the essays
that follow.

But ideology for Frye is always a secondary or a derived
value, and so he is unwilling to accept the current war cry that
ideology is all. What is primary, he argues, is mythology. It is
primary in the history of culture, as the earliest products of culture reveal. It is primary because it descends directly from what
Frye repeatedly in the pages that follow refers to as the basic
human concerns. And it is primary, finally, because, as a product
of the imagination, it can lift us clear from whatever ideologies
happen to be in vogue. Our relationship to culture is always for
Frye a continual dialectic between engagement and detachment.
If we throw all our energies into political or social commitment,
then we become trapped on the treadmill of history, and art becomes parasitic on something else. But if we see art as unrelated
to social concern, then we trivialize the products of culture. That
the critical enterprise for Frye is a matter of both/and rather than
either/or is one of the primary subtexts of these essays, and it
suggests, at least to the editor of this volume, that Frye's conception of criticism remains more inclusive than the versions of contemporary critical thought that are sometimes heard whispering
from the margins of these pages.

In a collection such as this, where the occasion of the address
often defined the topic, we should naturally not expect the plan
of the whole to be a stubborn structure. The arrangement of the
essays into thematic clusters is, therefore, somewhat arbitrary,
and because Frye keeps circling back to the same issues, the
reader will see that other patterns of organization are possible.
Still, some explanation of the present grouping is called for. The
essays in section one center on the fundamental building blocks
of literature—the myths, metaphors, symbols, and cosmologies
out of which, according to Frye, literature is made. Those in
section two examine generally the relationship between literature
and mythology, on the one hand, and social concern and ideology, on the other. Because one of the primary ends of the educational contract in Frye's view is to make us aware of our
mythological conditioning, I have also included in this section
two essays that focus on education. The recurring theme

throughout these addresses is the social function of criticism. The essays in section three focus on literature itself—its critique of the purely analytic faculties, its relation to the visual arts, and two of its recurring metaphors (the stage and the journey). The four addresses in section four are all about Frye's long-standing preoccupation with the literary shape of the Bible. In the final section, which should lay to rest the complaint frequently heard that Frye neglects particular literary works, he turns his attention to books by Thomas More, Castiglione, William Morris, Wagner, and Joyce. The second principle I have used in organizing the collection is, therefore, the general movement from theoretical to practical criticism.

The initiative for all but one of the essays was an invitation for Frye to address a conference or some other gathering. I have not removed the features that point to these occasions. I have, however, deleted several paragraphs, not crucial to the argument, from two of the essays that repeated material found elsewhere in the volume. Still, as one might expect in a collection such as this, there will be occasional repetitions. But I have not tampered with these, because the echoes that remain will be heard in different contexts. As Frye says in the preface to *Spiritus Mundi,* "Some things need to be stated more than once to fit into their different settings."[5]

I express my gratitude to Northrop Frye for again permitting me to bring together a selection of his occasional pieces, to the publishers and journal editors who have consented to the reissue of those essays that have already made their way into print, and to Gerald Trett, my editor at the University Press of Virginia. Finally, the dedication page records a very large debt, intellectual as well as personal.

---

5. *Spiritus Mundi: Essays on Literature, Myth, and Society* (Bloomington: Indiana Univ. Press, 1976), vii.

I

The Koine of Myth: Myth as a Universally Intelligible Language

T HE WORD *myth* is used in such a bewildering variety of contexts that anyone talking about it has to say first of all what
his chosen context is. Mine is the context of literary criticism,
and to me myth always means, first and primarily, *mythos,* story,
plot, narrative. The words *story* and *history* were originally identical, but they are now distinguished, and the word *story* seems
to lie along an axis extending from history to fantasy. In theory,
we have at one extreme the "pure" history which is all "true," in
the sense of being a verbal structure that corresponds closely, or
satisfactorily, with events that actually occurred. At the other
extreme we have stories that are not intended to possess "truth,"
but are "just stories," which may be fantastic enough to be im-
probable or so far as we know impossible.

Obviously, such extremes do not really exist. The most pedestrian history must not only select its material, it must also
have some principle of selection. So a form-content type of distinction arises between the historian's sources and whatever it is

that enables him to arrange what he finds there into a sequential narrative. This sequential narrative, which is not present in the nonverbal events themselves, is his *mythos*. My stock example for this has always been Gibbon's *Decline and Fall of the Roman Empire,* where the phrase "decline and fall" indicates the mythical principle that controls the selection of material and various other factors, such as the tone used in presenting it. A myth, in nearly all its senses, is a narrative that suggests two inconsistent responses: first, "this is what is said to have happened," and second, "this almost certainly is not what happened, at least in precisely the way described." It is this latter aspect of myth that has given it the vulgar sense of something simply untrue, something that did not occur. Even Gibbon's *mythos* contains an element of something imposed from outside on the material: very few of the people he discusses had much notion that they were declining and falling.

There is a more positive side to this "untrue" aspect, however. The phrase "decline and fall" is a fairly literal translation of the word *catastrophe,* which is a technical term in literary criticism, and suggests that Gibbon's *mythos* is in part an imaginative construct, something the historian has in common with the poets. We notice that as the purely historical element in Gibbon's scholarship dates, as historians discover more and more about the period, his book tends insensibly to shift from the historical to the literary category. It now becomes something of a poetic meditation on the theme of decline and fall as illustrated by the Roman Empire, and its "truth" has, on Aristotelian principles, shifted from the particular to the universal.

As we follow the spectrum leading away from the historical, we find ourselves in literature properly speaking, and at the end of the spectrum is fantastic romance, like the works of science fiction where the history and the geography have both been invented. There is no reachable extreme here either. A fantasy completely discontinuous with its social context would be impossible to write: nobody's mind is capable of getting so detached from its social milieu. Even the writings of psychotic or similarly disturbed people are still bound to their surroundings, however off-course their interpretations.

Now that we have located the center of gravity of myth as the narrative of literature, we can see that such narratives descend directly from myth in its more customary sense of a story

4

about a god which is frequently employed in connection with ritual. Being a story, it is always potentially literary, and very soon becomes actually so, or has close relatives that do. Two categories of stories crystallize in most societies. At the center is a body of "serious" stories: they may be asserted to have really happened, but what is important about them is not that, but that they are stories which it is particularly urgent for the community to know. They tell us about the recognized gods, the legendary history, the origins of law, class structure, kinship formations, and natural features. These stories do not as a rule differ in structure from other stories that are told simply for entertainment, but they have a different social function. The less serious stories become folktales, travelling over the world through all barriers of language and culture interchanging their motifs and themes with other stories. Their literary life is at first nomadic, and only later, often not until the rise of writing, do they become absorbed into the general body of literature. The more serious stories, on the other hand, become the cultural possession of a specific society: they form the verbal nucleus of a shared tradition. The stories of the Bible had this distinctively mythical status for Christian Europe down to the eighteenth century at least; the stories of Homer had it for Greek and much Roman culture.

One should not exaggerate this, of course: myths can also migrate, just as two of the world's greatest mythological systems, the Christian and the Buddhist, have moved outside their places of origin. In the *Odyssey,* we meet Odysseus on Calypso's island, resisting her importunities to marry her, which include the promise of immortality if he does. Later we learn that Odysseus has spent a year with Circe, after he was enabled to overcome the enchantments by which she had turned his companions into animals. In the Gilgamesh epic, many centuries earlier, the hero resists a similar proposal from the goddess Ishtar, telling her that she had not only abandoned her earlier lovers but had turned them into animals and birds by enchantment. The older story brings us much closer to what Robert Graves calls the White Goddess cycle, where the Earth Mother takes a new lover each year and then abandons or sacrifices him, renewing her virginity and destroying her memory before the next year begins. The similarity of theme points to a good deal of mythological diffusion in the intervening centuries. It does not follow, incidentally, that we can always reach the most authentic form of a myth by tracing it backwards in time. Shakespeare's *Winter's Tale* brings a complex richness out of the Demeter and Proserpine myth that is unique in its history, and the same is true of Wagner's treatment of the Parzival story.

The response to a narrative, of whatever kind, has two stages to it, the first being most frequently described in metaphors of hearing, the second in metaphors of seeing. Someone who is about to tell a joke may say, regrettably, "Stop me if you've heard this one," indicating that what follows is addressed primarily to the ear. But if we "see" the joke, the joke is all over, and we are considering the afterimage of its total structure. The metaphors should not prevent us from realizing that we can have a narrative presented in visual terms, such as a ballet, or a response presented verbally. But nonetheless there does seem to be a movement in time, which is the *mythos* properly speaking, up to and followed by an act of understanding where the *mythos* is "seen," or apprehended as a unit. It is this final act of understanding the whole, which for a complex work is more ideally than actually present, that has made the word *structure* so pervasive a metaphor in literary criticism, although the traditional term *anagnorisis* seems to me less misleading. The apprehension of a total structure may exist on any level from the simplest to the most profound. We hear a joke, but as soon as we "see" the joke we do not want to hear it again. We read a detective story to reach the identification of the murderer, but as soon as we reach it we do not normally want to continue studying the story, at least not until we have forgotten how, as we say so significantly, it "turned out." But in something like a play of Shakespeare there is an indefinite sequence of these final apprehensions: as soon as we have reached one, we become dissatisfied with it and try to regroup our forces for a new and, we hope, better understanding. The kind of literary work we describe as a "classic" could perhaps be defined as one in which the process goes on through the whole of one's life, assuming that one keeps reading.

This conception of two phases of apprehension, one metaphorically aural and the other metaphorically visual, helps to explain the connection of religious myth with ritual. Many types of ritual begin with the reciting of a myth, as the creation myth was read at the festival of Marduk in Babylon, telling again the story of how Marduk created the present world out of the body of the dragon (or whatever she was) Tiamat and then imposed laws on mankind, or the only part of mankind that mattered, the Babylonians. Here the reciting of the myth is part of a ritual which, so to speak, epiphanizes or makes present the myth, that is, repeats the original assumed event in the present. Sometimes the ritual centers on the exhibiting of a visual symbol. In a Christian mass the reciting of the Creed, the summary of mythical events recounted in the Gospels, leads up the elevation of the Host, and the initiations at Eleusis are said to have reached their climax with the exhibiting of a reaped ear of corn. Zen Buddhism has a legend that after the Buddha had preached a sermon, he held up a golden flower, which caught the eye of the only auditor who got the point, that auditor being, of course, the founder of Zen.

At this stage it becomes clear that myth is inseparable from another verbal phenomenon, the metaphor. A typical metaphor takes the form of the statement "A is B," examples being found in Jacob's prophecy of the twelve tribes of Israel in Genesis 49: "Joseph is a fruitful bough," "Issachar is a strong ass," "Naphtali is a hind let loose." Here again, as with the myth, we have two contradictory messages presented. There is, or seems to be, an assertion that A is B, along with an undercurrent of significance that tells us that A is obviously not B, and nobody but a fool could imagine that it was. Joseph is clearly not a fruitful bough, and the metaphorical attributes seem purely arbitrary and interchangeable. Here again, as with the myth, there is a more positive side to the obvious unreality of what is being said. "Joseph" is an element of personality, and "fruitful bough" a natural object. Metaphor, then, suggests a state of things in which there is no sharp or consistent distinction between subject and object. That is, a metaphorical statement is not so much an assertion that A is B as an annihilation of the space separating A and B. I shall return to this in a moment: just now we must note that the myth does to time what the metaphor does to space. It does not say so much "this happened long ago" as "what you are about to see, or have just seen, *is* what happened long ago." The present becomes a moment in which, in Eliot's phrase, the past and future are gathered.

In watching, say, a historical play of Shakespeare, we discover that Shakespeare has, as we say, taken some liberties with the historical facts, such as making Prince Hal and Hotspur the same age when they were in fact twenty years apart. So we say

7

that the *mythos,* the total story being told in Shakespeare's play, "follows" history except for certain "poetic licenses," which we allow to poets for much the same reason that liberty of speech used to be allowed to court fools. But if we stop to think, we can see that the *mythos* is not "following" history at all: it includes a historical theme, but it twists it around so that it confronts us in the present. It shows us the glorious English victory over the French; it also shows us the misery of France and the low morale of many of the English soldiers. It shows us a triumphant young king about to marry a foreign princess; it also indicates that this king died almost immediately and left a legacy of sixty years of unbroken disaster for England. It is neither patriotic nor ironic: it simply presents all imaginative aspects of a historical situation. The departures from historical fact are in the direction of giving greater symmetry to the story, that is, of throwing emphasis on the unique form of *this* story, rather than on the content of a historical episode which is like so many other episodes. Similarly, the story of the Crucifixion of Christ is presented mythically in the Gospels, although there is no reason to doubt that a historical event forms the kernel of it. But as a historical event, the Crucifixion of Christ is like any other execution, one more manifestation of the continuous psychosis of brutality and stupidity that is human behavior. It is only as a myth that it has the power to confront us in the present tense, and tell us that what was done then is what we are doing now.

The metaphor, by saying "A is B," is not being logical, the identity of two different things being an impossibility, but neither is it antilogical. It is counterlogical; it introduces us to a world where the inevitable movement from cause to effect, the inevitable separation of one thing from another thing, no longer exist in the same way. A creation or deluge myth, by saying at once "this happened" and "this didn't happen quite like that," is not being historical, nor antihistorical. It is counterhistorical, which I take it is what biblical scholars mean by the term *Heilsgeschichte:* it opens up a world whose laws are quite other than those of this world of differing and deferring. The Elizabethan critics used the Horatian tag *ut pictura poesis,* poetry as a speaking picture, to emphasize this quality of representing and recreating something otherwise out of reach.

A *mythos,* a story being told in time, is what Jacques Derrida would call logocentric: it suggests the presence of a teller of the story, even if it is presented as a drama. But when we reach the end, it turns into something for which some visual metaphor, like Derrida's own term *écriture,* expanded, as he expands it, from writing to any visualizable system of meaning, is what seems appropriate. This something, this simultaneous pattern to be apprehended all at once, is itself a cluster of metaphors, images and events linked together in identity by the previous movement of the story. Sometimes this metaphor cluster is expressible by a diagram, a pictorial design, or a single image. For example, as Gibbon's *Decline and Fall* moves increasingly from the historical to the literary category, we begin to see it more and more clearly as an eighteenth-century book. That is, there is an act of simultaneous apprehension of the whole theme which Gibbon could have attained only in the eighteenth century, when he could look at the story of late Rome as a growing descent from the Antonines into the triumph of barbarism and religion, after which history struggled out on the other side to a plateau of enlightenment from which Gibbon could survey the whole process and pass his vision on to us. What we see is a U-shaped curve declining and falling until it reaches its nadir with the fall of Byzantium, after which a Renaissance begins to bring history up again to something like the original level.

After absorbing Gibbon's vision of history, we may turn to Ruskin's *Stones of Venice* in the next century, and learn that in fact the shape of that period was precisely the opposite, an inverted U beginning in the "servile" art of the late Romans, rising to a pinnacle of disciplined spontaneity with decorated Gothic, and declining through what Ruskin calls the "fall" of the Renaissance. Both visions are true, just as both the comic and the tragic visions are true: they merely select different data. It is in this metahistorical form that history reaches the general public. Not everyone has read Spengler's *Decline of the West,* but everyone has unconsciously absorbed a good deal of his application of the "decline and fall" *mythos* to our own culture. Similarly with the cyclical myth of Vico, the progressive myth advanced in the democracies from Condorcet on, the revolutionary myth of Marxism, and so on. Here again the ambivalence of myth, in saying "this happened" and "this isn't the whole truth about what happened" at the same time, continues to operate. All these myths are oversimplified diagrammatic formulas, and the advance of scholarship has a great deal to do with qualifying their symmetry by pointing to more complicating factors. And yet the advance of scholarship itself seems also to move toward the reconstruction of some such vision, however more flexible.

What I have said about historical narrative applies in general to dialectic, or philosophical narrative. Philosophers themselves point out that their philosophy is a kind of garment woven over a far more primitive and naked vision. Philosophical narrative, like historical or fictional narrative, does more than narrate: it reaches an end and stops, and where it stops it points to a simultaneous structure of how, say, the world looked to Spinoza in the seventeenth century or Kant in the eighteenth. This simultaneous structure is a kind of cosmology, and a cosmology is *écriture* in the sense of being a structure of meaning written over the heavens. As usual, we can see this more clearly in religious or imaginative literature. Most religions, including the biblical ones, begin with a creation myth. But creation, at any rate in the Book of Genesis, is not a story of how the order of nature came into being, but a vision of nature as *écriture,* as an interlocking system of signs. "Let them be for signs," is what God says when he creates the sun and moon. Every cosmology is a renewed effort to see the creation as an end rather than a beginning.

As a book to be read consecutively, the Christian Bible is logocentric, a continuous discourse, traditionally ascribed to God speaking through his prophets and scribes, and reaching a climax in the Incarnation, which though visible was invisible to practically everyone. But what it all points to is an apocalypse, or ultimate vision of creation, the world-book with its seals taken off. Within the Old Testament, the climax of the narrative is the return of Israel to its Promised Land, after its bondage in Egypt and its forty years in the desert. Here the leader, Moses, climbs a mountain and sees, without entering, the Promised Land. The inference is that nobody actually saw the Promised Land except Moses, because as soon as it is entered it turns into Canaan, and another cycle of history begins. At the end of the Book of Job, God makes a long speech ending with hymns on the animals behemoth and leviathan, which are presented, again, in visual metaphors: "Behold now behemoth," etc. Job responds: "I have heard of thee by the hearing of the ear, but now mine eye seeth thee." In Dante we reach the corresponding point when Beatrice finally resigns her oral school-mistress role and points to the Virgin Mary. In Milton, whose theme is tragic, we go in the opposite direction and end with a logocentric summary of human history, as recorded in the Bible, after which human experience as we know it begins.

Let me give one fairly extended example of how narratives lead up to some sort of visualizable emblem, myth or narrative frozen into a complex metaphor. Mythology from primitive times to Tolkien and beyond has always thought of the world we live in as a "middle earth," with two other theaters of reality above and below it. "Above" and "below" are once again spatial metaphors, but they are no less pervasive for that. So we get the image of climbing to a higher sphere of existence, represented usually by a ladder, sometimes by a mountain or tree.

In the Bible we have the ladder, or rather staircase, seen by Jacob in his dream at Bethel. Angels go up and down the ladder, but the ladder is clearly not of human construction. It has a demonic parody in the story of the Tower of Babel, built by arrogant man himself to reach the heavens. The Tower of Babel in its turn is related to the Mesopotamian ziggurat, the temple in the midst of the city that provided the means of ascent to the gods, a kind of artificial mountain transplanted to a flat country. Here we have a recessed building with a stairway going up, usually in a spiral form. The image of the spiral, suggesting among other things the organic process of birth from nothing and death into a second nothingness, gets associated with ladders and mountains very early. Brueghel's painting of the Tower of Babel, and Blake's of Jacob's ladder, show them as spirals. There were spiral staircases in Solomon's temple, even though it was only three stories high. According to Herodotus, Babylon and Ecbatana had more elaborate temples, seven stories high, with each stairway colored differently to represent the seven planets. On top was the chamber of the bride, who was placed there to receive the embrace of the descending god: the myth of Danae, courted by Zeus in a shower of gold, seems connected with this. In Egypt the step pyramids may have had a similar reference, and one of the names for Osiris was "the god at the top of the staircase."

The Tower of Babel illustrates a problem in mythology that troubled both Judaism and Christianity. How was one to explain the close resemblance between biblical and nonbiblical myth and imagery, if the adherents of the biblical religion claimed a unique revelation? The simplest answer was the hard-line one: all nonbiblical myths had been invented by the devils to deceive mankind by a close simulacrum of the truth. But gradually a more liberal view prevailed that nothing need necessarily be demonic unless it is attached to false belief or cult, and that classical myths and images, purely as that, could be taken as metaphorical analogies of the myths and images that revealed God's actual purpose in history.

Even so, the central emphasis on the ladder image in Mithraism, where the soul's ascent through the seven planets was so much insisted on, provided a good deal of imaginative rivalry with early Christianity. But by Dante's time it was clear that the ladder had been fully absorbed into the victorious religion. Dante's Purgatory is a vast ziggurat, a mountain on the other side of the earth, up which the souls of the redeemed ascend spirally to the top. There are the traditional seven complete turns around the mountain, and progressing through each turn removes one of the seven deadly sins. The laborious climb reminds us that man's ability to raise himself in the scale of creation is limited, as he cannot fly to heaven. John Donne remarks in a sermon how the angels, who traditionally can fly, still are demurely plodding up and down a ladder in Jacob's vision. At the top of Dante's Purgatory is the Garden of Eden, the home originally destined for man. The female figures that appear here, first Matilda and then Beatrice, indicate the descent of the theme from the ancient bridal chamber. The Virgin Mary does not appear until later in the poem, but in contemporary iconography she was, at the time of the Incarnation, the "garden enclosed, the fountain sealed" of the Song of Songs, or Eden in an individual form. Her mythological connection with Danae is frequently noted by poets: Francis Thompson and Ezra Pound both provide examples. With the *Paradiso* comes the climb through the planetary spheres, and in the sphere of the last of the planets, Saturn, we see Jacob's ladder again, symbolizing the final ascent to the presence of God. As the Greek word for ladder, *klimax,* reminds us, it is the last step on the ladder that is the crucial one. Perhaps it is worth noting that the word *climax* entered the English language originally as a term in rhetoric, a name for a certain way or arranging words.

Dante's poem also reflects the two great cosmological ladders that dominated the thought of his time, the chain of being, polarized by form and matter, that extended from God to chaos, and the Ptolemaic universe, extending in a parallel fashion from the primum mobile through the heavenly bodies and the four elements to the earth we stand on. The conception of a ladder of elements goes back to pre-Socratic times. Heraclitus appears to think in terms of a soul struggling upwards from soggy wet mud at the bottom to the dry light of the *logos* or shared consciousness at the top, and of this again as part of an incessant process of ascent and descent, one in which we live each other's deaths and die each other's lives. With the Renaissance, the ladder of Eros in Plato's *Symposium* began to reenter the European world picture, on a more heterosexual basis than Plato provides, but still one where the driving force is a love rooted in the human body in a way that Christian love (*agape*) is not. Sometimes the two aspects of love are united: in Dante's *Commedia* Beatrice is purely an agent of *agape,* but her original appearance in Dante's soul, as described in the *Vita Nuova,* was the work of Eros.

We noted that the Bible contains both an ideal and an ironic version of the mounting image. The classical counterpart of the ironic version is the story of the revolt of the Titans, the sons of earth who piled mountains on top of each other to reach their enemy in the sky. There are also widespread folktales that associate the attempt to build a ladder to heaven with futility. One such tale is current among British Columbia Indian tribes, where there is an original war between the Sky People and the Earth People, the latter being apparently animals. One animal or bird, generally the wren, shoots an arrow into the moon; another shoots a second arrow that hits the notch of its predecessor, and so on until there is a complete ladder of arrows from earth to sky. Then the animals climb up, until the grizzly bear breaks the ladder by his weight. One is reminded of Blake's sequence of drawings called *The Gates of Paradise.* One of these drawings has the caption "I want! I want!," and shows a young man starting to climb a ladder leaned against the moon. There is a young couple making a gesture toward him, but he ignores them, no doubt in the spirit of Longfellow's mountain-climbing youth, shouting "Excelsior!" when invited to sleep with an Alpine maiden. There is an ominous bend in the ladder, however, and we are not much surprised to find that the next engraving, with the caption "Help! Help!," shows him fallen into water, like his prototype Icarus.

In the Bible the difference between Bethel and Babel is the difference between a stairway created by God between heaven and earth and an attempt to build one up from the earth by man. In Milton, where naturally the emphasis on divine initiative is always primary, we encounter, in the third book of *Paradise Lost,* the "paradise of fools" on the smooth surface of the primum mobile, or circumference of the universe, where those arrive who have tried to take the Kingdom of Heaven by force or fraud. A reference to the tower of Babel precedes this description, and indicates its archetype. There follows a vision of stairs descending from heaven to earth, which, Milton tells us, were "such as whereon Jacob saw" the angels of his vision. These stairs are let down from heaven and drawn up again at God's pleasure: Satan, on his journey to Eden, arrives at a "lower" stair, from which he descends to earth by way of the planets.

The ladder cosmology of the chain of being and the geocentric universe began to fall apart in the eighteenth century. By then the centered perspective had vanished, and it became increasingly obvious that the conception had held sway so long because it was a structure of authority, and rationalized the religious and secular structures that claimed to embody it in society. The chain of being was still in place for Pope, early in the eighteenth century, but Voltaire was very doubtful about the *échelle de l'infini,* which he realized to be a weapon in the armory of the social establishment. However, the ladder remained in the center of thought, though it took other forms. Hegel's *Phenomenology* is called a ladder by its author, but it is really a tower or mountain stood on its head, its apex the concept that can hardly be found between subject and object, but steadily broadens until it becomes absolute knowledge. Such a structure could not exist in nature, only in thought, and perhaps only in Hegelian thought at that. But with the coming of evolution pop science broke out in another rash of ladders, all designed to show that Nature had been patiently climbing one until she reached her supreme and once-for-all masterpiece, namely ourselves. In the meantime, the ladder had settled into place in the two great workshops of models, science and the arts. The Latin word for ladder, *scala,* has given us "scale," the techniques of measurement on which all the sciences depend, and which inform the arts as well, notably music.

If we had asked in 1930 who were apparently the most significant writers in English at the time, most critics would have included T. S. Eliot, W. B. Yeats, Ezra Pound, and James Joyce in their list. In Eliot the staircase is an almost obsessive image in the earlier poetry, and *Ash-Wednesday* (1930) recounts an ascent up a spiral stair to the enclosed garden of the Virgin at the top. The choice of image is not surprising, given the poem's open and avowed debt to Dante's *Purgatorio,* but around the same time Yeats, from a very different point of view, was collecting his poetry in books entitled *The Tower* (1928) and *The Winding Stair* (1933), and finding spirals not only in staircases but in human history and the afterlife. Yeats even went to the point of buying one of the round towers, with a spiral staircase, that still exist in Ireland, although he did not spend much time living in it. After completing *Ulysses* (1922), Joyce went on to construct his epic on the story of Finnegan, the drunken hod carrier who fell off a ladder, an event identified on the first page of the book with both the fall of Adam and the flood of Noah. Falling off ladders reminds us of the story of Elpenor in the *Odyssey* which enters Pound's first Canto, and even the terrible experience of being confined in a cage at Pisa did not destroy Pound's ambition for his poem, which was, he says in the opening lines of the Pisan Cantos, "To build the city of Dioce whose terraces are the color of stars," a reference to the ziggurats mentioned in Herodotus.

One could go on for a long time with these images, and others closely related, such as the tree that stretches into the heavens, whose fruit is the planets, or descending staircases and whirlpools leading to worlds below. Nearly all of these are images of what is called the *axis mundi,* the vertical dimension that connects our world with the others above and below it. About the *axis mundi,* we can say two things, first, that it is not there, and second, that it won't go away. The difficulties in such a metaphor begin with projecting it, thinking of it as something with an independent being, and nothing could be more obvious, in this context, than Yeats's remark that all ladders are planted in the foul rag-and-bone shop of the human heart. But to psychologize or subjectivize such an image is equally misleading, as it simply emphasizes the other half of the subject-object split. Such images are not subjective or objective: they are units of creative activity with words, the roots of a language spoken from China to Peru that never affirms and can never be refuted, but always makes its own kind of sense. They belong to the world man builds out of nature, not to the order of nature itself.

Our next and final step takes us back to metaphor. I said a

moment ago that such a metaphor as "Joseph is a fruitful bough" asserts an identity between something personal and something natural. There is no question of belief or reader's involvement here, except that originally the reader was assumed to be an Israelite who would be, however distantly, a relative of Joseph or his tribe. But this kind of literary metaphor is a later development of a type of metaphor that links together a divine personality and an aspect of nature in which he has a particular interest or function. To say, for example, "Neptune is the sea" would be a genuine identity for those who accept the cult: the statement would in fact be almost a tautology, like saying that Elizabeth II is queen of England. The identity of Neptune and the sea is the base of a triangle with its apex pointing to the social group that addresses prayers or sacrifices to Neptune when starting on a sea voyage.

Such a god is, so to speak, a prefabricated metaphor: it unites a personality and a natural object, and is the entering wedge of that union between subjective and objective worlds that all creative activity depends on. It is part of the function of literature, more especially poetry, to keep alive in society the metaphorical habit of mind, and gods are invaluable to poets because they are traditional and recognized metaphors. Gods are supposed to be immortal in contrast to the mortality of man, but in practice the situation is reversed. After all the temples to Jupiter and Venus had been closed down and their cults abandoned, Jupiter and Venus continued to live a far more intense imaginative life than ever before within literature.

More psychologically primitive than such literary or imaginative metaphors, if not necessarily earlier in time, is what we could call ecstatic metaphor, the sense of being actually linked with a divine power, as in the worship of Dionysus in Greece or in states of direct inspiration or possession by a god. Theseus in Shakespeare's *Midsummer Night's Dream* speaks of "the lunatic, the lover and the poet" as the people who take metaphor seriously. The inclusion of the lover is a throwback to ecstatic metaphor, as lovers traditionally attempt to create a single soul out of two bodies. In Shakespeare's day it was conventionally assumed that a poet began by fixing his whole mental and emotional life on a lady, whose disdainful repelling of his advances forced him into poetry as an outlet for his frustration.

Behind the lover the rather limited horizon of Theseus con-

16

tains only lunatics. Today we think also of, say, members of totemic societies who feel an identity with the totemic animal, primitives who engage in ritual dances and initiation ceremonies, shamans who make journeys to upper and lower worlds. All these have their present-day counterparts, as the popularity of yoga and Zen meditation and of such books as those of Carlos Castaneda shows. Mystics, too, though they also show a great affinity for climbing ladders and mountains, like the Mount Carmel of St. John of the Cross, arrive at an ecstatic union with the divine, the precise degree of union being determined by the dogmas of whatever religion commands their allegiance.

These ecstatic or directly experienced metaphors are not crude forms of the literary metaphors we encounter in literature and in religions no longer believed in, but the extension into life of their meaning. A genuine progress in the study of literary or religious mythology would not "outgrow" or impoverish the ecstatic stage but reabsorb it. Moments of ecstatic union, or "peak experiences," as they are often called, may come and go like flashes of lightning, but such moments are, we said, the frozen or simultaneously grasped aspects of a *mythos* or continuous narrative. Within the limitations of human life, the most highly developed human types are those whose lives have become, as we say, a legend, that is, lives no longer contemplating a vision of objective revelation or imprisoned within a subjective dream. The New Testament presents the ultimate human life as a divine and human Logos, but the Logos has transcended its relation to logic and has expanded into *mythos,* a life which is, so to speak, a kind of self-narration, where action and awareness of action are no longer clashing with each other. I conclude with this reference because the New Testament was written in a *koine* in the ordinary sense, a simplified Greek understood over most of the Mediterranean world. What it had to say with this language was a *mythos,* a story of immense scope and suggestiveness which was the spearhead of its advance through the Western world. Anything that proposes to become a significant part of human consciousness today will have to use the same kind of mythical *koine,* narratives with a verbal shape that can inform other arts and sciences as well, and draw them together in a unity of thought and action.

Literary and Linguistic Scholarship in a Postliterate World

✧

THE TITLE of this paper is not mine: I do not know what the word *postliterate* means, and I have finally decided to take it as a synonym for education itself. Society supports compulsory education because it needs docile and obedient citizens. We must learn to read to respond to traffic signs and advertising; learn to cipher to make out our income tax. These passive acquirements make us literate, and society as such has no great interest in education beyond that stage. Teachers take over from there: their task is to transform a passive literacy into an active postliteracy, with the responsibility and freedom of choice that is part of any world we want to live in.

A hundred years is not a long time, geologically speaking: I have been teaching for nearly half that time myself, and for well over a third of it I have belonged to the MLA and watched its letters come increasingly to stand for Miscellaneous Linguistic Activities. In 1883 the picture of a scholar reading a book was a fairly adequate icon for the humanities. It was a Cartesian icon, a thinking subject confronting a mechanically produced object. However, as the MLA has grown, it has become clear that texts, like dragons or beautiful princesses in romance, attract a great variety of visitors. Some want to devour the text; some want to surrender to it; some want to read it; some want to misread it; some want to extract its essence; some want to proclaim its existence; some critical engineers want to build bridges connecting the images; some critical developers want to build new structures in the empty spaces.

It is apparently the policy of the MLA, as of most such gatherings, to allow all of these a share of time on the program, in the hope that the procession will eventually shake down into some sort of community, or group of communities. The fact that a relatively stable text becomes the focus of a community is so patent now that the old individualized reader, shut away from the community to read in quiet, begins to look like a self-dramatizing abstraction. In the process it has also become generally accepted that criticism is not a parasitic growth on literature but a special form of literary language.

It would be unreasonable for me to object to this development, when I have been advocating so much of it for so many years. But it is still only postliterate communities that are involved, and they still operate within a society that neither sees nor much wants to see the importance of what they are doing. The critics in turn seem to have equally little interest in trying to demonstrate it. It is curious, considering the brilliance of the leading scholars in the field, how much critical theory today has relapsed into a confused and claustrophobic battle of methodologies, where, as in Fortinbras's campaign in *Hamlet,* the ground fought over is hardly big enough to hold the contending armies. One very central critical question, it seems to me, is that of the social authority of the writer, but we seem to be unable to deal with this. Yet it is a very old question: when Dante expounds the meaning of a verse in the Psalms, and then says that his own *Paradiso* is written on the same principle, he is not simply describing a critical method but trying to find a place for his authority as a poet by attaching his work to another text that already has it.

It is easy to see in science, say in Galileo or Darwin, how the integrity of the science itself commands a loyalty and a commitment from the scientist even when it conflicts with social concerns and demands. It seems much more difficult and complex to locate the source of the social authority of the writer. We know that there is often a core of authentic vision at the heart

19

even of writers who admittedly also wrote a good deal of blith-
ering nonsense. We know how hideously powerful perverted
rhetoric can be, and how a deliberate debasing of language can
wipe out all genuine freedom and culture in a society. We also
know—and this is the center of the issue for me—how many
writers of recent years have faced ridicule, persecution, even martyrdom, in order to remain loyal to a vision that they felt had
been entrusted to them. Many writers have been suppressed or
exiled or murdered for ideological reasons, and many have committed suicide through social and political as well as psychological stress.

What I am speaking of is not a question of the last century
only. Writers have always been torn by the conflicting demands
of their own craft and those of a society that usually finds something quite different more acceptable. One thinks of Petrarch,
spreading the gospel of the frustrations and sublimations of love
throughout Europe, yet writing in his *Secretum* a rueful dialogue
between himself and St. Augustine, a mother-fixated saint whose
view of the workings of Eros in human life was seldom genial,
and yet who stood much closer to the center of spiritual authority
in Petrarch's day. One thinks of Chaucer and his retraction, dis-
owning his allegedly sinful tales, as though his Friar and Summoner were after all to be taken at their own valuations. One
thinks of any number of self-conflicts, ranging from Tasso to Gogol, from Rimbaud to Yukio Mishima, that have nearly or quite
destroyed the creative powers of those in whom they raged.
Around us today we see a great variety of social groups, Christian, Marxist, Moslem, anarchist, liberal, conservative, all of
them full of hard-liners who simply deny, in the interests of their
own dogmas, that poets have any authority except what they
might derive from whatever ideology the dogmatist himself
wants to advance. Their confident and self-hypnotized assurance
has influenced many of the more timid critics to believe or assume that if there is any value in the study of literature, it cannot
inhere in literature itself. And if we speak vaguely, as Auden does
about Yeats, of a "gift" for "writing well," we are only going
around in circles.

It should go without saying—but it doesn't, so I have to
say it—that the social authority of the critic and the literary
scholar is inseparably a part of the same question, because text

and reader can no longer be thought of as standing in a simple object-subject relationship. I know too that the word *authority* will sound disquieting to many. I use it because it is impossible to raise the issue of the social function of writing without a complete redefinition of authority, and such a redefinition would have to extend to every aspect of social life. In a world where authority now resides in power structures that are confronted by one another and by most of their own citizens with equal apprehensiveness, this reconsidering of authority would take us quite a long way. It might conceivably give the MLA itself a new kind of social relevance.

Literature develops out of mythology, a body of stories with a specific social function, and mythology in its turn is an outgrowth of what I call *concern,* a term that I hope is self-explanatory. There is primary concern, and there is secondary concern. Primary concern is based on the most primitive of platitudes: the conviction that life is better than death, happiness better than misery, freedom better than bondage. Secondary concern includes loyalty to one's own society, to one's religious or political beliefs, to one's place in the class structure, and in short to everything that comes under the general heading of ideology. All through history secondary concerns have had the greater prestige and power. We prefer to live, but we go to war; we prefer to be free, but we keep a large number of people in a second-class status, and so on. In the twentieth century the dangers of persisting in the bad habits of war, and of exploitation both of human beings and of nature, have brought humanity to a choice between survival and extinction. If we choose survival, the twentieth century will be the first period in history when primary concerns have some real chance of becoming primary.

Poets are the children of concern: they normally reflect the ideologies of their own times, and certainly they are always conditioned by their historical and cultural surroundings. Yet there has always been a sense of something else that eludes this kind of communication. Gerard Manley Hopkins speaks of an overthought of syntax and an underthought of metaphor and imagery, a distinction between what is said and what is shown forth. What is said may sometimes be only a perfunctory disguise, a concession to the censor in the reader, burglar's meat for a watchdog, in Eliot's phrase. But even what is shown forth by the figurative structure, if more distinterested, may be a choice among alternatives, which are repressed but still in some sense there.

As we pursue this question, one landmark after another begins to disappear. The writer disappears as an individual, and the question of authority shifts from him to the authority of literature as a whole. Then we see that there are no clear boundaries between literary and other verbal structures, so that the question becomes one of the authority of language. Similarly the reader merges into the community of criticism and scholarship, which again cannot be separated from what it acts on. Every effort of criticism is a recreation. So we are left only with language and users of language. But on further reflection we can no longer be sure whether it is humanity that uses language or language that uses humanity.

It might be prudent to stop here, with the retrospective view appropriate to a centennial, surveying our progress from the scholar and book of a century ago to the reduction of all solid elements into a heaving sea of melted-down categories. But if there are any members of the larger social public I mentioned earlier who are waiting to have the significance of all this explained to them, they are still waiting. And even if they have gone home, we, if we survive, need something to keep us going for another hundred years. So I have to venture on one more step.

Primary concern is clearly not confined to life and the pursuit of happiness; it is not confined even to the leisure, privacy, and freedom of movement that for most of us indicate the higher levels of culture. It includes also the concern of a conscious being to enlarge that consciousness, to get at least a glimpse of what it would be like to know more than we are compelled to know. In short, conscious primary concern is postliterate, in the sense I have given to that word.

Just as there is primary and secondary concern, so there is primary and secondary mythology. Primary mythology sees the environment in terms of the human impulse to expand into it. The chief instrument of this expansion is metaphorical identification. If we look at the drawings of bisons and stags in Paleolithic caves, and consider the conditions of positioning and lighting under which they were done, we can see that the titanic strength and urgency of the motivation involved is something we can no longer find words for. Such words as *aesthetic, magical,*

22

religious, or words relating to social solidarity or survival, are merely thrown at it: they express nothing of the intensity of identification involved. Later we find the metaphorical imagination expanding into the worlds of dream, belief, vision, fantasy, ideas, as well as human society and nature, and annexing them all to the enlarging consciousness.

But every society is structured, and there is always another or secondary tendency to attach what is imagined to the ideals of some ascendant group or class. Thus medieval and Renaissance romances were attached to the aristocratic or monastic ideals of their time; nineteenth-century fiction to contemporary bourgeois ideals: every age shows the same pattern. We never get a work of imagination which is wholly primary or secondary: it is invariably both at once. Yet the two aspects are still two: primary mythology is anthropocentric; secondary mythology is ethnocentric. Much of the critical process revolves around the effort of distinguishing them.

For instance, when Shakespeare presents the career of Henry V, he supplies his audience with their own prefabricated prejudices. He traces his hero through his madcap disguise as prince, his emergence as responsible king, his invasion of France and his victory, leaving him as he is about to marry the French princess. He throws in Falstaff as comic relief to diversify the same ideology, and removes him when he has served his purpose. But if we listen carefully to the progression of images and to other things said which are subordinated but still audible, we can see and hear how many other things are happening. We become aware of the misery of France, the fact that Falstaff is a powerful presence whatever his moral status, the shaky morale of many of the English soldiers. Above all, we become aware of the way in which Henry's victory is shot through with the illusions of fortune, and of the fact that he died almost at once and left a legacy of sixty years of disaster for England. This does not mean that the play is a palimpsest with a perfunctory patriotic message on top and an ironic one underneath to be discovered by cleverer students. It means that as we progress in understanding, the play's expression of primary concern, as a metaphorical vision of life, begins to become distinguishable from an ideology of patriotism which is also there.

In our day, this distinction is so clear that we now instinctively think of a "mythology" as a structure of phony ideas that embodies the entrenched interests of some ascendant or pressure group, whether its vehicle is advertising or propaganda. It is obvious too that if there is a strong tension between two political powers, the greatest long-term danger, so far, comes less from what either power directly does than from the mythology that each projects on the other. Hence there would clearly be some point in trying to develop a technique of making ourselves more aware of our mythological conditioning, of removing the ideological cataracts from our social vision. Using the criticism of literature as a remedy for the abuses of ideology is unreliable and hazardous, and in practice it has hardly ever worked. But that is true of criticism as it is, not as it could be, and I see nothing else that has any chance of working at all.

Henry V is a history play, and it builds up a sense of an irresistible historical destiny and of cause-and-effect logic. These things are realities, or seem so until the total annihilation of everything they bring before us shows that they are also illusions. What we notice increasingly is, first, the immense power of counterlogic in the metaphorical structure, and, second, the equally powerful counterhistorical movement in the myth, the total story being told. We begin by thinking that the myth of the play follows history except for a number of poetic licenses. But it does not "follow" history: it absorbs the historical movement and then confronts it.

We are reminded of Nature's judgment at the end of Spenser's *Mutabilitie Cantos,* where she decides against Mutability's claim to be the supreme power in the universe. If, says Nature, we are ruled by change, there is only mechanical repetition leading to death, the normal drift of time and space into entropy. But we can reverse the movement and rule over change, making repetition a progress toward freedom, as repeated practice sets us free to play the piano or tennis. This latter repetition, she says, is a working of our own perfection, a dilation of our own being. *Dilate,* incidentally, is also a rhetorical term referring to the writer's copiousness or creative energy.

It seems to me that all creative impulses, including the literary one, begin in the sense of the unreality of time and space in ordinary experience, where the central points that we call here and now never quite come into existence. The counterlogical and counterhistorical movements of metaphor and myth have to do with trying to establish or reconstitute a sense of a present moment and a spatial presence as the basis of whatever significance the verbal imagination can find in life. I conclude with an example or two of what I mean.

In Plato's dialogue *Phaedrus* we first meet Phaedrus himself, deeply impressed by a speech about love given by the rhetorician Lysias. As Socrates begins to ask him about the speech, it becomes obvious that it is the personal impact of Lysias' oral address that has impressed Phaedrus rather than the content. So he pulls a written copy of the address out of his pocket to refresh his memory of it. At the end of the dialogue we are told that the god Thoth, having invented writing and proclaimed its virtues as an aid to the memory, was informed by his critics that his invention had far more to do with forgetting than remembering, and that it would only encourage mental laziness. Beginning and end fit together exactly. For Phaedrus at the beginning and for Thoth's critics at the end, writing is a vestige of a presence that has vanished, and in fact was continually vanishing even while it was appearing. The same principle would apply to the oral discourse of Socrates, in that context.

But in addition to the Socratic irony which pervades the dialogue, there is a Platonic irony inherent in the arrangement of the dialogue itself. In the middle of it we hear Socrates taking off into the blue in one of his wonderful mythical journeys, telling us of the power of Eros, how it pushes us upward in a staggering chariot drawn by two unequal horses, how it crashes again to the earth as we are reborn once more in a cycle of thousands of years. He also says that Lysias' speech has no shape: his points simply follow one another as minute follows minute, whereas a *logos* or discourse ought to be also a *zoon,* a living being from which nothing can be taken without injury. Socrates is speaking to that unified and organic awareness that is one of the things he means by equating knowledge with recollection: our response to him should be, in part at least, that of the narrator in Eliot's "Marina": "I made this, I have forgotten / and remember." The implication is that Socrates' speech does not merely follow Lysias: it does not even merely confute him. It reverses his movement; it is a tide coming in again after low ebb.

In the New Testament the gospels record the words uttered orally by Jesus. Few if any scholars believe that the authors of the gospels were eyewitnesses, or rather earwitnesses, of the original utterances; they are recording after a lapse of time. The orthodox doctrine says that they were inspired to give a definitive transcription of what Jesus said. The critical principle involved is that the text is not the absence of a former presence but the place of the resurrection of the presence. Or rather, it is not a place but what Wallace Stevens calls a description without place, a description he identifies with revelation or apocalypse. In this risen presence text and reader are equally involved. The reader is a whole of which the text is a part: the text is a whole of which the reader is a part: these contradictory movements keep passing into one another and back again. The Logos at the center, which is inside the reader and not hidden behind the text, continually changes place with the Logos at the circumference that encloses both.

In Donne's poem "The Extasie" two bodies joined in sexual union produce two souls that merge into a single entity. The barrier between subject and object disappears, and the single entity is thereby enabled to enter an experience that is not wholly in time. But of course the clock still goes on ticking in the ordinary world, the united soul dissolves and returns to the two bodies, and ordinary experience is reestablished. It is obvious that Donne is not talking exclusively about sexual union: in such concluding phrases of the poem as "the body is [love's] book" and "dialogue of one," he seems to be glancing at some of our own concerns. Similarly, in another poem, "The Canonization," there is a sexual union in which "we die and rise the same," but which moves from there into metaphors of text and reader. In the sexual union two separate egos form a soul that is still not quite a body; in the reading process the object as book and the subject as reader merge into an identity equally fragile and temporary. But the reader belongs to a community of readers, the text to a family of texts, so that both text and reader have the support of an extending world of a kind that sexual experience, confined as it is to two individuals, cannot provide.

In each of these examples certain beliefs are suggested: reincarnation in Plato, plenary inspiration in the New Testament, a dichotomy of soul and body in Donne. But in the full critical operation there must always be a catharsis of belief, which belongs to secondary concern and secondary mythology. What they all open up to us is a world of recovered identity, both as ourselves and with something not ourselves. That does not mean that we ever escape from paradox into certainty: paradox and self-contradiction are if anything greater than they were before. But these new paradoxes come from the countermovements of myth and metaphor against the annihilations of time and the alienations of space, and one cannot only live with such paradoxes, but live more intensely with them.

Our fondness for words beginning with *post* and *meta* whether we are speaking of the postliterate or the poststructural, of the metaphysical or the metaphorical, indicates the importance we place on the renewing aspect of tradition. We look for the son who comes after the father, bringing a youthful vision of revived hope in place of stability and fixed order. The real reference in *post* and *meta,* however, is less to the future than to another dimension of the present, where time flows back on itself and space collapses in upon itself, and where a sense of reality replaces, for however brief an instant, our normal fear of the unknown.

The Symbol as a
Medium of
Exchange

✧

THE WORD *symbol* is a term of such protean elusiveness that
my instinct, as a practical literary critic, has always been to
avoid it as much as possible. However, the title of this conference, "Symbols in Life and Art," indicates, quite correctly, that
it is a word of major importance in an aspect of criticism which
has also been central to my interests, the linking of the arts,
including literature, to other social phenomena, and the study of
the place and function of the arts in social life. *Symbol* comes, we
are told, from the Greek *symballein*, which means to put together, or, in many contexts, to throw together. A *symbolon* was
a token or counter, something that could be broken in two and
recognized again by the identity of the break. By an easy derivation it acquired the meaning of a ticket, say to a theatrical
performance. Emily Dickinson writes:

> *I never spoke with God,*
> *Nor visited in heaven;*
> *Yet certain am I of the spot*
> *As though the checks were given.*

"Checks" means railway checks, which validate the ticket and
guarantee that one is going to the right place. The word is a
symbol that takes us back to one of the most ancient and primitive senses of the term.

There was also a closely related masculine noun *symbolos*,
which means an omen or augury, such as predictions made from

entrails of birds or the position of the stars. This brings us a little closer to the "throwing" meaning in *ballein,* the sense of something random or accidental which partly reveals something not fully understood. When Mallarmé tells us that a dice throw does not abolish chance, and ends his poem on the subject by saying "Toute pensée émet un coup de dés," he is using a symbol that takes us back to its other primitive sense. In these two Greek words we can see the beginning of a distinction in our conception of symbolism that has run all through its history. A *symbolon* is something that is not complete in itself, but needs something else, or another half of itself, to make it complete. A *symbolos,* in contrast, links us to something too complex or mysterious to grasp all at once.

In the chapter on "Symbol and Myth" in his book *Poetic Process,* George Whalley remarks that "a symbol, like a metaphor, does not stand for a 'thing,' or for an idea; it is a focus of relationships." This is true of the literary context of the word *symbol* with which Whalley is concerned: it is not true of all its contexts. It is very common to use a symbol to stand for a thing or an idea: every noun in language represents a thing or idea in one of its aspects, and every verb an action or event. The relation between a word and the thing or event it represents is arbitrary, or more accurately fixed only by convention. But if we are going to use words in this way we must employ the words that convention has decreed to be the suitable ones. In medical diagnosis, for example, the doctor studies a set of symptoms and tries to find the verbal *symbolon* that unmistakably fits them. Such *symbola* of course need not always be verbal: in driving in traffic, red and green lights are symbolically related to actions that the driver must complete by performing.

But if we turn to other symbols, such as national flags, we find ourselves moving closer to the *symbolos,* the omen or portent. A Greek flag on a ship may be a simple sign telling us that the ship is Greek in origin. But a nation is a very complex entity, and its flag can be used in any number of contexts with any number of possible responses. Here we are definitely in the area that Whalley describes as "a focus of relationships." Flags belong to a group of what may be called metonymic symbols: the symbol is *put for* a cluster of phenomena indicating what kind of social contract a certain body of people has been born into. If Joe Snitch the cat burglar is on trial for stealing, his case is called *Regina vs.*

Snitch. Everyone knows that the queen has never heard of Snitch or has the least awareness that she is going to law with him: the metonymy is there to show (among other things) that the Canadian social contract has a central British and monarchical strain in its cultural traditions. Similarly with religious symbols, like the cross in Christianity or the symbols that appear on the flags of Israel and South Korea.

When such symbols are simple visible or audible stimuli, like a flag or a slogan, they possess a tremendous condensing power. Their focusing of relationships can act as a burning glass, kindling a flame of response from the heat of a myriad social concerns that they draw together into a single impact. At the same time they are displacements of those concerns: they are not the concerns themselves, with all our conflicting and critical feelings about them. The words *condense* and *displace* remind us of Freud's conception of the dream symbol. And certainly there is something dreamlike about a social symbol of this kind. Like the dream image, it is a mirror of our own identity: it looms up out of a mass of vanished or submerged impressions, and speaks to us from a context of silence. Like the dream image, again, it bypasses all mental conflict. Once seen, it is to be accepted (or rejected, if it is a symbol of something hostile to our concerns) and accepted on a deep emotional and uncritical level. Such symbols may be essential to social unity, especially in a crisis, where their function is to stop debate and initiate action. But because of the uncritical element in the response to them, there are lurking dangers in their use. Such words as *flag-waving* express our awareness of these dangers.

Secular loyalties, however, have the built-in safeguard that they cannot be believed to have an ideal form. A sufficiently ferocious tyranny may prevent its citizens from expressing all criticism of it, but that merely makes it more obvious that such criticisms are possible. It is different with religious symbols. Take the symbol of the Christian church in a well-known hymn:

> *We are not divided,*
> *All one body we:*
> *One in hope and doctrine,*
> *One in charity.*

Anyone who had been, let us say, on an ecumenical action committee might well wonder how even a hymn-writer could bring

himself to write this appalling blither. But such a perfectly unified church of pure love and compassion not only could conceivably exist, but according to its own doctrine it does. Hence it is
possible to define the church in a way that would have, to a
visitor from Mars, not the slightest discernible connection with
that building on the corner advertising a rummage sale. This fact
has in the past given a peculiarly venomous quality to disputes
over religious symbols, and it is all the more essential to keep in
mind that a spiritual church, so far as ordinary experience is concerned, is the same thing as a dream church in a dreamworld.

One of the best known discussions of symbolism occurs in
Carlyle's chapter on symbols in *Sartor Resartus*. The chapter begins with a praise of silence and secrecy as the atmosphere in
which all creative work takes shape, and goes on to say "in a
Symbol there is concealment and yet revelation: here therefore,
by Silence and by Speech acting together, comes a double significance." I have tried to show that this is true of the metonymic
symbols I have been discussing, and why it is true. Carlyle then
goes on to distinguish extrinsic from intrinsic symbols: symbols
without value in themselves, like the flags mentioned above, and
symbols that have inherent value. These latter include, first,
works of art, and, secondly, charismatic personalities, heroes,
leaders, prophets, and finally Jesus of Nazareth. The implication
is fairly clear that the intrinsic symbol is the reality to which the
extrinsic symbol points.

It seems to me that in this conception of an intrinsic symbol
Carlyle made the fatal misstep that sent him on the downward
journey to becoming a prophet of fascism. A human personality,
whether of Jesus of Nazareth or of our local member of Parliament, is not a symbol but a presence. Certainly some persons
incorporate many symbolic attributes, like the queen or the
pope, but the symbolism is still extrinsic to them so far as they
are persons. In the title of Kantorowicz's great book, the king
has two bodies: if they are not separable, we have a human leader
who claims a more than human authority, which I think is one
of the things that the New Testament means by Antichrist.

In his inclusion of works of art among intrinsic symbols,
again, it seems clear that Carlyle, as in fact we know from his
other writings, thinks of the work of art as essentially its creator's
personal rhetoric, a by-product of the artist's life. It is true that
in poetry, at least, there is a constant association of the poem

with the poet speaking. But this is a literary convention based on the fact that the poem is being referred back to an original performance. If we ask a poet what his poem means (or, in still clumsier language, what he meant by it), the only truthful answer he could give would be to recite the poem. The poets themselves, from the authors of the Homeric Hymns involving the deity they were celebrating to T. S. Eliot invoking a catalyzer in a chemical laboratory, have insisted that their poetry was not their personal rhetoric but something that seemed to emerge with an origin of its own. The poet, then, like the king, has two bodies, one a maternal body where the poems are gestated and born, the other the person who is, in Yeats's phrase, the bundle of contradictions that sits down to breakfast.

We have now to turn to the question of symbols in works of art, and the obvious art to begin with is literature. Every word is a verbal symbol with two contexts. First, it is half of a *symbolon* which must be matched up to its other half, its conventional meaning, in memory or in a dictionary. Second, it is a *symbolos*, with a meaning related to its context which will give us one more clue to the sense of the whole verbal design of which it forms part. What makes a word a word is its difference from all other words, but what makes verbal arrangement, or syntax, possible is the opposite: a prehensile quality that words have of linking up with one another. To speak in the romantic idiom of early theories of social contract: no sooner has a noun discovered its identity as a word apart from all other words than it also discovers that it is in fact a subject, and must go off looking for a predicate. The predicate meanwhile has been searching for an object; adjectives and adverbs leap in to extend the world of things and actions into a world of qualities and universals and values, and so on until finally an articulated verbal society takes shape. But in, say, a poetic structure, where the bonding of words is so concentrated, there is a second level of linking up which may cooperate with the syntactic links or may override them. This is the level of metaphors and other figures of speech.

The double nature of the symbol, as something completed both by its context and by its relation to something outside the world of words, still remains: as long as it continues to use words, literature can hardly become as abstract, as removed from all direct representation of what is external to itself, as painting or music can. We see this in a late development of the theory of

32

symbols, Eliot's conception of an "objective correlative": "The only way of expressing emotion in the form of art is by finding an 'objective correlative'; in other words, a set of objects, a situation, a chain of events which shall be the formula of that *particular* emotion; such that when the external facts, which must terminate in sensory experience, are given, the emotion is immediately evoked." There are many things wrong with Eliot's conception: it contains an unnecessary mechanical metaphor (the word *automatically* occurs in a sentence following the quotation), and it is a theoretical principle invoked to rationalize a bad value judgment. It occurs in an essay on *Hamlet* in which Eliot asserts that *Hamlet* is an artistic failure because Hamlet's personal disgust and nausea is in excess of the "correlative" it is projected on, namely his mother. But the excess of Hamlet's feeling is precisely what the play is about, and the hinge on which the tragedy turns. Nonetheless the conception is a useful one, and is closely related to such metonymic images as the flag and the dream symbols that we have just been looking at.

We most frequently find such correlatives in the titles of works of fiction, where a central symbol conveys what the author feels his book is "about," what its main theme is. The Canadian novel *White Narcissus,* for example, tells the story of a young man whose love for a young woman is frustrated by the latter's parents, who are emotional vampires: for some reason they have quarreled and have retreated into a mutual sulk in which they communicate only through their daughter, while the mother spends her energies raising white narcissi. Clearly the flower, with its sickly-sweet smell, funereal color, and mythical affinities conveys the sense of psychological deadlock more clearly than any description would do.

We may take the metaphor, perhaps, the statement or pseudostatement that A is B, as the basic form of verbal figure, perhaps the essential figure of which all the others are variants. Let us look at the following verse from Isaiah (55:12): "For ye shall go out with joy, and be led forth with peace: the mountains and the hills shall break forth before you into singing, and all the trees of the field shall clap their hands." Passing over for the moment the rhythm of parallelism which makes the whole verse poetic, we can accept the first part of it as a more or less conscious syntactic statement. The concluding part seems to come from a less conscious part of the mind which is nonetheless linguistically structured. Our normal response to such a statement as "the trees of the field shall clap their hands" is something like "Of course we can't take this literally, but—." What follows the "but" is usually some qualification that turns the response into "This doesn't make sense, or appear to make sense, and yet it does make its own kind of sense." What we have to do with such a metaphor is look into the empty space between what it appears to be saying and what is obviously untrue about what it is saying. What we find in that empty space is, first, a *symbolon,* the counter or other half of the first or more conscious part of the total statement. Second, it is a *symbolos,* a portent or augury of a state of existence in which nature is totally humanized and responsive to human life.

Syntactic and metaphorical meanings, the meaning conveyed by statements or quasi statements and the meaning conveyed by the sequence of imagery, have long been distinguished. Gerard Manley Hopkins speaks of them as overthought and underthought. In very ironic structures the stated meaning can even be a disguise for the figurative one, or, in Eliot's phrase, a piece of meat thrown by a burglar to keep a watchdog quiet. The watchdog in this case is the anxiety of a reading or listening public. If we listen to the opening scenes of Shakespeare's *Henry V,* for instance, we hear, superficially, what the original audience wanted to hear, the patriotic nobles of England urging a heroic king to invade France and clean up on a lot of foreigners. If we listen more closely to the metaphorical imagery, we hear something much more ominous and foreboding. England, says the Archbishop of Canterbury, a century earlier sent the king of Scotland a prisoner to Edward III, then fighting in France:

> To fill King Edward's fame with prisoner kings,
> And make her [England's] chronicle as rich with praise
> As is the ooze and bottom of the sea
> With sunken wrack and sumless treasuries.

It is also generally recognized that the metaphorical texture is less under the control of the conscious will than the syntactic one. Ever since Aristotle's *Poetics* it has been said that the ability to think metaphorically is the distinguishing mark of the poet, what he must be born with, and is the one thing that he cannot learn from others.

If we examine these two levels of meaning in a major poet,

34

we usually find that the syntactic meaning is infinitely varied and flexible, but that the metaphors used are much less so. They tend to cluster around certain repeating images, as though they were building up a kind of structure based on recurring units. Let us look at a sonnet by Sir Thomas Wyatt, written in the reign of Henry VIII:

> My galley, chargéd with forgetfulness
> Thorough sharp seas, in winter nights doth pass
> 'Tween rock and rock, and eke mine enemy, alas,
> That is my lord, steereth with cruelness;
> And every oar a thought in readiness,
> As though that death were light in such a case.
> An endless wind doth tear the sail apace
> Of forcéd sighs and trusty fearfulness;
> A rain of tears, a cloud of dark disdain,
> Hath done the wearied cords great hinderance;
> Wreathéd with error and eke with ignorance.
> The stars be hid that led me to this pain;
>   Drownéd is Reason, that should me comfort;
>   And I remain, despairing of the port.

This poem is based on a sonnet of Petrarch, and is sometimes said to be a translation, though "paraphrase" is more accurate. I think it a tighter and more completely realized poem than Petrarch's. It was first published, not in Wyatt's lifetime, but fifteen years after his death in an anthology known as *Tottel's Miscellany*. The Tottel editor, besides doing his best to destroy the subtleties of Wyatt's rhythms (presumably in the interest of a metrical smoothness which he never achieves anyway), provides the poem with a fancy title: "The Lover Compareth his State to a Ship in Perilous Storm Tossed on the Sea." This suggests that the poem is an allegory, a narrative illustrating a concept. Perhaps it is: it certainly uses allegorical techniques, such as personification ("Wreathéd with error and eke with ignorance"). But I should prefer to think of the controlling design as analogical metaphor. Two vivid pictures, of a despairing lover and a foundering ship, are set up facing each other, each reflected in the other, with occasional points of coincidence such as the "lord," who is both the master of the ship and the god of love, and the hidden "stars," which are both the concealed stars of a stormy sky and the averted eyes of an indifferent or absent lady.

The narrative of the sonnet proceeds straight ahead, glancing at a great variety of entities on its way. But its metaphorical meaning, its underthought, is totally absorbed into this single structure of two reflecting pictures. We note that the specifically poetic features in the sounds of the poem reinforce the metaphorical rather than the syntactic organization. Rhyme emphasizes recurring and echoing sounds; meter recurring and echoic movement. There is also an unobtrusive imitative harmony, as "'Tween rock and rock, and eke mine enemy, alas," where the *k*'s stick up like rocks, or "Thorough sharp seas," where the sibilants hiss like wind in sails. The relation between words and the things they describe is arbitrary: the effect of these devices is to minimize the arbitrariness, to suggest an incantation with some hidden link between what is said and the objective world it is, so to speak, said *at*. Modern free verse may dispense with formal devices like rhyme or meter, but its discontinuous rhythm breaks up the syntactic structure into meditative fragments. Instead of a suggestion of a magical connection between words and the world, it suggests, not exactly that reality is verbal, but that our only possible contact with reality must be verbal, or something closely related to the verbal, such as the pictorial or the musical. In modern poetry, reality is absorbed into what Wallace Stevens calls "a world of words to the end of it."

One inference from all this is familiar to students of literature. Poetry speaks the totality of language, the language of the subconscious as well as the language of consciousness; the language of emotion as well as the language of intelligence. The units of this language, whether words or images or even letters, are symbolic in relation both to their own verbal context and to the external entities they represent. The Romantic poets, beginning with Blake, adapted the word *imagination,* which had previously had the general meaning of hallucinatory vision, to express this linguistic union of conscious and unconscious, the language of reason united to the language of feeling. One principle that emerges here is that every conscious verbal construct, such as a metaphysical system, is founded on less conscious metaphorical ones, usually diagrams of some kind. The other is that criticism cannot deal with literature unless it recognizes the creativity of metaphor in poetic language, and recognizes also that metaphor cannot be described except by another metaphor.

Sometimes a metaphorical understructure of thought

changes without notice. The Romantic critics put metaphorical above syntactic language, a "higher" against a "lower" reason. In this post-Freudian era, aware of the connection of creative power with repression and dream states, we tend to put it below. In between came the *symboliste* movement in France, which put them side by side, with their backs turned to each other. It is common knowledge that *symbolisme* was a development mainly in French literature, influenced by Wagner and Baudelaire, and, through Baudelaire, Edgar Allan Poe. *Symbolisme* emphasized how words made their own kind of reality, and were not merely servomechanisms calling up nonverbal elements of experience. It reacted against rhetorical poetry, and often seemed hermetic and puzzling, because it insisted that the reader should think metaphorically, instead of regarding metaphor as "poetic license," a concession to immature intelligence.

Earlier critics, such as Edmund Wilson, had an easy way of writing off this movement: they described it as a movement of almost total subjectivity, where reality consists of one's own moods and perceptions, which have to be indirectly suggested or evoked rather than described. Certainly the subjectivity is there, to a degree that is occasionally funny or grotesque. For example, Des Esseintes, the hero of Huysmans's *À rebours,* who admires Dickens, decides to take a trip to England. He packs his bags, takes a train to Paris, and a taxi to Galignani's, where he buys a guide to England, and visits a restaurant that caters to English tourists, where he eats an English meal surrounded by people he identifies with characters from Dickens. Then he goes home. He does not have to get sick on a channel crossing, endure any more English weather (it is pouring rain in Paris), or eat any more English food. He has had all the pleasure and none of the trouble of a trip to England, and to follow this symbolic journey with a real one would be most pedestrian and literal-minded.

In Villiers de L'Isle-Adam's dramatic romance, *Axel,* there is a somewhat grislier version of the same principle. The hero is sitting on top of a vast treasure: he goes down to it and finds the heroine about to plunder it—how she got there would take too long to explain. She tries to kill him, but they fall in love instead. The hero decides that, again, they have had the one moment worth living for in their lives, and to go on to consummate their union, or, worse still, go on the extended honeymoon that the heroine proposes, would be simply anticlimax. So the hero proposes mutual suicide: "As for living," he says, "our servants will do that for us." It is not said what the surviving servants are to live on.

The conception of "peak experiences," as they have come to be called, is found in other writers too, notably Pater. Such experiences are symbolic, and reflect our two traditional meanings of symbol: they are portents or auguries of what life could be, and it is worth any amount of commonplace life to purchase one of them. But *symbolisme,* the movement that produced Mallarmé and Laforgue and Valéry and Rilke, is very much more than merely a paradoxical cult of introversion, and it gives the conception of "symbol" a new dimension. The earlier poetry of Rilke, for example, the poetry of the *Neue Gedichte* of 1907–8, is a poetry full of "things," of emotions let loose in a world of Eliot's "correlatives" ready to respond to and complete them. The main influences on him at that time, Rodin's sculpture and Picasso's blue-period painting, are representational, even to some degree realistic. Rilke then fell into a long period of silence, and at the end of it came two works, the *Duino Elegies* and the *Orpheus* sonnets, almost simultaneously. According to a long letter he wrote at the time, the world of things had to be interiorized, the visible world transmuted into the invisible, before the later poetry could take shape. Man's spiritual evolution has to proceed in the direction of moving from a physical into a symbolic world. In the elegies the symbol of the "angel" appears, representing the kind of being for whom this transcendence has been accomplished, and of course Orpheus is preeminently the artist who can transform his physical environment at will. Rilke emphasizes that his conception is not Christian, but it is clearly religious in most senses of the term, an almost Neoplatonic or Gnostic effort to find through words, and through the symbolic relationships of words, a more intense mode of life and experience.

In Mallarmé it is clearer that what Rilke calls an invisible world is a verbal world created in a certain way. In one place Mallarmé speaks of "transposition" and "structure" as characteristic of the poetic process. The poet has to use the same words that everyone else uses, but as they do not belong in ordinary syntactic structures, words in poetry become as distinct from their everyday use as the tones of a violin are from noises in the street. The verbal world is the form for which external reality supplies the material. But there is a single verbal or symbolic world, not just a pile of poems, and this symbolic world, or "supreme fiction" as Wallace Stevens calls it, is forged in defiance of external reality. The world of reality dies into nothing; the symbolic world is born from nothing, for a symbol to begin with is nothing apart from the context that forms around it and completes it.

So although Mallarmé speaks of God as an old scarecrow whom he has at last overcome, he also speaks in his letters of a symbolic death and resurrection that he has attained through his search for a pure poetry, and speaks also of the poet who creates in the teeth of *the* creation, so to speak, as though he were the vehicle of a holy spirit. "Man's duty," he says, "is to observe with the eyes of the divinity, for if his connection with that divinity is to be made clear, it can be expressed only by the pages of the open book in front of him." He also describes himself, in a letter to Cazalis, as "one of the ways the Spiritual Universe has found to see Itself, unfold Itself through what used to be me."

Mallarmé's monologue drama, or whatever it is, called *Igitur,* depicts a man (though he is said to be a young child) descending to the tombs of his ancestors, where he blows out his candle, throws dice, and lies down on the ashes of his ancestors. A throw of dice does not abolish chance, Mallarmé says, but it is a gesture of defiance against the totality of chance: it defines a world where chance and choice are one, in Yeats's phrase. So the ashes may be phoenix ashes after all. Igitur does not commit suicide (if he does) merely because, like the lovers in *Axel,* he is afraid that the rest of his life will be an anticlimax. He has entered the world of nothingness because it is there that everything has to renew itself. Mallarmé's symbolic world, then, is not a Platonic world above the physical one, nor a world of buried treasure below it, nor a private world inside it. It is the world where human creation comes to be, where meaning is, where chance is not abolished but where a world that within itself is not chance has taken shape. It is not a subjective world, because, as Rilke says, all poets are manifestations of the same Orpheus. Symbols intercommunicate: they are not, like dream symbols, parts of a code to be interpreted by unknown or repressed desires within a dreamer. So although we have become increasingly aware, in the last century, of the close connection between dreaming and the poetic process, it seems to me that Keats's principle that "the poet and the dreamer are distinct" still holds up.

It should be becoming clearer that a symbol is a unit of meaning, that is, an image *plus*. If someone knowing nothing of physics examines the traces left in an atom-smashing cloud chamber along with a physicist, or if someone knowing nothing of geology goes for a walk with a geologist and sees a mountain-side exposing a series of rock strata, the two see the same images, but only the trained eye sees them symbolically, as units meaning something in the context of its knowledge. Freud became one of the great pioneers of contemporary thought as soon as he realized that dream images were dream symbols, in the subjective context I just mentioned. On the other hand, there is probably no human society that has not attached some kind of symbolic value to dream images. So perhaps the ability to see the image as a symbol, as a unit to be completed by an understander or by a context, may be, as Cassirer among others suggests, the distinctively human element in consciousness.

The word *symbol* enters the English language in the fifteenth century in the sense of a dogma, or articulated doctrine of religion. We find "the credo and symbol of our faith" in Caxton. This meaning of the word is a late derivation of *symbolon* through Latin. Since then, the meanings of symbolism and faith have widely diverged: symbolism now means to us something that may or may not suggest a belief, but bypasses belief, and does not commit us to acceptance of any specific body of values. It is in their doctrines or conceptual languages that religions disagree: symbols form part of a universal language. And yet a historical religion does establish a framework of understanding that confers symbolic meaning on images, and such a framework may persist unconsciously however strongly repudiated by the consciousness. In studying poets who have talked about symbolism, I find those who, like Mallarmé and Rilke, explicitly repudiate the association with doctrinal Christianity most useful, because it is in them that the historical Christian shape of the framework organizing their conceptions emerges most clearly, more clearly than it does in, say, Claudel or Auden. It is not surprising in any case to find that the whole program of nineteenth-century *symbolisme* was anticipated in the seventeenth century by Andrew Marvell, the Puritan member of Parliament for Hull, in the familiar lines of "The Garden":

> *Meanwhile the mind, from pleasure less,*
> *Withdraws into its happiness:*
> *The mind, that ocean where each kind*
> *Does straight its own resemblance find.*
> *Yet it creates, transcending these,*
> *Far other worlds, and other seas,*
> *Annihilating all that's made*
> *To a green thought in a green shade.*

I have now come within sight of my title, "The Symbol as a Medium of Exchange." The basis for the title is an aphorism of Heraclitus: "There is exchange of all things for fire and of fire for all things, as there is of wares for gold and of gold for wares." Heraclitus is concerned with the perennial theme of the one and the many, the world of "all things" and the sense of unity that the mind constantly struggles for, which emerges in some form in practically every effort to make sense of a pluralistic world. Heraclitus' teaching appears to include some metaphorical conception of a ladder of elements. Earth, wet mud, and water are at the bottom of this ladder: people with undisciplined emotions and undeveloped intelligence are soggy and moist. As they rise in the scale of being they become drier and warmer, and capable of sharing in the common light of experience that Heraclitus calls the *logos*. On the top level of fire, where there is dryness and light, we begin to experience the unity of things instead of simply their plurality. But unity, the oneness of things, cannot be expressed except by such a symbol as the word *fire* provides. Heraclitus apparently does not think that we go up to an "other" world where, in Yeats's phrase again, we stand indefinitely in God's holy fire. Sooner or later the descent back to the world of things takes place, and we begin to sink from the dry light of fire to the mud-vision of the dreaming ego. Perhaps everything consists of these two movements: of death passing into nothingness, of new life coming to birth from the same nothingness. We live each other's deaths and die each other's lives, he says: we move from "all things" to the unity they symbolize, and find that the symbol of unity, the fire, is also the symbol of all things. If

41

so, then the illustration of buying wares with gold is to be taken seriously: we may have one or the other, but not both.

And yet, it is possible that he is speaking of an interchange rather than simply an exchange. "All things" are wholes, yet surely every one of them must have something of what Heraclitus symbolizes by fire in it. What he calls fire, on the other hand, is a whole which may illuminate "all things" rather than causing them to disappear. Let us go back to the early English meaning of symbol as dogma. One of the central dogmas in Christianity is that of the Eucharist, which develops from Paul's conceptions of both being in Christ and of having Christ in himself. Christ is a whole of which we are parts, and at the same time we as individuals are wholes of which Christ is a part. The rite of the Eucharist expresses this paradoxical interchanging of part and whole, the world of fire and the world of all things. The Reformation did not change this doctrine, so far as its symbolism is concerned, but it put more emphasis on another aspect of it. We exist in Christ as the Word of God; as individuals reading the Word of God in the Bible, we are wholes of which the Word is part, so part and whole interchange again.

These are statements of belief, because they are attached to the center of a specific religion. They could be loosely or vaguely attached, as in Edgar Allan Poe's cosmological essay *Eureka,* which ends in the contemplation of "this Divine Being, who thus passes his Eternity in perpetual variation of Concentrated Self and almost Infinite Self-Diffusion." Poe puts in the word *almost* because he will not concede the infinity of the universe. But they could be stated with no such attachments at all, and then they would cease to be statements of belief, or gestures toward it like Poe's, and become simply statements of experience. The teachings of Zen Buddhism have been summarized in the formula "First there is a tree and a mountain; then there is no tree and no mountain; then there is a tree and a mountain." First, simple images, then a state of enlightenment in which particulars vanish, and finally a return to the world of images, now not the less images for having been transformed into symbols of enlightenment. Whatever the English word *enlightenment* may translate from Sanscrit or Japanese, the word itself is clearly not far away from Heraclitus' "fire." Every creative achievement is an invention, and to invent something is, subjectively, to construct it, and, objectively, to find it. A scientist discovers something new

42

in his science, alone, or, more likely nowadays, with the help of forty or fifty colleagues, collects his Nobel Prize, and adds something to the total structure of the science in his time. Before long the entire world picture of which that scientific structure forms part begins to change, in the manner set out in Thomas Kuhn's now classical study, *The Structure of Scientific Revolutions*. I have only to add that no scientific revolution is confined to science: there are invariably parallel and closely related revolutions going on in all other areas of culture, even though they may come at slightly different times. Whenever they come, that curious union of thing and meaning that we call a symbol shows once more that it is neither static nor arbitrary, but part of the continuing presence of our own becoming and being.

✧

The Survival of
Eros in Poetry

✧

EVERY SOCIETY is characterized by concern, a term so broad
that it is practically equivalent to conscious awareness itself,
or at least to the awareness that life is serious, both on its individual and its social sides. The verbal expression of such concern
is, in modern times, mainly conceptual and theoretical, taking
the form of political, religious, psychological doctrines. Before
the rise of conceptual language, however, such verbal expression
would most naturally take the form of stories, stories tending to
explain or identify the gods, the structure of authority in the
society, the legendary history, and the like. It is obvious that a
great many societies would have two categories of stories, one
"sacred" or particularly serious and important, telling the society
what it essentially needs to know, and one more relaxed and secular, stories told for entertainment or mere sociability.

Our own culture, by which I mean essentially the culture of
Western Europe from the beginning of the Christian era to the
present day, along with its descendants in the New World and
elsewhere, was characterized, for many centuries, by a group of
sacrosanct stories derived from the Bible. These stories had consolidated into a mythology, a reasonably coherent account of the
relations of God to man from creation to, in the future, the end
of the world; and the metaphors within the mythology had taken
the form of a cosmology. Like most mythologies of concern, its
primary function was to illuminate and rationalize the structure
of authority, both spiritual and temporal, within its society. Although its cosmology, in some respects, was admitted to be metaphorical, still most of it enjoyed the prestige of a science for a

44

long time. But the cosmology remained essentially related to the sense of concern about man's duties and destiny that had inspired it, and it was not really a protoscience.

This cosmos of authority envisaged a universe on four main levels. At the top was a heaven in the sense of the place of the presence of God. The word *top* is a metaphor, but it was so pervasive a metaphor that it got into practically every type of reference to God, who was invariably thought of as "up there." This God was a Creator, the creation myth of the Bible being an artificial creation myth in which the universe is made by a divine Sky Father, in contrast to others where it is brought into being by an Earth Mother. Such a God could have created only a perfect world, with no sin or death in it: this perfect world is described in the Book of Genesis in its first chapter, and in the story of Adam and Eve in the Garden of Eden. An alienation myth or fall is necessary to account for the difference between this originally perfect world and the one we are now in. The latter forms a third level, also part of the order of nature, and below it is the demonic world or hell—again a metaphorical "down," but an inescapable metaphor. There are, then, a divine presence above nature, a demonic world below nature, and two levels of the order of nature itself, or the created world.

The third or "fallen" world is the one we are born into, and animals and plants seem to be relatively well adjusted to it, but man is not. His natural home is the perfect world God originally created for him and intended him to live in. Nothing remains of this world physically except the stars in their courses, along with the legends concerning the stars, that they are made of quintessence, that they move in perfect circles about the earth, that they give out an inaudible music. Otherwise, the original home of man is no longer a place, but may to some degree be achieved as a state of mind. Man's primary duty, in fact, is to move upward on the scale of being, coming as close to his original state as possible. Many things are "natural" to man that are not natural to any other organism: the wearing of clothes, the being in a state of social discipline, the practice of religion and law, the possession of consciousness. Everything good for man in religion, law, and education has for its end his promotion from the lower to the higher level of nature. Man's pilgrimage is a purgatorial one, whether an actual doctrine of purgatory is involved or not.

If we take such a period as the Elizabethan age in English

45

literature, we can soon see how impossible it is to understand, in many crucial aspects, without realizing that for Spenser, Sidney, Shakespeare, and their contemporaries there are two levels of nature, an upper level of human nature, where nature and art are much the same thing, and a lower level of physical nature, from which man's essential humanity feels alienated. Thus Sidney says that nature's (i.e., lower nature's) world is brazen, in contrast to the poet's golden world, and that (on the higher level) art is a "second nature." In *King Lear* the nature whom Edmund accepts as his goddess is lower nature; what Lear's own references to nature are concerned with is an order of nature that Edmund has shut out of his mind. Such a conception of nature, it is obvious, is one that throws a very heavy emphasis on the aspect of nature called *natura naturata,* nature as a structure or system.

This emphasis derives from the biblical horror of nature worship, that is, of finding anything numinous in nature to adore. This is primarily what the Bible means by idolatry, and the corollary of its condemning of idolatry is the principle that man is to turn away from nature and seek his God through human institutions. Nature was of course created along with man, and the traces of its original perfection may still be seen in it, but whatever we find to admire in it must be instantly referred back to its Creator. Everything God has created possesses two impulses: an impulse to die or decay, which is inevitable in a fallen world, and an impulse to return to its creator, something that only man can do consciously.

Not that man can set out to do such a thing of his own volition. In this cosmos all the initiative comes from above, the initiative that in human life is known as grace. Even a revolutionary thinker in this period, such as Milton, could not think of liberty as anything that man can achieve for himself or even wishes to achieve. Liberty is good for man because God wants him to have it, but without grace no man wants it. There is a current of love flowing from God to man, and it is man's duty to accept that love and communicate it to his neighbor. That is Christian love in its pure form of *agape* or charity. Whatever springs from the sexual instinct is mainly something that belongs to the behavior of a gregarious animal.

All of this represents a very considerable divergence from the tradition of classical literature, starting with Plato and continuing through Virgil and Ovid, which assigns a powerful impetus in human life to Eros, the energy of a love rooted in the sexual instinct, which can be a destructive passion or an ennobling power. It is profoundly significant, for the central question in literary criticism of the social function of the arts, that poets from the medieval period on simply inserted Eros into their cosmos, as something the religious and philosophical authorities had left out, and ought not to have left out.

There is no need to rehearse in detail the familiar story of courtly love in medieval poetry. Influenced largely by Virgil and Ovid, the poets worked out an elaborate correspondence between sexual love and Christian *agape.* One might be living one's life carelessly, in complete freedom from the perturbations of love; then the God of Love, Eros or Cupid, would suddenly strike, and from then on one was Love's abject slave, supplicating the favor (usually) of a mistress. Sometimes, as in Dante, the cult of Eros is sublimated, in other words assimilated to the Christian one. It is Eros who inspires Dante with his *vita nuova* that started from his first sight of Beatrice, but Beatrice in the *Paradiso* is an agent of divine grace. In another great medieval epic, however, *The Romaunt of the Rose,* the climax of the poem is a clearly sexual allegory, and in Petrarch, who did far more than Dante to popularize the theme, at least in English literature, the love for Laura is rooted in Eros throughout, even though again it is sublimated, involving no sexual contact and easily surviving her death.

In these sublimated forms the love of a mistress forms a parallel quest to the purgatorial one: it is what inspires a hero to great deeds and a poet to great words. A poet who attempts poetry without experiencing the power of Eros is conventionally assumed to be a rather poor creature. Sublimation usually means that the mistress is an inspiring object but not a sexual one; love poetry, however, covers the whole spectrum from idealism to bawdiness. What is essential, normally, is a long period of frustration during which the mistress is proud, disdainful, cruel, and the like. Lovers who die or go mad through such frustration are the saints and martyrs of the God of Love: in Chaucer's *Legend of Good Women,* meaning women good by Eros's standards, we find Helen of Troy, Cleopatra, and Dido. The question has been raised of whether Romeo's suicide would, in the minds of Shakespeare's audience, involve him in damnation. Most of the audience would recognize that Romeo has his own religion, which does not con-

47

flict with Christianity but nevertheless goes its own way: when Romeo speaks of "my bosom's lord" he means the God of Love, and he dies a martyr in the odor of erotic sanctity.

Although the main sources of such love poetry are classical, there are certain biblical allusions that reinforce it and help to assimilate it to other types of poetry. The Song of Songs, whatever the commentators had done to it, still remained a great monument of poetry inspired by sexual love, and there the bride is described as "a garden enclosed, a fountain sealed." The imagery of trees and water reminds us of the Garden of Eden, and there too the love of Adam and Eve before the fall remains a pattern of sexual union, even though not everyone shared Milton's view that sexual intercourse as we know it took place before the fall. Let us glance at a familiar lyric of Campion:

> There is a garden in her face,
> Where roses and white lilies grow;
> A heav'nly paradise is that place,
> Wherein all pleasant fruits do flow.
> There cherries grow which none may buy
> Till cherry-ripe themselves do cry. . . .
>
> Her eyes like angels watch them still;
> Her brows like bended bows do stand,
> Threat'ning with piercing frowns to kill
> All that attempt with eye or hand
> Those sacred cherries to come nigh,
> Till cherry-ripe themselves do cry.

The theme of forbidden fruit is associated with sex; the biblical image of the angels forbidding entrance to Eden after the fall is assimilated to the lady's disdain; echoes of the garden of the Hesperides mingle with the memories of Eden suggested by such words as *paradise* and *sacred*. Similarly with Fulke Greville:

> Caelica, I overnight was finely used,
> Lodged in the midst of paradise, your heart;
> Kind thoughts had charge I might not be refused,
> Of every fruit and flower I had part.
>
> But curious knowledge, blown with busy flame,
> The sweetest fruits had in down shadows hidden,
> And for it found mine eyes had seen the same,
> I from my paradise was straight forbidden.

48

The "heart" is invariably a respectable suburban address: if the lover moves into the downtown business section other complications arise. More accurately, the theme of forbidden knowledge is given an even more explicitly sexual connotation than it has in Genesis.

Another association involved here is that between the mistress's body and the garden itself. If we look carefully at the imagery of *Paradise Lost,* we can see how subtly but constantly Milton associates the Garden of Eden with the body of Eve. Marvell's well-known poem "The Garden" describes a union first of the body and then of the soul of the narrator with the garden, and then goes on to make the paradoxical point that the garden itself was the only mistress that Adam needed, the creation of Eve being the beginning of the loss of paradise. A different aspect of the same kind of identification appears in Bartholomew Griffin's *Fidessa* sequence:

> *Fair is my love that feeds among the lilies,*
> *The lilies growing in that pleasant garden*
> *Where Cupid's mount, that well belovéd hill is,*
> *And where that little god himself is warden.*

The first line contains an echo of the Song of Songs, but "Cupid's mount" can hardly be anything but the *mons veneris.* The same imagery, according to most Spenserian scholars, appears in the Garden of Adonis episode of *The Faerie Queene,* where the gardens are also referred to as a paradise. In a very long poem called *Loves Martyr* by Robert Chester, best known now because a group of rather better poets, including Shakespeare, wrote pendants to it (Shakespeare's contribution was called "The Phoenix and the Turtle"), a conventional feature of such poems, the detailed description of the heroine's body, is provided. In case our attention relaxes, the author places in the margin the feature of the lady's anatomy he is talking about: we begin with "Hair," "Brow," "Eyes," and the like, and finally work our way down to "Bellie." Just as we are beginning to get a flicker of interest in this dreary poem, the next stanza has in the margin merely "Nota," and the stanza itself talks about the four rivers of Eden. If the author had been a distinguished poet, we might assign this to a quirky originality, but when he is Robert Chester we can be sure that nothing but straight convention is involved.

Shakespeare's "Phoenix and the Turtle" is a different matter:

there the biblical metaphor of two people becoming "one flesh" in marriage is applied, in an erotic context, to the union in "death," which can mean sexual union, of a red bird and a white bird on St. Valentine's Day. Some of the paradoxes resulting from two things becoming the same thing almost read like parodies of the Nicene creed on the persons and substance of the Trinity. Donne uses the same kind of imagery, especially in "The Canonization" (the title means that the narrator and his mistress have become saints in Eros's calendar):

> The phoenix riddle hath more wit
> By us: we two being one, are it.
> So to one neutral thing both sexes fit,
> We die and rise the same, and prove
> Mysterious by this love.

And, of course, the same biblical paradisal imagery, the same identification of God-created garden and the body of his bride (or virgin mother) could occur in a straightforward Christian poem with no courtly love overtones at all. Thus in Henry Vaughan's "Regeneration":

> With that, some cried, Away; straight I
> Obey'd, and led
> Full East, a fair, fresh field could spy
> Some call'd it, Jacob's Bed;
> A Virgin-soil, which no
> Rude feet ere trod,
> Where (since he stepped there) only go
> Prophets, and friends of God.

The epigraph to this poem is again the passage in the Song of Songs that includes the reference to the enclosed garden and the sealed fountain.

The points I have been making up to now are not particularly novel; my purpose in making them is to bring out certain aspects of historical criticism that are less frequently discussed. One is the status of allusions to classical mythology. From the very strict orthodox point of view, all the resemblances between classical and biblical stories and images result from the activity of the devils, who seized control of the classical oracles (Cowley, for example, speaks of "the fiend of Apollo") and instilled demonic parodies of the sacred myths in the minds of the heathen.

Such demonic parodies may be called negative analogies. But there are other classical myths that can be regarded as positive analogies, as moving, from the poet's point of view, in counterpoint to the sacred texts. It was a commonplace in the Renaissance period that many of the classical myths, especially those in Ovid's *Metamorphoses,* could be used contrapuntally in this way. Thus Giles Fletcher:

> *Who doth not see drown'd in Deucalions name*
> *(When earth his men, and sea had lost his shore)*
> *Old Noah; and in Nisus' lock, the fame*
> *Of Samson yet alive; and long before*
> *In Phaeton's, mine own fall I deplore:*
>   *But he that conquer'd hell, to fetch again*
>   *His virgin widow, by a serpent slain,*
> *Another Orpheus was than dreaming poets feign.*

The story of the worldwide deluge in Ovid, which Deucalion and Pyrrha alone survived, is a positive analogy of the story of Noah in Genesis; the story of "Nisus' injur'd hair," as Pope calls it, has resemblances to the Samson saga; the story of the fall of Phaethon is an analogy of the fall of man; the descent of Orpheus to hell to reclaim his bride Eurydice is an analogy of the harrowing of hell by Jesus and his rescue of his bride the Church. The final phrase about "dreaming poets" is an example of the traditional ingratitude of Christian poets who levy such tribute on the classical writers while officially denouncing the truth of their stories. Similarly, in the first canto of the *Paradiso,* Dante uses the classical images of Marsyas, who was flayed alive for challenging Apollo to a contest in flute-playing (the Olympians were notoriously poor losers, but Apollo had not even the excuse of losing), and of Glaucus, who ate some miraculous grass that turned him into a sea-god. The images are exquisitely precise: Marsyas stands for the divesting of the garment of flesh in paradise and Glaucus for the plunge into a new and unknown element. But the touch of grotesquerie in the same images still keeps a hint of negative analogy or demonic parody.

To understand this more clearly we may turn to the passage in *Paradise Regained* in which Satan suggests that Jesus, if he does not want earthly power of any kind, might become one of the great Athenian philosophers. Here Jesus, in a passage which has troubled many of Milton's commentators, rejects the whole of the classical tradition as worthless. Its taproot is the theology and culture of hell described in book 2 of *Paradise Lost,* and Jesus must reject every atom of it if he is to proceed with his ministry. But having rightly rejected it in the right context, he thereby redeems it, at any rate for his followers. In the *Nativity Ode* all the heathen gods are put to flight by the rising sun of the Incarnation. Our own sympathies are divided: nobody wants Moloch back, and he will always be a demonic parody, but we have more sympathy with the "parting Genius" who is "with sighing sent" from his habitation. Milton can use Moloch only as a devil, but the "Genius" is a positive analogy of a Christian guardian angel, and appears as such in *Lycidas, Arcades, Comus,* and *Il Penseroso.*

The cult of Eros in medieval and later poetry, then, is a special case of the imaginative conquest of the classical poetic mythology, sometimes in the teeth of religious opposition, but steadily increasing the range and power of poetry in the Western world. As society became more complex and sophisticated, other types of analogies grew up: in Protestant England, for example, Jewish or Catholic imagery could be used either as types or as aesthetic analogies of what would be acceptable to authority. In Milton's *Il Penseroso* the narrator, choosing to live in the melancholy tonality, so to speak, for the rest of his life, speaks of dwelling among cloisters, stained glass, Gothic architecture, organ music, and finally a hermitage. All these were deprecated in strictly Puritan circles, but in a mood poem, where aesthetic feelings are so important, they are acceptable as aesthetic analogies. It is probable, but not absolutely necessary, that the nun who is the Muse of this poem is more of a classical vestal virgin than a Christian nun. The poem closes with a phrase that delicately indicates the analogical nature of its imagery, specifically in the passage about becoming a hermit: "Till old experience do attain / To something like prophetic strain."

To anticipate a little, a poet with strong Christian commitments might use classical imagery as analogical to Christian themes, but he would do so, presumably, with the assumption that the Christian theme was primary and the classical one peripheral. Thus Francis Thompson, in *Assumption Maria:*

> *I am the four Rivers' Fountain*
> *Watering Paradise of old;*

Cloud down-raining the Just One am,
Danae of the Shower of Gold.

The same imaginative link between the Virgin Mary and the story of Danae is made by Ezra Pound, in the fourth Canto, but this time there is no sense of the greater reality of one story as compared to another: they are simply two themes in poetic counterpoint:

upon the gilded tower in Ecbatan
Lay the god's bride, lay ever, waiting the golden rain. . . .
Across the Adige, by Stefano, Madonna in hortulo,
as Cavalcanti had seen her.

Cavalcanti has a poem which tells us that the miraculous cures ascribed to a picture of the Virgin were the result of the fact that the model for the Virgin was his mistress: a further secularizing piece of counterpoint.

The general principle this argument is leading to may be expressed as follows. In the earlier stages of a culture, there is usually a dominating myth of concern which controls the arts. In the Middle Ages, for example, the ecclesiastical authorities who were the main patrons of painting prescribed the subjects to be painted and the way they were to be treated, stated which saints were bearded and which clean-shaven, which ones barefooted and which shod, and insisted on certain conventions, such as clothing the Madonna in blue. As painting grew more complex and its patronage widened, the artist became increasingly aware of technical discoveries to be made in the art of painting itself, which might command his loyalties no matter what his patrons wanted. By the time we reach the *Salon des refusés* of the French Impressionists, we have gone a long way in this direction. The principle is more easily illustrated by science. Galileo and Bruno felt a commitment to the scientific conception of a heliocentric solar system even when the anxieties of the time demanded a geocentric one. So did Darwin and Huxley, opposing Bishop Wilberforce on the question of evolution and creation. Today the authority of science is generally recognized, even though the lethal dangers of our time indicate that the conflict of science and social concern is a two-way street, that concern still has its own case, and that there can be such a thing as socially irresponsible science.

53

But society is much less willing to grant literature or the other arts any degree of inner authority of this kind. Certain Marxist regimes, such as Stalinist Russia with its "social realism" and the so-called gang of four group in China, deny such authority as a matter of dogma, and insist that the arts, including literature, must be hitched to the bandwagon of ideology. In theory, of course, there is no ideology, merely the natural creativity of workers released from the constraints of other ideologies, but it would take a fairly gullible observer to accept that. There have been some startling outbreaks of hysteria in the democracies, too, that indicate similar feelings there, even when not expressed in government action. In the period that we have been looking at, there were certainly tensions between the anxieties of the prevailing social concern and the poet's loyalty to his own craft, though their expression was necessarily very oblique. In the thirteenth-century French romance *Aucassin and Nicolette,* for example, Aucassin is warned that his uncompromising pursuit of his lady may place him in danger of hellfire. He replies that hell is clearly the only place to go, because everything that makes life worth living seems headed for it, whereas nobody cares about heaven except a few old crocks who are fit for nothing else. For all the gossamer-light humor, there were contemporaries of the *Aucassin* poet who would have said the same thing in grim earnest. An even more familiar example is the "Retractation" at the end of Chaucer's *Canterbury Tales,* where the poet repudiates those of his tales "that sownen into synne," a phrase that takes his Friar and Summoner at their own valuation. There is a strong aroma of "sign here" about the Retractation, but if it is a voluntary composition of Chaucer's it merely demonstrates the conflict of concern and craftsmanship within the same mind, a conflict that has raged in many great poetic minds before and later. Tasso and Tolstoy are obvious examples.

It seems to me that the question of the authority of poetry within a culture, which is much the same thing as the question of the social function of poetry, is a central problem of critical theory. It is obvious that such authority has no direct or simple connection with content. Most literary critics would recognize a core of authority in the essential visions of Pound or D. H. Lawrence, while admitting freely that they talked a good deal of nonsense as well. As W. H. Auden apostrophizes Yeats: "You were silly like us; your gift survived it all." But what constitutes

54

a "gift"? If we accept the poet's own answer, the ability to write well, we are simply going around in circles.

Around the latter part of the eighteenth century the era of Rousseau, the older cosmos of authority began to break down. What was at issue, as far as literature was concerned, was not the objectively true but the rhetorically convincing: within literature, the word *truth* is a term in rhetoric, and means what carries one along in emotional agreement. The cosmos of authority could not outlive the authority that supported it; and the American Revolution, the French Revolution, and the later Industrial Revolution were cracking up the authority on all sides. Let us look first at the metaphorical association of the presence of God with the upper heavens. After Newton's time, it was no longer believed that the stars were made of an imperishable substance, that they moved in perfect circles, or that they symbolized the underlying harmony of the universe. A universe held together with gravitation suggests a mechanism, not a design, and within literature there is a sharp difference between the two. In Romantic thought the superiority of the organism to the mechanism is a central principle: there being no visible organism in the skies, the upper world becomes increasingly a symbol of alienation, as it still is, for the most part, in science fiction.

More central to our present argument is the poetic treatment of Eros, which from this period on begins to acquire a larger reference. Human sexuality comes to be seen increasingly as an aspect of the neglected *natura naturans,* nature as a vast reservoir of life and reproductive power. Such nature is indissolubly linked to man: man is, therefore, as much a child of nature as he is of God. And so another cosmos began to grow up in poetry, with much the same set of levels as before, but, in effect, the older world stood on his head. At the top was empty space, filled by an emotionally meaningless world of stars. This world suggested nothing to the human imagination except the involuntary and mechanical: hence the sky-god in Romantic and much later poetry, Blake's Urizen, Shelley's Jupiter, Hardy's immanent Will, becomes a source of tyranny. Below this is the world we live in; below that again is a nature, huge, mysterious, morally ambivalent, an otherness that is nonetheless an essential part of our own identity. In more optimistic writers, this "nature" is what man needs to complete his own being, a wise and benevolent teacher, as normally in Wordsworth. Elsewhere it is a sinister image, predatory, ruthless and totally indifferent to human values, but man is inescapably attached to it nonetheless.

In the older construct the two levels of nature were arranged so as to put the ordinary world we are all born into—or thrown into, according to some—metaphorically below an ideal or paradisal world where man was, at one time, fully integrated with his natural surroundings. In the newer Romantic construct the world of ordinary experience sits on top of a world in which man rediscovers his integration with nature, but does not necessarily find this a beneficial discovery. Some writers in the Rousseau orbit associated the natural with the rational and assumed that a natural society would also be a rational one: it is this attitude that changed the word *artificial* from a term of approval to a deprecatory one. In Shelley a relation of sexual love normally involves a reintegration of nature: thus in *Epipsychidion:*

> *Let us become the overchanging day,*
> *The living soul of this Elysian isle,*
> *Conscious, inseparable, one.*

Such an integration with nature as environment would have been impossible for, say, Donne, with his conviction that there is nothing paradisal outside the regenerate human mind. Elsewhere the sense of otherness in nature is associated with its size and strength: the feeling of awe that produced the "sublime" in Romantic and pre-Romantic aesthetic. I have elsewhere spoken of the curious "drunken boat" construct in nineteenth-century thought, where the world of experience seems to float precariously on something immensely powerful that both supports it and threatens it. Examples are the world as will in Schopenhauer, the world of unconscious impulse in Freud, the world of the excluded proletariat in Marx, the world of evolutionary development in Darwin and the social applications of Darwinism. In some of these constructs the lower world contains only monsters of the deep; in others there is a submarine Atlantis to be reached.

It is particularly the latter group who revive the ancient theme of the quest of descent, which had been kept alive because of the prestige of Virgil's *Aeneid* and the extraordinary vision of its sixth book, but which in Christian constructs was usually demonized. With the Romantic period there begins that inner quest to something oracular in the depths of the mind which has developed, among other things, the technique of fantasy. In De Quincey, for example, particularly in the great mail-coach essay, there is, first, a long diffuse and digressive piece of reminiscent writing, as though the author were scanning the ground for clues; this suddenly tightens up into a moment of intense action, except that the action is not performed but observed by him, and after that it funnels into the dreamworld in a descending spiral. The dreamworld is, like all the levels of the Romantic cosmos, morally ambivalent: the *Confessions* ends with two sections, one on the pleasures and the other on the pains of opium, the good and the bad trips, after which there is a succession of visions representing the fact that the greatest intensity of the imagination is to be found at the bottom rather than the top of experience, as in the classical oracles, which were also assisted by drugs or narcotics. In the mail-coach essay the experience described dramatizes to the writer the essential weakness of human consciousness as based on observation, and hence on the lack of a crucial spontaneity where action is needed. Perhaps, De Quincey concludes, the central thing that dreams are trying to tell us is that man's rational and observing consciousness is his original sin:

> Upon the secret mirror of our dreams such a trial
> is darkly projected, perhaps, to every one of us.
> That dream, so familiar to childhood, of meeting
> a lion, and, through languishing prostration in
> hope and the energies of hope, that constant se-
> quel of lying down before the lion, publishes the
> secret frailty of human nature—reveals its deep-
> seated falsehood to itself—records its abysmal
> treachery. Perhaps not one of us escapes that
> dream; perhaps as by some sorrowful doom of
> man, that dream repeats for every one of us,
> through every generation, the original temptation
> in Eden.

We are reminded of the fact that the *Confessions* ends with a line from the end of *Paradise Lost* about the angels expelling man from Eden, and, by anticipation, of the dream of Finnegan, or rather of HCE, in Joyce, with its feelings of primordial guilt as the unreached source of the dream pilgrimage itself. For modern literature the essential link between man and nature seems to be the sexual one, and the great battle between sexuality and self-consciousness, or what Lawrence called sex in the head, is so prevalent a theme in literature now as to suggest that the integration of Eros is close to the center of whatever new cosmos will replace the Romantic one.

I spoke at the beginning of concern as one of the essential elements of all civilization. It seems to me that there is primary concern and secondary concern. Primary concern is based on what can be expressed only in the baldest and biggest of platitudes: the sense that life is better than death, happiness better than misery, freedom better than slavery. Secondary concern has to do with the structure and source of authority in society, with religious belief and political loyalties, with the desire of the privileged to keep their privileges and of the nonprivileged to get along as well as they can in that situation. I think the present age, with its threats of nuclear warfare and environmental pollution, is an age in which secondary concerns are rapidly dissolving. Down to the Romantic period, and for many poets later than that, the cosmos within which most writers worked was either the cosmos of authority already described, or the cosmos of revolt, which we said was essentially the same kind of structure upside down. As the sixteenth-century Anabaptist theologian Hans Denck remarked, after publishing a list of antithetical statements culled from scripture: "Whoever leaves an antithesis without resolving it lacks the ground of truth."

Occasionally one discovers a writer who is not satisfied to inhabit his world unconsciously, or by instinct, or whatever the right term is. Thus Poe's *Eureka* is an essay on speculative cosmology which sounds as though it were using scientific or philosophical language, but which Poe himself says at the beginning he wishes to be considered as a poetic product. Paul Valéry's note on *Eureka* remarks that cosmology is primarily a *literary* art: it is based, not on the scientific or philosophical ideas of its time, but on metaphorical analogies to them that appeal to poets. The purpose of such cosmologies is to give us some notion of the kind of context within which literature is operating, the imaginative counterpart of the worlds explored by intellect and sensation. Since then, a good many such speculative cosmologies have emerged, some disguised as historical or scientific treaties, and

58

eventually, one hopes, we shall have a clearer notion of what kind of world our creative writers are living in.

Such a world is dominated by forces that were originally gods, Eros, Prometheus, Cybele (perhaps the closest approach to Graves's white goddess), and others. In consequence some modern writers have accepted a polytheistic outlook: Hölderlin did, and Ezra Pound often talked as though he did. But it is only a nervous habit that keeps us calling such forces gods: they are states of the human mind with metaphorical identities in nature. More important, they are the shaping powers of poetry, the authentic Muses. In Greek myth the Muses bore the names of literary genres and were in the aggregate daughters of memory, that is, of literary convention. In our day they bear names like Anxiety, Absurdity, and Alienation, and they are the daughters of Frustration; but their power is as great as ever, and their cultural achievements could be as impressive as ever.

II

The View
from Here

✧

I SUPPOSE a certain amount of reminiscence is appropriate to
this occasion, but I shall try not to overdo it. If one has remained for a long time in the same place, one gets some curious
kinds of bifocal vision. It is disconcerting, or was at first, to find
that the student in front of you is the grandchild of one of your
classmates. There is also a confusing foldover in time, because at
my age the classmate of the past is more vivid in the memory
than the student of the present. I have kept going by putting
together the two great axioms of the Book of Ecclesiastes: "there
is nothing new under the sun," and "there is a time for all
things." The first axiom refers to knowledge and to history: many
things go in cycles, and that fact tends to even out one's moods.
Good times do not last, but bad times do not last either. The
second refers to experience: each stage of the cycle, when it
comes round, is a fresh and unique phase of life.

Over the last half century, however, I can see social changes
that suggest bigger cycles than those of a single life. In my own
undergraduate days, a great many students came from small
towns, mainly in western Ontario: there was of course no Waterloo then, no Guelph apart from O.A.C. [Ontario Agricultural
College], and no McMaster in Hamilton. Coming to a bigger
city was an essential part of one's cultural education, even grant-
ing that Toronto was something of a hick town then compared
to what is available in it now. It says a good deal about the
essential nastiness of my disposition that what I seem to remember most clearly is Bertrand Russell responding to a question
with "Read my books," Paderewski playing the Chopin "Butter-

fly" Etude with the most exquisitely bad taste, and a number of movies, silent and audible, sufficiently corny to be regarded now as primitive classics.

The lectures, at least in English literature, were rambling and digressive, because there were no courses in contemporary or Canadian literature, and any reference to what was going on around us had to be, so to speak, bootlegged into a lecture on something else. I first heard about the Group of Seven in a lecture by John Robins on the ballad, and about contemporary Canadian poets and novelists in Pelham Edgar's course in Shakespeare. Fortunately, Pelham rather disliked Shakespeare, so I learned a good deal about Canadian literature while reading Shakespeare on my own.

At that time, Toronto was a very homogeneous town; the names of Victoria students read like a Belfast phone book, and the public food was as bad as it is in most right-thinking Anglo-Saxon communities. Shortly after the Second World War, a social worker told me that one out of every seven people in Toronto had been there less than a year. Canadians are often scolded for their diffidence and lack of sense of identity, but the positive side of that is, I think, shown by the ability of Toronto to absorb this tremendous and cosmopolitan influx with what seems to me a minimum of tension. The fact that the public food improved dramatically may have had a soothing effect.

Canada had, I think, one of its few advantages in starting out with two European cultures and languages. Nobody could ever say what a hundred percent Canadian was, except that he would obviously have to be bilingual, which in 1929, when I first came to Toronto, would have eliminated practically the entire city. Here there certainly has been tension, but even in the worst days of separatist terrorism a dozen years ago I never saw in Canada anything like the *mort aux flamands* graffiti that I have seen in Belgium. And while there are many disadvantages in being trapped in the middle of a big city, Toronto seems to have escaped the worst of the problems that have beset Chicago and Columbia.

One soon learns that many social issues that we at first consider moral are really nothing more than convention, and can evaporate like the morning dew almost unnoticed. What has always been to me a very moving spectacle, the meeting at reunions of graduates of fifty years back with the present undergraduate body, shows how easily a continuing institution can get over generation gaps. In my undergraduate days there was still prohibition, and very strong feelings about it, especially at Victoria. This reflected the rural-based society of nineteenth-century Canada, where it did tend to be true that people either took to drink or stayed off it, and where temperance organizations were politically liberal, even radical, centers of activity. But as manners became more urbanized this issue simply disappeared. That was merely a change in social pattern: whether we call it an improvement or not depends on our selection of evidence.

Some things I note with at least tentative satisfaction. I am concerned with language, and among other things with the dialects within the same language that indicate where the social barriers are. There are slight differences between the vocabularies, inflections, and linguistic assumptions of men and of women: a century ago those differences were very marked. They pointed to a social situation in which women were given a certain protected status in order to keep them out of the decision-making processes of society. The speech of what are called adolescents differs from both the speech of children and of adults. In times of great social tension, like the late sixties, some young people would express their dissidence by refusing to speak the ordinary language, or by reverting, like certain other social groups, to the starvation-budget vocabulary that consists in the repetition of two or three obscenities. Even in more placid times, the English teacher is often handicapped by a shyness, almost a feeling of shame, on the part of young people about speaking articulately at all.

I think this reflects that very ill advised development of the early part of this century, the deliberate creation of the "adolescent" or "teenager" as a means of keeping young people off the labor market and consigning them to an intermediate limbo where they were neither children nor grown-up. Their situation was similar to that of women: some protection and privilege at the price of exclusion from a good deal of adult life. In the 1920s the cult of adolescence extended into the university, where the typical undergraduate was supposed to be a case of arrested development in a coonskin coat. My sister was teaching then in a working-class area near Chicago, and she reported that she had no luck at all in persuading parents of even the brightest children to send them to college. They had acquired their notions of college from the movies; the movies had told them that college was a middle-class playground, and they would not have their children declassed in so humiliating a way.

Sixty years ago is not as remote as it may seem. A few weeks ago a neighbor's son, a boy of eleven, came in to see me with a questionnaire his teacher had given him. His first question was: "What sort of image comes into your mind when you think of a teenager?" I said none whatever: I thought it was not only silly but morally wrong to form stereotypes of large and miscellaneous groups of people. He said that if that was my attitude there was no point in going on with the questionnaire. But I knew well enough what his teacher meant, and I hope that more flexible methods of involving high school and university students in the operating of their institutions will minimize both the social and the linguistic differences.

What I am circling around here is the fact that the more homogeneous the language, the fewer social barriers there are. A century ago the language of domestic servants in *Punch* or of black people in comic strips was supposed to be automatically funny, like pidgin English, which I understand was developed partly to make non-English speakers of English sound foolish. I should be very pleased to think, if it were true, that teachers of language may have had something to do with a growing thinning of class barriers, and that speech is being used less and less as a form of aggression, whether of class or sex or age. In this process I think it important to understand the extent to which language can neutralize or fossilize, that is, help along this minimizing of aggressiveness by a kind of inertia.

Every language picks up metaphors from the social phenomena around it, and retains those metaphors long after the phenomena have disappeared. We don't have cockfights any more, but we still say "crestfallen" and "showing the white feather"; we don't shoot with flintlock muskets any more, but we still speak of "hanging fire" or "a flash in the pan." Retaining these metaphors in the language gives us no nostalgia whatever for the return of cockfights or flintlock muskets. In the same way traces of ancient feuds and intolerances may survive in language without reviving dead emotions. If I speak of a member of the Society of Friends as a Quaker, I am using a term that was originally hostile or derisive, but it has become so sanctioned by usage now that it no longer conveys any sense of hostility to any listener. Similarly a doctor may speak of an abnormal arrangement of chromosomes as "mongolism" without reference to the idiotic racism that originally suggested the word. In the seventeenth century there were Puritans who refused to pronounce the word *Christmas* because the last syllable was "mass," and there are people today who refuse to pronounce the word *chairman* for much the same reason. However, people kept on saying *Christmas,* and Christmas did not turn Roman Catholic in consequence: it merely turned pagan. It seems to me superstitious to assume that words can never fossilize, but must always keep reminding us of their origin.

It is not difficult to show that social changes are reflected in changes of language. What interests me more is the reverse possibility: that the teaching of language, and the structures of literature in which language is contained, may foster and encourage certain social changes. This is what I should like to discuss briefly now.

Not long ago I was asked to speak to a group of alumni in a neighboring city, and a reporter on a paper in that city phoned my secretary and asked if this was to be a "hot" item. My secretary explained that Professor Frye was what Marshall McLuhan would call a cool medium of low definition, and that he could well skip the occasion, which he did with obvious relief. The incident was trivial and typical, and I wanted nothing less than a reporter on my trail looking for hot items, but it started me thinking about the curiously topsy-turvy world of "news" as reported today.

What would the historians of the future, say of the year 2283, assuming the human race lasts that long, make of the history of Canada in the 1980s? In that remote future it is most unlikely that there would be any historians left who would still regard newspapers as historical documents. If there were any such, they would have to report that in the 1980s there were clearly no functioning universities in the Toronto area, otherwise the papers would refer to their activities, but that there must have been some conception of the university, because every month or so these same papers would run an item asserting that there was no particular advantage in attending one. There might also be, in that future, some anthropologists with a historical bent, and they might have some interest in studying the assimilating of children's and adult activities during this period. They would point out, for example, that in the phrase "adult entertainment," the word *adult* had already come to mean infantile, and they might trace out the similarities of pattern between, say, the leadership conventions of political parties and children's games, like pinning the tail on the donkey.

But the real historians of that period would know very well that nothing of any historical importance whatever was taking place in Canada during the 1980s except what was happening in the universities, and in certain specific fields outside that were directly reflected in and by the universities. These fields would vary widely: there would be environmental control, related to the biological area of the university spectrum; computer technology, related to engineering and physics; literature and the performing arts, related to the humanities, and so on. If Canadian universities continue to be underfunded and supported so badly that they can no longer function effectively, Canada will disappear overnight from modern history and become again what it was at first, a blank area of natural resources to be exploited by more advanced countries. This is not empty rhetoric: it is a verifiable fact, just as the destructiveness of the hydrogen bomb is a verifiable fact. In neither case should I care to become known as the person who verified it. What is connected with the universities is what is really happening: the political and economic charades also going on are what are called pseudoevents, created for and blown up by the news media. The human lives behind these charades, of the people losing their jobs or finding that they can no longer live on their pensions, certainly do not consist of pseudoevents. But they are not hot news items either.

The humanities in particular have for some time been fighting a rearguard action, constantly faced with supercilious questions that take the general tone: assuming that your area of interest is an expendable luxury, what are the serious things in society you can attach it to in order to defend its continued support? There are only two answers, so far as I know. One is the utterly futile Vicious Circle argument: we have to go on teaching this stuff to younger people so that they will grow older and teach it again to the next generation. The other is the National Interest argument. If we are going to trade with Latin America it might be useful to know Spanish; if Ronald Reagan's hardware fails to perform on schedule it might be handy to have some elementary Russian grammars around. But one should not try

68

to argue by accepting the terms of people who have got it all wrong.

The basis of my own approach, as a teacher of the humanities, has always been that we participate in society by means of our imagination or the quality of our social vision, and that training the imagination and clarifying the social vision are the only ways of developing citizens capable of taking part in a society as complicated as ours. Society supports compulsory education up to the point of producing passive, docile, obedient citizens. We must learn to read in order to read traffic signals and government handouts; we must learn to count to make out our income tax; we must learn to write to sign the income tax form. Obviously learning to read and write on this level is as essential for living in the modern world as food and shelter, and we periodically hear public complaints that the schools are not enabling children to grow up in a real world. So we get such slogans as a "back to basics" movement. The "basics," however, are not bodies of knowledge: they are skills, and the cultivating of a skill takes lifelong practice and repetition. All genuine education starts with the passive knowledge of elementary reading and writing and then tries to transform this passivity into an activity, reading with discrimination and writing with articulateness. Without this background of practice and repetition, one may be able to read and write and still be functionally illiterate. It is, admittedly, discouraging for a student to find that he has reached university and is still totally unable to say what he thinks. It is even more discouraging to realize that the real trouble is that he cannot think, thinking being a by-product of the skill developed in the practice of language. When he is in that condition there may be some relevance in a literature course that shows him the amount of reading, pondering, experiencing, and revising that has gone into the making of a serious writer, whose books are like the tip of an iceberg, the little that has emerged from a sunken mountain of torn-up drafts.

A skill may be difficult to acquire without having social authority: articulate speech and writing does have authority, though critics have hardly begun to examine its nature. Every society, if it is to hold together at all, has to develop a body of concerns, assumptions in various areas, political, economic, religious, cultural, that are generally agreed on, or sufficiently agreed on for members of that society to communicate with one another. As society gets more complicated, various bodies of knowledge appear within it: these bodies of knowledge develop their own authority, and that authority may conflict with the concerns of society. We can see this most easily in the sciences. Galileo upheld a heliocentric solar system when the anxieties of a panic-stricken church were screaming to keep the geocentric one. That meant a conflict of loyalties in Galileo's mind, one to his science and the other to society as a whole. As I understand it, there was not as yet, in Galileo's time, an overwhelming body of evidence on the heliocentric side. Galileo was simply taking what some writers on religion, such as Pascal and Kierkegaard, call a leap of faith. Not every leap of faith is a religious one.

It is not hard to see that the sciences have their own authority, to which a scientist is committed even when their authority conflicts with that of social concern at the time. It is harder to see that literature and the arts also have their own authority, that a writer may have to persist in his loyalty to the demands of what he writes even when threatened with censorship or personal persecution. Marxism, in fact, whenever it comes to power, simply denies, as a point of dogma, that literature has any authority of its own at all. Literature in a socialist country, it says, should reflect and follow the demands of socialist concern, otherwise it will turn into the neurotic, introverted, decadent, etc., kind of literature produced in the bourgeois countries. The United States has no actual dogmas on the subject, but there have been startling outbreaks of hysteria, from Anthony Comstock in the 1890s to Joseph McCarthy in the 1950s, and it is clear that such hysteria is constantly there, waiting for someone sufficiently evil to get it organized.

The whole question of the authority of culture is complex: there are no easy answers, and certainly social concern does have its own case. Nuclear bombs, the energy crisis, the pollution of the environment and the choking off of the supply of air, all indicate that scientists have a profound social responsibility for everything they do, and that ignoring it is treachery to their science as well as to society. In literature, too, I think that there is such a thing as a moral majority, though I certainly don't believe that the people who call themselves that represent it, which a serious writer has to respect. Once when I was very young I found myself on a train with nothing to read, and in desperation bought a thriller from a news agent. It told me, in effect, that practically all the Chinese in North American cities were engaged in drug-running and in kidnapping or seducing young white women. It would be against the law to distribute such stuff in Ontario today, and I thoroughly approve of the law.

Nevertheless, almost all movements of censorship are mistaken, because they spring from an instinctive hostility to anything that seems to threaten one's habitual reflexes. Hence censorship almost always fastens on the most serious writers as its chief object of attack, whereas the serious writer ought to be considered the ally of social concern, not its enemy. I can remember a time when even university professors (none of them at Victoria, I should add) would tell their students that D. H. Lawrence and James Joyce were degenerates wallowing in muck. The real concerns of society are not anxieties, which merely resent the authority that comes from the fresh and expanded vision of the serious writer. The failure to grasp this results in some very grotesque situations: people in Canada snatching Canadian books out of high school libraries that are read and studied with the greatest enthusiasm in a dozen countries in Europe.

What emerges from this is, I think, that there are two levels of social concern. There is a primary level which is instinctively exclusive, suspicious of outsiders, and very wary of any new developments from within. Left to itself, this primary level becomes a lynching mob, where every clearly defined individual, simply by being that, becomes a marked-out victim. Above this is a higher level of concern, reached occasionally by the professions and some of the trades, but much more clearly represented in the arts and sciences. The achievements of a society's culture always have a quality of authority about them, however foul the anxieties of the society out of which they emerged. We return again and again, with the same shuddering delight, to the opening of *Macbeth:* "Thunder and lightning: enter three witches," even though we know that these witches were contemporary with the most hideous and pointless tormenting of harmless old women. Perhaps the witches were put into *Macbeth* to amuse King James, who was an ardent and gullible supporter of witch-hunting, but the authority of the play is unaffected by that. However, this upper level of authority has no power: it is spiritual authority only, and is an ark precariously perched on Ararat when there is still no evidence that the flood is receding.

This is not to say that the study of the arts and sciences will make us better people: it can, and it should, but it would be nonsense to claim that it invariably does. Nothing works by magic. Reading the Gospels, and contemplating the quiet dignity and unwearing kindliness of its central figure, one would say that it would be impossible that any religion founded on such an influence could develop mob hysteria, ferocious persecution, torturing of suspected dissidents, or public burnings of "heretics," but unfortunately the record of history indicates otherwise. Still, there is potentially the greatest experience to be ordinarily had in life in attending a university for several years. The university is a community in which the intellect and the imagination have a continuously functional place, and so gives us a sense of what human life could be like if these qualities were always functional in it. The phrase "alma mater" does, or could, mean something: in taking one's first degree there is a genuine *rite de passage,* an acceptance of a new motherhood in which the maternal spirit is one of companionship rather than protectiveness or externalized authority.

I think Canada is a good training ground for the detachment, without withdrawal, that the university gives, because it is a secondary and necessarily observant country. Ordinarily we associate authority with leadership, but Canada is the sort of environment in which we can see most clearly that leadership is a conception that modern society is trying to outgrow. A bad metaphor blocks us here. Convocation addresses frequently refer to graduates as young people facing forward into the future, but of course nobody faces the future: we face the past and back into the future, and what knowledge of the future we may have, or think we have, we glean from a study of the past which is really a form of divination. Statistical tables replace the guts of chickens, and statements by public figures take the place of riddling oracles, but the process remains much the same.

The leader is needed in competitive situations, where he faces, not the future, but the opposite leader. War is competition pursued to its limit, hence military leaders are needed in wartime; competitive business similarly, and Marxist countries are more preoccupied with leadership than we are because they feel an urgent need of competing with capitalism. Under ideal social conditions, we should not have leaders but representatives of public opinion, who do not pretend to face the future but retreat gradually into it, one hopes with a sufficiently sensitive backside. Intellectuals often do not make good politicians because they construct their social vision by themselves, without waiting for the input of Tom, Dick, and Harry. The intellectual tends to be aware only of the higher level of culture, just as the demagogue is aware only of the lower one. Real political guidance, of course, is constantly aware of both.

In the course of my teaching I have gone through two cycles of student radicalism. One was in my graduate student days, when, in the wake of the depression, a number of left-wing groups crystallized on the campus, of which the Stalinist Communists had the most effective control of most youth organizations. The second cycle was in the late sixties, which was much more anarchist in tone, and drew its main inspiration from the cultural-revolution or gang-of-four Maoism in China. Crude and simplistic as student radicalism has usually been, such movements have their importance in illustrating the fact that universities form something of a counterenvironment in society, that they dramatize a state of free criticism of that society from the inside. It is the same principle that has developed the system of tenure appointments for the staff. Tenure may look now as though it were merely a form of job security, but those who remember the frantic efforts to get rid of Professor Underhill in the 1930s will understand that it has often been much more than that. Underhill had said only what everyone takes for granted now, that Canada had effectively ceased to be a British country and had moved into the American orbit, but the generators of local hysteria at that time were immediately activated.

Not long ago I read a book called *The Origin of Consciousness in the Breakdown of the Bicameral Mind*, by Julian Jaynes, who is at Princeton, though the book was published by the University of Toronto Press. This book tells us that man was not really conscious in ancient times, in, say, the Old Kingdom in Egypt, in Sumeria, in the oldest strata of the *Iliad*. That is, he had no sense of a continuous self existing in time, where experience moves along a central egocentric base, so that our verbal expression instinctively takes a narrative form that imitates the continuity of the self. Ancient man, we are told, had a divided or two-chambered brain, one hemisphere controlling immediate and practical actions, the other getting along with hallucinations and autonomous voices, assumed to be of or proceeding from a god or other symbol of authority. By the time we reach the Greek oracles and the Old Testament prophets, these voices and visions are heard and seen with increasing difficulty, and are increasingly associated with mental disturbance as a unified consciousness takes over. Today the ancient two-chambered experience survives in schizophrenia and the like.

It is an interesting book, but it presents consciousness as a recent form of evolution, and suggests the reflection: seeing what a ghastly mess our egocentric consciousness has got us into, perhaps the sooner we get back to split brains and hallucinations the better. And in fact something very similar in feeling to this forms one of the major cultural trends of our time. It is widely felt that our present form of consciousness, with its ego center, has become increasingly psychotic, incapable of dealing with the world, and that we must develop a more intensified form of consciousness, recapturing many of Mr. Jaynes's "bicameral" features, if we are to survive the present century. It is interesting to compare the history of the word *imagination*. In Shakespeare's day imagination was mainly a pathological term, seeing what is not there, the sense that survives in our word *imaginary*. With the Romantics, beginning in England with Blake, *imagination* reversed its meaning and became the thing that made man a creative being, in fact the power that unified his consciousness. The Romantics tended to ascribe the power of creating to an inspiration or genius that dwelt in mysterious and inaccessible areas of the mind, where it fitfully emerged from time to time, much as though the brains of creative people were two-chambered. This conception of the Romantics was, perhaps, the direct ancestor of the consciousness movement of today, or what I think of as the Zen industry, which by meditation, paradox, even physical violence, attempts to dissociate the linear ego and liberate us from helplessly dragging along after it.

It was a similar intuition that started off the work of Marshall McLuhan, who also contrasted a linear, causality-bound, tunnel-vision type of perception with a simultaneous type capable of taking in many aspects of a situation at once. He associated the linear perception with the reading of print and the simultaneous one with the more many-sided appeal of the electronic media. I think these were the wrong referents, because it is only the preliminary process of reading that is really linear: once read, the book becomes a focus of a community, and may come to mean, simultaneously, any number of things to any number of people. The electronic media, on the other hand, vanished so quickly in time that we can make no sensible use of them without falling back on the continuous ego. I think McLuhan also realized very quickly that these were the wrong referents, but by that time he had been ground up in a mass-media blender and was unable to set the record straight.

What is involved here is a prodigious change, extending over the last three or four centuries, in our views of what is or should be "normal" and of what deviates from it. Some time ago I was reading a rather dull academic book when Samuel Johnson's phrase about Addison floated into my head: "He thinks justly, but he thinks faintly." This started me thinking, no doubt faintly, about what is really meant by the phrase "he thinks justly." Would any contemporary critic use such a phrase as a commendation? To think justly implies, it seems to me, thinking from out of a center of established assumptions, agreed upon by practically the whole educated upper middle class of a society with clear lines of authority running through it. Johnson himself, Gibbon, Hume, even Macaulay in a latter age, however widely they may have differed among themselves, all think justly in this sense, and they all write, in consequence, with an assurance that they are addressing consistently rational readers. They speak for a world in which society establishes the criteria for what is rational, and where a deviating individual is a crank. I spoke earlier of young people who feel almost a sense of shame in speaking articulately. I think part of the trouble is that we still tend to think of this kind of continuously rational prose as normal prose, whereas the student knows that for him it is a dead language.

If we had asked anyone in the universities in Shakespeare's day, or Milton's, or even Johnson's, what writer we should study to give us a clear sense of civilized and humane values, he would almost certainly have urged us to devote our days and nights to the study of Cicero. For many readers of our day, interested in the more prominent twentieth-century writers, Cicero is the pits: they would see nothing in him but platitude and cliché and sonorous nonsense, at best a certain amount of pop philosophy. This seems strange: critical readers today live in a linguistic age, and one would think that stylistic mastery of Cicero alone would hold their interest. But Cicero was admired for so long because nobody spoke with greater assurance out of that center of authority in which one "thinks justly." He is a secondary writer today for the same reason. The people who have interested us most, from Rousseau onward, have been mainly people who thought unjustly, who went off exploring on their own, broke with customary assumptions, exaggerated some questions and blandly ignored others. Behind this is a revolution in our assumptions about society, the individual, the normal mind, and the intellectual deviate.

For Johnson, the consensus of society established the criteria of sanity. Society as a whole could not be mad; only the individual could, and Johnson was ready to accuse even himself of disorders of mind near to madness. After the French Revolution the notion that society as a whole could go mad became more conceivable. When Johnson published his essay on Addison, William Blake was in his late twenties, and Blake was a typical example of the deviating individual who could be dismissed as an eccentric too close to madness to be taken seriously. Well, Blake's biographer tells us that the Blakes once had a visitor, and that, as they could not afford a servant, Blake went over to a nearby pub and brought back a supply of beer. On the way he met a successful artist, a Royal Academician, who had met him at a dinner a few nights earlier, and was about to shake hands. But, seeing that Blake was carrying the beer himself instead of getting a servant to do it, he replaced his hand in his pocket and cut Blake dead. Eminently sane from his point of view: he was simply doing what his social conditioning told him to do. But I imagine that today the question Which of those two men was the real neurotic? would get a very different answer.

After the almost unimaginable horrors we have seen in this century, we have reached a manic-depressive psychosis in which we swing wildly from a despairing conviction that the human race is near its own extermination to euphoria about a coming age of Aquarius when everything will be for some reason wonderful. (I can hardly imagine a gloomier donkey's carrot to pursue than the precession of the equinoxes, apart altogether from the fact that Virgil predicted a new Golden Age for the period of Pisces, and could hardly have been more wrong.) When Russian and American spokesmen both tell us that nobody would start an atomic war because there would be no sense in such a thing and nobody could gain anything at all from it, we are not reassured. We simply do not believe that human society is as sane as that any more. Only the individual can be sane, though at great cost and effort, and even then he would be helpless. So it is not surprising that so many should feel today that nothing but the developing of a higher consciousness can lift us out of our present history.

It was a sense of this that made me say, a great many years ago, that the aim of education was to make people maladjusted, to destroy their notions that what society did made sense, and that they had only to conform to it to make sense of their own lives. I was also, I think, fortunate in coming to Blake so early in my scholarly career. I learned from him that society is not, beyond very narrow limits, qualified to say whether a man is sane or not. Society cannot distinguish between the individual above its standards and the individual below them. Blake also indicated a simpler way out of the impasse than any of our gurus and spiritual exhorters have provided. Blake was a poet and a painter. That meant that, like his split-brained ancestors, he could hear and see things that most of us cannot hear or see, and yet what he heard and saw it is profoundly profitable to us to look at and listen to. In short, works of art constituted for him what they have always been since Paleolithic times, a focus of meditation, a means of concentrating consciousness.

The poem or painting is in some respects a "hallucination": it is summoned up out of the artist's mind and imposed on us, and is allied to delirium tremens or pretending that one is Napoleon. Blake would say that such creative hallucinations are spiritual visions, and that what they present is more detailed, more vivid, and more accurate than anything that normal eyesight affords. In other respects a work of art is like a dream, but it does not introduce us to the ordinary dreamworld, where we retreat from reality into our withdrawn selves. It takes us into the world of social vision that informs our waking life, where we see that most of what we call "reality" is the rubbish of leftover human constructs. It speaks with authority, but not the familiar authority of parental or social conditioning: there will always be, I expect, some mystery about the real source of its authority.

Continued study of literature and the arts brings us into an entirely new world, where creation and revelation have different meanings, where the experience of time and of space is different. As its outlines take shape, our standards of reality and illusion get reversed. It is the illusions of literature that begin to seem real, and ordinary life, pervaded as it is with all the phony and lying myths that surround us, begins to look like the real hallucination, a parody of the genuine imaginative world. The glimpses I have had of the imaginative world have kept me fascinated for nearly half a century, and no one life can begin to exhaust the fascination. What that may say about the actual dimensions of life would take me too far beyond "the view from here."

✧

Framework and
Assumption

✧

As THIS conference is concerned with convention and knowledge, I should like to begin by talking about the role of convention in literature. A convention is an aspect of the identity of a work of literature: it is what makes it recognizable for what it is, and it is also the aspect that welcomes and invites the reader. Conventions may appear in minor roles within other conventions. In *Romeo and Juliet,* for instance, the great courtly love convention that dominated so much of the Middle Ages extends only to the Romeo-Rosaline affair that precedes the action of the play. Convention can even be merely a traditional custom, like the *topoi* used so much in medieval literature or the fourteen lines of the sonnet. When the convention is big enough to include the entire work, we call it a genre, and this is the aspect of convention I shall be mainly concerned with. A genre establishes the identity of a work of literature in two ways: it indicates what the work is, and it suggests the context of the work, by placing it within a number of other works like it. Any large bookshop will illustrate the role of genre in reading by dividing its stock into sections labeled science fiction, detection, romance, westerns, and the like. Such divisions continue the role of convention in inviting the reader: if you want this kind of book, the label says, here is where you find it.

In ordinary speech convention implies that a thing is just like a lot of other things. This may be a reason for feeling indifferent to certain conventions: it is also a reason for feeling interested in certain others. I know of no reason, beyond the whims of personal taste, why members of one convention should impel

79

us to say "they're all much the same," and why members of another should rouse our interest in distinguishing all the variety we can. The only criterion I can think of is the number of normal conventions that have to be sacrificed to keep a central one intact.

For example, I was once in the shop of an old and cranky bookseller who had put up his labels according to his own reactions, which were precritical. One such label read, simply, "Filth." There were some books approaching pornography in this section, and they started me thinking about pornography as a genre. Most pornography plays down the traditional conventions of story line, characterization, description, and comment, and confines itself to a prodding of certain reflexes or an evoking of certain fantasies. Such things are always formulaic, and the formulaic represents convention at its most primitive, a level at which the work may emerge, like the popular songs in Orwell's *1984,* untouched by human intelligence. I notice too that in bookstores and publishing houses the categories of genre have been uninfluenced by critical theory. I glanced at a row of books by Carlos Castaneda recently, and saw that the earlier books were labeled "nonfiction" by the publisher and the later ones "fiction." I daresay an interesting story lies behind that, but as the earlier and the later books appeared to be generically identical, the distinction was of little critical use.

There is a certain amount of snobbery among some readers tending to assume that a book is of minor importance if its genre is easily recognizable, like the science fiction and detective stories just mentioned. The detective story, in particular, is written in a convention that follows certain prescribed rules, and so resembles a game, like chess. That is nothing new in literature, though earlier rules-of-a-game conventions were usually smaller in range and mostly confined to verse. At present there is a widespread impression that flexible conventions are a mark of serious writing. The days are gone when Jane Austen could protest against the snob phrase "only a novel," and point out that a "novel" could be on the same level of seriousness as any book of sermons. But of course she had her conventions: there are no writers who are unconventional or beyond convention. Sometimes a writer may seem unconventional because his readers are accustomed to different conventions and do not realize it, or else assume that what they are used to is the normal way of writing. Such reactions to convention may vary from Samuel Johnson's dictum "Nothing

80

odd will do long: *Tristram Shandy* did not last" to the claim of a twentieth-century formalist critic that *Tristram Shandy* was the most typical novel ever written.

Browning's poem on Andrea del Sarto, called "the faultless painter," makes the point, among others, that faultlessness can itself be a fault. The reason is that if a painter can be called faultless it means only that the particular convention he followed has come to a dead end. When this happens, all the critics who decided that other painters were "faulty" because their grasp of the convention was less complete are swept into the dustbin of the history of taste. Today we try to be more liberal and eclectic in our responses, but government and other boards entrusted with the duty of giving grants to promising artists still often respond only to certain fashionable conventions, so that artists who are interested in different conventions have to go without grants until the fashion changes. The word *beauty* has become suspect as a critical category, because it has meant, so often and for so long, conforming to an established convention. In the nineteenth century there were still critics who assumed that the Greeks had invented beauty in their statues and architecture, and that everything pre-Greek or outside the Greek tradition was deliberately and perversely ugly.

Thirty years ago, when I wrote the *Anatomy of Criticism*, I paid some attention to the question of genres, because I felt that lack of careful attention in that area made for many confusions and illiterate critical judgments. The wheel of fashion that moves the history of taste has turned since then, though that does not mean that the issues involved have turned with it. I now frequently encounter objections to my alleged passion for ticketing and labeling things, where reference to an excessive toilet training in my infancy is clearly being suppressed with some reluctance. But when I turn to other areas of critical theory, and am informed, for example, that the privileging of interdiscursivity problematizes the differentializing of contextuality, I do not feel that I am being released from an obsession. I only feel that I am facing different conventions about what it is important to find names for.

I think of literature as a specific field of imaginative activity, but the metaphor of "field" I have in mind is something like a magnetic field, a focus of energy, not a farmer's field with a fence around it. I also think of genres as fields in the same way. A literary genre being a part of literature, that means, as long as we hang on to the farmer's field metaphor, a smaller field with a smaller fence. Hence we instinctively think of Shakespeare, for instance, as a poet who wrote mainly plays, rather than as a dramatist who used mainly verse. That will sound like a quibble only to those who do not understand the issues involved. A modern reader of Shakespeare may be put off by the dullness he finds in the Henry VI plays, the brutality of *Titus Andronicus,* the anti-Semitism of *The Merchant of Venice,* the sexism of *The Taming of the Shrew,* and so on through a large part of the canon. The point is that all these plays, whatever our present ideological values, are superb theater, and with Shakespeare the actable and the theatrical always come first. If we had been Shakespeare, we feel, we would have used the theater for higher and nobler purposes. Shakespeare never used the theater for anything except putting on plays, which is one reason why he is Shakespeare. The surrender to the genre, the entering into its conventions as they were at his time, is the mark of the professional craftsman, who outlasts most of the well-meaning amateurs.

In Shakespeare's day schoolboys were trained in the three parts of trivium, grammar, meaning Latin grammar, rhetoric, and formal logic. Deductive logic became increasingly arid with the rise of science and its more inductive attitude, along with the growing suspicion that the syllogism yielded no new knowledge. The decline of rhetoric continued through the eighteenth century and was fairly complete by the Romantic period. Grammar, even English grammar, declined in the twentieth century, partly through the influence of linguists who maintained that the English grammar taught in schools was still Latin grammar, English analyzed in a way that had no relevance to the real structure of English.

I have thought about this a good deal, and my present view is that the linguists were pedagogically wrong: I think that English grammar should be taught from the point of view of a more highly inflected language, Latin being the obvious one. Such a training gives an insight into the structure of English that cannot be obtained from English alone, and it also provides an elementary introduction to philosophical categories, the concrete and abstract, the universal and particular, and the like, which the student will be encountering all his life. But this is by the way: the essential point is that in the twentieth century writers learn

82

to write mainly by instinct and practice, supplemented by the study of older writers who had, or took, greater educational advantages, such as Joyce and Pound. As a result the conventions of writing are acquired but not learned, and while this may be an advantage for some kinds of writers, it makes the general bulk of contemporary writing more conventional than ever. A writer who has studied and practiced certain conventions may develop more distinctive and individual ways of handling them; a writer who does not know that he is being conventional becomes a mass voice in a mass market.

As a result of the collapse of the trivium there grew up an attitude to the arts represented by the title of a book by Herbert Read, *The True Voice of Feeling*. This was a refinement of the Carlyle view that all writing was the personal rhetoric of the author. Jacques Derrida would quickly recognize it as one more way of using writing in order to denigrate writing. I spent ten years reviewing poetry in Canada, where the doctrine of the true voice of feeling was the established one, and had ample experience of the monotony that resulted. I noted with interest the other day that one or two Canadian poets were talking of basing more of their poetic themes on the routine work of their society, on the jobs people held and the way their social functions affected their imagination. They had finally realized, after a steady downpour had been going on for half a century, how many Canadian poets were still as obsessed by certain sexual themes as the most pedantic Elizabethan sonneteer.

This is a far cry from the day when a poet would begin his work by making an appeal to the Muses. The great advantage of the Muses was that they were confined to specific generic categories: if you wanted to write a love lyric there was a Muse for that (Erato), but you wouldn't call on Calliope or Clio, otherwise it might take you twelve books to get to your first orgasm. The poet who is his own Muse, regarding his own imagination as an unconditioned will like Calvin's God, gains a facile victory over nothing: he has no angel to fight with, like Jacob. Walter Benjamin connects this autonomous aesthetic with fascism: I would not go as far as that, though I can see some of the affinities. And I would certainly not want to leave the impression that all Muses are soft cuddly nudes: some of them are ravening harpies who swoop and snatch and carry off, who destroy a poet's peace of mind, his position in society, even his sanity.

83

I think I understand what Derrida means by the use of writing to denigrate writing, though I hesitate to draw the portentous inferences from it that some of his disciples do. What I find much more difficult to understand is the continuous use of criticism to denigrate criticism, the continued assumption that literary criticism has no skeleton, and cannot stand up unless some philosophical or psychological construct provides one. If we start by regarding criticism as parasitic on literature, we invariably end by regarding literature as parasitic on the other verbal structures that convey actual information. Again, language is certainly one of the contexts of every verbal discipline, but to obliterate all distinctions between reader and poet, between criticism and creation, between literature and other verbal structures, because they are all forms of language, seems to me to fall under the law in the Book of Deuteronomy that says "Cursed be he that removeth his neighbor's landmark." There are many distinctions that may be difficult, even impossible, to establish in theory that are nonetheless essential to employ in practice. Ignoring them transforms all the products of language into a vast alphabet soup in which those two essential letters, Alpha and Omega, in the beginning and the end, are nowhere to be found. There is no reason in the mind of God or the design of nature why I should now be in an area called Massachusetts, but life would get very confusing without such arbitrarily designated areas.

I noticed that an increasing number of literary critics are moving outside the literary field and developing interests in other verbal disciplines. Some of them, including myself, are following the lead of Kenneth Burke's pioneering study, *The Rhetoric of Religion*. Of the many reasons for my growing preoccupation with the Bible, two are particularly relevant here. One is that a literary critic, in studying metaphor, is confined to the hypothetical metaphor of literature, the statement of identity that remains purely verbal and simultaneously denies what it asserts. The Bible expands metaphor into what might be called existential metaphor, the actual identifying of a conscious subject with something objective to itself. As Shakespeare's Theseus ought to have said, every human being is of imagination all compact. The other reason is the double perspective the Bible presents: from one point of view it is a completely unified whole of metaphor and imagery, and from another it is totally decentralized. It continually, in other words, constructs and deconstructs itself.

I see a writer of a work of literature as at the center of a cross like a plus sign. The horizontal bar represents his historical and cultural situation, the assumption that he was bound to make as a man of his time, the ideology he was bound to reflect when he wrote. The vertical bar represents the literary tradition from which he descended and the continuing of that line of descent to ourselves. Let us look at the horizontal line first. It runs in theory from complete acceptance of the social and ideological environment the poet is in to its complete rejection. In practice nobody could live continuously at such extremes, and there is always some conflict within the mind of the writer himself. This, rather than the influence of a predecessor, seems to me to constitute the primary anxiety besetting a poet. Certainly an influence can also be an anxiety, but I should call this a special factor in a writer's struggle with his contemporary culture, rather than putting it on the socially isolated Freudian basis that Harold Bloom does. Gerard Manley Hopkins, for example, found himself in conflict with the prevailing ethos of Victorian England, and adopted a dogmatic Catholic position partly in opposition to it, partly for the positive values it supplied in place of the negative reaction. But the religious position he adopted was a terrifying anxiety in itself, however much we as readers may profit from the tensions it created. Other poets, Tasso, Gogol, Rimbaud, have had their lives shattered or drastically altered by similar tensions.

Of course it is obvious that we cannot keep horizontal and vertical dimensions separate: Hopkins's Catholicism had also a great deal to do with the literary traditions he attached himself to. But again there are practical distinctions. To take the next step I must return to a point made in the *Anatomy of Criticism*. Young writers huddle together in schools and issue manifestos, announcing their conventions as something new, or as about to produce something new. As they grow older and acquire more authority, they do not become less conventional, but their notions of convention become more deeply rooted in the history of the art and are less a reflection of a contemporary fashion in ideology. It is at this point that the really crucial form of originality comes into view. Painters of the Barbizon school in nineteenth-century France followed certain easily recognizable conventions, though they achieved a great deal of individual variety within them. When we come to Manet, we feel that we have got past those conventions and are on something new. But after a while we realize that the new, though certainly new, is also deeply traditional. There is a deeper link with certain painters of the past, Goya, Velasquez, Rembrandt, being established. This aspect of tradition forms the vertical bar of my diagram: it refers to the traditions of the art rather than to contemporary situations. But, unlike the more obvious conventions linking the Barbizon painters with one another, there is a discontinuous quality in the larger historical tradition. Something that has disappeared for years or centuries may suddenly reappear; conventions long ignored or forgotten suddenly materialize again, like the angels who traditionally do not move in time or space but simply become visible somewhere else.

It seems to me that this historical relationship is an integral part of an artist's or writer's relation to us. What might otherwise be an insoluble mystery, the way in which a writer incredibly remote from us in time, space, social conditioning, and cultural assumptions, can still make imaginative contact with us, becomes intelligible when we remember that we are still living within the history of literature and the other arts, and can recognize the current of that history flowing into us. It should go without saying that this current is not only that of the Western tradition, but includes Oriental and other cultures as well. If we are interested in our ancestry, it is natural to trace our direct ancestry first, but we all know that we eventually come to a point at which everyone alive was an ancestral relative.

If we keep this cross diagram in mind, it may give us some understanding of the artist's situation vis-à-vis his own time. In studying, let us say, Shakespeare, we confront a dramatist working around 1600 in a society with very different assumptions and organization from ours. We cannot study him intelligently without noting the nuances that the differences in social rank among his characters bring into the dialogue, nor without allowing for the prejudices and cultural preferences his audience brought into the theater with them. Without this context of Shakespearean scholarship, we simply kidnap Shakespeare into our own age, and judge him by all the prejudices and assumptions that "we" bring into the theater with us. At the same time, there is still the mystery of how such a writer does communicate with us, and for that we need a different dimension from the one provided by a knowledge of Elizabethan ideology. That communicating ability, it seems to me, is the other half of the historical relation to the dramatists and other writers of earlier ages, starting with his immediate precursors of the Greene and Lyly period, and going back to the great Greek writers. This is a genuinely historical relationship, but it cannot all be reached by historical methods, as Shakespeare did not know the Greek tragic writers directly and knew the formulas of Menandrine comedy mainly in prose romance distortions. Here only a comparative generic analysis will establish the relation.

I can understand the fascination of what Roland Barthes calls the zero degree of writing, the impulse to rid oneself of all conventions and confront one's subject directly. I can understand Picasso's remark that it was easy to learn to paint like Raphael but very difficult to learn to paint like a child. In a related field, I can understand the nostalgia of Husserl for an abandoning of preconceived mental categories and an unimpeded view of things in themselves. In painting, again, we prize the work of the so-called primitives because of their freshness of insight, their freedom from second-hand formulas, from stock pictorial quotations and allusions. But if we look at a collection of primitives, we see the same doll-like figure drawing, the same psychedelic coloring, the same crowding of detail in the composition, over and over again. Directness of vision is not for us: everything objective is also in part a mirror, the human creation is an ontogenetic development that must recall its phylogenetic ancestry before it can bring it to life once more. Adam may have had a direct vision of reality on the sixth day of creation, but after the seventh day the world became conventionalized to God himself. I think the cult of unmediated vision really relates to something quite different.

I have often enough insisted that every human society exists within a cultural envelope that separates it from its natural environment: that there are no noble savages, and no men sufficiently natural to live in a society without such an envelope. Most people call this envelope an ideology, which is accurate enough for fairly advanced societies. The word *ideology* suggests argument as well as ideas, because of the Hegelian principle that every proposition contains its opposite. That is why a writer living in his own ideology is subjected to stress and anxiety: thesis

87

and antithesis are bound to be in his mind at once. I suggest that an ideology is a secondary and derivative structure, and that what human societies do first is make up stories. I think, in other words, that an ideology always derives from a mythology, as a myth to me means *mythos,* a story or narrative. I am speaking of course of story types, not of specific stories.

It is mythology that we find in primitive societies, and mythology that we find at the historical beginnings of our own, and it is again mythology that underlies our present ideologies, when we examine them closely enough. In Shakespeare's day the Christian ideology his contemporaries accepted was a derivation from Christian mythology, the story Christianity had to tell from its sacred books. In our day we are surrounded by various historical ideologies, progressive and revolutionary, Jeffersonian and Marxist, but these go back, in their inception, to various forms of comic plot superimposed on history. I think also that the poet, in particular, has an instinct for the mythological core of his culture and goes directly to it to try to recreate it so far as he can. The quest for unmediated vision, then, is really a quest for the recovery of myth, the word-hoard guarded by the dragons of ideology.

The growth of an ideology in society is a product of concern, a word that I find very difficult to define or even describe, but that I hope is to some degree self-explanatory. It is our concern for living in social units that builds up societies into nations to be defended in war, into religious confessions to be maintained by enforced agreement and the persecution of dissidents, into class structures where the different strata of society have different rights and privileges. These are, it seems clear, secondary and derivative concerns, and the ideologies that maintain them are based on rationalization. The primary concerns underlying them are simpler: they are the concerns for food, for shelter, for sexual relations, for survival; for freedom and escape from slavery; for happiness and escape from misery. Paul Tillich distinguishes the religious concern as "ultimate": it may be that, but it can hardly be primary. One cannot live a day without being concerned about food, but one may live all one's life without being concerned about God. At the same time one hesitates to rule out the conscious and creative concerns from the primary ones. When a society comes close to the level of bare subsistence, and has no leisure or technology for the so-called frills, the arts, including the literary arts, do not disappear: they leap into the foreground among the essentials for survival. Examples range from Paleolithic cave drawings to Inuit (Eskimo) life today. Again, the opening sentence of Aristotle's *Metaphysics*, "All men by nature desire to know," seems to me to put the expanding of consciousness, too, on its proper primary footing.

All through history secondary concerns have taken priority over primary ones. The primary concern for survival has to give way periodically to going to war; the concern for a sexual partner gives way to the demands of celibacy enforced by a religion or by certain other types of social calling. I say "all through history," and in fact history itself is created by the continuity of such secondary concerns. Literature obviously reflects these ideologies in every period, but they enter literature as elements of content, not as forms or shaping principles. The conventions and genres of literature are essentially untouched by them: these seem to look back to the earlier mythological time, some of them, like the pastoral, looking very longingly and nostalgically to them. Certain mutations of genres take place as the social structure alters and the reading public changes: it is clear, for instance, that the classical novel as we know it rose along with a certain kind of bourgeois reading public in the eighteenth century, and will disappear with the disappearance of that class. But the middle-class novel was not a new entity in literature: it was a new format for storytelling, and the shape and pattern of the stories told remained much the same.

What we said earlier, that ideology is primarily an anxiety to a writer and not a guide to the form of what he should write, makes it not surprising that so many of the best and most influential writers, Balzac, Dostoyevsky, Ezra Pound, D. H. Lawrence, should have adopted such bizarre, even perverse, forms of ideology. It is clear that their mythological interests, the kinds of imaginative themes that preoccupied them, fitted very awkwardly and uneasily into the ideological structures confronting them.

The historical nature of ideology makes it quite feasible to study the history of ideas, but, as explained earlier, the history of mythology is more discontinuous. The best we can do with mythology is to try to sketch out the large interlinking patterns in it, and when we do this we find a curious affinity between mythology and primary concerns. Because of the unorthodox methods that are essential, those who deal with the informing role of mythology in literature often seem close to being cranks. Frazer's *Golden Bough,* for instance, while it is by no means as fundamentally wrong and full of holes as some anthropologists and classicists say, is still a very valuable book. Nonetheless it retains its fascination as a book that brings an astonishing number of mythological patterns into alignment with one of the primary concerns: the food supply, more particularly the agricultural supply. Frazer's dying god cycle has an intimate connection with a female figure who usually represents the earth as the dying god does the vegetation. Frazer leaves out most of her mythological role: Graves's *White Goddess,* another vulnerable book, attempts to fill this in. However, the primary sexual concerns of humanity are reflected more directly by modern psychologists when they touch on mythology, as they often do. The work of Freud and his followers, orthodox and heretic, is of course indispensable here. Jung moved further away from the sexual concern than most of the others, even though his biggest, most complex, and most totally unintelligible book is called *Mysterium Conjunctionis.* Some works in archaeology, such as G. R. Levy's *Gate of Horn,* deal with the primary concerns of providing shelter for the living, the dead, and the gods.

Because the history of mythology rides on top of, or gets submerged under, actual history, it suggests a state of innocence or Golden Age that we do not look for in actual history. Every age had cruelty and horrors parallel to our own, but we can still read their literature and look at their visual arts with pleasure. This is partly because the creative imagination suggests an intimacy with the natural environment which emerges in the metaphorical structures of poetry, metaphor being the language of identity. In its more pastoral and romantic genres it creates a nature that responds to human desire; in its more tragic and ironic ones it surveys the human situation from a point of detachment. The language of ideology is metonymic: it urges that this particular structure of authority is the closest we can get to the ideal one, and so is being "put for" the ideal.

The twentieth century saw in its earlier years a very explicit and conscious revival of mythological themes in its literature, especially in the group of writers who peaked around 1922, the year of *Ulysses* and *The Waste Land.* What happens in the arts indicates what is going to happen in the world a generation or so later, and from midcentury on we have come to realize, from the nuclear bomb and from the polluting of the supply of drinkable water and breathable air, that our age is the first in history to exhibit clearly the principle: primary concerns must become primary, or else. Some people in various parts of the world, including this one, may still think it highly desirable to go to war to smash somebody else's ideology, but the primary concern with human survival tells us that we cannot afford such gestures any more. And for the first time the primary concern is beginning to speak with authority.

It seems, then, if this argument has any cogency, that criticism, the theory of the language of myth and metaphor in which primary concern expresses itself most directly, is very far from being the game of trivial pursuit that it so often appears to be. In the title of my paper, "Framework and Assumption," the "framework" is the ideological structure, or the great variety of them, surrounding us in the contemporary world. Such frameworks, whether religious or secular, are reasonably well known in their general outlines. Studying the assumptions on which they are based brings us to the mythological structures from which they are derived, and which literature recreates directly. We have no coherent surveyed maps of the "here be dragons" type. It has been recognized at least since Sir Philip Sidney's time that because literature, the mythological imagination at work in the world, makes no assertions, it escapes from argument and refutation. In criticism, of course, and in any theoretical field, disagreement is as essential and as creative as agreement is. Subordinating it to primary concern means only that it should be kept impersonal. Nonetheless the vision of a created order where, in Blake's phrase, "no dispute can come," is essential to the total picture.

If we are working solely on the basis of ideology, and regard it as the basis from which literature and the other arts emerge, we shall eventually come to a vision of humanity as a crazy Oedipus obsessed by two overmastering desires: to kill his father God and to rape his mother Nature. By "his father" I mean the source of his life, whether we call it God or not. For such a rabid animal, as Gulliver's Houyhnhnm master told him, reason is simply a faculty that intensifies his viciousness. With the mythological perspective, we can see ourselves capable of creation as well as destruction, with reason a means to an end of ultimate consensus, however distant. In that perspective, what this conference is studying, the role of convention in knowledge, becomes more intelligible. The two meanings of the word *convention* coincide: the convention is the agreed-on place of meeting for a community, where variety and difference are always needed, where individual distinctiveness is as prized as it is anywhere, but where the total disruption caused by wholesale commitment to secondary issues cannot break in.

The Dialectic of
Belief and Vision

✧

I APOLOGIZE for a somewhat forbidding title, which was extracted from me in a hurry, and I hope most of the argument will lie down in pleasanter pastures. I am continuing the debate with myself that I started in my book *The Great Code,* which was a tentative exploring of the question What place does the creative imagination, and the kind of response that we make to a work of literature, have in the study of religion in general, or of the text of the Bible in particular? As I have said in that book and elsewhere, the Bible is as literary as it can be without actually being literature, and hence the response to literature must be in some degree a model of the response to the Bible. I am not denying that there could be other models, including those more familiar to the theologian, the pastor, or the historical critic. But the imaginative model is a genuine and relevant one, too little considered by either literary or religious scholars, at least until very recently.

If one turns from literature to the wasteland of critical theory, one finds that the Bible is obviously relevant to nearly all the major issues that criticism is concerned with, and throws a quizzical light on its currently fashionable doctrines, including the doctrine that there aren't and shouldn't be any doctrines. In the course of making a few suggestions here, I hope I can recycle such old and tired words as *faith* and *vision* to fit some kind of critical context. A predecessor of mine in this series of lectures, Wilfred Cantwell Smith, has distinguished the terms *belief* and *faith* in a recent book: I think I understand the importance of the distinction, but have room here only for the crudest form of it.

Belief to me refers to a state of mind, *faith* to its expression in action.

Whenever we read anything, literary or not, we are following a narrative movement, starting at the upper left-hand corner of the first page and gradually working our way down to the lower right-hand corner of the last page. After that, there comes a second effort of attention, the effort of understanding what one has been reading as a whole. This effort has of course been accumulating during the reading, but cannot be adequately expressed until all the words are in. Two sets of metaphors get entangled with this approach. One is the metaphor of hearing and seeing. We "listen to" the words as they come past us one after the other, and then, we say, we "see" what it all means. The other set are metaphors of time and space. We read sequentially, moving in time from one word to the next; we understand what we have read in a simultaneous (*Gestalt*) pattern, in conceptual space as it were. For the first stage, there are conventions that what the poet is uttering is not words but music, the art that most obviously moves in time, and that the prose writer is actually speaking. For the second stage, the word *structure* has entered criticism largely because it is a metaphor drawn from the stationary or visual arts, notably architecture.

Such metaphors have produced many confusions in literary theory, which I think remain confusions, even if my attempts to indicate what they are may be thought oversimplified. In Marshall McLuhan, for example, the book is equated with the linear process of reading, and the electronic media are associated with the total or simultaneous vision. This account of the matter overlooks the fact that the book has to be understood as well as read, and that it patiently waits around, repeating the same words however often it is consulted, until its readers proceed from the linear stage of attention to the next one. The electronic media, more particularly television, greatly foreshorten the linear process, but still they do require us to follow a narrative as well as make an effort at apprehension, which means in practice that many television programs make a strong immediate impression and are soon forgotten afterwards. McLuhan came to understand this very quickly, and warns us constantly about the dangers of "media fallout," the panic caused by the impact of sense impressions that our minds have not been adequately prepared to receive. But in the meantime he had been ground up in a public relations blender and was unable to correct, or even modify, his absurd popular reputation as the man who said that the book was obsolete.

In the work of Jacques Derrida, and still more in that of his American followers, there is an opposite extreme of emphasis on writing, the *écriture* to which Derrida gives a special meaning. According to this school, most if not all philosophers are engaged in a gigantic conspiracy to use writing as a means of abusing writing. The philosopher's model is one of speaking orally to a group of disciples, and he uses writing as a necessary evil, a substitute for a speaking voice and a visible presence. There is a very complex theory here that I have no time to do justice to, but it seems to me that its kernel is a metaphor and a convention taken in the wrong context. For one thing, prose, which all philosophers now use, is based on writing, and oral speech is associative in rhythm. Oral speech often enters into the design of prose in order to informalize it, but prose remains radically a written medium, a form of *écriture,* whatever the author wants it to be or says it is. It is the written structure, not the speaker's presence, to which the response is made: the speaking presence is a conventional pretense. We may compare the parallel convention I just referred to, of the poet's pretense that he is really producing song, or music, rather than words. The epilogue to Milton's *Lycidas* tells us that the narrator has been simultaneously singing and playing a wind instrument. This would be a most impressive feat to watch, but something tells us that if we pursue the matter further convention and metaphor will lead us astray.

The metaphorical use of *structure* has also led to confusion. It is often said or assumed that the effort to understand a work of literature as a whole is really seeking the destruction of that work, as once something has been completely understood there is nothing left of it. But the notion that one has attained such understanding is always an illusion. There certainly are structures in words that can be dispensed with after we have understood them, but the classics of literature are not among them. If what we have read is on the level of Plato or Dante or Shakespeare, our first efforts of structural understanding will be inadequate and immature, but we continue to make further efforts. This continuity of efforts may go on all through our lives, if we are professionally concerned with literature or philosophy. Even then understanding it never becomes definitive: we grow, but the

Republic or the *Purgatorio* or *King Lear* do not shrink. The work itself has acquired a history: it has picked up centuries of former readers, and brings something of their reading down to us as a part of its own meaning. It will also go on into the future, so that definitive understanding at any stage is not even theoretically possible. Every such work adumbrates something of the paradox of incarnation, the enclosing of the infinite in a finite form. Some literary critics mention this analogy in order to deny or attack it, on the ground that it makes them nervous, but it is still a datum of critical experience.

One reason why the metaphors of hearing and seeing enter into this aspect of criticism so persistently is that in some areas hearing and seeing become actual sense experiences. One such area is religious ritual. One thinks of the Collect of the mass followed by the elevation of the Host; of the words spoken in the mystery religions followed by the exhibition of a visual emblem—at Eleusis, apparently, a reaped ear of corn—and similarly in other contexts. Zen Buddhism has a legend that after the Buddha had preached a sermon, he held up a golden flower, the only member of the audience who got the point being, of course, the founder of Zen. Zen appears to be, or include, a technique of becoming "enlightened" (another visual metaphor) by evading the preliminary address to the ear—an obvious reason for its popularity in the West in the age of television. Going back to metaphor, one thinks also of the climax of the Book of Job, when Job says: "I have heard of thee by the hearing of the ear: but now mine eye seeth thee."

In reading a work of literature, no process of belief, in the ordinary sense, is involved. What is involved is a continuous process of acceptance. We accept every word given us in the text without question (unless we are textual editors), and withhold our response until the end. Literature differs from descriptive or factual verbal structures in the degree of emphasis it places on this postponing of response. There are also different degrees of response within literature. A response to a novel of Trollope or George Eliot would include some consideration of the way it illustrates the life and social conditions of its time, but to *Alice in Wonderland* or Rider Haggard's *She* there would be little response of that kind.

If, on the other hand, we are reading a newspaper, the acceptance of what we read is continuously involved with tentative reactions of belief, positive or negative. This item may well be true; this next one may be a rumor; a third one may be slanted by rhetoric and partisanship. Whether such news stories are true or only made up is a primary issue, and so we continually compare what we read with what we guess or have read elsewhere about situations in the world outside the newspaper. The fact that no clear or unambiguous truth in such matters is possible makes the degrees of approximate truth attainable all the more important.

These differing reactions emerge clearly in the confusions over the phrase "literal meaning." Traditionally, literal meaning has applied to the newspaper type of reaction, where the acceptance of the words is accompanied by some belief or disbelief in their substantial relation to historical events or doctrines. But a body of words cannot be literally anything but a body of words, and literal meaning seems to me to apply only to the sense of a verbal structure in itself, not to its correspondence to something outside itself. In reading the Bible we find ourselves following a verbal structure intensely metaphorical in its language and full of events that seem to have no counterpart in actual history or in ordinary experience. For Samson's feats with a jawbone, for Jonah's maritime adventures, for Elisha's accomplishments in magic, for Jesus' feeding five thousand with five loaves and two fishes, afterwards gathering up the fragments that nothing might be lost, it seems clear that the literary model of acceptance is better than the newspaper model of tentative belief for the appropriate response. The postponing of commitment until after the linear stage of acceptance seems to me to be one of the things that Paul is referring to when he speaks of the analogy or proportion of faith (Romans 12:6).

In the past, when science was embryonic and objectors were silenced by secular authority, the elements in the Bible that contradict ordinary reason and sense experience were less problematic. If faith fulfilled sense experience and reason, well and good; if it violated them, so much the better: God would approve of the sacrifice of the intellect involved, and would attach special merit to accepting the incredible as factual. Of course in some contexts there is a good deal to be said for Tertullian's axiom, "I believe because it is absurd and inept," because that stretches the mind to accommodate paradox, and resists the drift to narcissism in all habitual mental processes. But in the twentieth century a totally uncritical response is bound to create a latent hysteria in the believer's mind, leaving an impression that there are aspects of his mind that do not agree with much of what he says he believes, but that they are being internally shouted down or rationalized into silence.

In the more extroverted "literalists" one may see hysteria in the staring glazed eyes, the loud overconfident voice, the forced heartiness, that accompany so much expression of conviction on this level. In more introverted and speculative types there is a high rate of intellectual mortality: a "crisis of faith" frequently occurs sooner or later, and a crisis of faith is normally followed by the total loss of it. I pass over the more pathological and racist forms of such attitudes, merely saying that hysteria, by insisting that an inner state of mind is united when it is actually divided, is bound to project its frustrations sooner or later on some outward scapegoat who symbolizes the objecting inner self. The assertion "I believe that" is not simply meaningless but actively dangerous when we still don't know who "I" is or what "that" is.

Belief of this sort has no way of distinguishing what one believes from what one thinks or believes one believes: the same confusion that led Don Quixote into so many sad predicaments. I have often had occasion to notice that a man's beliefs are not revealed by any profession of faith, however sincere, but by what his actions show that he believes. In this respect practically everyone has a belief of some kind, if it is only belief in the importance of one's own interests. Faith, then, is whatever consistency one's behavior exhibits throughout one's life, and one's lifestyle is the continuous revelation of one's real faith. And faith, even the most limited or antisocial kind, must be powered by some kind of vision. One who believes only in the importance of his own interests will still have some rudimentary vision of what he thinks those interests are. To use terms that have been extensively employed ever since Hegel, faith is the continuous struggle of a time-bound man to pursue the *for itself* which is the burden brought into the world by consciousness. Vision is focused on an aspect of a model world which is the *in itself*, a model that is ineffective if separated from the *for itself*.

Perhaps we are now in a position to confront the definition

of faith in the New Testament. The Epistle to the Hebrews tells us that faith is the *hypostasis* of the hoped-for and the *elenchos* of things not seen. *Hypostasis* is among other things a Greek philosophical term of which the Latin counterpart is *substantia,* and the Vulgate so renders the word, followed by the 1611 Bible, which says "substance." Modern translations usually render it as "assurance," because Paul uses the word in this sense. But Paul is not the author of Hebrews, and "substance" seems to me closer to what is meant here (see also Hebrews 1:3). The believer is being told that he has got something, not being reassured that he is eventually going to get it. Similarly, the word *elenchos* is usually rendered "proof" or "evidence," and commentators often explain that this refers to the inward certainty that requires no external confirmation. But this seems oversubjective, and "proof of the unseen" is an awkward expression. Something like "manifestation" or "visible form" seems closer to the context. I have often noted that the Bible shows relatively little interest in the invisible world as a separate order: it tends to regard the invisible as the medium for the visible, much as the invisible air makes it possible for us to see anything at all. The author of Hebrews in fact goes on to say this a verse or two later.

Again, if faith is the substance of the "hoped-for" (*elpizomenon*) faith and hope, two of the three great theological virtues named by Paul, are essentially connected. It is impossible to separate hope from a visionary quality: hope is not a mere subjective yearning but the construction of a model or ideal in the mind that our actions move toward realizing. "Fear and Hope are Vision," said Blake. Everyone with any social function has some model community in his mind in the light of which he does his job, such as a community of better health for the doctor, of clearer judgment for the teacher, or fewer wrecked and wasted lives for the social worker. The model so constructed is a myth or fiction, and in normal minds it is known to be a fiction. That does not make it unreal: what happens is rather an interchange of reality and illusion in the mind. Most of what we call objective reality is a human construct left over from yesterday: much of this could do with improvement, and the model that hope constructs shows up a good deal of this construct as both undesirable and removable, and to that extent unreal. The touchstone of reality is the fictional model vision. The Epistle of James talks about "works" as the complement of faith, but it seems to me a better metaphor to regard faith and hope, belief and vision, as the parents of which works are the offspring.

Faith, then, as distinct from professed faith, is the activity of realizing a visionary model in the mind suggested by hope. I am aware that this collides directly with the traditional view, in which the visionary model of faith is the professed faith, the Apostle's Creed or what not. I shall give my reasons in a moment for thinking that this self-enclosed conception of faith is inadequate, but what concerns us just now is the need for two elements, a program of work and a model to work from. Belief without vision, the ordering of one's life without a clear notion of what it should be ordered to, soon breaks down, within religious bodies, into anxieties over secondary moral issues. When we talk with some members of those bodies, we find all too often that anxieties over liquor, contraception, divorce, dietary ordinances, absence from church, and the like have blotted out most of the religious horizon for them. Parallel forms of blindness are found in the secular world, such as that of the politician who has forgotten what his party ever stood for in the effort to circumvent the intrigues that surround him. Vision without belief produces what the philosopher Sartre calls, very accurately, "bad faith." This is as a rule the contemplation of a timeless body of truth *in* itself, with none of the limitations of a specific temporal and historical conditioning *for* oneself taken into account. No human being is in a position to gain any benefit from that kind of vision, and the truths such a vision express soon shrivel into platitudes, which are true only because they are too vague to be opposed.

I think that creeds and dogmatic formulations of faith, however important they have been historically and however much modernized in vocabulary, are written in the wrong language for the twentieth century. It so happens that the Bible suggests, in its structure, what the more appropriate language is, but to understand this we have to return to the distinction between preliminary hearing and final seeing that we began with. According to the opening of Genesis, God placed in Eden every tree that was pleasant to sight, and evidently made himself visually available to unfallen humanity. After that comes the fall and the plunging of the human race into history. Here there is no difficulty about hearing the voice of a speaking God, either directly or through his prophets, but any suggestion that God has actually been seen is surrounded by editorial euphemisms and expurgations. With the coming of Jesus in the Gospels visibility is attached to the Godhead, but it is a curiously disguised visibility: the Gospels make it clear that most people in Jesus' vicinity, including the disciples themselves, were confused about many of the things they experienced. Like their descendants down to our own time, they were obsessed about what was happening historically and getting nowhere, and so overlooking the unique importance of what was happening mythically. The transition from hearing to seeing, however, and from time and history to something beyond both, is achieved in the final Apocalypse, the account of a second coming when, it is promised, "every eye shall see him."

What the Apocalypse proves to be is not a summary of biblical doctrines or even a summary of its historical narrative. It is primarily a vision of a body of imagery, where the images of every category of being, divine, angelic, paradisal, human, animal, vegetable, and inorganic, are all identified with the body of Christ. That means that all the images are metaphorically related, metaphor being expressed as a statement of identity, in the form "this is that." Whatever is not part of the body of Christ forms a demonic shadow, a parody of the apocalyptic vision in a context of evil and tyranny. This ultimate separation of vision from shadow, the heaven-world and the hell-world, is alluded to in the Gospel parables as a separation that human society cannot attain to in a world of time, but will see as the revelation that comes with the ending of time. Meanwhile, every unreality that the vision of hope in the mind perceives in the world around us is part of an apocalyptic judgment on that world.

The unwillingness of so many religious temperaments to try to grasp the reality of a revelation in any but doctrinal terms recurs in a number of religious communions. It accounts for the divergence in emphasis between, say, the Talmudic and Cabalistic traditions in Judaism, the scholastic and mystical developments in medieval Catholicism, a parallel difference in Islamic thought, and the Calvinist and Anabaptist traditions in Protestantism. The Reformation was founded on the doctrine of justification through faith, but conceiving faith as something to be expressed in the language of creed or thesis minimized the visionary element in it. We notice that Calvin could make very little of the Book of Revelation in his biblical commentaries: in spite of its dense texture of allusions to the Old Testament, the quality of its language eluded him. I have now to try to put that language into its cultural context.

Literature, like the mythology from which it descends, expresses primary concern, but it may express it positively in romantic fantasy or negatively in irony and satire, and in our day irony and satire strongly predominate. Further, while the great writers of literature understand that they are committed to mythology, it is inevitable, when the theory of criticism is so confused and so dominated by ideologies, that many writers should also be confused about how their social function operates and what their authority as writers is based on. Hence their myths all too often emerge in the perverted form of obsolete or discredited ideologies. Examples are W. B. Yeats, Ezra Pound, and D. H. Lawrence, all of them great writers with much essential to say about the human condition, all of them apt to turn into cranks or fanatics when their myths decline into ideology. Here is one of the terrible final fragments of Ezra Pound's *Cantos,* written after the wrecking of his life had finally begun to erode his belief in the value of what he had done:

> *M'amour, m'amour*
> > *what do I love and*
> > > *where are you?*
> *That I lost my center*
> > *fighting the world.*
> *The dreams clash*
> > *and are shattered . . .*
> *and that I tried to make a paradiso*
> > > > *terrestre.*

What, we may ask, does the vision of an earthly paradise have to do with the extraordinary mélange of Confucian philosophy, social credit, Provençal poetry, the economic policies of John Adams, the history of Renaissance princes, and hundreds of other things that make up the pastiche of the *Cantos?* The meaning of the passage is quite clear in the mythological context of poetry. The "center" of a poet is the body of what he loves, or what Blake calls his emanation. Searching for this center, which he has lost sight of in his ideological turmoils, this poet realizes, among the shattered fragments of his dreams, that he had once wanted to express the central mythological vision of the earthly paradise. Myth has to do with the primary concerns, with the food supply, the restoring of sex to love, as distinct from exploiting the genital machinery, with the building of dwelling-places for living people, for the gods, and for the dead. But the limit of the mythological vision is not the achievable but the conceivable: it provides a context for these concerns in which nature is infinitely closer to humanity, and human beings to one another, than we have ever experienced in history.

The ideological imagination, though it may accept the vision of unfallen humanity as a traditional mythological datum, cannot incorporate it into its orbit of thinking. It cannot go behind Adam after his fall, struggling to extract a living from an alienated nature, his link with his creator fatally impaired, his lethally feuding family going off to found cities and start more feuds. As long as this vision of ideological man stays within the traditional religious and mythological framework, something of the original myths may cling to it. But now, when the struggle with nature seems to have reached a plateau of independence, and divine origin seems more and more irrelevant even to those who accept it, we are finally achieving a clarified view of what ideological man is. We may now see him as a crazy Oedipus obsessed by two overmastering impulses: one to murder his father God, the other to rape his mother Nature. By "his father" I mean the source of his life, whether we call it God or not.

If there is any substance in this argument, one thing is clear: in the contemporary world of ideological deadlock, the worst thing we can do is to try to "demythologize" anything, in or outside religion. I see it as the essential task of the literary critic to distinguish ideology from myth, to help reconstitute a myth as a language, and to put literature in its proper cultural place as the central link of communication between society and the vision of its primary concerns. Every ideology, because it is or includes the rationalizing of a claim to social authority, tries to get itself established as the right or "orthodox" one. In our day there is an obvious need for an ecumenical source of power that will cut across all these claims, and it seems equally obvious that one must look for such a power source within the visionary aspect of these ideologies, the aspect that links them with mythology. It is only mythology, I feel, that can really express the vision of hope, the hope that is focused on a more abundant life for us all, not the hope of finally refuting the arguments of Moslems or Marxists.

Ideology is argumentative, but a dogmatic basis for ideology renders it impervious to argument, and creates in the world not so much iron curtains as a series of unbreachable Maginot lines. Certain forms of academic religious ideology are more flexible than this, in the sense that they understand how propositions contain their opposites. In learned journals concerned with religion one finds that thinkers who have repudiated all religious connections, Marx, Freud, Heidegger, Nietzsche, seem to be quite as useful and are certainly as frequently referred to as the accredited theologians. But one wonders if this is not partly because there is as yet no political crunch in this field. One should not overlook the importance of ecumenical movements either, but they again are subject to the same difficulty as the United Nations and parallel secular assemblies, of being aggregates of sovereign bodies whose delegates are likely to be recalled if they seem about to infringe on that sovereignty. Meanwhile, no literary critic can be in doubt about the intolerance of secular ideologies to myth, considering the very large number of twentieth-century writers who have been driven into silence, exile, imprisonment, suicide, or judicial murder by ideology-obsessed governments.

One large gap in our argument remains—at least one that I can see. I have tried to explain why I think it essential to separate faith from professed faith, and to conceive of genuine faith as a continuous sequence of committed actions guided by a vision. I also said that vision without belief leads to Sartre's "bad faith," the contemplation of objective "in itself," an unchanging reality that we are not and never can be a part of. In a culture where mythology is largely ignored except for works of disinterested imagination, how is it possible to connect such a mythology to any kind of active faith? Here again I think we have to look at the structure of the Bible for a clue.

At the beginning of the Bible, we said, we have the contrast between the mythical vision of an earthly paradise, and the subsequent vision of man alienated from his God and from nature, subject to sin and death, and about to begin the history that Byron calls the devil's scripture. We said that it took the mythological imagination of the poet to recreate the paradisal vision, whether positively, as in Eliot's rose-garden or Yeats's Byzantium, or ironically and elegiacally, as in Dostoyevsky's *Dream of a Ridiculous Man*. One feature that we notice about the Eden story is that nature, the external environment, is not simply regenerate but seems to be identified with the humanity that lives within it. All the animals are brought to the "adam" to be named; the trees are pleasant to sight and good for food. The element in experience that we call aesthetic, the ability to see the world around us as beautiful, is not here purely in the eye of the beholder, but is an objective fact as well. The world makes human sense, but there is nothing of the fallacy of trying to reduce the beautiful to the functional: there is rather that sense of purposiveness without purpose that Kant recognized as central to beauty.

Again, the Old Testament word for God, *Elohim*, with its plural form, however assimilated to a strict monotheism, seems still to contain a slight sense of plurality in the godhead. Certainly there seem to be other spiritual beings than man whom God addresses, and Milton, in *Paradise Lost*, not only has an angel paying a social call on Adam and Eve but makes Adam say to Eve, with all the accumulated wisdom of being her senior by half an hour or so: "Millions of spiritual creatures walk the earth Unseen, both when we wake and when we sleep." The great imaginative power of the gods of pagan polytheism lay in the fact that they suggested a relation of identity between a personality and an aspect of nature: there were sea-gods, sun-gods, earth-gods or goddesses, and the like. We feel that the unfallen state included some sense of identity with nature, and that to recover or attain such a state would be to return to it, or, as Emily Dickinson says: "He will refund us finally / Our confiscated gods."

But it is the other end of the Bible that I want particularly to look at now. One gap between mythological and ideological imagination I have placed as the point of the fall, where the beginning of history separates from a state of being which is clearly not historical. We see already that myth is not second-hand history, though it sometimes uses historical material to transpose a remote past into a present that confronts the reader directly. At the other end of the Bible, the ideological imagination conceives in the immediate future a millennium, the inaugurating of a Messianic kingdom when justice and peace will spread across the earth. The dream of this imminent kingdom seems to be all over the New Testament, and as the years passed and it failed to materialize it changed into an indefinitely postponed future event. Here again the mythological imagination deals not with a millennium but with an apocalypse, a total transformation of reality which has no more direct connection with the future than the Eden story has with the past, but confronts us with the imperious invitation to drink of its water of life.

The apocalypse, we suggested, was a vast metaphorical structure in which all categories of reality, or what was later called the chain of being, are identified with the body of the Messiah. The golden city which is the New Jerusalem, the trees and rivers of Eden, the final union of bridegroom and bride, are all there, and much besides. The metaphor, which, we said, normally comes to us as a statement of identity of the "this is that, A is B" type, develops out of a phase of consciousness where there is as yet no consistent sense of the separation of subject and object, but rather the easy mingling of personal and natural presence that we find in the god. In literature, the metaphor is the commonest of all verbal figures, so common that perhaps it is part of the function of literature to keep the metaphorical habit of thinking in identities alive. And yet in literature as we know it there are no real identities: all literary metaphors are verbal associations only. In literature we may say something like "Now is the winter of our discontent / Made glorious summer by the sun of York." Which, in literature, means: "It is *as though* our discontent were a winter, and the House of York a summer sun." Everyone knows that such metaphors mean nothing at all in the actual world.

But in the Bible the conception of "word" is greatly extended from spoken or written language, and perhaps the metaphorical structure in the Bible can be extended also, moving back to recapture some of the existential force that the metaphor once suggested. No one can read far in, for example, mystical literature without feeling the urgency of the question of whether there is an identity of the kind that the verbal metaphor suggests but does not assert. In fact some sense of ultimate identity, of the kind implicit in the Hindu formula "thou art that," seems to lie behind nearly all the profoundest religious feelings and experiences, whatever the actual religion, even when the ideological censor forbids its expression as a doctrine.

For the present audience it is perhaps unnecessary to add that two things happen at the next stage in this development of imaginative identity. One is that Paul's third great virtue, *agape* or love, makes its appearance, not as a third virtue but as the only virtue there is. Outside its orbit, faith and hope are not necessarily virtues at all: the same machinery of action conforming to a model vision goes into operation when we are embezzling funds or murdering our spouses. The other is that the sense of initiative reverses itself. So far we have spoken only of what the human subject is trying to do, but we soon realize that at a certain point we enter into a vaster operation where human personality and will are still present, but where the self-begotten activity no longer seems to be the only, or even the essentially, active power. The initiative is now usually seen to come, not from some unreachable "in itself" world, but from an infinitely active personality that both enters us and eludes us. To go further than this would require another paper that I am not qualified to write. I stop with saying that pursuing the dialectic of belief and vision until they merge seems to be the first step on the ladder that Jacob saw in the "dreadful place" of the *mysterium tremendum,* the mystery that is really a revelation, and mysterious only because its revelation has no end.

✧

The Expanding World of Metaphor

✧

LET US start with literature, and with the fact that literature is an art of words. That means, in the first place, a difference of emphasis between the art and the words. If we choose the emphasis on words, we soon begin to relate the verbal structures we call literary to other verbal structures. We find that there are no clearly marked boundaries, only centers of interest. There are many writers, ranging from Plato to Sartre, whom it is difficult, or more accurately unnecessary, to classify as literary or philosophical. Gradually more and more boundaries dissolve, including the boundary between creators and critics, as every criticism is also a recreation. Sooner or later, in pursuing this direction of study, literary criticism, philosophy, and most of the social sciences come to converge on the study of language itself. The characteristics of language are clearly the essential clue to the nature of everything built out of language.

The developments in linguistics and semiotics in the last quarter-century have shown us how language both expresses and structures our consciousness in time and space. I speak of these developments only in passing, because there are many scholars who can speak about them with more authority than I can. In this area of study a word is primarily a signifier, related arbitrarily, or more precisely by convention, to what it signifies. What makes a word a word is its difference from other words, and what gives words a public meaning for a community is the disentangling them from the associations of those who use them, including the author. Jacques Derrida in particular has emphasized that this attitude to language is one in which writing or printing is logically prior to the spoken word. In oral discourse the words are still, in a manner of speaking, unborn, still attached to an enclosing presence or speaking personality.

We can also, however, turn to the other emphasis on the *art* of words, where we begin with a practical commonsense distinction in which, say, Keats and Shelley are poets and not philosophers, and Kant and Hegel philosophers and not poets. Again there are no definable boundaries, and no one asserts that there are, but we do have, in practice, a distinctive area in which literature has the same kind of integrity that music has when distinguished from songs of birds or noises in the street. The painter René Magritte painted a highly representational picture of a pipe and gave it the title *This is not a Pipe,* and one can see very well what he means. The center of the art of words is poetry, and from here on I shall be speaking of poetry.

In poetry, accidental resemblances among words create sound patterns of rhyme, alliteration, assonance, and meter, and these have a function in poetry that they rarely have outside it. The function of these sound patterns is to minimize the sense of arbitrariness in the relation of word and meaning, to suggest a quasi-magical connection between the verbal arrangement and the things it evokes. Puns and different or ambiguous associations bound up in a single word seem to be structural principles rather than obstacles to meaning. Above all, in poetry we are in the area of figurative language, where the status of the word as a word is called to our attention, and the relation of that word to its context has to be given special treatment. Of course we use figurative language everywhere, but in poetry what seems to be dominant in importance is not so much the relation of signifiers to signifieds as the *resonance* among the signifiers.

The poet may be very remote in time, place, language, and cultural context from his reader. Hence there are two directions in the study of poetry. One is an attempt to determine, so far as is humanly possible, what a poem meant in its own original context; the other tries to see what the qualities in it are that make it still communicable to us. The critical reader of a poem is one of a large number of people who have read it; hence he cannot dream of any definitive criticism of it, for the simple reason that he is not all those other people. He is a spokesman for a community of readers, and fails if he replaces the poem with himself. But his reading is only his, and it may range in motivation from devoted discipleship to a kind of ritual murder of his poet. We might say that the reader invents his text, the word *invention* having its double meaning of something subjective that we make up ourselves and something objective that we find outside us. An invention comes out of an inventor's mind, but an invention that works must have some roots in the external world. It is normally best to begin reading our poem in a mood of Leibnitzian optimism that the words chosen for that poem are the best of all possible words.

So far, there is not much difference between the role of the reader of poetry and that of any other reader. But the poem (one might have to modify the statement in regard to prose fiction) seems to be radically an *oral* production, an utterance. This utterance is not a direct address to the reader; it is broadcast, like a radio program, and is separate from both reader and poet. Poets have always said that they did not feel that they were making their poems; they felt more like mothers bringing an independent life to birth. The written poem comes into being partly because of this independence. If there is anything to be said for Marshall McLuhan's axiom that the content of any given medium is the form of a previous medium, then the content of written poetry is the form of oral poetry, which seems invariably to precede it historically. The subordinate and secondary status assigned to writing, of which so many poststructural critics complain, is derived from a literary convention, but within literature the convention is rooted in the facts of literary experience.

The source of the convention is the fact that the poem, like a musical score, but unlike other types of verbal structure, is being referred back to an actual performance. If we want to know what a poem "really means," we have to read the poem itself aloud. The poet may be replaced by a reciter, as Homer is by Ion in Plato, or the oral reader may not be present at all, except as a minor element in a silent reader's response. But, except in poetry where literature is encroaching on the visual arts (as in concrete poetry, shape poems, and typographical designs like those of E. E. Cummings), there is always a priority of utterance to writing. This convention is closely related to another convention within poetry itself that the spoken words are actually being sung or played as a musical composition. Thus Milton says halfway through *Lycidas,* "But now my oat proceeds," "oat" meaning a reed, or a kind of rustic oboe, and at the end "Thus sang the uncouth swain to th' oaks and rills." The impossibility of singing and playing a wind instrument at the same time does not bother Milton. The written text of a poem is a kind of charm or spell: a spell that, so to speak, knows and repeats the *names* of the poem, and has the power to summon an absent present into reappearance.

Of all figures or rhetorical devices that emphasize the relation of signifiers to one another, the simplest and most direct is the metaphor, the figure that tells us that one signifier *is* another signifier, even if each term keeps its own conventional relation to a signified. That is, the metaphor is usually presented in some variant of the grammatical model "A is B." Our first problem is, what is the point of saying that A is B when anyone can see that A is not B?

Let us first try to put the question into some form of historical perspective. We notice that a typical metaphor, such as "Joseph is a fruitful bough," identifies some aspect of human personality or consciousness ("Joseph") with some aspect of the natural environment ("fruitful bough"). If we were to think of a permanent relationship of this sort which we might in some contexts have to "take seriously," we should come to the conception of a god, or, at least, a nature spirit. The god is an early form of socially postulated metaphor, but the god has many mutations and derivations, such as the totemic animal in totemic societies. The Bible does not accept gods or nature spirits, but still "Joseph is a fruitful bough" is a development of the same mode of thinking that elsewhere identifies Neptune with the sea or Baal with the fertility of the land.

Metaphor, then, arises in a state of society in which a split between a perceiving subject and a perceived object is not yet habitual, and what it does in that context is to open up a channel or current of energy between human and natural worlds. The gods are not simply projections of the human mind on nature: they are evocations of powers of nature as well. The starting point of metaphor, then, seems to be what I propose to call, taking a term from Heidegger, ecstatic metaphor, the sense of identity of an individual's consciousness with something in the natural world. I say an individual, but of course a social or group consciousness is what is almost always primarily involved. If we look at the cave drawings of animals in Altamira or Lascaux, and think of the fantastically difficult conditions of lighting and positioning in which they were done, we can get some sense of the titanic will to identify that they represent. We can distinguish certain aspects that seem more reasonable to us, such as the magical wish to evoke by art a supply of animal food, but the will to identify is what is in the center. Similarly, the chief "primitive" use of music seems to have been ecstatic, designed to merge the consciousness with another kind of being, like the Dionysus cult in Greece that has given us the word "enthusiasm," and the school of prophets in the Old Testament whom King Saul briefly joined (1 Samuel 10:5–6).

Such forms of ecstatic identification survive in modern religion, and have left many traces in literature. In drama, for example, we require the actor to be ecstatically identified with his role. But gods suggest a more stabilized social relationship of a sort that produces cults, statues, temples, myths, prayers, and sacrifices. Any such metaphor as "Neptune is the sea" is the base line of a triangle with its apex pointing to the group of worshippers who acknowledge the identity. The sense of a subjective consciousness separated from the physical world seems to become continuous around the time of the earliest civilizations, although some would put it much later. In proportion as it does so, the ecstatic response becomes individualized: the social conditioning is of course still there, but its workings in the individual mind become harder to trace. Along with this goes the specifically "literary" response to metaphor: the sense of it as assumed, as putting something in a way that does not assert or deny anything about the "real" world. Poetry thus becomes a form of play, to use Francis Bacon's term, or, as we should now say, there is an ironic distancing between literature and experience. I am not sure that the modern phrase is an improvement on Bacon.

Literature thus becomes detached from the kind of commitment that we call "belief." In the poetry of the Christian centuries Jupiter and Venus are readily absorbed, the more readily because they are not believed in. Of all works of classical literature, the one that had the most pervasive influence over the next thousand years was probably Ovid's *Metamorphoses*. The metamorphosis, in Ovid, is typically a story of the disintegrating of metaphor, the breaking down of some conscious personality into a natural object, as when Daphne becomes a laurel tree or Philomela a nightingale. When Jupiter assumes the form of a bull or a swan for one of his amours, the original story may have actually identified the god and the animal; but in the age of poetry he is merely putting on a disguise to fool Juno, usually without success.

A literary age tends to think of ecstatic forms of identification as primitive and something to be outgrown, as modes of behavior that would seem hysterical in our society. Such terms as Lévy-Bruhl's *participation mystique* suggest an attitude of keeping them at arm's length. We are afraid of losing our sense of the distinction between fiction and fact, like Don Quixote at the puppet show, and the tendency of younger readers to identify with (or, in the fashionable euphemism, relate to) some figure in a book or movie or rock band they admire we think of as immature. Yet it seems clear that one of the social functions of literature is to keep alive the metaphorical way of thinking and of using words. So our next problem is, Why should it be kept alive?

I have often reverted to the lines from *A Midsummer Night's Dream* in which Duke Theseus summarizes the three types of people who, from his point of view, take metaphor, as we say, literally or seriously: "The lunatic, the lover and the poet / Are of imagination all compact." We see that the word *imagination* already contains the twofold emphasis it still has in the contrast between "imaginary" and "imaginative." Theseus' emphasis is on the whole on the pathological side: lunatics, lovers, and poets for him are people disturbed emotionally who see things which are not there. He goes on to say that lunatics see more devils than hell can hold, and that the poet's eye moves from heaven to earth and from earth to heaven, suggesting that the poet is essentially a lunatic on a good trip. The inclusion of the lover is particularly interesting, because sexual love is a throwback to ecstatic metaphor. The sexual drive is symbolically toward a union of two people in one, or, as Sir Thomas Browne says, "United souls are not satisfied with embraces, but desire to be truly each other." He goes on to say, however, "which being impossible, their desires are infinite, and must proceed without a possibility of satisfaction." It seems to Browne, as perhaps to most of us, safer to stay with embraces.

The association of lover and poet is what enables John Donne to write such poems as "The Extasie" and "The Canonization," which begin with a celebration of sexual union and end with images of books and sonnets. It also accounts for the hundreds, if not thousands, of poems bewailing the cruelty and indifference of a poet's mistress. Few poets in medieval or Renaissance times would set up as poets without declaring themselves head over heels in love: a poet not a lover is conventionally a rather poor creature. The same convention assumes that poetry is the normal result of frustration in love: Eros is the presiding genius of the awakening of the imagination, and poetry is written as what biologists now call a displaced activity, the baffling of love by a lady's cruelty. But Eros is still the driving force of the poetry, and Eros does not care how casual or inappropriate any given metaphor may be: he only wants to get as many images copulating as possible.

Behind the lover, the practical and rather commonplace mind of Theseus sees nothing but lunatics. But even in this paper we have already seen that many of the most intense forms of human experience take some form of ecstatic metaphor. The hypothetical nature of literature, its ironic separation from all statements of assertion, was as far as I got in my *Anatomy of Criticism,* published nearly thirty years ago. The literary imagination seemed to me then, as in large part it does now, to be primarily a kind of model-thinking, an infinite set of possibilities of experience to expand and intensify our actual experience. But the *Anatomy* had led me to the scripture or sacred book as the furthest boundary to be explored in the imaginative direction, and I then became increasingly fascinated with the Bible, as a book dominated by metaphor throughout, and yet quite obviously not content with an ironic removal from experience or assertion. Clearly one had to look at other aspects of the question, and reconsider the cultural context of metaphor, as something that not only once had but may still have its roots in ecstatic experience.

I had noticed, for example, that many of the central Christian doctrines (e.g., Christ is God and man) were grammatically expressible only in metaphor. At that time, however, existential questions of "commitment" and the like were still in the ascendant, and in that cultural frame of mind, committing one's beliefs and values to metaphor seemed like crossing a deep gorge on a rope bridge: we may put all our trust in its ability to get us across, but there will be moments when we wish we hadn't. At the same time I was not happy with the merely "let's pretend" or "let's assume" attitude to literature. Nobody wants to eliminate the element of play from literature, but most poets clearly felt that what they were doing was more complex.

The complexities begin when we realize that metaphor, as a bridge between consciousness and nature, is in fact a microcosm of language itself. It is precisely the function of language to overcome what Blake calls the "cloven fiction" of a subject contemplating an object. In the nineteenth century the German philosopher Humboldt had arrived at the principle that language was a third order of reality, coming between subject and object. Saussure, the founder of modern linguistics, also spoke of a world of "signification" in between the signifier and the signified. Language from this point of view becomes a single gigantic metaphor, the uniting of consciousness with what it is conscious of. This union is Ovid's metamorphosis in reverse, the transfiguring of consciousness as it merges with articulated meaning. In a more specifically religious area this third order would become Martin Buber's world of "Thou," which comes between the consciousness that is merely an "I" and a nature that is merely an "it."

To turn now to a slightly different aspect of the subject. We started with the conception of the god as a socially stabilized metaphor. The metaphor "Neptune is the sea" becomes a social datum if we build a temple to Neptune or address prayers to him when starting on a voyage. The next step in this social stabilizing of a god is the story or narrative (*mythos* in Greek, whence "myth" in English) that is associated with a god and gives him a specific character and activities. We find such myths in the Homeric Hymns in an unusually concentrated form. Such myths, or stories about gods, are a normal part of every society's verbal culture: in structure they hardly differ from folktales, but the social use made of them is different. Folktales may be told for amusement, and tend to lead a nomadic existence, wandering over a wide area through all barriers of language. But myths, though they also travel widely, form in addition a central body of stories that it is particularly important for a specific society to hear, because they set out what are regarded as the essential facts about its gods, its history, and its social structure. Hence myths, in contrast to folktales, have a higher proportion of stories about recognized deities in them, and they also unify into a mythology and form the core of a body of shared imaginative allusion and shared experience for a society. They add the dimension of history and tradition to a society's verbal culture.

The myth, like the metaphor, conveys two contradictory messages. One is "this happened." The other is: "this almost certainly did not happen, at least in precisely the way described." The latter aspect has given us the common but vulgar sense of myth as simply a false statement. In Western culture the biblical myths formed an inner core of sacrosanct legend, where, in contrast to classical or other nonbiblical stories, the assertion "this happened precisely as described" was maintained for centuries by brute force. Thus at the end of the seventeenth century Bishop Burnet's *Sacred Theory of the Earth* explains how the world was originally smooth and uniform, without mountains or sea, until human sin provoked the Deity into causing the deluge, after which Nature appeared in its present preposterous and asymmetrical shape. The Last Judgment by fire will start with volcanic explosions in which Great Britain will burn faster than most of the world, because it has so much coal. However, in expounding these matters his orthodoxy was suspected and he lost an official job under William III, an example of the way in which people of that time, especially if they were clergymen, were effectively disqualified from trying to think seriously about such subjects as ancient history or the earth sciences. But as, later, people became freer to speak of creation, deluge, and even gospel myths, the positive as well as the negative side of myth became clearer.

A myth is a story, a word now distinguished from history, and of course many stories are "just" stories, making no claim to be anything else. But consider what happens when a great poet treats a historical subject. In studying Shakespeare's plays on Henry IV and Henry V, for example, we can see that Shakespeare used the historical sources available to him, but made some deliberate changes, such as giving Hotspur and Prince Hal the same age when they were in fact twenty years apart. So we say that the myth, the story, of Shakespeare's plays follows history except for some deviations which are permitted only to poets, and are called poetic license, poets being assumed to be too weak-minded to handle documents accurately.

But let us look again at, say, *Henry V.* We see the victorious king winning Agincourt and becoming king of France; we also see something of the ghastly misery of France, the greatness of personality which still remains in the abandoned Falstaff, the fact that Henry is being merely pulled upward on an automatic wheel of fortune, that he died almost at once and that sixty years of unbroken disaster in England resulted. This growing "alienation," as Brecht would call it, means that the myth or story of the play is not "following" history at all. It incorporates a good deal of historical material, but it twists the events around so that they *confront* the audience. The audience is compelled to respond to a dimension of time that is no longer purely sequential. That is why the changes that poets make in their sources are so often in the direction of providing a greater symmetry in the narrative.

Similarly, the crucifixion of Christ was a historical event, or at least there is no discernible reason for its not being one. It is presented mythically in the Gospels, and that implies a certain amount of arrangement and contrivance, such as the way in which the sensibilities of Roman authorities are clearly being soothed down. But to concern ourselves only with the negative aspect of myth, its departure from history, would be to miss the whole point. As a historical event, the crucifixion of Christ is merely one more manifestation of that continuous psychosis which is the substance of human history, the activity of what Cummings calls "this busy monster, manunkind." It is only as myth that *this* crucifixion has the power to confront us with the vision of our own moral bankruptcy.

Poets, on the whole, prefer to work within their own history. That history tells us that the central event in the past was a ten-year siege of Troy by the Greeks, that Rome was founded as an aftermath of that siege, that Britain was settled as a later aftermath, and that out of the British settlement there arose the titanic figure of King Arthur, with whom no other British sovereign can compare for an instant in majesty and power. Tennyson closes his account of that king's passing with the somber lines: "The darkness of that battle in the West, / Where all of high and holy dies away." It would be difficult to write with this kind of resonance about an actual event, where the chaotic untidiness and continuous anticlimaxes in human behavior would be bound to get in the poet's way.

The value and importance of getting actual history as accurate as possible is not, of course, in question here. But our ordinary experience in time has to struggle with three unrealities: a past which is no longer, a future which is not yet, a present which is never quite. The myth is presented to us now, a present moment where, as Eliot would say, the past and future are gathered. Similarly, in metaphors of the type "A is B," the "is" is not really a predicate at all. The real function of the "is" in "Joseph is a fruitful bough" is to annihilate the space between the "Joseph" who is there, on our left as it were, and the "bough" which is there, on our right, and place them in a world where everything is "here." And as it becomes increasingly clear that the words *infinite* and *eternal* do not, except in certain aspects of mathematics, simply mean space and time going on without stopping, but the reality of the "here" and "now" that are at the center of experience, we come to understand why all language directly concerned with the larger dimensions of infinite and eternal must be mythical and metaphorical language.

My next step begins with what may sound like a digression. Several best-selling books lately have been telling us how the most advanced societies of our time, that is to say our own, are moving from an industry-based to an information-based form of social organization. This thesis doubtless appeals strongly to a middle management who would rather issue memoranda than produce goods at competitive prices. But what is really curious about such books is the conception of information involved. Surely everyone knows that information is not a placid river of self-explanatory facts: it comes to us prepackaged in ideological containers, and many of these containers have been constructed by professional liars. There is such a thing, of course, as a genuine information explosion, but in even the most benevolent forms of acquiring information, such as research in the arts and sciences, most of the work involved consists in extricating oneself from a web of misinformation, after which the researcher hands over to posterity what he has put together, with *its* quota of mistakes and prejudices. The issue here has a direct bearing on the social function of writing.

A mythology is not a protoscience: it does not, except incidentally, make statements about the natural environment. It is a structure of human concern, and is built out of human hopes and fears and rumors and anxieties. When a mythology is looked at spatially, as a unified construct of metaphors, it turns into a cosmology, and in that form it may include or imply pseudoscientific fallacies. The cosmologies of Dante and Milton are full of what is now pseudoscience, but that does not affect their worth in the literary structures they inform, because, as Paul Valéry remarks, cosmology is an aspect of literature. It still often does not matter to a contemporary poet whether his cosmology is in accord with the science of his day or not. Twentieth-century poets continue to talk about four elements and phases of the moon and other such features long excluded from the scientist's universe. In fact, as Valéry also says, the word *universe* itself, with its suggestion that all the millions of galaxies out there turn around one point, is mainly a word to be consumed on the licensed premises of poetry.

There is primary concern and there is secondary concern, and correspondingly there is primary mythology and secondary mythology. Primary concern is based on the simplest and baldest platitudes it is possible to formulate: that life is better than death, freedom better than slavery, happiness better than misery. Secondary concern is what we call ideology, the desire of a particular social group, or a class or priesthood or bureaucracy or other special interest within that group, to preserve its ascendancy, increase its prestige, or proclaim its beliefs. Every work of literature, as something produced for its own time, is in part an ideological document. The relation of a poet to the ideology he expounds or reflects is the genuine form of the "anxiety of influence," and it affects all writers without exception. The psychological and Freudian aspect of it celebrated by Harold Bloom seems to me mainly a by-product of the law of copyright.

What we call classics are works of literature that show an ability to communicate with other ages over the widest barriers of time, space, and language. This ability depends on the inclusion of some element of insight into the human situation that escapes from the limits of ideology. Thus Shakespeare's *Henry V,* just referred to, contains the kind of ideology that his audience would want, and shows a heroic English king victorious over a swarm of foreigners. It was still exploiting that ideology in the

Laurence Olivier film version in the Second World War, where the invasion of France became an allegory for a second front against Nazi Germany. At the same time the immense variety of events and moods in the play, which show us the context of such a war in the total human situation, constitutes a vision of life in terms of its primary concern with the struggle against death.

All through human history secondary concerns have kept an ascendancy over primary ones. We prefer to live, but we go to war; we prefer to be free, but we may accept authority to the point of losing our freedom; we prefer happiness, but may allow our lives to self-destruct. The century that has produced atom bombs and a pollution which threatens to cut off the supply of breathable air and drinkable water is the first period in history we know of when humanity has been compelled to face the conclusion: primary concerns must become primary, or else. Surely this suggests that it is becoming a central task of criticism, in literature or outside it, to try to distinguish the disinterested vision from the interested ideology. As the critic has his own ideology to become aware of, this is very difficult to do, and it is very natural for him to regard his own ideology as the Aaron's rod turned serpent that will eventually devour all its rivals. But as it becomes clearer that all the ideologies presented by political, economic, and religious bodies fall short of a genuine mythology of primary concern, it becomes more and more urgent for critics to increase the awareness of their own and of others' mythological conditioning, and thus take up some of their real social functions.

And what good would it do if they did? I wish I had a glad confident answer to this. Previous decades in this century assumed that revolutionary action, self-determination on the part of third-world colonies, and the like, could revitalize our social consciousness, but that has led to one disillusionment after another. Today it is hard to dodge the fact that any form of intensified ideology is pernicious if it leads to another excuse for war or for exploiting either other men or nature. In the late sixties a state of mind developed that we might characterize as a feeling that the old subject-object consciousness, in which the individual is merely one of a social aggregate, had to give way to a new and heightened form of consciousness. Hence many forms of ecstatic metaphor reappeared. Certain drugs seemed to bring about something close to a sense of identity with one's surroundings;

teachers of yoga and Zen forms of concentration became immensely popular; folksingers and rock music festivals seemed to symbolize a new conception of comradeship. It was a period of neoprimitivism, of renewed identity through ecstatic music or contemplation of a visual focus. McLuhan suggested that the physiological impact of television and other electronic media would create a new sensibility, forming bodies of social awareness in which nations and states as we know them would wither away and be replaced by a revitalized tribal culture. In the seventies he became less sanguine about this, but something of his earlier view survives as a vague hope that some technological gimmick will automatically take charge of the human situation.

At the same time it seems clear that metaphorical and mythical habits of mind are much more taken for granted today than they were thirty years or so ago. There seems little interest in reviving gods or nature spirits: in contemporary academic journals references to Nietzsche and Heidegger are all over the place, but nobody seems to want to buy Nietzsche's Antichrist Dionysus or Heidegger's murky and maudlin polytheism. The feeling is rather a new awareness of a common identity of human consciousness engaged with a total nature. This conception of a total human consciousness is central to all the more serious religions: in Christianity it takes the form of the vision of Christ as total man, as the Word or total intelligibility, and consequently as the key to all metaphor as well as all myth, the identity of existing things. But it extends so far beyond Christianity as to strain our best "ecumenical" efforts. The notion of an antithesis between the religious and the secular-humanistic does not work any more, if it ever did. Everyone knows that all religious social phenomena have a secular aspect to them, and the same principle holds in reverse. The specific entity pointed to by the word *religious* seems to me to be closely connected with the principle of ecstatic metaphor that I have been expounding. What a man's religion is may be gathered from what he wants to identify himself with, and except perhaps for those who are devoted one hundred percent to pursuing their own interests, all activities have a religious aspect as well as a secular one.

In reading contemporary criticism, I have been interested to notice how the religious origin of many critical questions still peeps out of odd corners: in the tendency to capitalize *Word*, in the theological subtleties of distinctions among *verbe, parole, lan-*

gue, and *langage,* in the pervasive uncertainty about whether human consciousness is using language or is being used by it. Similarly with poets: Wallace Stevens speaks of a "central mind" or "major man," which or who includes all other minds without destroying their individuality. He also has a poem in which a fisherman, with his river and his fish and the doves cooing around him, consolidate into one form, though, again, the individual forms remain. One thing that is interesting about this poem is its title: "Thinking of a Relation between the Images of Metaphors." Scientists too: the physicist Erwin Schrödinger, the founder of quantum mechanics, informed an audience at Cambridge about thirty years ago that "consciousness is a singular of which the plural is unknown."

Well, of course, there are those who emphasize, quite rightly, the social and cultural conditioning that underlies every thought or experience we have, and they could just as readily say that consciousness is a plural of which the singular is unknown. But the real significance of such statements is in a different category from assertions that anyone can instantly refute. What is involved is rather the interchange of reality and illusion that language brings about. We start with the notion that the perceiving subject and the perceived object are the essential realities, brought together by the fictions of language. But in proportion as subject and object become illusory, the world of intelligibility connecting them becomes reality, though always the sort of reality that Wallace Stevens, again, calls a supreme fiction. To the extent that the subject-object relation is the sole reality and the metaphors and myths connecting them illusory, the poet will be a relatively unpopular leisure-class entertainer with a limited function and no authority. To the extent that the subject-object relation grows illusory and the fictions connecting them real, the poet begins to recover something of the social authority which, according to tradition, he originally had. But we can never understand the poet's authority without Vico's principle of *verum factum,* that reality is in the world we make and not in the world we stare at.

I mentioned Bishop Burnet and his discussion of the deluge myth, the story of how human sin and folly caused the entire world to be destroyed. His treatment of the myth may seem to us naive, but the myth itself seems far less so now than it might have done not so long since. If the human race were to destroy

122

both itself and the planet it lives on, that would be the final triumph of illusion. But we have other myths, myths telling us that time and space and life may have an end, but that the sense of identity with something other than these things will not, that there is a word which, whether flesh or not, is still dwelling with us. Also that our ability to respond to what it says is the only sensible reason yet proposed for our being here.

The
Responsibilities
of the Critic

✦

MANY NINETEENTH-CENTURY writers, including Burke, Carlyle, and Arnold, were badly shaken by all the revolutionary talk about the "rights of man" following the French Revolution, and were fond of insisting that men have no rights, only duties. Similarly, the academic critic represents the practical arts, notably literature, within the university, and it is safer for him to talk about his responsibilities than about his privileges. Many poets and novelists wonder why, if he must thrust himself in front of students to talk about literature, he cannot confine himself to the dead, and let them make their own impact unimpeded. Most academic critics would prefer to do so, but the assumption involved is that students can be left to read contemporary literature on their own, and students are so little inclined to do that that they often regard their teachers as under a moral obligation to devote themselves as much as possible to the living. The university administrator may sometimes feel gratitude to the humanists because their financial demands are less than those of science and technology, but high price and high regard go together, and he more often echoes the attitude of a public who queries the "relevance" of the humanities. The critic has no relevance except what he creates himself, though I suspect that that is equally true of the rest of the human race.

Let us start with the tradition that begins with Aristotle, as a way of introducing the real subject of the critic, the subject that Aristotle calls poetics. I speak of an Aristotelian tradition rather than of Aristotle, because the *Poetics* is a very elliptical treatise, and the notetaker to whom we owe it seems to have been seized with writer's cramp at the most inappropriate times. Whenever we read anything, we have two things to do with the words: fit them together, and relate them separately to what they mean in the world outside the book. As though this were not complicated enough, we also have two aspects of words to struggle with, the unity and the units. The unity is expressed by the narrative, the sequential ordering of the words from the first page to the last. The units consist mainly of the images, the words with their conventional meanings, of which the most prominent are the nouns and the verbs, the names of things and of actions. We may call these two aspects of narrative and imagery the structure and the texture.

At a certain point we may come to feel that what the words mean, outside the book, is taking precedence over their relations to each other. That is, we have a verbal structure which is meant to be set up against something else, to which it is related as an imitation to an original. There are two large and important classes of such verbal structures: those that imitate *praxis,* or human actions, and those that imitate *theoria,* or human vision and thought. These can be called the historical and the discursive verbal structures. Here the narrative reflects a corresponding area of action or thought and is subject to the criterion of "truth." Truth here means truth of correspondence: a verbal structure is compared with a body of phenomena outside it, and is called true if it is a satisfactory verbal counterpart of it. The correspondence may be only occasional and fitful, or may come to be increasingly so in the course of time. This causes us to say that there is "some truth in" what the writer says. The images correspond to the things they conventionally mean: words have to be used in accustomed and consistent senses, and the smaller units are subject to a related but different criterion, the criterion of the factual.

On the other hand, we may come to feel that in what we are reading the interrelations of the words come first, that we have a verbal structure set up for its own sake. In that case it is a secondary verbal imitation of action and thought, and belongs to the group that we call poetic or literary. In the literary work the unifying narrative is simply that, a narrative, *mythos* in Greek, not subject to the criterion of truth of correspondence, or detailed agreement with anything outside it. As an imitation of action, the narrative is not a history but a story, something read for its own sake. Aristotle suggested that in the process the narrative moves from representing the particular to representing the universal. When we go from the early history of Scotland to *Macbeth,* we go from what happened to what happens, to a vision of something recurrent and never finished within human life. The word *vision* implies that *theoria* is involved as well as *praxis,* which is why Aristotle says that poetry is more philosophical than history.

The *Poetics* says next to nothing about the relations of literature to representations of thought, and in English criticism it is not until the time of Coleridge that this question begins to be dealt with. But the same general principles hold. Primary imitations of thought are made up of predications, particular statements which again are judged by the truth of correspondence. Poetry may use philosophical material, just as it may use historical material, but when it does the context is different from philosophy. On the simplest level, the poet has a peculiar concern for felicity of statement, for saying, in Pope's words, "What oft was thought but ne'er so well expressed." The poet has always been admired, and still is much more than we often realize, for a sententious quality in his work, his ability to produce the quotable or easily recognized phrase. If we look more closely, we see that this results from a greater concreteness in his medium. On a more continuous level, a philosophical poet, as compared with a philosopher, is less interested in a system or the relating of ideas, and more in elaborating the metaphorical pictures or diagrams out of which the system comes. Thus Poe's *Eureka,* which talks a good deal about electricity and gravitation, develops these concepts into a positive and negative alternation of movement in the universe, and ends with a vision like that of the days and nights of Brahma in Hinduism. A perhaps more obvious example is *Sartor Resartus,* which elaborates the clothes-and-body metaphor implicit in Kant and Fichte. In long and complex literary works, like the epics of Dante and Milton, such world pictures expand into cosmologies, cosmology being, as Valéry says, one of the literary arts.

In literature, then, the narrative is a pure *mythos,* or, in English, a myth, and there are two general types of literary myths, story myths and conceptual myths. As for the units or images, in literary works these are related primarily to each other rather than separately to things in the world outside. When two images are related primarily to each other we have some form of metaphor: thus a work of literature has a structure of myth and a texture of metaphor.

The Aristotelian view of verbal structures, which modulated into the Coleridgean one around 1800, served us very well down to the beginning of this century, and seems to me still solid and useful. Its main deficiency, apart from the lack of historical perspective, was less in itself than in the fact that it left criticism open to some very dubious social and cultural assumptions. In spite of Aristotle's use of the term *universal*, it seemed to imply that the really serious business of words was to tell us the truth about what was going on in time and conceptual space. Hence literary structures were not very serious, unless they had been written in dead languages, where the effort to decipher them, and the obscurity surrounding the effort, helped to make them more so. The real function of literature, it was assumed, was to supply a kind of emotional resonance to the truths that history and philosophy could convey. It is these cultural inferences, not the Aristotelian theory itself, which has fallen to pieces in our day.

We no longer have the same naive confidence in the unlimited ability of words to express all possible phenomena of experience, or show us every kind of reality in a flawless mirror. We realize more clearly how easy it is to talk about things which are not there, or cannot be shown to be there, to discuss the nine orders of angels as concretely as the stratification of rocks. More important, we realize the extent to which words keep twisting away from reality back to their own grammatical fictions, and so entice us to believe that subjects and predicates and objects are built into the nature of things. As a result philosophy in our time has shifted a good deal of its attention from what words tell us, or seem to tell us, to the linguistic structure itself, and the powers and limitations of that structure as a communicating instrument.

Thus we have Heidegger, in *Was heisst denken?* and in his essays on Hölderlin, minimizing the difference between the poetic and the philosophical thinker. Both, for him, elaborate self-contained verbal structures, and his most typical philosophers are Nietzsche and Parmenides, both of whom could equally be described as poets. Wittgenstein, a very different philosopher, is more concerned with the negative aspects of verbal structures and in defining the limits of their capacities, but similar interests are reflected in him. When a verbal structure is called true because it is thought to correspond to a body of phenomena, it becomes univocal; that is, language is being used as pure communication. The *Philosophical Investigations,* in particular, explore the immense difficulties involved in oversimplifying this situation. More positive questions are also involved. As long as literature continues to use words in their accustomed senses, it can never be as abstract or nonrepresentational as music is, or as painting and sculpture can be. On the other hand, there must be another aspect of the kind of truth that can be conveyed by words, a truth of implication, a truth emerging from inner coherence rather than external reference.

There is thus a growing realization, among critics, philosophers, even social scientists, that what words do best, do most accurately, and do most powerfully, is hang together. The ability of words to inform the external world makes them extremely useful, but it seems to be limited as compared with mathematics, and to be to some extent derivative. It would be easy to exaggerate this tendency out of reaction, but it has gone so far that we seem to be nearing a critical situation in which the verbal structures can be thought of as literary or as subliterary. This year, 1976, we celebrate the bicentennials of Adam Smith's *Wealth of Nations* and the first volume of Gibbon's *Decline and Fall.* These books were originally historical and discursive accounts of economics and the history of Rome. As such, they "date": accepting them as that would drag us back to outmoded conceptions of their subjects. But as self-contained verbal structures they are more important now than they were in their own day, because they have been graduated to the higher, or literary, category.

Two corollaries follow. One is that when a work survives through such a literary quality, it also acquires a historical dimension. This is what the word *classic* primarily expresses. The fact that the books of Adam Smith and Gibbon are still readable makes them valuable also as eighteenth-century documents, perspectives of another age. We have to look at things sometimes from the point of view of other ages, precisely because they are not our own. Why else does this university celebrate a centennial, and the country it is in a bicentennial? The other is that every writer, to the extent that he succeeds in producing a coherent verbal structure, is not only a "creative" writer, but, if we are using the word in a proper critical sense, a poet. A third corollary ought to follow, but does not. This is that literary criticism occupies a central place in everything that has to do with words. Why it does not follow is something we cannot deal with until we have looked at the historical or genetic dimension of the subject. This will take us from the Aristotelian tradition into the eighteenth-century Italian philosopher Vico, with his great vision of the development of social institutions out of what he calls "poetic wisdom," or an original mythology.

The importance of Vico to our present argument is that he grasped so firmly two points: first, that a mythological structure is a poetic structure, whatever nonliterary uses may also be made of myth, and second, that this poetic mythology precedes the development of historical and discursive writing. This is the historical side of the principle that verbal structures are primarily made to hold together rather than reflect: the holding-together aspect is not only primary but primitive, the one that came first. One assumption involved here is that the poetic always precedes the prosaic in the history of literature, which is obviously true, but at once destroys what I have often attacked as the Jourdain fallacy, the notion that prose is the language of ordinary speech. Such a fallacy is particularly foolish at a time when so many students in university cannot write or speak prose, and when we are near the point of seeing the smear word *elitist* applied to anyone who habitually does.

Vico sees poetic mythology as something used in society to control human action on the one hand and human thought on the other. The control of human action is achieved through law, though law in this context includes custom and ritual. Society begins in an age of gods, where laws are assumed to be of divine origin and are interpreted by oracles and divination; it then moves into an age of heroes, where laws are drawn up in the interest of an ascendant class, then to an age of the people, where man is assumed to be responsible for his own laws, and finally to the various stages of a *ricorso* which starts the sequence over again. The great example of the *ricorso*, for Vico, was the return of the age of gods and heroes after the fall of the Roman republic.

This growth of law is a nonliterary development of mythology, and it involves a new allegorical recreation of the mythology at each social phase. When we pass from an age of gods to an age of heroes, the actions of the gods become an allegory of the actions of an aristocracy or privileged class. When we pass to the age of the people, the actions of the aristocracy become an allegory of what we should now call a class struggle. Each reinterpretation is an effort to say what the original myth "really means." By doing so, it destroys the myth as a structure and replaces it with the new meaning. The evolution of the inner mythology of law into a parable of exploitation is what Vico himself is mainly interested in, and he begins the tradition followed later by Michelet, Marx, and Sorel. Vico's normal habit of mind is allegorical, and he insists that the true allegories of the original myths are univocal and historical.

But the original mythology was a product of poetic, or what we should call imaginative, thinking, and hence, along with the movement in which mythology mirrors the course of social action, there goes a reshaping of the mythology itself in its own imaginative patterns, a reshaping which is structural and not allegorical, which works by recreation rather than by destroying one meaning and setting up another. This structural reshaping of myth is what we call literature. As the age of gods becomes the age of heroes, the myths of the gods modulate into romances about human champions; as the age of heroes becomes the age of the people, romance becomes more plausible and realistic. But the same mythical structures, the same devices for beginning and developing and ending the story, persist throughout.

The literary development of myth is also different from another development in which myth forms the embryo of philosophy and science. Mythology is not really a form of conceptual thinking, and the development of science, like the development of law, involves destroying and replacing rather than the restructuring myth. Thus seventeenth-century astronomy replaced mythological with scientific space, and nineteenth-century biology and geology replaced mythological with scientific time. We still use the words *sunrise* and *sunset,* but we now think of them as allegories of a very different situation. We need, therefore, a third social development of mythology, one which, unlike the other two, preserves its inner imaginative structure, to account for the continuation of the poetic and mythological habit of mind in literature.

A cyclical view of history is in itself a rather pessimistic one, and the ideal course that nations run, under the benevolent eye of a divine providence, is summarized by Vico thus: "Men first feel necessity, then look for utility, next attend to comfort, still later amuse themselves with pleasure, thence grow dissolute in luxury, and finally go mad and waste their substance." It seems to follow that if there is any sense or moral to history, or even to the study of it, that moral must be connected with the question of how we can arrest the cycle at what seems to us the most desirable point. For most of us this point would be the age of the people, and that appears also to be Vico's attitude. He even seems to suggest that the effort of analysis represented by his book might do something to work against the fatality of another *ricorso*. Perhaps, to borrow a celebrated maxim, it is only those who will not learn history who are condemned to repeat it. The ouroboros might straighten out if it began to feel actual pain while chewing its tail.

In Vico the cycle of history begins with a thunderclap, the noise from the sky that the primeval giants after the flood took to be the voice of God, interrupting their intercourse with their women with what was assumed to be disapproval. The frightened giants got up off their women and dragged them to the caves instead, thus beginning private property. This was the feature of Vico that attracted James Joyce, who was also terrified by thunderstorms. In *Finnegans Wake* Joyce seems to be associating Vico's myth with that of another great eighteenth-century masterpiece, Sterne's *Tristram Shandy*, where the hero ascribes his misfortunes in life to his mother's having interrupted his father, in the act of coition, by asking him if he had wound the clock. Sterne, along with St. Augustine, is clearer than Vico in that the anxieties of sex and time go together.

Vico's thunderclap, however, also symbolizes a historical and social problem that we do not have the conceptual tools to deal with: the problem of whether, and if so to what extent, cultural developments are founded on some forgotten, suppressed, or misinterpreted trauma. Myths of the fall of man or, still more obviously, myths of a major deluge, like the story of Atlantis, seem to indicate something like this. Freud suggests the rite of killing a primal father as the source of a traumatic myth of a similar kind. But for the most part we leave these questions to such speculators as Däniken and Velikowsky, who follow Vico's suggestive but somewhat free-wheeling mythopoeic style. It may seem inherently likely that the real answer, if there is an answer, would be something less picturesque than visits from outer space or the birth of the planet Venus. But the reason for the popularity of such writers in our day opens up another aspect of the problem, and explains why I am putting so much emphasis here on Vico.

Every age, of course, thinks it is the fulfillment of everything up to itself, and tries to interpret history not as cyclical but as evolving towards its *telos* in the present moment. Vico himself, living in the eighteenth century, lays a good deal of emphasis on the improvement of life since giants wandered the world in a state of promiscuous anarchy. Similarly, the popular progressive myths of fifty years ago feature a "caveman" who was much closer to nursery tales of giants and ogres, and closer also to Vico, than to anything that the caves of Lascaux and Altamira actually suggest. But there is so strong a sense today that we are in the last stages of the cycle Vico traces, when luxury gives way to a mad squandering of resources, that our progressive and evolutionary myths have become overlaid by something much more apprehensive.

Of course anyone over thirty may feel that the existence of so many people under thirty constitutes in itself a threat of return to the Dark Ages. But a great intensifying of an otherwise normal feeling seems to pervade our time, and to affect the younger generation even more than the older one. The feeling that another trauma or thunderclap is directly in front of us, as something that will come within a generation, extends from depressive fears of a nuclear holocaust to manic forecasts of an age of Aquarius. It is related to the sense of being near the end of a cycle, close to what Blake's *Mental Traveller* calls the birth of the babe. Naturally language and literature are affected by the same feeling. Vico's *ricorso* period was accompanied by the breakdown of language, as Latin turned into the Romance vernaculars. The elaborate communication machinery of our time holds together a traditional normalized form of English which without that machinery would fly off in all directions into every variety of dialect and idiom. I often find in young people a sense of diffidence, almost of something like shame, in speaking this traditional language, as though it implied an attitude to participating in society that they do not share.

Vico tells us that history is made by men, which means that all the gods born of the fear of the thunderclap are human creations too. This is the main reason why he is compelled to bracket the whole biblical tradition as outside the history he surveys. We can hardly follow him in this, nor am I sure that he wants us to. In the first place, Jehovah, who drowned the whole human race, is quite as much of a thundergod as Zeus, and the story of the Exodus has cultural trauma written all over it. The real relation of Hebrew to Egyptian culture can only be guessed at: we may note some shrewd guesses in Freud's *Moses and Monotheism,* and a comment in Melville's journal after a visit to the pyramids: "I shudder at idea of ancient Egyptians. It was in these pyramids that was conceived the idea of Jehovah. Terrible mixture of the cunning and awful." Second, and more important, the culture born in so mysterious a way had a revolutionary character that makes it unique in the ancient world, as well as the direct ancestor of a line of revolutionary religions, Judaism, Christianity, Islam, and Marxism. It begins with God telling Moses that he is giving himself a name and entering on a specific and highly partisan historical role. The belief in a revolution starting in a definite time and place, the acceptance of a canon of sacred books, the dialectical habit of mind which polarizes every issue and excludes revisionist or compromising or liberal elements: these are characteristics of a revolutionary religious movement, and they recur in all the progeny of the burning bush. The revolutionary monotheism of the Hebrews is quite different in social reference from the imperial monotheism that appeared early in Egypt and later in Persia and Rome. Biblical monotheism is that of a small and beleaguered nation: its god is invisible, and in contrast to Egypt, where the Pharoah was always the high priest and an incarnation of Horus, the Hebrew tendency was toward a separation of spiritual and temporal authority. The main reason for this separation was that the Hebrews possessed, in the institution of prophecy, a third form of authority which, though it often served the kings or priests, was distinguishable from both. The function of prophecy was to remind the people of their contractual relation to their god, in other words to keep restating the original myth.

Out of the teachings of the prophets came the development of the law and the later wisdom literature. But although the Deuteronomic code assumes great differences of wealth and station in society, including slavery, the prophetic insistence on preserving the form of the original direct relation to the god seems to exert an equalizing force. The explicit teachings of the prophets, of Amos, for instance, are full of denunciations of the "great houses" and of the rich grinding the faces of the poor. It is as though the age of the gods and the age of the people were linked in something of a common cause against the tyranny of heroes. Similarly, the tyranny of heroes is what revives with the failure of nerve which starts off the *ricorso,* when the power of the people is surrendered to dictators or Vico's "kings."

The biblical tradition, then, if I am right, has the three elements of mythology that I have tried to extract from Vico, or see implicit in him: the two centrifugal developments of law and wisdom, and an inner imaginative restructuring of the original myth in prophecy. The structures of law and wisdom are, so to speak, horizontally related to society: they are sustained by what I think of as the anxiety of continuity. Hence the emphasis, for example, on hereditary succession in monarchies, and on the next election and the new leader in democracies. Similarly, in religion, where the constant repetition of the same rite is the motive force. Prophecy, on the other hand, breaks vertically and discontinuously into society: it presents a transcending vision of the social order out of which it has come. Its biblical symbol is the prophet in the desert, the voice crying in the wilderness.

But once a prophetic revelation is accepted and established in society, there can be no more prophets, in the sense of transcendental visionaries, within that establishment. The structures of law and wisdom take over entirely, and social change takes place within an evolutionary and continuous development. Medieval Christendom had its High King and its High Priest, in the emperor and pope of Rome, but no recognized prophetic tradition. The liberty of prophesying was one of the things that the Protestant Reformation was all about, but Protestantism can hardly be said to have achieved that liberty: its prophets were preachers, who continued within the priestly orbit, or, as Milton said, new presbyter was old priest writ large. Within any social order, however established, there may be improvement and development, new strategies for new occasions, social criticism, individual or mystical recreations of the original vision. But by definition and hypothesis, nothing can transcend the revelation of the Torah or the Gospel or the Koran or the writings of Marx: whatever appears to do so is only a heresy, an old fallacy in a new disguise.

134

Such a feeling is intolerable to the mood of many people today, at least in the democracies, and one of the features of our age is an anxious search for some kind of prophetic or transcending vision of the social order. Here again is an intensifying of something that has been with us for a long time. Protestantism, I said, did not succeed in liberating prophecy, but it did produce some remarkable prophetic figures, including Milton. Milton's *Areopagitica* seems to me to represent a turning point in the history of Western culture so far as our present subject is concerned. It is an attack on censorship and a defense of the liberty of the press which is important perhaps less as that than as the first suggestion that the power of prophecy is starting to come from the printing press rather than the pulpit, from secular rather than sacerdotal contexts. This may be expanded into the general principle that the prophet is most likely to emerge from an unrecognized quarter of society, from a place that society has overlooked or forgotten to enclose and protect.

Ever since the Romantic period, at least, we have tended to recognize a prophetic authority in literature, and in the arts generally. Some writers, notably in the T. S. Eliot and T. E. Hulme generation, have made a good deal of renouncing this attitude, but they usually turned out to be only prophetic plainclothesmen. The original prophets were ecstatics who went into trances and spoke with different voices, and their prestige had much to do with the primitive reverence for such abnormal states of mind. Thus Samuel says to Saul: "It shall come to pass, when thou art come thither to the city, that thou shalt meet a company of prophets coming down from the high place . . . and they shall prophesy: And the spirit of the Lord will come upon thee, and thou shalt prophesy with them, and shalt be turned into another man." The fact that creative powers come from an area of the mind that seems to be independent of the conscious will, and often emerge with a good deal of emotional disturbance in their wake, provides the chief analogy between prophecy and the arts. The creative people that we most instinctively call or think of as prophetic, Nietzsche, Rimbaud, Blake, Van Gogh, Dostoyevsky, Strindberg, show the analogy very clearly. Some people pursue wholeness and integration, others get smashed up, and fragments are rescued from the smash of an intensity that the wholeness and integration people do not reach.

Then too the prophetic aspect of the arts is reflected in the great difficulty that society has in absorbing its creative people. The fierce persecution of so many of the best Russian writers by the Soviet bureaucracy comes readily to mind, and there are many parallels in the democracies. At the same time, if the prophetic voice so frequently comes from the outsider, it follows that society's most effective defense against prophecy is toleration. The realization of this, in our society, has helped to create an almost obsessive preoccupation with the subcultures or countercultures of various minorities, blacks, Chicanos, homosexuals, terrorists, drug addicts, occultists, yogis, criminals like the holy and blessed Genet—wherever it may still be possible to make out a case for social hostility or discrimination. Similarly with the revival of dada and other movements in the arts that spill over into anarchistic activism. We read in the Old Testament of prophets who used various emblematic devices to make their oracular points: "And Zedekiah the son of Chenaanah made him horns of iron: and he said, Thus saith the Lord, With these shalt thou push the Syrians, until thou have consumed them." There seems to be some analogy here to the brief vogue of the "happening," when, for instance, large blocks of ice were set up in various street corners in Los Angeles and left to melt, presumably as an emblem of California civilization.

Again, many great writers have been not simply neurotic but called mad, like Blake, or confined in asylums, like Ezra Pound. The assumption in the word *mad,* which is a social judgment, is that society as a whole is always sane, a difficult assumption to accept in the twentieth century. We are now told by R. D. Laing and others, not only that schizophrenia, for example, may be a quite normal reaction to a mad society, but that the primitive sense of the prophetic authority of madness, the ancient linking of the manic and the mantic, may have been more nearly right than some of our notions about mental illness. But however useful the self-criticism involved in exploring every corner of society in search of yet unheard oracles, it may be well, before we settle permanently into a second-coming syndrome, to remember that there is another and more traditional side to prophecy.

Milton's *Areopagitica* has another importance for us in this connection. It was written while Milton was pondering the subject of his epic, and was slowly shifting over from the story of Arthur to the story of Adam. *Paradise Lost* retells one of the original myths of Milton's culture in such a way as to make it a parable of the failure of the revolutionary movement of Milton's time and, by implication, of the failure of all efforts of an age of the people to maintain its own freedom without help from the kind of power that the Son of God symbolizes in the poem. Significantly, that failure went around in a circle, from revolt against Charles I to acceptance of Charles II. However right or wrong his views, Milton's poem illustrates the curious link, which he found implicit in Vico's argument, between the age of the gods and the age of the people. For the story of Adam is the story of Everyman, excluded from Paradise and wandering in the circles of lost direction all through history, yet never quite losing the hope of an eventual return to something that is not the beginning of another cycle. The hero of *Paradise Lost* is a human trinity made up of Christ, Adam, and Milton himself. Adam is man in the cycle of history; Milton is the prophet who restructures the myth and makes Christ and Adam his own and our contemporaries; Christ represents the fact that although man does not much want freedom, there is a power, identical with his own creative power, which is determined to force it on him.

The story of Arthur, on the other hand, is a theme belonging to the Homeric convention, in which the poet's chief function is to glorify a hero. The hero, to revert again to Vico, is one of the ascendant class of rulers who appear as feudal overlords at one end of the cycle of history and as divine Caesars or charismatic dictators at the other end. The glorifying of the hero thus implies acceptance of the cycle with its *ricorso* as the ultimate horizon of human existence. No comparative value judgments are involved here, but Milton's final choice of subject was an act of criticism, and helps us to understand the place of criticism in the literary process. The critical principle involved is the identifying of something in the literary tradition with the activity that we have been calling prophetic.

The work of most middle-class people today consists mainly in the polluting of paper, or what is known as filling out forms. I struggle hard to keep up with the avalanche of poetry and fiction produced in Canada, and the bulk of this, however interesting in itself, consists of filling out conventional forms, no less than filing an income tax return. Similarly with the routine of the critic's work, editing texts, commenting, and researching into historical background. But there is something in the whole enterprise that is different. A work of art is an effort at imaginative communication: if it succeeds in being that, it becomes the focus of a community. The critic is there, not so much to explain the poet, as to translate literature into a continuous dialogue with society.

The word *critic* is connected with the word *crisis,* and all the critic's scholarly routines revolve around a critical moment and a critical act, which is always the same moment and act however often it recurs. This act, I have so often urged, is not an act of judgment but of recognition. If the critic is the judge, the community he represents is the supreme authority over the poet; all human creation must conform to the anxieties of human institutions. But if the critic abandons judgment for recognition, the act of recognition liberates something in human creative energy, and thereby helps to give the community the power to judge itself. If the critic is to recognize the prophetic, of course, he needs to be prophetic too: his model is John the Baptist, the greatest prophet of his age, whose critical moment came with recognizing a still greater power than his own. I do not mean by this that the critic's function is to wait for a great poet to come along and then recognize him: practically everything the critic will ever recognize accurately is already here. Still less do I mean that the significant critical act is to recognize the supremacy of poets over critics. That points to an utterly muddled and misconceived notion of the critic's role.

The cultural trauma that Vico symbolizes by the thunderclap is projection, the accepting of a mysterious power outside man which is first called the will of the gods, then incarnated in a ruling class. As the sense of power transfers itself to the people, guilt feelings left over from earlier phases may continue unresolved: every scandal and crime may contribute to a growing sense of failure and muddle and self-contempt, until before we know where we are the charismatic leader is there again. That is why the inner self-transforming of the original myth is so important. In the age of the gods we learn that God made the Garden of Eden for man, that man fell out of it through his own fault and is now shut out of it forever. In the age of heroes we learn that there are huge parks or enclosures set aside for our great men, where they may hunt and enjoy themselves, but which the rest of us must keep out of. In the age of the people we begin to learn, at last, something of what is meant by the metaphor of "creation."

The world around us is not necessarily a creation: there is no reason why the actual world should have a beginning or an end. But everything human is created: man has created his gods, his rulers, his institutions, his machines, and it is only when he enters the created world, through a door that someone's imagination has opened, that he can participate in this and feel that the word *subject,* in all its contexts, no longer applies to him. The sense of freedom and release that we can get from entering the created world is so great that we can also understand why religions and political organizations are so anxious about the creative process, and use every pretext to regulate or control or get rid of it. But the critic is constantly trying to find his and our way back to the original lightning flash which the trauma of the thunderclap has caused us to forget. The door to our Eden is still locked, but he has a key, and the key is the act of recognition.

I began by separating the use of words to illustrate something in action or thought from the self-contained body of words which exists for its own sake. These, I said, are not two kinds of structures: every verbal structure has both aspects. We might distinguish them as what the words mean and what the words say. The psychologist Eric Berne, in a popular handbook called *What Do You Say After You Say Hello?,* remarks that when a child is picking up patterns of behavior from his parents, he listens not to what is said to him but to the imperatives implied in what is said to him. The principle is very similar to that of Frege, referred to by Wittgenstein, that every assertion contains an assumption, the assumption being what is really asserted. Society does the same thing with a revelation: it asks not "What does it say?" but "What does this tell us to do?" The prophet, on the contrary, is first of all a sayer and an asserter, even when he does not think of himself as the primary source of what he says.

As a structure of meaning, every body of words is an ideological document, the product of a specific social and historical condition in the cycle of human life. In this context there is nothing really prophetic in any human utterance, outside the group that accepts it as a revelation. Isaiah has a tremendous vision of God treading the winepress of wrath, but that, historically, is only a squalid jingoism gloating over the future discomfiture of a hated enemy. Elijah hears a still small voice after the earthquake and fire, but, historically, all that the voice tells him to do is to liquidate the opposition, exterminate the priests of Baal. Similarly, the great prophetic figures of modern literature, Rousseau or Swift or Kierkegaard or Dostoyevsky, may often not have been much more than wrong-headed neurotics in their historical and biographical contexts. What the critic tries to do is to lead us from what poets and prophets meant, or thought they meant, to the inner structure of what they said. At that point the verbal structure turns inside out, and a vortex opens out of the present moment, from the world of the Viconian cycle into the created world.

Literature, including all structures in words which come to be literary in the course of time, shows an extraordinary conservatism and sense of tradition and convention, along with an equally extraordinary power of renewing itself. It thereby suggests that the real course of human life may be neither a closed circle nor a straight line going off into unknown directions and hazards, but an expanding and open-ended cycle, the stages of which may be simultaneous as well as temporal. The ages of gods and of people are opposite poles of the cycle. At one end is a sense of infinite and eternal mystery, at the other a sense of unlimited possibilities. All through literature the tone I have been calling prophetic keeps echoing the sense of the infinite and eternal, not as what is meant, but as what is said in spite of what is meant. In the Bible there are references to a prophecy which has to be sealed up and hidden away until its time has come. That time comes when in the age of the people the gods become names for human powers that belong to us, and that we can in part recover. Ultimately, all criticism is social criticism, and while it is the part of the creative imagination to say, with Eliot, "Do not think of the fruit of action," it is the part of the critical intelligence, by recognizing and responding to it, to ensure that something at least of the essential act of creation does bear fruit.

✧

Some Reflections
on Life and Habit

✧

I T IS a great privilege to be giving a lecture in honor of my old
friend and colleague Professor Priestley. That should go without saying, which is a phrase we use when we mean that it is
very important to say it. When the invitation came to me, I was
reading Samuel Butler, the nineteenth-century satirist, and *Life
and Habit* is the title of the book of his I happened to be reading.
But the fact that it got into the title of this lecture was not pure
accident. Another book of Samuel Butler's, the Utopian satire
Erewhon, was featured in a course in nineteenth-century prose, an
excellent course while it lasted. For many years the course was
taught by Professor Priestley at University College and by me at
Victoria College. My successor in teaching it at Victoria was Professor John Robson, the first Priestley lecturer. I think it was also
taught at St. Michael's College by the late Marshall McLuhan: in
any case there are several echoes from Butler in McLuhan's books.
But while a lecture devoted entirely to Samuel Butler might be
appropriate for the scholar I want to honor, it might be less so
for a public occasion. I have therefore attempted a compromise,
starting with Butler and working out to more contemporary concerns.

I was reading *Life and Habit* for two reasons. One, its first
hundred pages or so are a brilliant and witty piece of writing,
and if the entire book were on that level it would be one of my
favorite books. Two, those hundred pages are essentially a theory
of education, which naturally concerns me as a teacher. Butler's
theory was not new, but the formulation and context for it were
new in his day. The context was Butler's intense interest in Dar-

winian evolution: he was a contemporary of Darwin, and realized that the issue raised in the *Origin of Species* in 1859 was the central scientific issue of his time. Darwin's account of the evolutionary process, in which variations are thrown out by a species at random until one proves to have better survival value for its environment and becomes the channel for a new development, fascinated Butler but dissatisfied him too. He felt that the degree of precision and skill shown by even the simplest organisms, along with their immense variety, pointed to a directing will within them. The title of another book of his, *Luck or Cunning?*, indicates his attitude. Here he was reverting to an earlier view, proposed by the botanist Lamarck in France and by Darwin's own grandfather, Erasmus Darwin, in England.

Biologists oppose this view on the ground that it appears to depend on the inheritance of acquired characteristics, and that there is no evidence, or not enough evidence, for this. As Butler went on, he became increasingly hostile to Darwin, and more and more insistent on introducing elements of will, design, and purpose into evolution. The consensus of biologists was that the Darwinian explanation described the process, the *how* of evolution, and that that was the whole business of biological science. The other elements, they said, belonged to speculative philosophy or theology, and could not be experimentally studied.

So Butler fell out of fashion, and became known as an amateur who blundered into a scientific controversy without really knowing what he was talking about. His reputation was further affected by the fact that his chief disciple was Bernard Shaw, whose doctrine of "creative evolution" in my opinion rather vulgarizes Butler's views. This is particularly true of his interminably gabby play, or series of plays, called *Back to Methusaleh*, in which the human race evolves from Adam and Eve to a whirlpool of pure thought in something like twenty hours. More recently, there was the attempt of the pseudoscientific politician Lysenko, in Stalin's Russia, to set up Russian biology on a Lamarckian basis, which proved an abysmal failure.

Well, as it happens, I am rather interested in people who are out of fashion, because they often indicate the limitations of the age that considers them so. If I knew more biology, I should not be surprised if many of Butler's speculations, such as his identifying heredity with memory, were eventually to come back on center stage. In short, I doubt that the luck-or-cunning issue is entirely closed. But it is clear that many aspects of that controversy have been put out of date by new discoveries about the DNA molecule and the transmission of genetic codes, and many of the things that Butler says should now be read as remarkably prophetic insights into these developments. He speaks, for example, of the embryo's "ability to compress tedious and complicated histories into a very narrow compass remembering no single performance in particular."

Butler's word *habit* recalls the medieval Latin *habitus,* an educational term meaning the accomplishment of a skill. In the Middle Ages a person who could read Latin was said to have the *habitus* of Latin. *Habitus* in its turn was the Latin equivalent of the Greek word *hexis,* which in Aristotle means something like stabilization, the way in which a thing continues to preserve the quality that makes it what it is. In Butler "habit" refers to the learning process in which a skill moves from the conscious into the unconscious. When we begin to learn a language, we consciously pay attention to every new word, to the grammatical rules of syntax and inflection, to the nuances of pronunciation and accent. When we can speak a language fluently, the attention to detail disappears from consciousness, but it is obviously still there. A first-rate pianist may play thousands of notes in a few minutes, attending to every rest, dynamic shading, and predominance of one voice over another. He does not consciously attend to each of these details, but there must have been a time when he did.

The principle involved is that complete learning is unconscious learning. When consciousness is brought into play, it means doubt, hesitation, and imperfect knowledge. It also sets up interference patterns against the smoothness and perfection of unconscious learning, once the latter has been attained. Anything like conscious choice or free will disappears with the advance of learning, and if we are playing the piano and still exercising free will about whether we shall play the right or the wrong notes, we are not playing very well. So Butler's "unconscious" is a form of distilled intelligence, or intelligence moving so fast that we can no longer perceive the details. The pianist cannot consciously remember all the notes he played, but there is a data bank inside him which is vastly more efficient than his conscious memory.

In Butler's view the unconscious memory is part of our biological inheritance, but because we are conscious there can still be conflicts within it, a whole parliament of ancestral voices where some dominate and others are repressed. Long before Freud, Butler realizes that the unconscious could speak, and that when it spoke it defined the speaker much more clearly than his conscious speech did. He quotes a famous evangelical preacher named Spurgeon as praying publicly that God would change England's rulers "as soon as possible," and pointed out that those last four words showed that while Spurgeon's consciousness may have been evangelical, his unconscious was clearly aesthetic.

But such anomalies are a feature of conscious uncertainties. The learning skill is perfect when we have reached the stabilization, the *habitus* or *hexis,* where no such conflicts remain. On this principle the best educated would be those who do not even know that they are educated. To Butler, as a nineteenth-century middle-class Englishman, the principle that unconscious knowledge is perfected knowledge meant that the best-educated people in England in his day were the aristocracy. They had been accustomed to rank and privilege from birth, not counting centuries of heredity before that, and could live a privileged life with a spontaneity and ease that was the despairing envy of any jumped-up businessman or politician who tried to imitate them by voluntary effort. If the noble lord happened to be as stupid as the pheasants he shot, that showed that he was even better educated: he had nothing of the uncertainty and hesitation that go with the investigating of new things.

It is clear that in this argument there are two levels of education involved. One is the education we acquire through our evolutionary heredity: we display most of this within a few hours of birth, but its afterglow remains all through our lives in our social and personal relations. The other is the specifically human education we develop from the fact that we are conscious beings. A little girl with a skipping rope would be a model of the first stage of education; a wise man telling us to take no thought for the morrow and to consider the lilies as an example of living would represent the fulfillment of the second stage.

One of Butler's most celebrated remarks is that a hen is simply an egg's way of making another egg. Why should this statement seem so paradoxical to us, when the reverse statement, that an egg is what a hen makes, seems so self-evident? Butler explains that the development of an egg into a hen is a matter of growth through repetition of previous growths. Every detail of this development can be, and has been, studied by embryologists. But when a hen makes an egg she cackles, and we are very impressed by noise, which we always associate with some kind of meaning. Also, we see an egg where there was no egg before, and that gratifies our impatience to get something tangible without having to wait too long for it. So when the Bible begins by saying that everything started with a revolutionary act of God in suddenly making the world out of nothing, we feel that that is the proper and inevitable way to begin a story of nature. In Genesis the cackle and egg are perhaps below the dignity of Holy Writ, although there are eggs in Hindu and Greek creation myths. But even in Genesis there is a spoken utterance and what seems like a brooding bird. However, God's ways are not our ways, and human creation is much more a matter of eggs trying to be hens in the hope of producing future eggs.

The real paradox in Butler comes from the fact that words are instruments of the conscious mind: they mean exploration, discovery, experiment, and consequently imperfect knowledge. The unconscious knowledge he is talking about is wordless. We do not feel complete confidence in the skill of a craftsman until he can no longer say how he does what he does. When we turn from human beings to plants and animals, this paradox increases enormously. A snail builds its shell and a warbler its nest with an unerring precision, exactly as though they knew what they were doing. Why, then, do we deny the term *know* to them? A good deal of Butler's wit comes from his applying terms of knowledge and consciousness to organisms that simply behave with the appearance of knowledge and consciousness. He says, for example, that the lichen could not grow on the rock unless it thought it could, and could not think it could unless it could, yet it does very well for itself in spite of arguing in a circle.

An organism struggles to achieve some kind of equilibrium with its environment, and so develops some patented skills to enable it to keep on absorbing nutriment and reproducing its kind. In a human being this is largely accomplished within a few days after birth. Butler says that a baby a day old sucks, which involves a profound practical knowledge of the laws of pneumatics and hydrostatics; it digests; it oxygenizes its blood millions of years before oxygen was discovered; it sees and it hears—all most difficult and complicated operations, involving a similar knowledge of optics and acoustics. Before that, it was an embryo constructing eyes and limbs and performing other fantastically complex feats of engineering.

If we say "nature" does this, we are using a superfluous metaphor: there is no such thing as nature, no mother goddess who does things for us. The metaphor means that behind what the embryo does is a long evolutionary process through which it learned how it does it. Why, says Butler, should we say of a man that he has never amounted to anything? He got himself born, and that is about 97 percent of everything he can ever hope to do. Society confirms this view of unconscious knowledge: we admire healthy, handsome, and fortunate people; athletes get far more news coverage than specialists in semiotics; people with conventional views, or people able to get along with conventions, are the sensible, the nice people, the people it is comfortable to be with. We also cherish an intense if sometimes grudging admiration for billionaires and dictators, because we spring from an environment in which the predators are the aristocracy.

One of Butler's inferences, that there must have been a time when there was something like intelligence and a learning process in the organism, takes him into biological speculations where it is hard to follow him and where at present we do not need to follow him. It is the analogy with human education that I am concerned with here.

We sometimes say of a student when he has got whatever degree he is pursuing that he has "completed his education." But of course we know that this is only a way of talking, and a rather loose way at that: no human being can ever finish an education as long as he has any sort of brain to process his experience with. It is only such organisms as the lichen on the rocks and the medusa jellyfish who have finished their education, and even they might be caught short by a change in the environment. Humanity, alone of all organisms, has elected to transform its environment instead of simply adapting to it, and so only human beings have a lifelong commitment to experiment, trial and error, uncertainty, and all the other burdens of continuing knowledge.

Does this mean that we are still evolving, and if so, toward what? In my view this question is not simply unanswerable but can be profoundly misleading. In the first place, the fact that we are adapting the environment to ourselves instead of ourselves to the environment has totally changed the rules of the game, so perhaps the word *evolution,* in its traditional sense, no longer means anything as far as our own future is concerned. This does not prevent us from using a lot of conceptions of change and development that we call evolution, even though the word is only a metaphor for most of them, and very probably for all of them. In Butler's day the German philosopher Nietzsche preached the gospel of the evolving of man into a "superman," who sounds like a remarkably unpleasant human being, however admirable as a god. Then there was the doctrine of progress, a doctrine much older than Darwin.

Some people who wanted to believe in progress thought that evolution had furnished scientific proof of it. But of course evolution is a principle in biology, and cannot be directly applied to human history except as an analogy. Whether we believe in progress depends entirely on what factors we select as evidence for it. Thus the processes known in some areas as pollution and in others as development, such as destroying a community by building a highway through the middle of it, are often rationalized by some such phrase as "you can't stop progress." "Progress" here is clearly an idol of some sort, and in totalitarian states, where thousands of people can be shot or starved to get a more efficient system of agriculture or industry in the future, we get some notion of how horrible such idolatry can be. Whatever ideals we may frame, in education or anywhere else, will take time to reach, and so will relate to the future, but a real future has to be built on what is available at present. To sacrifice the present, which exists, to a future which does not exist, and certainly will never exist in any presently recognizable form, is as perverse a notion as any in history.

In my student days, during the depression, it was widely believed that capitalism would evolve into socialism, with or without a revolution, socialism being assumed to be both more efficient and morally superior. A secondary assumption was that evolution never made a mistake, but always tended toward improvement. On the other side was the movement sometimes called social Darwinism, which was really a rationalizing of imperialism, taking on the white man's burden in Africa and south Asia. It asserted that there were developed and primitive soci-

eties, and that the developed ones were following the evolutionary laws of a competitive nature in enslaving or exterminating
the primitive ones. "Developed" in this context meant that their
military technology was deadlier. In our day there has been an
invasion of teachers of yoga, Zen, kundalini, and other techniques of meditation, which often carry ideologies of evolution
along with them, promising developments of consciousness that
will usher in a new phase of human existence. Nobody can object
to the teaching of these techniques, but the evolutionary metaphors seem, once again, to be mere analogies.

Our present mood in regard to education, however, is past-
centered rather than future-centered, and is more inclined to ask:
"Are we doing as well as we used to do?" This is mainly a reaction
to elementary and high school educators who do not understand
why we should transform our environment by reading Shakespeare when we can so easily adapt to it by reading Stephen
King. I was recently looking through a book which has been on
the best-seller list for a long time, and which propounds the
thesis that students have been cheated out of their education,
socially and morally as well as intellectually. I thought, in reading it: somebody writes this book every ten years; I have lived
through four or five cycles of similar protests, and have in fact
contributed to some of them. (On this last point I think I am
speaking for Professor Priestley also.) Such books are often, like
this book, warmly received and are accompanied by a feeling that
something should be done. Nothing ever is done, so there must
be something that the protest has failed to reach.

Two points occur to me in this connection. One is that there
is seldom any recommendation for action in this field except to
prod the educational bureaucracy. And a bureaucracy, as Mr.
Gorbachev is undoubtedly discovering, cannot be improved by
prodding: it can only be left alone and when possible bypassed.
The other is that what the public picks up from such books is
what literary critics call a pastoral myth. There was a simpler
time, the myth runs, when things were a lot better, so let's get
back to them. But just as the future does not yet exist, so the
past has ceased to exist, and an idealized past never did exist. I
distrust all "back to the basics" slogans because I distrust all
movements that begin with "back to." It is more profitable, perhaps, to inquire into the reasons for the dissatisfaction with what
our education has achieved, and this takes us "back to" Butler.

Here the phrase "back to" is in its right context, as it refers to something in the past that can still be brought into the present.

The author of the book I refer to was clearly still smoldering from the anti-intellectual movement among students twenty years ago in the late sixties. I remember this period very well: it was a time when, although practically all students merely wanted to keep on doing what they should have been doing, there was a small group caught up in an adversarial trend that I think was almost entirely created by the news media. I notice that the news media are sniffing around this period again, perhaps in some hope of reviving it in a new generation. The minority I speak of were students who felt they were revolting against middle-class values, and didn't realize how clearly they were expressing them. Much of their alleged activism consisted in dodging everything academic that looked difficult and repetitious. There were complaints about learning by rote, regurgitating lecture notes, plodding through memorization, and the like. They wanted every lecture to be an exciting existential event: they organized teach-ins with imported speakers who were usually left-wing political leaders giving one of their standard harangues, and they greatly resented the suggestion that these activities were entertainment and not education. Student representation, for them, did not mean sitting on committees but organizing sit-ins and demonstrations and disrupting meetings. Some of them were very agile in working out rationalizations for all this, and I am far from denying the good faith of the many idealistic students who believed passionately in what they were doing, and had no idea how or by whom they were being manipulated. But the movement was essentially one more outbreak of American anti-intellectualism, and it was discouraging to find it in the very place where it ought least to be.

Butler's theory of education follows the normal pattern in being based on the traditional emphasis on habit and practice. If we take piano-playing as a typical educational activity, it requires endless patient repetition until conscious learning is finally digested into unconscious skill. The unconscious cannot be hurried or forced or consciously invaded; some learn more easily and quickly than others, but everyone learns in essentially the same way. Obviously, a good deal of this sounds like the emphasis on discipline and routine which in the past has given so penal a quality to education, reinforced as it so often was by savage beatings and the like. If the unrest of the sixties had been a reaction against this, it would have been quite normal; but, while there had to be a good deal of pretense that such elements still existed, they had in fact disappeared at least fifty years earlier.

Of course a dull or plodding teacher can envisage only a dull educational process, and can make education a dreary enough operation. I have had teachers myself who took a squalid pleasure in making drill-sergeant noises about the moral benefits of plugging and slugging as ends in themselves. That was in the twenties of this century, and of course such teachers didn't realize that they were speaking for the capitalist work ethic and setting up the automatism of the Ford assembly plant as the model for it. Neither did I: I felt only that they were talking about their own mental processes and not about mine, and it was some time before I realized that the emphasis on routine was only the flip side of something very different.

Notice that we speak of "playing" the piano, just as we speak about playing tennis or chess, and just as we call dramas, even the most terrible tragedies, "plays." In ordinary speech we distinguish work and play, work being energy expended for a further end in view, play being energy expended for its own sake. Doing any kind of playing well, whether on the stage or at a piano or chessboard, takes an immense amount of work, but when the work has its end in play we can see the point in it much more clearly. Nothing gives greater pleasure than spontaneous activity, but the spontaneous comes at the end of a long discipline of practice. It never comes early except when it is something we have inherited as part of our previous evolutionary development—something our ancestors have practiced before us.

Education, then, is a movement toward the spontaneous, not a movement away from it. We speak of liberal education, which means essentially that something in us is getting liberated or set free. When we practice the piano, we are setting ourselves free to play the piano. The half-educated may follow rules or dodge around rules; it is only the thoroughly educated who can take liberties with rules. If we want to write, it is nothing very wonderful if we can produce acceptable or even remarkable poetry in early years: poetry at that age ought to be a natural secretion, like a pearl in an oyster. It is the writers who keep on writing who matter in the history of literature; and what their incessant practice aims at is a steadily purer and more direct simplicity. The simple, which is the opposite of the commonplace, is normally one of the last secrets of art to be mastered.

We often feel, ploughing through the gobbledygook and bumble of political speeches and the like: "Why can't they say what they mean?" Often, of course, they have excellent reasons for concealing what they mean, but the real answer is that lucidity is difficult. We may even be impressed by the kind of polysyllabic blather that merely throws words at the ideas instead of expressing them; we may feel that anything so hard to read must have been harder to think out. But eventually we realize that it is very easy to write this way: in fact it is the normal way to write when we are not thinking about what we are doing. It is the same with a kind of scholarly writing that we in the academic world are reluctantly familiar with, and which infallibly indicates a lack of understanding of one's material.

It should be clear from what we have said that two kinds of memory are involved in education, and that their roles are often confused. There is Butler's unconscious memory, a continuing of the evolutionary process we hooked into at the beginning of our lives, which is fostered by habit and practice, and there is conscious memory, the recall of an event of the past into the present. Conscious memory is certainly essential, as we soon realize if we talk to someone who has lost it. It supplies the continuity without which no learning is possible, hence the strong emphasis on the use of the conscious memory in education. But conscious memory is primarily an adjunct to unconscious memory, a means of getting hold of it and supplying the energy of the conscious will for continuing it. Only when conscious memory is treated as an end in itself does education become a treadmill of repetition.

Certainly there have been societies that approached education in this way, handing on traditions from the past without change, and demanding from the student only the acceptance of them through rote learning and repetition, no criticism or re-creation of them being tolerated. There can be nothing here of the progressive developing of a skill or the setting free of undeveloped abilities, only of stagnation. The contrast between this and real education is not unlike the contrast between superstition and faith. The root meaning of superstition is vestigial survival.

When we keep on doing something without understanding why we are doing it, but have only a vague feeling that something awful will happen if we stop doing it, we are in a state of superstition. Superstition of this kind is a frozen ideology, a pathological social condition that obstructs the developments in the arts and sciences, and so frustrates the central aim of education. Its usual cause is a fear that something in these developments will conflict with something else thought to be beyond the scope of argument. Evolution itself, as we all know, had to contend with superstitions attached to false readings of the biblical creation myths.

The wise man who wrote the book in the Bible called Ecclesiastes made two remarks that are very important for the theory of education. One is "there is nothing new under the sun," the other "to everything there is a season." He was speaking of two areas of the learning process, knowledge and experience. Knowledge may be new to us or to the entire human race, but new knowledge is not yet knowledge: we do not know anything until we have recognized it, that is, placed it into a context of what we already know, rearranging the familiar until the unfamiliar is fitted into it. It follows that we cannot know the unique as such. When we come to the phrase "to everything there is a season" and its corollary, "there is a time for all things," we are in the realm of experience, where everything is new and unique. The function of knowledge is to set free the capacity to experience. The repetition and constant practice that underlies the acquiring of a skill, then, is, or certainly ought to be, a process of continuous discovery: the knowledge is not new, but the experience of getting it is. Knowledge that tries to do without experience becomes paranoid; experience that tries to do without knowledge becomes schizophrenic.

The anti-intellectual trend which is so deeply rooted in American life is linked to a tendency in American education to emphasize experience at the expense of knowledge. I say American because the same tendencies have extended to Canada, perhaps as much here in the West as further east. The tendency is often associated with the name of John Dewey, although it seems hardly fair to blame him for all the imbecilities of his disciples. But certainly such slogans as "learning by doing" can do a great deal of damage when they ignore the fact that thinking is also doing, and one as totally dependent on habit and practice as any other skill. There is a semantic difficulty here: we often speak, with Thurber's Walter Mitty, of daydreaming or woolgathering as thinking, and when we repeat prejudices acquired from our friends or the morning paper we often imagine that we are thinking for ourselves. But thinking, again, is like piano-playing: how well we do it depends primarily on how much of it we have progressively and systematically done already, and at all times the content of thinking is knowledge. The age of hysteria in the sixties I spoke of developed the emphasis on experience over knowledge to great lengths. Drug cults, for example, were pursued as novel modes of experience, although they totally failed to link up with any genuine knowledge or creativity. Today the pendulum has swung the other way, and political leaders at least are required to have as narrow and conventional a background of experience as possible. Unfortunately, a lack of knowledge seems to be as highly prized as ever.

Samuel Butler was a humanist trying to relate, as a humanist should, what he observed in his reading to the quality of human life, actual or potential. His satire *Erewhon* depicts a society that has destroyed all its machinery. They had been persuaded to do this by a writer who told them that machines were not simply becoming more efficient, but were actually evolving as a new species, and evolving far too fast. They were, he said, just on the point of overcoming the last obstacle in the way of their taking over and enslaving humanity. That obstacle was their inability to reproduce their own kind, but they were now beginning to use human beings for that, as flowers use bees. So unless we destroy our machines we shall have no future except to become their genital organs.

Today we are faced with machines of a complexity that Butler himself, to say nothing of his imaginary pamphleteer, never dreamed of. Butler was writing satire, and knew that to say that machines are evolving was a false analogy. (The satire was directed against Darwin, because Butler believed that it would not be a false analogy on strictly Darwinian premises.) Nevertheless, technological developments have certainly dragged us through several major social revolutions in this century, and many more are awaiting us. Hence they still illustrate the central question that Butler's view of education raises: the question whether we are to keep on transforming our natural environment for genuine human ends, or mechanically go on exploiting both it and one another until we arrive at total chaos, a cultural black hole from which no light can any longer emerge. So the need is greater than it ever was for humanist writers and scholars to keep fighting in the front line of the constant struggle of humanity to stay in control of its own lives and habits.

III

The Rhythms of Time

I AM not a scholar of the Romantic period, except by fits and starts, so it seems to me that what I can most usefully do is to provide some sort of context for the theme of "Time and the Poetic Self." The great difficulty about time, of course, has always been that it is the primary category of experience, the most important and fundamental aspect of life, and yet apparently it does not exist. Its center seems to be in the present moment, the now, but when we try to grasp this "now," we find ourselves pursuing an elusive never quite that keeps vanishing between the no longer and the not yet. As Dylan Thomas says: "The atlas-eater with a jaw for news / Bit out the mandrake with tomorrow's scream." We try to cope with time facing the past, with our backs to the future, and in relation to time human life seems to be a kind of untied Andromeda, constantly stepping back from a devouring monster whose mouth is the mouth of hell, in the sense that each moment passes from the possible into the eternally unchangeable being of the past. At death we back into a solid wall, and then the monster devours us too.

The time-honored way of dealing with problems we don't understand is to project them on God, who presumably does understand them. In the traditional view, as incorporated into medieval and later Christianity, the human experience of time has always been contrasted with what must be the experience of God, whose mind can be only in a pure present comprehending both past and future. Our ordinary experience of time, we have been assured ever since St. Augustine at least, results from the fall, when we acquired a consciousness that can attend to only one thing "at a time," from which this slippery linear perspective on time has been derived. As the Elizabethan poet Sir John Davies says, in his philosophical poem *Nosce Teipsum:*

> *But we that measure times by first and last*
> *The sight of things successively do take,*
> *When God on all at once His view doth cast,*
> *And of all times doth but one instant make.*

On the human level there are, according to this traditional Christian view, three kinds of temporal existence. At the furthest pole from the mind of God, where time is an eternal now, is demonic time, time experienced as simply one clock-tick after another, an unending duration without direction or purpose, of which we know nothing except that it annihilates everything, including us. Hell is usually conceived as this experience of time with death removed, and Macbeth's "Tomorrow and tomorrow and tomorrow" speech is the best known literary evocation of it. Above this is our ordinary sense of time as a mixture of linear and cyclical movement. We see time as the universal devourer, with a unique capacity for wiping things out of existence; but we also experience a rotary movement in which spring follows winter, dawn the darkness, and new life death. In these brief instants of renewal there is some sense of hope and confidence, some feeling that a benevolent power may after all be concealed in the machinery. But this view of time is founded on the alienation myth of the fall of man, so two other questions about time arise. One is, What was time like in the Garden of Eden, in the world God originally made for Adam before the fall? The other is, To what extent can this unfallen sense of time be attained in our present life?

A higher awareness of time must be connected somehow with the one reassuring aspect of time in our ordinary experience, the sense of renewal in the cycles of nature. This aspect is seen in its complete form in the revolutions of the heavenly bodies, where there is a cycle without decline or decay, a continuous renewal. The heavenly bodies represent, for us, not mechanical obedience to divine law, but the release of freedom that such obedience makes possible. Their rotation is something to be associated with music and the dance, a movement which brings the highest kind of pleasure with it, and which is symbolized by the myth of the "music of the spheres." We turn to Sir John

Davies's other long poem, *Orchestra,* where we have the finest and best-known treatment in English poetry of the creation of nature as a dance, a "harmony" of joyous and integrated rhythm which was the characteristic of the world as God originally made it. The experience of time in the unfallen state, then, would be the kind of experience represented by the dancer, whose world is not timeless but where time is the effect of exuberance, its cycles taking place, as Milton says, "for change delectable, not need." As Davies says:

> *How justly then is dancing termed new*
> *Which with the world in point of time began?*
> *Yes, Time itself, whose birth Jove never knew,*
> *And which is far more ancient than the sun,*
> *Had not one moment of his age outrun*
> *When out heaped Dancing from the heap of things*
> *And lightly rode upon his nimble wings.*
> *Reason hath both their pictures in her treasure,*
> *Where Time the measure of all moving is*
> *And Dancing is a moving all in measure.*
> *Now if you do resemble that to this,*
> *And think both one, I think you think amiss;*
> *But if you judge them twins, together got,*
> *And Time first born, your judgment erreth not.*

That is, time and dancing, the measure of movement and the movement of measure, are not the same thing, but time is a mode of the dancing existence, the ultimate context within which it operates, just as the ordinary kind of time is for life on this level.

Davies's poem is said to be sung to Penelope by the chief of her suitors, Antinous, during the absence of Odysseus. The reason is that Penelope's web was often taken to be an allegory of nature, its weaving and unweaving the process of change and mutation that goes on around us. What Antinous' song does is to bring out the inner secret of nature, the form that time assumes in its originally created state. The poet says:

> *So subtle and curious was the measure,*
> *With such unlooked-for change in every strain,*
> *As that Penelope, rapt with sweet pleasure,*
> *Ween'd she beheld the true proportion plain*

> *Of her own web, weaved and unweaved again:*
> *But that her art was somewhat less, she thought,*
> *And on a mere ignoble subject wrought.*

Somewhat less, because the world we live in, which her web symbolizes, is not equal to the great orchestra celebrated by her suitor. The poet uses an ingenious image to express this: while Penelope weaves, her hands are moving in the great dance, but if she were in a completely liberated world, her feet and whole body would be moving too.

The prevailing assumption, down to Milton's time at least, was that everything that is genuinely good for man, that is, in the largest sense of the term educational, tends to raise him from ordinary experience a little nearer to the unfallen level that he was originally created to live on. In this educational activity the cycles of the heavenly bodies symbolize a creative form of repetition, like the repetitions of practice. If we want to learn to play a musical instrument or to read the Latin language, we set ourselves free for these activities through practice, which builds up a habit ending in an extension of freedom. This kind of creative repetition was represented by the sacraments of the church in particular. A great deal of the measuring of time in this period was a by-product of religion, with clocks and bells marking the hours of worship or devotion. The two aspects of cyclical movement, the ordinary and the cultivated, are distinguished in Spenser's *Mutabilitie Cantos*: in fact, the distinguishing of them is the whole point of the poem. Mutability dominates our world, and nobody disputes her claim to it. But she also claims the starry heavens above, on the ground that they too move in cyclical rotation, and hence are phenomena of becoming and change. The evidence she brings forth is the evidence of the natural cycle: the four seasons, day and night, the twelve months with their Zodiacal signs, life and death. But nature decides against her claim to the upper world on the ground that there are two aspects to cyclical movement. The stars being made, not of the dissoluble four elements, but of immortal quintessence, their cycle is unchanging and not subject to decay:

> *I well consider all that ye have said,*
> *And find that all things steadfastness do hate*
> *And changed be: yet being rightly weighed,*
> *They are not changed from their first estate;*

But by their change their being do dilate:
And turning to themselves at length again,
Do work their own perfection so by fate:
Then over them Change doth not rule and reign:
But they reign over Change, and do their states maintain.

The line "Do work their own perfection so by fate" indicates the element of what we have called habit or creative repetition in the upper cycle: the rotation of heavenly bodies symbolizes not simply an unending cycle but a *telos,* a purposive movement back to their Creator. As elsewhere in *The Faerie Queene,* the top and bottom of the four levels of time are only hinted at. The top level is referred to explicitly only in the very last stanza of the poem as the "rest" or "Sabbath sight" which the poet prays to have at the end of his life. The demonic level is indicated in Nature's comment to Mutability: "For thy decay thou seek'st by thy desire"—that is, the ultimate thrust of the force of change and decay in time as we know it is into perpetual annihilation, the chaos of fluctuating chance that Milton says is "the womb of Nature, and perhaps her grave."

So far we have been following the poets in their purely religious themes. But outside the Christian mythology was Eros, the power of love that has a sexual basis, however sublimated it may later become. For the poets Eros was another force that could raise man to a higher awareness of time. Davies makes it abundantly clear not merely that his poem is a love song but that his conception of the cosmological dance is also a manifestation of Eros. Similarly, it is Dante's love for Beatrice that impels him up the purgatorial mountain to reach the unfallen form of his own existence, which is in the Garden of Eden on top of the mountain. Even unhappy, frustrated, or rejected love may have the same result. In Shakespeare's sonnets we hear a great deal about time as the devourer and annihilator of all being. But in the beautiful-youth sequence there are certain intervals—three in all—where there is a sense of renewed energy and power, obviously connected with the imagery of spring. At the beginning of the sequence the poet urges the youth to marry and beget a son, a futile effort to prolong his beauty in time; then the poet drops this theme and falls in love with the youth himself. After a great deal of suffering and misery, along with a few gleams of ecstasy, the total experience of love on the poet's part lifts him clear of the dissolution and decay in time. The beautiful youth is left to nature's "audit," in other words to age and death, but the poet's love is in a *ver perpetuum* like the Garden of Eden in Dante. "That it nor grows with heat, nor drowns with showers."

As nearly all the poets in this period, apart from the dramatists, represented themselves as lovers, they were able, even without a doctrine of creative imagination as such, to suggest that poetry itself was also a means of acquiring a higher awareness of time and coming closer to the exuberant pulsation of the dance which is its real form. The word *grace,* with its double set of associations in love and religion, was of great importance here. At the end of *The Faerie Queene* Spenser introduces himself, under his earlier pseudonym of Colin Clout, the lover of Rosalind, as evoking a vision centered on the four "Graces," Rosalind being the addition to the conventional three, and in her turn being placed "under the feet" of Queen Elizabeth, who usually took this role of fourth Grace. The implication is that Spenser, as lover, is able to create the entire world of "faerie" and enable his reader to enter it.

In modern poetry the Eliot *Quartets* give us once again this traditional view of time on four levels of experience. In "Burnt Norton," which owes a good deal to Davies's *Orchestra,* we begin again with the sense of overwhelming unreality in the ordinary experience of time, where nothing but the most rigid kind of fatalism can unite its three dimensions. Perhaps nothing can happen except what must happen, which means that the future has, in a sense, already occurred, and so is indistinguishable from the past. In this kind of fatalism there could be no redemption, for "all time is unredeemable": such a world would be hell if there were no death. Redemption requires a God, but a God within time is no better off than we are, and a God wholly free of time is of no use to us. Fortunately we have the Incarnation, the descent of something outside of time into time, and this creates in time the possibility of a genuine present moment. The recurrence of this moment, suggesting that it is continuously latent, is represented by the church's daily repetition of the Incarnation in the mass, and its possible emergence into life is the basis of the arts; hence the sense of a moment in which "past and future are gathered," when "all is always now," is one of the things that poetry is about. In "Little Gidding" the conception of Eros is added, for the sake of completeness and tradition, but Eliot is not much a votary of Eros, and the theological subordination of Eros to *agape,* or God's love for man, takes over and organizes the argument.

So the traditional view of time is still poetically viable, as Eliot shows. But its traditional symbol, the sky with its heavenly bodies, has lost most of its prestige. We no longer believe that the heavenly bodies are made of immortal quintessence, or that they move in intelligently guided perfect circles around the earth. In fact the heavenly bodies now, with their colossal distances from the earth and their obvious indifference to human concerns, are more likely to be a symbol of human alienation than divine providence. Eliot does give us the traditional cosmological dance, at the beginning of the second section of "Burnt Norton," with all the rhythms of nature pulsating around the "bedded axle-tree." But the old spatial metaphors of sky and mountain have largely vanished, the Incarnation-moment being a kind of vortex or shadow-mountain.

By a century after Newton's time, at least, the heavenly bodies were becoming increasingly an image of mechanism rather than of divine providence and the original condition of creation. Hence the number of evil or stupid sky-gods in Romantic and post-Romantic poetry, along with the use of the older construct for parody, as in Byron's *Vision of Judgment* and the Prologue to Goethe's *Faust.* When the movements in the sky become thought of as mechanical, we are left with the organism as the highest symbol of being, with man, the conscious organism, at the center. In the older construct man turns away from his natural environment and attaches himself, through love or religion, to an ideal form of human community. But now man is thought of as immersed in, first, his social, and then his physical, environment. His time-consciousness, first of all, expands into the more leisurely temporal rhythms of social continuity. The "short time" that so haunted Spenser is still short for the individual, but the individual's life is interpenetrated by instants when he becomes aware of the slow growth or decline of ideas, religions, institutions, and, of course, empires. A very obvious symbol of this enlarged view of time is the Wandering Jew who appears in Shelley's *Hellas.* It follows that both a specifically historical consciousness and a speculative consciousness of the future become elements of the Romantic awareness of time.

In the background are the still slower rhythms of nature, a nature which is not itself human, and yet contains something that complements human experience, where life and death assume different patterns and suggest different proportions. To take an example practically at random from *The Prelude,* Wordsworth sees a ruined convent as

> *a roofless Pile*
> *And not by reverential touch of Time*
> *Dismantled, but by violence abrupt.*

This complementary sense of time in nature develops from the eighteenth-century vision of the sublime, as manifested later in, for instance, the Mont Blanc that confronts Wordsworth, Coleridge, and Shelley, and inspires them to different and yet curiously interrelated reactions. The sublime, by definition, is not the lovable, and although, in Shelley particularly, the association of love and the poetic imagination may still be very close, the basis of the poet's enlarged time-consciousness is not in his role as lover but in his function as poet. Hence that function is separable from the poet's personality, real or projected. The barrage of scriptural echoes in the *Defence of Poetry* shows how deliberately Shelley is replacing the older construct with a new one: "Their errors have been weighed and found to have been dust in the balance; if their sins were as scarlet, they are now white as snow; they have been washed in the blood of the mediator and the redeemer, Time." This deification of time is parallel to Blake's conception of Los as both Time and the Holy Spirit.

To use a somewhat oversimplifying formula, the Romantic time-consciousness tends to be immanent rather than transcendent, and its emotional tone is not ecstatic so much as elegiac. The older ubi sunt theme, of time as the devourer, is of course still there, but it is qualified by occasional instants where our unconscious participation in larger rhythms of history and nature come to the surface and "We feel that we are greater than we know." The Romantic poet, working as he normally does without the professional rhetorical training that Spenser and Milton had, is well aware of the large involuntary element in creative writing, the time when the will to write must be employed to relax the will and let the slower autonomous rhythms welling up from the lower strata of the mind take over. These rhythms are often identified with historical or natural processes, as in *Prometheus Unbound,* where the liberation of Prometheus is part of a huge cosmological *culbute* in which Demogorgon, whose name is "Eternity," ascends from the depths of the earth on a car piloted by the "Spirit of the Hour" to pull Jupiter off his throne, in a kind of reversal of Eliot's vision of the Incarnation. Shelley's vision is in fact founded on the myth of resurrection, which is complementary to that of incarnation, though of course in Shelley it is not specifically the resurrection of Christ which is involved, as it is in Blake's *America,* for instance. Resurrection, where the power bringing the new sense of time comes from below, is most naturally a revolutionary myth, just as incarnation, which visualizes that power as descending from a higher world of greater order, is most naturally an authoritarian one.

Shelley's visions of liberation are comic visions and derive from the structure of comedy as we have it in *The Winter's Tale,* where the tragic complications are metamorphosed into a comic conclusion by the discovery of Perdita's identity at the appointed time. Time himself is a personified chorus in Shakespeare's play, and the play's main source, Greene's *Pandosto,* is subtitled "The Triumph of Time." The incarnation, on the other hand, repeats, on a voluntary and conscious level, the earlier fall of Adam into the lower world, the archetype of tragedy, the theme of which is regularly the theme of the breaking of time, the disruption of the proper rhythms by something violent and hurried. But the rhythms of both descent from above and emergence from below break into the continuity of our ordinary experience of time with something discontinuous. Eliot's *Quartets* make a good deal of the discontinuity that the real present, the still point of the turning world, makes in time. Eliot shows us that it is folly to try to unify our linear sense of time, to assume that we get wiser as we grow older, to think that we build a continuous structure of achievement out of our past that will follow us into the future. In "The Dry Salvages" popular myths of evolution and progress, along with the practice of fortune-telling through various occult means, are condemned as illusion and vanity, as compared to the humility which sees in every moment a fresh beginning, discontinuous with its predecessor:

> *Men's curiosity searches past and future*
> *And clings to that dimension. But to apprehend*
> *The point of intersection of the timeless*
> *With time, is an occupation for the saint.*

165

Auden's *For the Time Being* uses the Romantic mythological framework and sees the Incarnation as appearing in obscurity and darkness in the midst of a much more specifically historical situation.
Nonetheless, when it comes, it disrupts Herod's futile efforts to
establish continuity and progress in his society ("Yes, in twenty
years I have managed to do little"), and because it does, it turns
the well-meaning liberal into an enemy of God.

There are naturally an infinite number of issues involved
with these Romantic views of time, but time affects me as well
as the Romantics and allows me only one to conclude with. In
the *Defence of Poetry* Shelley speaks of a polarization in our awareness of time. On one side is the perception of the environment as
familiar and routine. The same things keep turning up, the same
cycles of nature go round and round, life is involuntary and death
invariable, and so a tendency develops to think of life in time
fatalistically, a passive acceptance of what must be. This corresponds in Shelley to demonic time. The poetic or creative faculty
pulls in the opposite direction: its vision is always a renewal of
the freshness and energy of man's view of nature. The next step
is to realize that there are two powers in the consciousness, one
analytic and the other synthetic, and that the latter is the poetic
faculty properly speaking. "Reason respects the differences, and
imagination the similitude of things." The poet constructs
wholes or configurations; these become in their turn part of the
one great poem that all the poets in history have helped to construct, that is, the mythological universe which is a model for
the world man wants to live in, as distinct from the world that
is there.

However, Shelley's separation of the analytic reasoning faculty and the synthetic or poetic one points to a curious paradox
in the Romantic treatment of history. History, qua history, is the
record of what actually occurred: the reason—sifting evidence
and rejecting whatever cannot have existed in the past—plays a
primary role in the awareness of it. What imagination, attending
only to the similitude of things, gets from the past is not history
but myth—the same thing that it gets from the future, as, according to Shelley, poets are "the mirror of the gigantic shadows
which futurity casts upon the present." Myth normally appears
in the form of romance when the genre employed is that of prose
fiction. In the Romantic period a good deal of fiction appeared
under the category of "historical novel," and we note that such

historical novels are actually romances, in which whatever is historical is inserted as a kind of tour de force. Thus in the Waverley novels, we get a lively characterization of James I in *The Fortunes of Nigel*, with probably some relevance to the original king. In *Ivanhoe* and *The Talisman*, however, the John Bullish patriot king Richard I has little resemblance to the obsessed gangster of history, whose only interest in the countries he ruled was to mulct them for crusades. Such things do not really matter: it is the form of romance that matters. The formulas of Scott are very close to the formulas of the late classical writers of the Second Sophistic, Heliodorus, Achilles Tatius, Longus, who also called their romances by such names as *Ethiopica* or *Babyloniaca* in order to claim some affinity with the historian. The same romance formulas reappear in contemporary science fiction, where the mythical shape is projected on the future rather than the past.

The writer of the period who really succeeds in giving us a sense of historical awareness is rather the writer who concentrates on the immediate data of sense experience and waking consciousness—in short, the compensatory form of Romantic whom we call the realist. By turning his back on history, the realist records the world in front of him, and in due course his picture of that world becomes something of a historical document. In the pastiche of Gibbon in Scott's *Count Robert of Paris,* or of Commines in *Anne of Geierstein,* there is little of much historical value, entertaining as these stories may be on other grounds. But in *Mansfield Park,* though of course the structure of comic romance is still there, the reflection of the life of the Regency period has a genuine historical importance. Later in the century, Oscar Wilde remarked, in *The Decay of Lying,* which is really a manifesto of romantic and mythical writing as opposed to realism: "M. Zola sits down to give us a picture of the Second Empire. Who cares for the Second Empire now? It is out of date. Life goes on faster than Realism, but Romanticism is always in front of Life." Put less polemically, we may say that, of the two categories of this conference, Romanticism deals with the recurring constants of myth and romance, Historicism with the specific features of an age, normally the age contemporary with the writer, which are most successfully recorded by those who most successfully resist the temptations represented by the word *Romanticism.*

◆

Literature as a
Critique of
Pure Reason

◆

THE WORD *irrational* is derived from "reason," and the word *reason* summons up the ghost of the old faculty psychology, in which "reason" is a thing man has, and frequently regards as uniquely his, to be distinguished from other things called "will" or "feeling" or "desire." These latter seem to be found among animals, or at least analogies to them are, and so "reason" has been traditionally considered the crown that man wears as the king of nature. It is the faculty that shows off man as the only organism in nature whose horizon is not wholly bounded by the needs of survival and adaptation. However, looking at the mind as an assemblage of parts or different capacities no longer seems very productive, and is generally thought of now as metaphorical, like the theory of four humors in medicine.

But calling such terms metaphorical hardly gets rid of them. Some time ago, in reading through Bertrand Russell's *History of Western Philosophy,* I noted a comment he makes in introducing Aristotle's conception of physics:

> To understand the views of Aristotle, as of most Greeks, on physics, it is necessary to apprehend their imaginative background. Every philosopher, in addition to the formal system which he offers the world, has another, much simpler, of which he may be quite unaware. If he is aware of it, he probably realizes that it won't quite do; he there-

fore conceals it, and sets forth something more sophisticated, which he believes because it is like his crude system, but which he asks others to accept because he thinks he has made it such as cannot be disproved.

A passage in Whitehead's *Science and the Modern World,* also about the Greeks, makes much the same point: "Every philosophy is tinged with the coloring of some secret imaginative background, which never emerges explicitly into its trains of reasoning." Whitehead connects this background, in the Greek period, with the Greek sense of the dramatic.

We get, then, from two highly reputable philosophers, a conception of philosophy as a verbal clothing worn over the indecent nakedness of something called its "imaginative background," so as to allow it to appear in public. It is this retreating nude that I have been trying to study all my life. I call it a metaphorical or mythological structure, and it seems to me that while a good deal of philosophy, as Russell and Whitehead say, consists in disguising it in various ways, literature approaches it more directly and recreates it, age after age. One major function of literary criticism, as I see it, is to help us to become more aware of this "secret imaginative background," as it has operated in the past and continues to operate in the present. I do not think that Russell and Whitehead are talking simply about the prejudices of one's upbringing: if they were they would not use the term *imaginative.*

Our primary thinking, then, is not rational but metaphorical, an identifying of subjective and objective worlds in huge mental pictures. Metaphors are statements of identity: they tell us, for instance, that the poet and the lady he loves are shadow and sun. Here two quite different things are said to be one thing. To say that A is B when A is obviously not B is absurd and illogical, and, as Russell says, it won't quite do, at least for argumentative purposes. But it is also a primary structural effort of consciousness. Metaphor does not evoke a world of things linked together by overstated analogies: it evokes a world of swirling currents of energy that run back and forth between subject and object. Such metaphor may be followed by, or even translated into, more continuous or rational thinking, but when it is, it is not superseded by rational thinking: it remains in the background as its constant source of inspiration. About two generations ago there was a vogue among philosophers, including Russell himself, for saying that no statement had meaning unless it was either empirical or analytic, and that if it had no meaning it was obviously not rational. The trouble with this position was that it was a dead end: it cut philosophy off from the metaphorical basis of its own creativity, and there was nothing to do but to scrap it and go on with something more fruitful. The present age seems fascinated by Nietzsche and Heidegger, and so we are unlikely to lose sight of the connection between the philosophical and the metaphorical as long as the present attention span lasts.

Let us ask ourselves, first of all: What are the customary metaphors applied to reason? One of them, clearly, is light: we instinctively think of an age of reason as an age of "enlightenment," and whatever we can add to the world's structure of rational knowledge we call throwing more light on it. Another is dryness, often associated with coolness. The dispassionate thinker rises above the tumultuous storms and tempests of the passions into the clear air, etc.—one can easily paint such metaphorical pictures by numbers. The same metaphors operate negatively for anti-intellectuals. Long ago I spoke of a popular prejudice about poets, of the type often called romantic, as based on a hazy metaphorical contrast between warm mammalians who tenderly suckle their living creations and the cold reptilian intellectuals who lay abstract eggs.

This metaphorical ambience of sunrise and mountain air surrounding the reason suggests that we highly approve of ourselves when we feel that we are rational beings. The metaphors were not born yesterday: they are all in Heraclitus, who associated his conception of Logos with "dry light," a contrast to the soggy moist sensuality in which most people are soaked for most of their lives. More important for historical influence, the same metaphors enter into the first two acts of creation in Genesis, which begins with a primordial light, followed by the separation of the dry land from the sea. The account of creation in the Bible does not describe the origin of nature, and was probably never intended to: if it were, it would have been a little cleverer, and not had the trees created the day before the sun was. Creation is rather the presenting to human consciousness of what Heidegger says is the first riddle of existence: Why are there things rather than nothing? The creation resulted also from a divine commandment: light and dryness appeared because they were told to do so. Metaphors of reason, then, are connected with an activity, one that we often distinguish as will.

This connection of reason and will, a connection implying both an identity and a distinction, is complex and confusing. The distinction is often linked to the difference between Hellenic and Hebraic influences on our culture. Many classical scholars, and some philosophers including Whitehead, think of reason as something uniquely developed by the Greeks, as though what we call philosophy in Chinese or Indian traditions rested only on some kind of analogy to the techniques of logic and dialectic introduced by Plato and Aristotle. Others, following Nietzsche's lead, have claimed that the conception of "will" is a Christian one, unknown before the New Testament and developed mainly by St. Augustine. But whatever historical constructs we adopt, surely reason has always been active and the will conscious, so that they are really aspects of the same thing, even if at times they seem to be separated. In traditional Christianity creation was not the product of the simple will of God but of the Logos of God, a reasoning and conscious as well as an active will. And it is clear in, for example, Plato's *Republic* that reason should be, and in the wise man is, the commander of the soul, not simply exploring or speculating about the environment but giving orders to the subordinate appetites. Plato expects reason to be what some psychologists call "top dog" in the wise man's mind, and a top-dog reason is clearly an executive. At the same time Plato was well aware that self-conflict would arise in the best-regulated minds, and Christianity can hardly have introduced a new conception in this regard, though it did place much greater emphasis on the psychology of self-conflict. But Paul's statement "what I hate, that I do" is not really so different from Ovid's "deteriora sequor."

Another kind of example also shows how inseparable "reason" is from a controlling activity, whether called "will" or not. Will is frequently associated with motion, and a man's impulse to move has developed a sequence of vehicles of transport, starting with domesticated animals and continuing with machines that can go faster and further than sound. We have also started to build computers that can calculate infinitely faster than the human brain by itself can do. This second development has created in many people a sense of the eerie and uncanny. "Surely," they protest, "a machine may calculate but it can't *really* think. That would endanger man's status as king of nature." Here again "will," as another aspect of "reason," seems to provide us with at least a verbal solution, which is perhaps all we need here. Whatever a machine may do, qua machine it has no will to do it. Leave an automobile in a garage unused, and it will rust away to nothing without the slightest sign of impatience. And so far no computer has exhibited a will to compute until it's plugged in by a human being, and I do not see how it can acquire such a will unless computers in the future come equipped with DNA molecules and genetic codes impelling them to fight every moment for their own survival and reproduction. We may notice in passing that when science fiction stories depict computers beginning to use their own powers for their own ends, like the computer HAL in *2001,* the effect is frightening, as it is intended to be, but the computer has nonetheless turned into a fellow creature. However sinister when in power, there is a genuine pathos in his destruction.

This example suggests that machines are both fascinating and frightening to us because they work without self-conflict. The behavior of many social insects, such as ants and bees, affects us in a similar way. When we think of the "irrational" in the modern world, we first of all think of such tyrannies as the Nazi movement in Germany, and then smaller but equally mad phenomena like the Jones debacle in Guyana or the Manson group in California. These impress us not simply as erratic behavior, but as mechanical behavior in which the mechanism has gone out of control, like an automobile with a blacked-out driver. Certainly there can be no doubt about the self-destructive element involved: when a mass suicide occurs in such groups, one feels that the essential suicide has already taken place, and the essential life already given up.

We may recall the impression given to Hannah Arendt by her experience of attending the Eichmann trial, as recorded in her book *Eichmann in Jerusalem.* What disconcerted her about Eichmann was not a sense of great wickedness or even of great stupidity, for either of which she would have been prepared. She felt rather that, so to speak, he wasn't there: something impossible to define, but nonetheless at the core of real humanity, was simply missing. She developed from this a conception of "the banality of evil," which, I take it, was a philosopher's way of putting clothes over the naked metaphor of "lost soul." Let us look more closely at the metaphor.

In Plato, we said, an active reason has to be top dog in the wise man's mind. As few of us are wise, our top dogs are usually capricious tyrants continually changing their moods, but even people who are wise may have underdogs who hate their wisdom and are ready to look anywhere except in themselves for a new master. An external master has a strong appeal because he puts an end to the sense of self-division in the soul. He makes the sense of responsibility unnecessary, if we have such a sense, or he releases us from self-hatred and self-contempt if we do not. Michael explains to Adam in the last book of *Paradise Lost* that there will always be tyranny in society because the great majority are tyrants to themselves, but prefer to project their tyrannical impulses on something or somebody outside. The affinity of such irrational movements as those we have mentioned with hypnotism, which depends partly on a willingness to be hypnotized, and with hysteria, which is an attempt to cover up something suppressed, has often been noted.

The active reason employs, as a part of itself, a thought police, hunting down and exterminating every lawless impulse, or else a brainwashing indoctrinator makes sure that no such impulses are formed in early life. Plato's remedy for self-conflict was a dictatorial one. The political side of Plato's *Republic,* at least, is not, in my view, its primary one: I think the just state envisaged there is really an allegory of the wise man's mind. But of course the political analogy is present, and there must be something wrong with a psychology that makes for such frightful tyranny when translated into political terms. Christian remedies, though they had a different context, were also dictatorial: whatever rebels against the active controlling reason is evil and must simply be stamped out. Here again the political analogies have tended to be authoritarian: it has been urged that man is so desperately wicked that the strongest possible restraints, secular and spiritual, are needed. In a Christian context such an attitude is arbitrary: the obvious political inference from original sin is democratic. There is no point in giving unlimited authority to others who by definition cannot be any better than we are.

It seems clear that the active consciousness we have spoken of is really human life itself, and choice and responsibility are aspects of biological survival. The presence of an inner commander is a sign of autonomy or freedom, and the hundreds of books demonstrating that we cannot be free-willers and ought not to be freethinkers may safely be ignored as containing, in Hume's phrase, nothing but sophistry and illusion. And yet a dictatorial maintaining of this inner authority is a panic-stricken attitude that soon ends in the very hysteria it is trying to fight. In society, irrational impulses may have at least a comprehensible cause, such as the vacuum left in the soul by the departure of political loyalty, religious faith, family affection, or social vision. In the individual, it would be more practical to regard the mind as more like a parliamentary democracy. The active reason should not be a dictator but a government in power which has, like the Liberal party in Canada, a divine right of reelection. The irrational or self-destructive impulse is the view of the honorable member from Redneck Gulch, representing a constituency from a more primitive area of the brain. What he says is not to be acted on, but it is better to know that he is there and holds the views he does. And gradually, as we listen to the parliamentary debate that goes on inside ourselves, and which we hear the instant we stop to listen, we begin to understand that while there are elements in the mind that are perhaps grammatically "irrational," they may not be self-destructive at all, and hence can coexist with reason, or even form a part of it.

In speaking of reason, we have come to characterize it as primarily something that maintains an inner freedom, rather than something that tries to arrive at an objective truth, which is the more conventional view of it. For most of us today, the word *truth* has a rather empty and rhetorical sound: what is true today will either be disproved tomorrow or carried on to another stage, and in any case may be only a choice among many truths, as we imply when we use phrases like "the real truth." To revert to *Paradise Lost:* when the yet unfallen Adam asks the angel Raphael whether or not other planets are inhabited besides the earth, Raphael discourages the question as a distraction. The primary knowledge for Adam is the knowledge Raphael gives him, the story of the fall of Satan which will help him to preserve and maintain his freedom in paradise. Knowledge of nature for itself, to satisfy the mere desire of knowing, has to take second place. For St. Augustine, much earlier, intellectual curiosity verged on a sin of presumption.

This attitude, so hard for us to sympathize with now, arose

partly because Christianity had come to think of all natural knowledge as a set of deductions in a vast synthesis of reasoning, with the primary revelations of faith acting as the major premises. The essential truths, those that tell us what we must do to be saved, have already been given us. Such a conception of knowledge, we may observe, is one that annihilates the distinction between reasoning and rationalizing, or carrying a reasoning operation to a predetermined goal. Rationalizing, apart from private and subjective contexts, has, as its primary aim, the bolstering of some ideology held in one's society, and is still with us in both sacred and secular contexts. The general attitude is: if you want to philosophize, don't just stand there. Do something socially functional, that is, work out proofs that your society is right in believing what it wants to believe. The principle formulated by St. Anselm, *credo ut intelligam,* I believe in order to know, is the axiom of this kind of rationalizing.

Most of us, nonetheless, feel that there is a difference between reasoning and rationalizing, however easy it may be to show that every point of view is culturally conditioned and subject to preceding social assumptions. We are now fairly sure that no deductive approach to knowledge founded on unquestionable premises is going to work. Any individual's line of reasoning, then, may achieve a break with the structure and tradition of the reasoning he started with: it may become a genuine mutation with a survival value for a quite new society. One sees this most clearly in scientific method. Science is an activity like anything else, and it has to begin in the same chaos of I-wonder-if and let's-see-whether that any activity would. But here the activity is directed toward the external world, which acts as the answering authority. Hence the activity is reinforced by an observant, sometimes almost a passive, receptivity in regard to the evidence coming from nature. If a cattle tick will wait for years to hitch a ride on a passing cow, the science that records this fact has to be equally patient.

The poet Browning, in his early poem on Paracelsus, the sixteenth-century doctor and occult philosopher who was a contemporary of Luther, Rabelais, and Erasmus, makes Paracelsus say, at the outset of his career:

> *There is an inmost center in us all,*
> *Where truth abides in fullness . . .*

> *and, to KNOW*
> *Rather consists in opening out a way*
> *Whence the imprisoned splendor may escape,*
> *Than in effecting entry for a light*
> *Supposed to be without.*

Browning may have thought of Paracelsus, as he did of Fra Lippo Lippi, as a spokesman for the new attitudes coming in with Renaissance humanism, the period he was particularly interested in. But Paracelsus, as we have seen, is speaking for the whole traditional attitude to knowledge before him in thinking of knowledge as primarily an activity directed by the subject towards the object. Browning himself, however, seems to assume that this attitude would be something of a paradox to Paracelsus's contemporaries. Here, I think, he is reflecting the growing ascendancy of a more receptive attitude to nature that had grown up since Descartes and had been codified by Locke's theory of knowledge. According to this, man is first of all equipped with five senses and is surrounded by a world which those senses must take account of. Hence there comes a strong emphasis on the inductive side of reasoning, on the receptivity of the scientific attitude, its impartial taking in of sense impressions, its uninvolved observation of phenomena, the patience with which it checks its data and repeats its experiments to make sure the observations are correct.

We have now a conception of two aspects of reason, one active and aggressive, the other receptive and suspending judgment. Scientific method on this basis has come to symbolize, for us, the typically rational procedure of our time. This method is founded on the Cartesian paradigm, where consciousness resides only in the perceiving subject, so that the object has to be treated as mechanical, and, by extension, as quantitative and measurable. In recent times there has been a growing chorus of objections to the Cartesian paradigm, asserting that what was a brilliant and innovative idea in the seventeenth century has become a positive danger in the twentieth, especially in the social sciences. It is argued that the active and passive aspects of reason are wrongly related: what is observed is affected by the observation, and when it is man himself that is being observed, a detached attitude is only a disguise for reactionary prejudice. Perhaps, then, there is not only an active and a passive side to reason, but different levels of it, the two aspects being closer together on higher levels.

In Hindu philosophy, as we have it in the *Bhagavadgita* and elsewhere, there is a conception of three "Gunas" or moods of the soul. Perhaps "modes" would be a better rendering than "moods." There is an active and aggressive "Rajas" mood, a passive and receptive "Tamas" mood, and a balancing or neutralizing "Sattva" mood which is superior to them both, because it includes them both, and which is the foundation of all genuine wisdom. All three, being modes of consciousness, are modes of reason as well, even though they include other factors. The "Rajas" or aggressive mood is typically what we have been calling the actively rational. The "Sattva" or balancing mood is closer to what we generally call the reasonable. For, as Samuel Butler pointed out over a century ago, the reasonable is often the opposite of the rational. The reasonable pursues the middle course that keeps life unified and integrated. Emotional and other factors are balanced and compromised with, but not ignored. The rational attitude, in contrast, pursues extremes rather than the middle way. It is fascinated by reason as a machine, and by the compulsions in it that seem to do away with self-conflict. If you accept A, then B necessarily follows and you must do that, however out of proportion to human life as a whole it may be.

Reason pursued in this exclusive way eventually becomes a mental cancer, fostering its own growth at the expense of the whole organism. A few steps further along, the excessively rational turns into the irrational, which, as we saw, is the rational gone out of control. As a modern French poet has said, the madman is the victim of the rebellion of words. Orwell's nightmare world of *1984* is a mad world, but a triumph of pseudologic also. Some years earlier, E. J. Pratt had used Orwell's imagery in describing the Nazi invasion of France as reason in the service of the irrational:

> *Seven millions on the roads in France,*
> *Set to a pattern of chaos*
> *Fashioned through years for this hour.*
> *Inside the brain of the planner*
> *No tolerance befogged the reason—*
> *The reason with its clear-swept halls,*
> *Its brilliant corridors,*

Where no recesses with their healing dusk
Offered asylum for a fugitive.

There is a Western analogue to the Hindu conception of two levels of reason in the psychology of Jung, where there are said to be four types of consciousness: thinking, feeling, intuition, and sensation. Jung suggests that people can be classified according to the proportion of these elements within them. The "thinking" type, if he is primarily that, is often a hard-driving aggressive person, impatient with the untidiness of people who never seem to understand that the shortest distance between two points is a straight line. He is the direct opposite of the "feeling" type, and it takes all the opaqueness of Jung's prose style to conceal the fact that by a feeling type he means a receptive thinker. Such a person would make a good chairman, collecting the sense of a meeting, or a good teacher, presenting the thoughts or events of the past, but his record of accomplishment in the world might be less impressive. For Jung there is an ideal of "individuation" beyond them both, and when we reach it one typical activity is an outbreak of symmetrical doodling, or drawing that Jung calls mandalas or geometrical designs.

To see the point of this we have to turn to Kant, for whom there are also two levels of reason, which he distinguishes as *Verstand* and *Vernunft*. If I have grasped the distinction correctly, *Verstand* is what we have called the Cartesian paradigm, a surmounting of clearly delimited problems by an alternation of active search and passive consideration of evidence. *Vernunft* is a freer activity of reason, concerned not so much with things as with consciousness itself, asking Montaigne's question "What do I know?" and limited only by the categories within which the mind operates. There is a distinction between "pure" and "practical" forms of *Vernunft,* corresponding to the distinction between the theoretical and active aspects of a commanding and executive reason, and consequently two critiques. For pure reason the world is objective and phenomenal; hence pure reason cannot make contact with the ultimate realities, including God. The practical reason, however, can feel its attachment to a divine or creative Logos that knows nothing of any distinction between pure and practical aspects of itself, and nothing of any limitations on either.

We are now back to the metaphor of creation in Genesis.

We notice that the climax of the creation was a day of rest, which God presumably spent in contemplating the "good" world he had made, which once finished had become objective to himself. On the previous day he had taken the precaution of making man among the other animals, so that there would be at least one member of an appreciative conscious audience. Man's imitation of the sabbatical aspect of creation is the subject of Kant's third critique, the *Critique of Judgment (Urteilskraft)*. Here the mind is neither reflecting on itself nor motivated by desire, but is studying that curious assimilation of nature and art that seems to underlie so much of what we call beauty, design for its own sake, purposiveness without purpose, as Kant says. There is no reason why we should feel that a snowflake has an exquisite and subtle design: we just do, and there is a feeling of wonder and mystery about this that mathematical explanations of the forming of crystals do not affect: they are made in a different area. The words *speculation* and *reflection* remind us of how deeply our view of nature is bound up with metaphors of mirrors, of seeing in nature, traditionally the second Word of God, the same free play of design that we find in our own consciousness. Hence, as Matthew Arnold insists, many things are not really seen at all until they are seen as beautiful, and this kind of perception is really the fulfillment of consciousness itself. Sir Thomas Browne goes much further, with an explicit reference to the Sabbath of creation: "I hold there is a general beauty in the works of God, and therefore no deformity of any kind or species of creature whatsoever. . . . Nature is not at variance with Art, nor Art with Nature, they being both servants of his Providence. Art is the perfection of Nature. Were the World now as it was the sixth day, there were yet a Chaos."

But as soon as we enter the world of design, beauty, play, and the assimilating of nature and art, we begin to wonder whether creation itself, rather than the exercising of consciousness within it, is not the primary human activity. The Romantics who followed Kant developed a conception of imagination, designed to express this. Imagination is a constructive, unifying, and fully conscious faculty that excludes no aspect of consciousness, whether rational or emotional. As such, it is for many Romantics the primary activity of human consciousness. In Blake, for example, the word *reason* usually has an unfavorable sense, because for him it means the Cartesian split between subject and object that all creation begins by trying to overcome. But the words *mental* and *intellectual* in Blake are consistently synonyms for imaginative. For Shelley, the language of imagination is the key to human freedom and equality, because it is purely construc- tive, in contrast to the language of assertions that carry their own negations along with them, and are consequently aggressive and hostile. For Coleridge, there is a "primary" imagination, an ex- istential consciousness very close, it seems to me, to Kant's prac- tical reason, and a "secondary" one which embodies itself in its artifacts.

This takes us back full circle to the metaphorical world with which we began, the world of the poets which is older than the world of the philosophers, and is still the verbal matrix of civi- lization. The Romantics tell us that to get to the furthest dis- tance from the irrational we have to move from the balance and prudence of the reasonable to the creative energy of culture, more particularly as embodied in, or symbolized by, the great works of art, music, and literature. The creative person or "genius," in the Romantic view, does not simply avoid the irrational but grapples with it and transforms it, dealing with the fantastic as well as the real, and often in the grip of neurosis himself. In creation the alternating of activity and receptiveness recurs: there is no question about the mental energy that creating works of art requires, but poets constantly tell us that much of that energy has to take the reverse form of allowing what is being created to assume its own independent existence without interference from the poet's conscious will. Many of Keats's most dazzling letters are concerned with the principle that "that which is creative must create itself."

Of course, especially in the theologically minded Coleridge, there is an analogy between man as creator of art and the Logos of God as the creator of nature. This analogy is not new with the Romantics: we find it in the Elizabethan critic Puttenham, writ- ing in the 1580s: "A Poet is as much to say as a maker. And our English name well conforms with the Greek word, for of *poiein*, to make, they call a maker *Poeta*. Such as (by way of resemblance and reverently) we may say of God; who without any travail to his divine imagination made all the world of naught, nor also by any pattern or mould, as the Platonics with their Ideas do fan- tastically suppose." Well, the Platonics may be fantastic, but it was they who supplied Puttenham with his metaphor. The word rendered "created" in the first verse of Genesis is never used in the Bible to describe anything that man can also do. But in, say, Plato's *Timaeus,* where the creator is a demiurge working by a model like a human craftsman, the way is wide open for such a parallel.

There are two obstacles here. In the first place, nothing that man makes is genuinely alive: Pygmalion's statue, in ordinary experience, never really becomes Galatea. Milton says that books are not absolutely dead things, but the very defensiveness of the phrase indicates that they are relatively dead things, mechanisms that repeat what they say. This is the point at which the Bible inserts its warnings against idolatry: an idol is a human artifact, therefore dead, or animated only by some spirit that has forgotten or ignored its real creator. Thus man invented the wheel thousands of years ago, and promptly turned it into an idol of external fate or fortune. An attempt to idolize human culture would be equally futile: the Romantics reach a conception of the elitism of genius, and many of them, even Blake, often speak as though they were content to leave it at that, but we cannot.

In the second place, metaphors of the dead or the mechanical seem to get attached even to God's creation in the Bible. God's making of Adam is very like the animating of a corpse, and man's occasional grumbles that he never asked to get thrown into so stupid and meaningless a world are supposed to be refuted by the statement that pots do not raise this sort of question with their potters. We find however that that remarkable Victorian novelist, clergyman, and writer of fantasy George Macdonald ends a short allegorical fable with a very unusual prayer dealing with precisely this point: "We thank thee that we have a father, and not a maker; that thou hast begotten us, and not moulded us as images of clay; that we have come forth of thy heart, and have not been fashioned by thy hands." To adopt the male-centered biblical terminology that Macdonald uses, can man beget as well as create? Or, more accurately, what do human beings bring forth that is alive?

Their children, of course, and by extension a new society. But if we bring something to life, we have to respect its freedom; otherwise it is not really alive. I am not speaking here of what is often called "permissiveness": that is not a genuine respect for freedom, but a deliberate prolonging of the frustrations of dependence. The adolescent or teenager is a twentieth-century invention, and a most ill-advised one. I am saying rather that there can be no progress in human life except progress in the formula "Live and let live," releasing more and more members of society from exploitation, from the inherited conditioning of conventions that keep us from dealing with change, from the panic that perverts all experience into a form of possession. Our word *manufacture* shows how deeply we are involved in the clutching, grasping, possessive activity of the hand, and we also speak of seizing or grasping ideas. The genuinely human reason for technology was the abolition of slavery, but slavery is partly a state of mind and can coexist with the most highly developed technology. I do not mean only human society: the domination and exploiting of nature is part of a slave economy too. I have occasionally wondered, in looking at the approaches to our cities, whether nature possesses the capacity to make a convulsive lunge of self-preservation that would rid her of this horrible strangling parasite of humanity once and for all.

The arts, whatever their limitations, have an essential role to play in the liberating of the human mind. They do not work by magic, and are not mind-altering drugs: they cannot make people better unless there is already a reasoning will to be made better. But the work of literature (the art we are at present concerned with) forms a focus for a community. It reflects the concerns of that community but is detached from immediate action, so that the community remains a community and does not turn into a mob. Literature cannot by itself prevent the total destruction that is one of the many possible fates in store for the human race, but I think that that fate would be inevitable without it. No one has really studied the function of literature in society, but it must be one of major importance. In Canada today, for example, with its demoralized government and chaotic economy, it seems to me only its lively and articulate culture that holds the country together. Everything else seems to me irrational, in the sense I have given the word of machinery out of control. But if we place the works of the human imagination in the center of the community and make sure they stay there, we shall be able eventually to see that community itself as the total form of what human beings can bring forth, their own larger life that continues to live and move and possess its inward being.

Literature and
the Visual Arts

⬦

I SHOULD like to approach the relation of literature to the visual arts through some of the general principles involved, and hence I am not confining myself to Italian examples. Also, if I am to keep the discussion contained within the limits of a short introductory paper, I shall be able to discuss only one of the visual arts: the one I choose is painting.

The verbal and musical arts that address the ear are presented as temporal experiences, where we move along with the presentation from beginning to end. Those that address the eye, including painting, sculpture, and architecture, are presented spatially. But before long we realize that there is something accidental about the presentation, that every art has both a temporal and a spatial aspect. We may, by studying the score, perceive a musical composition as simultaneous, spread out all at once in front of us, as it were. We may also see a painting or other spatial work of art as an instant of arrested movement. T. S. Eliot speaks of how "a Chinese jar / Moves perpetually in its stillness." Literature seems to be closer to the visual arts than music, as it depends on imagery as well as rhythm. We may think of it as midway between the musical and the visual. We experience this double context most obviously in drama, where we not only hear a narrative but often a background of music as well, along with seeing a spectacle on the stage. But even if we are silently reading a work of literature, there is still a metaphorical hearing and seeing that is never wholly out of our consciousness.

The metaphorical "hearing" of literature, more particularly

poetry, is often expressed in metaphors of music. Thus Milton's *Lycidas* has in its invocation the line "Begin, and somewhat loudly sweep the string," implying that the poem has a *mezzoforte* musical accompaniment on a lute or lyre. At the end we read

> *Thus sang the uncouth swain to th' oaks and rills*
> *While the still morn went out with sandals gray:*
> *He touch'd the tender stops of various quills*
> *With eager thought warbling his Doric lay.*

The word *quills* implies the use of a reed or a kind of rustic oboe, called an "oat" earlier in the poem. Milton had a good deal of musical taste and knowledge, but the impossibility of singing and playing a wind instrument at the same time does not seem to bother him. *Paradise Lost,* again, invariably uses the metaphor of singing whenever the poet appears in his own person.

But when the process of reading or listening to a body of words in time is ended, we make an effort to understand what the body of words conveys, in a simultaneous or comprehensive act that we metaphorically call "seeing." Someone about to tell a joke may begin with some such formula as "Have you heard this?" Once we hear it, we "see" the joke; we "grasp" (turning to another group of tactile metaphors) the essential point or meaning of the joke, or what Aristotle would call its *dianoia*. But once we "see" the joke we do not want to hear it again. Similarly, we may read a detective story in order to identify the murderer at the end, but once we "see" who the murderer is, we normally do not want to read the book again until we have forgotten his identity.

If, on the other hand, we are presented with something as complex as *King Lear,* we hear or read the play, and make a tentative effort to understand what it all means. This effort soon falls to pieces; its inadequacy becomes oppressive; we read or listen to the play again, and attempt a more satisfactory understanding. Such a process, if one is professionally concerned with studying literature or drama, may go on for the whole of one's life. Any feeling that we have "seen" the meaning of a work of literature in a final and completely adequate way implies a rather low estimate of it. This conception of "seeing" a body of words is so deeply involved in our response to literature that the metaphor of "structure," literature studied as a simultaneous pattern, has become a central critical term.

The metaphor of "seeing," however, has two frames of reference. It may refer us to a conceptual meaning, an understanding which is a gestalt of apprehension, but in itself, when expressed, is primarily another kind of verbal structure. Thus the fable is a story we listen to like other stories, but understanding it is a matter of understanding a "moral," the reconstruction of the story in conceptual or didactic verbal terms. Most allegories call for a response of this kind also. Here the seeing is a response of simultaneity that appears to take place in some kind of conceptual space. Sometimes a poet will indicate what kind of response he expects by providing a suggested moral of his own to his fable, as with Gray's "On a Distant Prospect of Eton College": "No more: where Ignorance is Bliss, / 'Tis Folly to be wise." Another example would be the "truth is beauty" proposition at the end of Keats's "Ode on a Grecian Urn," where the urn itself suddenly comes to life and speaks, in the figure of speech technically known as prosopopoeia. This is the same figure of speech that is employed in Anglo-Saxon riddles, where a visual object describes itself verbally and challenges the reader to guess its identity. The Grecian urn in itself, apart from the poem, belongs to the visual arts, and suggests that a verbal moral can be attached to a pictorial image as well as to a story. This is what is done in the emblem, where an allegorical picture is the occasion for verbal commentary.

Poetry depends heavily on concrete sense experience, and has a limited tolerance for the language of argument, thesis, or proposition. Within the last century we have had a series of manifestos directed against the moral and didactic type of writing where the act of understanding, being itself verbal, keeps the literary work "logocentric," in the current phraseology. Thus Valéry adjures the poet to "wring the neck" of rhetoric, meaning by "rhetoric" the alliance of poetry and oratory that seems to evoke only a verbal response. In English literature the early years of this century produced the movement known as Imagism, which demanded that the response to the total meaning, or what we may call the theme, of a poem should be at least metaphorically pictorial. Imagism was a minor movement in itself, but similar tendencies led Eliot, for example, to praise the "clear visual images" of Dante, contrasting him in this respect with the blind Milton to the latter's disadvantage. William Carlos Williams, though working in a very different idiom from Imagism, formulated the principle that forms the title of the last poem in Wallace Stevens's *Collected Poems:* "Not Ideas about the Thing but the Thing Itself." In prose fiction it is a very common device to have some visual emblem represent the simultaneous meaning or theme of the novel. Examples include Henry James's *The Golden Bowl,* D. H. Lawrence's *The White Peacock,* and Virginia Woolf's *To the Lighthouse.*

The geometrical shapes of the letters of Western alphabets make it difficult to assimilate the literary and pictorial arts as completely as can be done in the Orient, where calligraphy often seems to bridge the gap between writing and drawing. However, there are enough experiments with shape poems and concrete poetry to indicate a considerable interest in this area. There is much less to note on the musical side: poets are no longer as liberal with metaphors of harps or lyres or lutes, or even singing, as they used to be. We occasionally run across the term *voice* as a metaphor for hearing, as in Herbert Read's *The True Voice of Feeling* or Malraux's *Les Voix du silence,* but these are critical works.

But the combination of verbal and visual appeal, with each art functioning by itself, has had a long history in our tradition. Its more modern forms begin with Hogarth's sequential pictures on a verbal program, such as *Marriage à la Mode* and *The Rake's Progress,* and reach their highest development in the illuminated books of William Blake, where we have again a sequence of plates that may show any proportion of verbal and visual material, from a plate that is all text to one that is all design, and anything in between. These are not illustrated poems, for illustration punctuates a verbal text and brings it to periodic halts: in Blake there is a continuous counterpoint of the two arts from beginning to end. On a popular level an easy-going intermixture of drawing and text forms the staple of young readers today, the comic book, where one art continually feeds on the other, so that the deficiencies in each art by itself are less noticeable.

We next notice that in our cultural traditions the specifically biblical and Hebrew influence, the one that underlies the religions of Judaism, Christianity, and Islam, has in common a reverence for the spoken word of God and a corresponding distrust in any association of deity with the eyesight. Moses turns aside to see why the burning bush does not burn up: the visual stimulus is merely to awaken his curiosity, and it is the voice that speaks from the bush that is important. God constantly speaks in the Bible, and there seems to be no theological difficulty about hearing his voice. But the editorial and redacting processes in the Old Testament seem to get very agitated where any suggestion of a vision of God is concerned. We are solemnly adjured to make no image either of the true God or any of the gods concocted from nature, and this commandment has led to the practical extinction of representational painting in all three religions at various times, more particularly in Islam. In Christianity, any swing back to the primitive revolutionary fervor of the first Christian age has been normally accompanied by iconoclasm, in both Western and Eastern churches. In the *Clementine Recognitions* St. Peter enters a building decorated with frescoes, and it is noted with emphatic approval that he is totally indifferent to the impressions of pictorial art. Of course the Bible is full of imagery, as full as any work of literature would be. But apparently this imagery is intended to be internalized, and assimilated to the silent hearing which is the approved response to the Word of God.

The attitude of Plato toward the arts of *techne,* painting and sculpture particularly, was not greatly different: he began the critical tendency to regard the painter as simply a master of representational illusion that lasted until after the Renaissance. But in a polytheistic religion we must have statues or pictures to distinguish one god from another, and in Greek culture we see two powerful emphases on the visual: the nude in sculpture and the theater in literature. For, whatever the importance of the music and poetry heard in a theater, the theater remains primarily a visual presentation of literature, as its derivation from the Greek word for seeing (*theaomai*) shows. In contrast, the iconoclastic tendencies in Christianity are often accompanied by a strong dislike of the theater, and complaints about the moral indecency of portraying naked bodies need no elaboration of reference. Again, in Homer a god or goddess will appear to a hero in the guise of someone he knows well: the Christian notion of a uniquely portentous incarnation of a deity in a human form is very remote from the Homeric world.

At the same time the transition from hearing to seeing metaphors that we noted in the encounter with literature also seems to operate in religious texts and rituals. In the Christian mass the Collect or scripture readings are followed by the elevation of the Host; the Eleusinian mysteries culminated, we are told, in exhibiting a reaped ear of corn to the initiates; Zen Buddhism has a legend that the Buddha, after ending a sermon, held up a golden flower, the only member of his audience who got the point being, naturally, the founder of Zen. The Christian Bible ends with the Book of Revelation, a tremendous vision of the whole order of nature being destroyed and succeeded by a new heaven and earth. Though a very imperfectly visualized book, it is said to be a "vision," and clearly follows the religious tradition in which the crucial transition from physical to spiritual life is described in the visual metaphor or "enlightenment." Similarly Job remarks, at the end of his long ordeal, "I have heard of thee by the hearing of the ear: but now mine eye seeth thee."

When the relation of the art of words and the art of drawing and coloring becomes less metaphorical and more concrete, the tension between them greatly increases. The elaborate descriptions of paintings that are occasionally found in literary works belong to a specific rhetorical device, usually called ecphrasis, which is often considered a sign of "decadence," or whatever term we use to indicate that the writer has embarked on what we consider a misleading path. Many such descriptions belong to late classical fiction: the romance of Leucippe and Clitophon, by Achilles Tatius, is triggered by a picture, elaborately described, of the rape of Europa, which leads a bystander to tell his story to another bystander. However, when he ends the story eight books later, the author has forgotten his opening and does not return to it. It is usually a woman's nudity that a writer counts on to hold his reader's attention in such a device, but even so his resources are limited. Two heroines are exposed naked to a sea monster in *Orlando Furioso,* but despite the fullness of Ariosto's description, the reader is apt to conclude that, in a verbal setting at any rate, one luscious nude is very like another. In still more elaborate examples, such as the shield of Achilles in Homer, we quickly forget about the connection with the visual arts—that is, we stop asking ourselves if it is really possible to get all that on a painted or carved surface, and simply accept the shield for what it is: a description of a calm world at peace that forms a beautiful contrast to the weary hacking of bodies that is the foreground action. It has been a generally accepted principle, since Lessing's *Laokoon* at least, that one art cannot really do what another art is especially equipped to do. The principle involved here is quite distinct from the one implicit in Blake's illuminated poems: there we have two arts running side by side, each doing its own work, and not one art attempting to reproduce the effect of another in its own medium.

The same principle would apply to the attempt in painting to imitate verbal effects, but there the issue is more complex. In the Middle Ages, when the church was the chief patron of the visual arts, an elaborate code of iconography prescribed at least the content of the picture. There were verbal reasons for presenting one saint as bald and another with hair, and for supplying martyred saints with the instruments of their martyrdom—Catherine's wheel, Laurence's gridiron, and the like. When in the Renaissance the market for secular painting began to expand, the situation was not very different: painting the birth of Venus or the apotheosis of Louis XIV is equally a commitment to a verbal program. Still later come the anecdotal pictures of the eighteenth and nineteenth centuries, which are part of the development of the visual arts known as illustration.

We have said that verbal media internalize the imagery they use, so that the reader is compelled to build up his own structure of civilization. The illustration relieves the strain of this by supplying a readymade equivalent for the reader's mental picture: hence its proverbial vividness, as expressed in the journalistic cliché that "one picture is worth a thousand words." In the nineteenth century books were illustrated to an extent hardly conceivable today, when the development of film and television has obviated the need for most of it. What's the good of a book, inquires Lewis Carroll's Alice, without pictures or conversations? The same close association with words is present in paintings themselves: the Pre-Raphaelite movement in Britain, for example, was primarily a development of painting as illustration—to medieval romance, to Shakespeare, to contemporary life, to the Bible.

A contradiction seems implied in what we have said thus far. We have spoken of the iconic art of the Middle Ages, and also of the prejudice against representational art of any kind that pervades the biblical religions, and accounts for the recurring movements of iconoclasm. The explanation is that the Word of God, or doctrine of the church, being verbal, is, we said, supposed to be internalized, and the status of the painting or sculpture related to it depends on the previous existence of that internalization. If there is none, the picture or whatever could be an idol, something that brings us to a reverent full stop in front of something presented as both objective and numinous. But in the biblical tradition nothing objective can be numinous: art is a creation of man and nature a creation of God, and no deities lurk in either. If the internalized verbal structure is already there, however, the picture becomes an icon, intended to elicit meditation instead of closing it off. The same principle, working inside the Christian tradition, makes for a progressive domestication of the major religious figures. We go from the great Torcello Madonna, who seems a million years old with no sign of aging, through the highly stylized Byzantine figures like the Rucellai Madonna of Duccio to the comparatively humanized Madonna of Giotto, and from there to the still more familiar quattrocento Madonnas, who look so much more like simply attractive young women with their babies.

In later periods of painting we become increasingly aware of the principle stated by William Carlos Williams in relation to literature: "The classic is the local fully realized, words marked by a place." Substituting "pictures" for "words," we see the principle operating in Dutch realism, including the realism of landscape in Hobbema and Ruisdael, in the first generation of French impressionism, in the earlier Barbizon school, in the southern English landscape tradition headed by Constable. Such movements in painting are opposite in tendency to what is called the "picturesque," the search for a particular spot (often called "unspoiled") that lends itself to certain pictorial conventions, again usually verbal in origin. In our day the picturesque has been mainly taken over by photography, but a contrast remains between two approaches to visual art: that of the tourist looking in from the outside and that of the native looking out from the inside. Such contrasts are more familiar in culturally new countries, including Canada, but picturesque bandits and gypsies have been celebrated by European painters too. The picturesque is typically a conservative idealized vision, and hence rather distanced: if it comes much closer it turns into the genuinely realistic. John Ruskin, who in this respect was more of a lay preacher using pictures as moral documents than a critic making objective analyses of works of art, is full of denunciations of the picturesque that gets too close to its subject. Thus in *Stones of Venice* he contrasts Holman Hunt, who "loves peasant boys, because he finds them more roughly and picturesquely dressed, and more healthily coloured, than others," with Murillo's drawing of a beggar's dirty foot, which "is mere delight in foulness."

The issue involved here takes us a long way. Traditionally, the painter has been judged by his representational skill: there are Greek legends about painters painting grapes that birds would peck at, and the Elizabethan critic Puttenham says that the artist of painting or carving is "only a bare imitator of nature . . . as the marmoset doth many countenances and gestures of a man." It is somewhat chastening to realize how triumphant the tradition of painting has been, in the face of such infantile critical theories. The justification for the theories was that, as Sir Thomas Browne said in the seventeenth century, "Nature is the art of God"; hence in theory all the original part of the painter's work had already been done. And yet the painter often agrees with such critics, maintaining that he paints only what he sees, and just as he sees, without realizing how impossible this is. What he sees he sees from within the conventions of painting in his day, which in turn are determined by a cultural and social framework. Any frequenter of art galleries can determine, with a little practice, what century any picture he is looking at was painted in, and this clearly could not be done if it were true that any painter in any age could simply reproduce nature at second hand. The development of photography has complicated this situation, but has not essentially changed it: photography has its conventions and fashions also.

In any case the assumption that painting is essentially representation has persisted up to a century or so ago, and it is part of the assumption that the painter is permitted only selection, not recreation. The selective process is supposed to operate on a quasi-moral principle: what the painter selects to record should, traditionally, be the "beautiful." The trouble is not only that beauty, at least the beauty that is connected with erotic feeling, is proverbially fleeting, but that conventions of beauty are fleeting also. Whatever is considered beautiful in any given period of culture tends to imprison itself within an increasingly narrowing convention. A beautiful body should be only a body in good physical condition between the ages of eighteen and thirty, and in a white society it must be obviously white. Even in the nineteenth century it was widely assumed that the Greeks had invented beauty, and that Asian and African artists had deliberately made a cult of the grotesque and hideous out of sheer perversity.

This constant closing off of the beautiful in academic dead ends and blind alleys is accompanied by a corresponding exhaustion of resources in the techniques of producing it. We recall Browning's melancholy monologue of "the faultless painter" Andrea del Sarto, obsessed with a sense of futility and disillusionment not merely in his personal life but in his painting as well. It has been remarked that probably nobody in Andrea's own time would have understood that faultlessness could itself be a fault: the point is, however, that technical perfection implies a convention narrowing so rapidly that there is soon nothing left to explore within it. When such perfection is reached it becomes mechanical, and there is nothing to do but abandon the convention and try something else. Nobody would call Magnasco, or for that matter even Caravaggio, a faultless painter, but they were exploring pictorial conventions that Andrea del Sarto could not have dreamed of.

We should not be surprised to find a fairly consistent tradition of revolt in the painting of the last two centuries or so, first against the tyranny of verbal conventions, then against the assumption that the painter's primary function is to represent nature, which makes the content of the picture and the "accuracy" of its representation functional elements in criticism. The landscape painters in England, Turner, Constable, Bonington, and their impressionist successors in France, were in the forefront of the struggle against too exclusive a demand for emblems, illustrations, and other forms of subservience to the verbal. By the end of the nineteenth century this resistance had spread to the dominance of representation itself. One of the commonest stories about twentieth-century painters, ascribed to both Picasso and Matisse and doubtless many others, is the response to the complaint that a picture, let us say of a fish, was not a fish: "Quite right: it is not a fish, it is a picture." The issue at stake here is, of course, the autonomy of painting, the right of the painter to deal only with the pictorial shapes and colors that belong to his art.

The development of the verbal arts has followed parallel directions, though the sequence is harder to trace because as long as literature uses ordinary words, it can never be as abstract or autonomous as painting or music can be. Some representational aura will still cling to the words, however strong the embrace of their metaphorical context in poem or story. Also, the external forces trying to dominate literature mostly take the form of other verbal structures. But the same resistance to conventionalizing standards of beauty, to an idealizing representationalism that stays well away from its subject (unfortunately there is no exact literary equivalent of "picturesque"), to the tyranny of religious or political anxieties, has operated in literature as well as in the visual arts.

One result of this is that instead of making a sterile and canonized ideal beauty the model for the artist, the entire spectrum of cultural traditions, from the most primitive to the most sophisticated, from the most immediate to the most exotic, is spread before him as a source of possible influences. A contemporary artist without a strong sense of inner direction would be more likely to suffer from agoraphobia than claustrophobia. A by-product of the same expansion has been the breaking down of the barrier between the work of art and the ordinary visual object. The *objet trouvé* may be not only the subject for a picture but the art object itself; in collage the picture is not painted but assembled from pictorial data; pop art and similar developments are based on the principle that anything may become a work of art when a consciousness is focused on it. In the Renaissance it was assumed, not only that nature was the art of God, but that the order of nature was a metaphorical book, a secondary Word of God, and that the properly instructed man could read its riddles for almost any purpose, magical, medical, scientific, or religious. A rather similar assumption, that nothing exists merely as itself, seems to inform the visual arts today, however different the context. A well-known picture by Boccioni, *The Street Enters the House,* may serve as an allegory for an age in which the separation of works of art inside buildings from miscellaneous objects outside on the street is breaking down.

The oldest paintings we possess, and the oldest works of any art by many thousands of years still extant, are the Paleolithic paintings and drawings in the caves of southern France and northern Spain. The firmness and assurance of the drawing would be impressive anywhere, but in such surroundings, with such formidable difficulties of positioning and lighting, they are little

short of miraculous. There were doubtless representational motives for drawing the animals of the hunt on which the food
supply depended, but this can hardly have been the entire motivation, as some of the figures are human beings, probably sorcer-
ers, clothed in animal skins. Wherever we turn in studying this
art, we are constantly brought up against the cave itself, as a
shrouding maternal womb containing the embryos both of human society and of the beings of the natural environment to
which that society was most closely related. The persistence of
the cave setting for fresco painting in Anatolia, India, Etruscan
Italy, and many other places makes us wonder whether painting
may not have a special relationship to the sense of something
embryonic, present within the human imagination but suggesting the outlines of a human civilization not yet born.

Whatever may be thought of this, the sense of something
unborn and embryonic turns up recurrently in the history of
painting. We see it in the grotesque fantasies of Hieronymus
Bosch and Brueghel, in the naive staring faces of primitive painters, in the melting or deliberately incongruous shapes of the sur-
realists, in the spidery childlike scrawls of Miró and Klee. It is
as though, in Klee's words, the painter "places more value on the
powers which do the forming than on the final forms themselves." We are very far away here from the notion of the painter
as a supermonkey reproducing the art of God in nature. In the
cultural history of Canada painting was the first of the arts to
come to maturity, and it formed a very important aspect of the
exploring and settling of the country. Perhaps a worldwide metamorphosis of the visual arts indicates the coming of a new age in
man's attitude to the globe he inhabits.

A corresponding metamorphosis of the verbal arts would
probably come later, though some elements of it can already be
glimpsed. In the Western tradition literature seems to have run
through a cycle beginning with myth and romance and ending
with an ironic realism which disintegrates into various forms of
paradox, such as the theater of the absurd. In our day we see
many signs of the cycle being repeated: the retelling of the great
myths, the reshaping of romance formulas in a science fiction
setting, the revival of a primitive relation to a listening audience
in rock and ballad singing. But nothing repeats exactly in history, and in any case the end of a cycle does not compel us to

repeat the same cycle, but gives us a chance to transfer to another level.

It is obvious that most of the movements in the arts mentioned above are political statements. Many of them are regarded as bourgeois erosions of socialist values in Marxist societies, even though they often assert those very values in a democratic setting. It seems to me that behind the political statement lies a fundamentally antipolitical attitude, an anarchism tending to break down all social mythologies devoted to promoting special social interests. Such an attitude may be unrecognized by the individual artist himself, or may even be the exact opposite of what he thinks he is trying to do. The movement known as dada, which arose after the First World War, was explicitly anarchist in this sense as a total movement, whatever the variety of social opinion within it. At present we are confronted by a movement in all the arts which, for all its tremendous creative variety, has incorporated the spirit of dada within it. Such a movement is to be welcomed, as long as we see it not as a kind of extreme unction for the bourgeois soul or as a morbid preoccupation with chaos for its own sake, but as the opportunity for renewed imaginative energy and a new freedom in seeing the world.

The Stage Is
All the World

✧

THE PROVERB "All the world's a stage" was a commonplace in Shakespeare's day, partly because it had come down from classical times and should be quoted in Latin: *Totus mundus exerceat histrionem*. The Globe theater, the one popularly associated with Shakespeare's plays, bore on it the motto *Quod fere totus mundus*, etc.: nearly all the world's a stage. Apparently the Globe architects made the curious blunder of getting an academic, or conceivably a lawyer, to write out the phrase for them, which he was unable to do without a qualification. The aphorism is used a good many times in various contexts by Shakespeare and other dramatists. What I should like to do here, with your permission, is to look at some of the uses of the phrase, mainly in Shakespeare, to see what is implied about the conception of personality in them, and, more broadly, how a dramatist looks at personality. Also to see whether the statement is reversible, as the nineteenth-century New England writer and physician Oliver Wendell Holmes claimed when he said: "The world's a stage, as Shakespeare said one day: / The stage a world, was what he meant to say."

The reason why it is possible to say that all the world's a stage is simple enough. All our social and personal relations are dramatic ones, even theatrical ones. If a friend comes into the room where we are, we instantly throw ourselves into the dramatic role that our knowledge of him and his orbit of interests suggests. True, the dialogue is improvised rather than memorized, as it is in the form of drama known as the commedia dell'arte, which I shall come back to in a moment. That means that we are continually thrown back on our own repertoire of ideas and suitable responses. There are two influences making for the conventionalizing of what is said, and the pressure of these influences is strong enough to make most dialogue of this sort fairly predictable. Occasionally we recognize that what someone says is identical with a standard dramatic convention, and we say that he is putting on an act. If the dialogue is being carried on in a police state and the room is bugged, the last difference between conversation and theatrical performance disappears.

In ancient times actors usually wore masks, and we have derived two words from the metaphor of the masked actor: hypocrite and person. Hypocrite is from Greek, and refers to an actor looking through a mask; person is from Latin, and refers to his speaking through one. So everything connected with "personality" has ultimately to do with a mask of some kind. We often use the word *persona* nowadays to mean the social side of the psyche, its aspect in relation to other people. The poet Yeats even extended the metaphor to writing, saying that the writing personality was a mask for the ordinary one. However, such metaphors often have misleading associations, and the metaphor of a mask is misleading when it suggests that one can remove the mask and disclose the real person underneath. Hamlet, for example, is a character who quickly wearies of social relationships, and likes to get by himself and soliloquize. But in a soliloquy one simply dramatizes oneself to oneself, one invisible mask conversing with another. Contemporary pop psychologists would perhaps say that Hamlet's soliloquies were top-dog monologues, addressed to a cowardly underdog who doesn't want to get on with skewering Claudius. But the top dog is equally unwilling to do the same thing, and in fact keeps talking in order to keep on avoiding it, and Hamlet soon realizes this aspect of his top-dog self too, and then goes on talking about that, and so on until in due course Shakespeare's longest play emerges.

In short, the mask metaphor fails us if it assumes that there is a real me underneath the mask I put on. There is no core to that onion: there is never anything underneath a persona except another persona. When we are alone, we have not walked away from a theatrical situation; we have walked into another one of a different kind. Each man carries inside him an entire Ottawa of politicians jockeying for power, civil servants struggling with routine, mass demonstrators organizing temper tantrums, secretaries trying to transcribe the inner turmoil into some kind of self-justifying narrative. In the physical world, scientists postulated, very early on, the existence of an "atom," that is, an indivisible unit of matter. We still keep the word, but we have split what we now call an atom, so that the reason for continuing to use a word that means the unsplittable turns out to be a fallacy. Similarly, we use the term *individual,* the undivided and undividable unit, for the hundred billion cells and bacteria that add up to John or Joan Smith. Never was there a sillier word. Let us say that we have just made a decisive action, of the kind that reassures us about how well integrated we are. But the decision may have emerged from a group of momentarily concurring moods, or a single mood taking a chance and seizing its opportunity, or a compulsion left over from the age of two. Still, the fact that we have adopted the word *individual,* and other words like it, shows how strongly we want to believe in some kind of hidden inner essence that remains stable and consistent, even though we may run through a dozen personal masks in an hour or so.

If we do, though, the result may become confusing even to us. Most of us simplify our lives by developing routines and habits, in conversations as in other things, to help us recognize ourselves as ourselves when we talk. Let us take the simplest of Shakespeare's uses of the phrase we're discussing. At the beginning of *The Merchant of Venice* the hero Antonio tells us that he feels sad, without knowing why. He goes on:

> *I hold the world but as the world, Gratiano,*
> *A stage where every man must play a part,*
> *And mine a sad one.*

Shakespeare's audience would have no trouble with that remark. The part you play in the drama of life is conditioned by your temperament, and temperament, at that time, meant the proportioning of four liquids or humors in the body. Antonio has, at the moment at any rate, a large proportion of one of these liquids, known as black bile or melancholy, in him: that makes him inclined to be observant and withdrawn from strenuous action. It's a mood only, as Antonio is basically a healthy man. In more extreme cases a character may be totally bound by the domination of one humor, and able to react only through it.

This is the principle underlying Ben Jonson's invention of the "comedy of humors." Jonson starts with the medical conception, as it was then, of temperaments dominated by one humor, and becoming melancholy or sanguine, phlegmatic or choleric, as a result. But he extends this in the direction of what we'd now call a conditioned reflex. A Jonsonian humor is a character who has a uniform response to every situation. A miser in a Jonson play can do and say nothing that isn't miserly or in some way connected with saving money. In his comedy *Every Man Out of His Humor* a miser named Sordido tries to hang himself because there's been a good harvest and he won't be able to foreclose many mortgages. There's a reference to something similar in the Porter's speech in *Macbeth*. His servants get to him in time and cut him down, and the first thing he says on coming to is to ask them why they had to cut an expensive rope instead of just un-tying it. In *The Silent Woman* the whole action turns on the fact that a central character, named Morose, hates noise of all kinds, and is delighted at the prospect of getting a dumb wife, who, of course, explodes into a deafening clatter of talk the instant she's married. If you find the suspense unbearable, I can tell you that the situation is resolved by the fact that she's a boy in disguise.

The comedy of humors, whether called that or not, is an extremely durable type of comedy. Molière used similar formulas in an even simpler way than Jonson: in all his famous comedies the action revolves around a character with one of the standard comic humors: a miser in *L'Avare*, a hypochondriac in *Le Malade imaginaire*, an ambitious snob in *Le Bourgeois gentilhomme*. In the eighteenth century, when Pope called Jonson's humor "the ruling passion," the same recipes were used for satire, and in the early twentieth century the philosopher Bergson wrote a book called *Le Rire*, in which he postulated the observing of someone bound to a mechanical routine of behavior as one of the main sources of the laughable. Assuming, that is, that the mechanical routine is voluntary and self-imposed. This type of humor is funny because we recognize in it, say, 97 percent of what we all do, and because of our feeling that we have another 3 percent or so of free and unpredictable response. This feeling may be an illusion: if it is ever proved conclusively to be one, nearly all comedy as we know it will disappear from human life, as the reactions of Archie Bunker, for example, would then be no more funny than the gestures of a spastic or paraplegic.

The mechanical nature of such behavior enables a type of drama to evolve which can depend on improvised dialogue. The types in Jonson's and Molière's comedies had descended directly from the Latin comedies of Plautus and Terence, and another line of descent, perhaps going even further back to the popular farces playing in Italy before Plautus, produced the Italian commedia dell'arte, well known in England in Shakespeare's time, and a major influence on Shakespeare, Molière, and Goldoni. There would be a company comprising the standard characters; a brief scenario, listing the props and outlining the main routines, would be posted up, and the action would go on from there. Similar devices are used in night clubs today, though more commonly in dialogue form.

The standard characters of the commedia dell'arte included Pantalone, a middle-aged wealthy Venetian who regularly took a dim view of his daughter's boyfriends, a Dottore, a professional man, often a Bolognese lawyer, pompous and pedantic, and Arlecchino or Harlequin, a clown who often pretended, like Hamlet, to split in two and hold dialogues with himself. As the form evolved and spread to other countries, we get the French clown Pierrot, the grotesque Pulchinello, who became the English Punch, the heroine Columbine, and the zanni or subordinate clowns who have given us the word *zany*. In the Gardiner ceramic museum in Toronto, there's a complete set of these characters in eighteenth-century porcelain. Also, when Brian Macdonald produced the Gilbert and Sullivan *Gondoliers* here at Stratford, he realized that Gilbert had written a purely commedia dell'arte story, with a Pantalone in the Duke of Plaza-Toro, a Dottore in the Inquisitor, and an Arlecchino in the twin heroes. You will remember a dance with puppets in that production, and the puppet play, where the mechanical nature of the behavior is so obvious, represents the basic theme of which humor comedies are variations.

I've spoken of our strong desire to believe in a stable and consistent entity underneath the variety of dramatic masks we assume. In the humor comedy this consistent entity appears in the form of parody: the humor is consistent only because he's conditioned himself to make the same kind of response every time. In some writers who have handled such characters with great skill—I'm thinking particularly of Dickens—we sometimes get the impression that the humor has conditioned himself to a minor obsession to avoid being taken over by a major one, just as one may develop a phobia about cats in order to conceal a

hatred of one's parents. In Shakespeare, where the great characters are so much more complex than they are in Jonson, the sense
of consistency comes from the limitations of their repertoire.
That is, Falstaff, for example, has a great variety of dramatic
functions—stage coward, braggart, jester, parasite, butt, vice—
but through all this variety he always sounds like Falstaff. We
know that there are limits beyond which he can't go, as when he
says, for instance, that he'll "purge, and leave sack, and live
cleanly as a nobleman should do."

To a professional dramatist, the axiom that the world's a
stage suggests the way he works. I said that there is no solid
essence or identity behind the various dramatic roles we assume
in life. If there were, the dramatist's creations would be what
Theseus, in *A Midsummer Night's Dream,* thinks they are: shadows, purely subjective entities dreamed up out of nothing. But
in practice the dramatist finds a fully inhabited world of impulses, moods, even things like personalities, inside his mind,
and sees an objective social world outside him with counterparts
of these things. Whenever we start to create, the creation hooks
on to something objective and autonomous, something with a
life and character of its own, so that we never know when we are
creating something and when we have invoked or summoned
something that is starting to recreate us. The drama is the most
obvious form of the objectivity of creation in words, because
there the fictional figures are taking the form of actual people on
a stage. The easiest way for a dramatist to proceed is to recognize
the largely mechanical element in social behavior that he also
finds in himself because he has to respond to it, and this creation
of the mechanical is the primary form of drama that I've been
dealing with, the humor comedy, the situation comedy, the improvised dialogue, and other developments of puppet theater.

But unless we are practicing dramatists, we begin to feel
that "All the world's a stage" is not a particularly cheerful remark. Antonio says it, we saw, because he is feeling melancholy,
and the much more famous use of it at the beginning of the set
speech on the seven ages of man in *As You Like It* comes from
Jaques, who is practically a professional melancholic. Let us
glance at the content of this speech first. Man goes through a
series of stages from infancy to old age, and each stage is an
actor's role. Some of these roles, the lover, the soldier, the justice,
are more or less voluntarily assumed: the man could have been

other things. But even in these some involuntary factor seems to be at work. Astrologers have noted the affinity of Jaques' stage with the sequence of planets—the lover and Venus, the soldier and Mars, the justice and Jupiter—and also the omission of the sun, the sign of a coordinating consciousness and will. One man in his time plays many parts, says Jaques. If we ask Which of these phases comes nearest to being the real man? it becomes clear that there isn't any real man, or if there is—and this is probably the answer that Jaques himself would give—we are closest to the real human essence in the mewling and puking infant at one end and the "mere oblivion" of total senility at the other. But we are asking the question wrongly. The identity of the real man, so far as there is one, is to be found, we said, in the limited number of roles that one can play.

The context of the speech is interesting. We are in the forest of Arden, a pastoral retreat of a quietness and simplicity like that of the Golden Age, except that it gets cold in winter. Two standard features of such pastoral retreats in literature are, first, remoteness from the injustices and absurdities of urban or courtly existence, and, second, deliverance from the tyranny of time. Jaques is introduced after being talked about as a character, and he sets out at some length a theory of the function of satire on urban or courtly life, along with some moralizings on the theme of time that he has picked up from Touchstone. Orlando comes in demanding food, is welcomed, goes out to fetch this servant Adam, and Duke Senior gives Jaques a cue:

> *Thou seest we are not all alone unhappy:*
> *This wide and universal theatre*
> *Presents more woeful pageants than the scene*
> *Wherein we play in.*

Jaques then weaves together the themes of satire and the passing of time into the seven ages speech.

The speech is totally ignored by the others: Orlando reappears with Adam and the company breaks into the wonderful "Blow, blow, thou winter wind" song. It seems merely a filler speech, designed to patch over a gap in the action, but one is usually mistaken in assuming that Shakespeare does things for second-rate reasons. The speech is rather what we, in this age of Brecht, might call an alienation speech. It reminds us that we are watching a play, or rather a play within the drama of the world, and a remarkably artificial and withdrawn dramatic scene at that. We become aware too that what seems the weak spot in Jaques' identifying of life with a series of actor's roles is what is really alienating in it. An actor has a life apart from his acting: Jacques' man going through his seven stages has no other life, but is simply an acting mechanism, a mechanism that soon wears out. After setting up this scarecrow, this vision of man as a dramatic puppet, in the magic forest of Arden, Jaques' function in the play is more or less complete: he says nothing of much interest after that until the closing lines, when he walks out of the artificial happy ending, looking for another kind of reality.

If we turn to a far more impressive melancholic than Jaques, namely Hamlet, we see how the axiom of the world as a stage can take on a tragic form. Hamlet exhibits an astonishing variety of moods, qualities, abilities, and sensitivities; but at the same time he is always Hamlet, and his identity as Hamlet depends, once again, on the limitations of his role-playing powers. Most of us come to terms with the fact that our identity, while not simply negative, is at least finite: because we are A we can't do what B and C do. The more active the intelligence, the more frequent the sense of frustration: if Shakespeare himself could speak of desiring this man's art and that man's scope, what price the rest of us? With Hamlet the frustration becomes claustrophobic: the world's a prison to him, and his dreams will not be bounded in a nutshell. The reason is that in contrast to Claudius, who is blocked by a crime in his past, Hamlet is blocked by his future, because the act of vengeance, if he accomplished it, would not fulfill but impoverish his life.

So in *Hamlet* we have perhaps the most impressive example in literature of a titanic spirit thrashing around in the prison of what he is, longing for death but suspecting that suicide will not release him any more than murder did his father. The duty of revenge makes it impossible for his inner and outer lives, however rich and eventful they are in themselves, to mesh gears. There is a good deal about plays and acting in *Hamlet,* partly because drama becomes for him a contrasting symbol of the integrating of the two worlds into a coherent unity of action. But Hamlet is not a dramatist: he merely wants to use a drama for a nondramatic purpose, something Shakespeare himself never did so far as we know; and Hamlet's observations on actors and what constitutes a good production have "amateur" stamped all over them. In the nineteenth century *Hamlet* seemed the central and essential play of Shakespeare, because it dramatized all the central Romantic and nineteenth-century problems: the conception of consciousness as the assassin of action, the sense of the disharmony of inner and outer worlds, the role of the creative imagination in overcoming the disharmony, and the obstacles and failures the creative impulse meets with. After about the Second World War in our century, the focus of what was felt to be Shakespeare's central play began to shift from *Hamlet* toward *King Lear.*

With *King Lear* we move over to the other side of our axiom: the stage as a world. The theater as a metaphor for the universe was extremely common in Shakespeare's day, and one reason was that the universe was assumed to have been intelligently designed by its Creator, and intelligent meant having some relation to human life. In *Romeo and Juliet* we meet Friar Laurence discoursing on herbs, the Friar being the kind of man who would know about herbs. Some herbs, he knows, are poisonous, but the assumption of his study is that God would never have made a plant that did not have some human function, if only a negative one. Similarly, the stars are not just up there: they have been put there to influence the character of living things. Even later than Shakespeare, Sir Thomas Browne could not understand why in the new continent of America there were poisonous snakes and the like, but not "that necessary creature, a horse." In so designed a cosmos all facts and all ideas are linked together, potentially in the human mind, actually in God's. The image of a totally participating theater begins to take shape. All facts and principles have their assigned and ticketed places, and step forward on the stage when needed. Courses in the training of memory were taught in which you constructed a theater-shaped encyclopedia in your mind, and remembered something by pulling it out of its numbered place in the auditorium. The scholar who did most work on these memory theaters, the late Dame Frances Yates, was convinced that the design of the Globe theater was influenced by them.

I have always been interested in the cultural frameworks of human societies, and I call such a framework a mythology. People have often asked me, not always politely, why I don't say ideology, like everyone else. The reason is that ideology to me suggests ideas, and a myth to me means a *mythos,* the Greek word for story or narrative. I know that we often assume that human beings build up structures of ideas, fitting them together logically if we believe in the ideology, pseudologically if we don't. But this is mostly illusion: what man does is what he has done from the dawn of consciousness: make up stories. All ideologies are derived from stories or story patterns. The Christian-centered ideology of Shakespeare's day that I've just spoken of came from Christian mythology, a story that was a comedy in its shape. The story of the salvation and redemption of mankind is a comedy because it comes out right and ends happily for all those whose opinion on the matter counts. Secular ideologies, whether progressive or revolutionary, are mostly comic plots imposed on history.

Occasionally a dramatist will remind us how we can get fooled by putting all our beliefs and values into a single story form. In Ibsen's *Ghosts* there's a dialogue between Parson Manders and Mrs. Alving, in which the parson informs Mrs. Alving how she should have gone about ordering her life. It's apparent at once that he knows nothing about the facts of her life, but he goes on talking anyway because he's commenting on the kind of drama he's assigned to God. God operates what he would call a Providence, which makes God a composer of sentimental domestic comedies. The fact that Mrs. Alving's life has been full of tragic irony doesn't get through to him: Providence would never go in for that kind of story. It's clear that Ibsen himself has no use for his parson, and the reason why he dislikes him so much is not just that he's smug and ignorant but that he believes in a God who's a third-rate dramatist: not a patch on Ibsen himself.

In a more recent play, *Amadeus,* the composer Salieri pleads with God to give him the reward of genius in return for a devout life. God ignores this plea and bestows all the genius on a grubby creep named Mozart. At the bottom of Salieri's mind was a notion that God would have bourgeois literary tastes, that the central bourgeois fable of the industrious and idle apprentice would be a favorite with him, and that he could always be counted on to enter into a dramatic situation that illustrated it. A glance at the Book of Job might have shown him that the divine mind was not confined in its choice of plots to the formulas of Horatio Alger, but such assumptions die hard, especially when they are not realized to be assumptions.

Returning to Shakespeare's theater, it is clear that there are difficulties in putting across a tragedy to an audience whose assumptions about life are unconsciously based on a mythology in the shape of a comedy. One ready-made way of meeting this difficulty is to give the tragedy a pre-Christian setting. Lear is a legendary king of Britain who was supposed to have lived around the seventh or eighth century B.C., and, although Shakespeare is as free-wheeling as ever in his allusions, introducing Saxon names like Edmund and Edgar and speaking of godsons and holy water, still there does seem to be a fairly consistent presentation of a society without Christian assumptions. The result is that the characters all make their own guesses about the shape and nature of things, or show by their behavior what they accept about it. The world-stage metaphor appears in Lear's "When we are born, we cry that we are come / To this great stage of fools."

The word *fool* is applied to practically every decent character in the play. The characters who are not fools are Goneril, Regan and Edmund particularly: for them the world is "nature," and nature is a jungle in which the predators are the privileged class. But Albany is called a "moral fool" by Goneril because he is unwilling to accept such a world; Kent is a quixotic fool because of his loyalty to an outcast king; the Fool himself is a "natural" who illustrates the proverb "Children and fools tell the truth." There is also a sense of the word that seems to be peculiar to Shakespeare: the fool as victim, as the kind of person to whom things happen. In this sense Lear calls himself "the natural fool of fortune," and it is in this sense, or a closely related one, that he speaks of the world as a stage of fools. Various characters make comments on the meaning of the events that occur to them: they are foolish comments in the sense of being the cries of victims who can't see their tormentors. Gloucester, at one point, speaks of the gods killing men for their sport; Albany, a well-meaning if rather weak man, keeps noting signs of a providence that will work out an approximate justice in things; Edgar searches for moral explanations of tragic events that make some sense when applied to Gloucester but none when applied to Lear.

In spite of all this, the action of the play seems to be heading for some kind of serenity and at least the peace of exhaustion, until there comes the final agonizing wrench of the hanging of Cordelia and the death of Lear. No one in the history of drama had ever taken such a chance before, and even Shakespeare barely got away with it. As is well known, the Restoration stage ig-

nored it and cobbled up another version in which Cordelia marries Edgar, and this version held the stage till the nineteenth
century. Even then, criticism, down to about the beginning of
the Second World War, kept talking placidly about the purgatorial shape of the tragedy, the amount of moral sense it made,
and what the good characters had learned from their suffering,
how Lear really dies of joy when he undoes his button, or Cordelia's button, and thinks she's coming to life again, and so on
and so on.

I said a moment ago that the nineteenth century put *Hamlet*
at the center of Shakespeare because it dramatized the preoccupations of the Romantics: in fact if there had been no *Hamlet*
there might not have been a Romantic movement. In the twentieth century *King Lear* came into the foreground with the exis-
tentialist movement that grew so rapidly after the French
Resistance, when it was fashionable to speak of existence as absurd. Absurd meant among other things that the providential
God who kept gimmicking his way through human history to
some kind of future happy ending was as dead as anything that
had never been alive can be. It also expressed what Browning
summed up a century earlier in the phrase "There may be heaven;
there must be hell." Justice and freedom may exist somewhere or
somehow; Hitler and Stalin are right there. The world-stage of
fools in *King Lear*, then, is the theater of the Absurd, where no
hidden benevolent design becomes manifest, where rebellion,
obedience, courage, loyalty, acceptance or rejection of religious
belief, all seem to be without direction in a world set up largely
to benefit the Gonerils and the Cornwalls.

I don't know what the central Shakespeare play will be in
the twenty-first century, assuming we reach it, but I'd place a
small bet on *Antony and Cleopatra*. Shakespeare wrote a lot of
plays on historical subjects, but it's obvious from the start that
he has no interest in anything that we call history. His play on
King John never mentions Magna Carta; his play on Richard II
never mentions the Peasants' Revolt. What he is interested in is
chronicle, the actions and interactions of the people at the top of
the social ladder. Along with this goes a close study of the kind
of dramatic performance required of a leader, especially a king.
We get an interesting sidelight on this from Henry IV, when he
is scolding Prince Hal for wasting his time carousing in the
Eastcheap tavern. He tells the prince that he is simply repeating

the follies of Richard II, who lost his crown because he was seen too often and not with the right people: "The skipping king, he ambled up and down . . . / Mingled his royalty with cap'ring fools." He says that while he was scrambling his way up to seize the crown from Richard, he put on a far better show. Its main principle was to appear in public very seldom, and, when appearing, always to make the maximum effect: "By being seldom seen, I could not stir / But like a comet I was wondered at." Well, this is his play, and perhaps it's unfair to look back to its predecessor, *Richard II*, where the report from Richard's headquarters about Bolingbroke's behavior is very different from what Bolingbroke himself later remembers of it:

> *Off goes his bonnet to an oyster-wench,*
> *A brace of draymen bade God speed him well,*
> *And had the tribute of his supple knee.*

If both Bolingbroke and Richard are right, we have the principle that the progress from hail-fellow democrat before election to austere dictator after it has been normal for many centuries.

Let's go back to what I said earlier about the two words derived from the masked actor, *hypocrite* and *person*. Hypocrite, of course, is a moral term, and person is not: it's accepted that we all need personalities, but we're not supposed to be hypocrites. At the same time, the ability to be constantly aware that one is saying one thing and thinking another requires as much self-discipline as a major virtue, and the man who can honestly say at his death that he has been a consistent hypocrite all his life has achieved an impressive ethical triumph. Unfortunately, what he is almost certain to have done instead is to start believing his own hypocrisies. But nobody, as Shakespeare presents history, can be a genuinely successful leader without the hypocrisy that goes at the very least with short views and inconsistent actions. Thus in *Richard II* Bolingbroke's first act of authority as the new king is his execution of Richard's favorites, Bushy and Green. One of his main charges against them is that they have separated the king from the queen, destroying their life together. An act or so later he is ordering a far more drastic separation of the king and queen himself, and their devotion to one another, despite Bushy and Green, is quite obvious. For leadership, especially if one is stealing a kingdom, moral principles can be dangerous hangups. New situations arise, and one does what fits the new situation, not what is consistent with what one did before.

Shakespeare, in short, would have agreed with Machiavelli, whom he had not read, that the appearance of virtue in a prince is infinitely more important than the reality. The dramatic show, the PR job, as we should call it now, must go over according to its own rules: what happens behind the scenes follows a quite different rhythm. Mark Antony in *Antony and Cleopatra,* who at times puts on a show of the greatest generosity, sends his general Ventidius out to defeat the Parthians, which Ventidius does. But when a subordinate suggests that Ventidius could win a far bigger victory if he really cleaned the Parthians up while they were demoralized and routed, he responds that if he did that Antony would soon see him as blocking his own "image," and get rid of him by some means or other.

If we ask what the motive is that keeps the leader resorting to such tricks, we can only answer in a dramatic metaphor: the desire to remain at the center of the stage. It may not even be as definite as a desire: it may be only a habit or instinct. Bolingbroke, whom Shakespeare studies carefully through three plays, owes his strength as a leader to his constant vigilance and his genius for short views. In the second part of *Henry IV* we see him tired, bothered, unable to sleep, and weary of watching the titled thugs around him with the suspicion that he'd be a fool to abandon. He breaks out once in a startling, eloquent, bitter, almost terrifying speech, in which he says that if a young man, for instance, were granted a long-term vision of his own life, seeing its progress to the end, he would simply lie down and die rather than try to live through it. His friend Warwick observes that there is a longer-range perspective to be seen within history, by which the stream of treacheries and intrigues and vicissitudes may at least look a bit more intelligible, and may even be up to a point predictable. Henry answers: "Are these things then necessities? / Then let us meet them like necessities" and goes back to his immediate problems. Bolinbroke makes a fairly impressive figure in history because he deliberately remains ignorant of history. He confines himself to the dramatic situation, and does not concern himself even with the underlying design of the play he is in. Once he took his eye off the processional aspect of the social drama, its narrative movement and changes of personnel, he would be swept off the stage. When York watches the crowd rejecting Richard II and hailing Bolingbroke as the new king, his mind goes straight to the inevitable image:

> As in a theatre the eyes of men,
> After a well-graced actor leaves the stage,
> Are idly bent on him that enters next,
> Thinking his prattle to be tedious.

In *Antony and Cleopatra* Shakespeare is confronted with a world totally unfamiliar to him, except for what his sources could tell him, but a mind like his doesn't miss much even when so handicapped. The cycles of time have brought us around to the Roman phase of history again, and so *Antony and Cleopatra* sets out a world that in most respects is much more like our world than like Shakespeare's. Here there is nothing of the Tudor mystique about hereditary succession and the lawful supremacy of the Lord's anointed: power is simply up for grabs. We are not in a closely knit kingdom any more: there is only one world, though it has two aspects. One aspect is represented by Rome, with its order, measure, law, discipline, and uniformity of action. The other aspect is centered in Egypt, the land of the over-flowing Nile, with its extravagance, barbaric splendor, and debauchery. Caesar is wholly in one world, Cleopatra wholly in the other, and Antony vacillates between them. Hundreds of messengers rush around this world bearing news, but nothing is really communicated. History of a sort is being made, and Caesar even says, when his victory has become a certainty: "The time of universal peace is near." But nobody is attending to the history: the attention is focused on the separations and reunions of a pair of horny lovers. The sexual relation, traditionally a private, even a secret relation, has become the spotlit center from which everything else radiates.

The real end of the action of the play is to take place after it concludes, with Caesar's final triumph in Rome when he returns. Caesar had naturally wanted Cleopatra to be the center of that triumph, but Cleopatra, who has spent five acts upstaging everyone in sight, is not going to be part of someone else's scene. She gets rid of Antony by Act Four and arranges the fifth act around her suicide, so that all Caesar can say, in the last lines of the play, is that his army will attend Cleopatra's funeral "in solemn show" before proceeding to Rome. The lives and fortunes of millions depend, quite literally, on the kind of motivation that inspires two or three people. The motivation turns out to be, first and last, a dramatic one: the motivation to put on a show. The stage is all the world, and human life has become what the stage is: a place where illusion is reality, with a procession of actors waiting to be applauded, nor for what they have been or done, but for what they have remembered in time to say.

The Journey
as Metaphor

A JOURNEY is a directed movement in time through space, and in the idea of a journey there are always two elements involved. One is the person making the journey; the other is the road, path, or direction taken, the simplest word for this being *way.* In all metaphorical uses of the journey these two elements appear. In pure metaphor the emphasis normally falls on the person; in proportion as we approach religious and other existential aspects of metaphorical journeys the emphasis shifts to *way.* I should like to begin with some common examples of the metaphor of journey, and see how they are intertwined with the still larger metaphors of the directions taken.

Journey is a word connected with *jour* and *journée,* and metaphorical journeys, deriving as they mostly do from slower methods of getting around, usually have at their core the conception of the day's journey, the amount of space we can cover under the cycle of the sun. By a very easy extension we get the day's journey as a further, perhaps more concentrated, metaphor for the whole of life, life being thought of as a cyclical process of birth, death, and renewed life. Thus in A. E. Housman's poem "Reveille":

> *Clay lies still, but blood's a rover;*
> *Breath's a ware that will not keep:*
> *Up, lad: when the journey's over*
> *There'll be time enough to sleep.*

Here the awakening in the morning is a metaphor for continuing the journey of life, a journey clearly ending in death. The prototype for the image is the Book of Ecclesiastes, which urges us to work while it is day, before the night comes when no man can work, and which is also dominated by the visions of life as a cyclical movement under the sun. The biblical vision includes a plug for the work ethic: in the much less realistic Housman the ethic seems to relate to war or adventure rather than simply the effort of life itself.

In the Housman poem there is also, in the background, the figure of the forking road, where one route leads to death and the other to a resuming of life. Such a figure may appear in any situation of extreme danger or despair, but it is also common in more ordinary ones: there is a famous and beautifully muted example in Frost's poem "Stopping by Woods on a Snowy Evening." Here a night traveller pauses to contemplate the stillness of the snow in the woods, which seems to express not only serenity but welcome, but he soon returns to his journey, because he still has "miles to go before I sleep." In Blake's poem "Ah! Sunflower," the flower that turns its face to the sun through its passage across the sky is the emblem of all those who have repressed or frustrated their desires to the point at which they all consolidate into a desire for the sunset of death: "Seeking after that sweet golden clime / Where the traveller's journey is done."

A journey is a movement from here to there, from point A to point B, and as a metaphor for life the two points are obviously birth and death. But this is true only of the individual: the containing way or direction is cyclical. When the cyclical movement enters the individual life, we have the form of journey we call the quest, where a hero goes out to accomplish something, kill a dragon, deliver a heroine from a giant, help destroy a hostile city, or what not. The hero of a quest first of all goes "away": that is, there must be some direction for his movement. Home, as Eliot says, is where one starts from. If the quest is successful, he normally returns home, like a baseball player, the great model for this returning journey being of course the *Odyssey*. The cyclical framework for the journey may have different emotional overtones. In a pure cycle the hero is trapped in a squirrel cage: there is nothing for him to do except to do it all over again. A rather silly example of this is in one of the romances that had some vogue in the wake of the success of Tolkien, Eddison's *The Worm Ouroboros*. The serpent with its tail in his mouth is a common emblem of an unending cycle, and when the heroes accomplish their quest in this book they invoke this emblem to repeat the whole performance, on the ground that it is so boring with nothing now to do. Other cycles are connected with evil: Psalm 12:8 tells us that the wicked travel in circles. At least, that is what the Septuagint and Vulgate say: the Hebrew and Protestant versions seem to me to make no sense.

The genuine quest-cycle is of the type in which the conclusion is the starting point renewed and transformed by the quest itself. In a way Virgil's *Aeneid* is a quest of this type: Aeneas moves from old to new Troy, setting up a new cycle of history with the same race of people. The cyclical movement is emphasized by the fact that the Trojans or Dardanides came from Italy to Asia Minor in the first place. Similarly with the biblical Exodus, the movement from Egypt to the Promised Land which is also a return to the Promised Land, and the quest of the Messiah as developed by Christian liturgy, where the Word of God begins as a person of the Trinity in the presence of God, then departs for the earth to redeem mankind, and returns to the same presence.

Let us turn to the word *way,* which is one of the commonest words in English, and is an excellent example of the extent to which language is built up on a series of metaphorical analogies. We are constantly using metaphors based on *way* without realizing it. The most common meaning of *way* in English is a method or manner of procedure, but method and manner imply some sequential repetition, and the repetition brings us to the metaphorical kernel of road or path. One *way* may be straight and another winding: such a phrase as "that's a funny way to go about it" indicates a winding one. If the situation is one where we get to the same destination whichever course we pursue, we use the word *anyway.* If we are speaking of a time when all possible journeys have been completed, we use the word *always.*

In the Bible *way* normally translates the Hebrew *derek* and the Greek *hodos,* and throughout the Bible, though very emphatically in the New Testament, there is a strong emphasis on the contrast between a straight way that takes us to our destination and a divergent way that misleads or confuses. This metaphorical contrast haunts the whole of Christian literature: we start reading Dante's *Commedia,* for example, and the third line speaks of a lost or erased way: "Che la diritta via era smarrita." Other religions are based on the same metaphor: Buddhism speaks of an eightfold path. In Chinese Taoism the word *Tao* is usually rendered *way* in English, by Arthur Waley and others, though I understand that the character representing the word is formed of radicals meaning something like "head-going." The sacred book of Taoism, the *Tao te Ching,* begins by saying that the Tao that can be talked about is not the real Tao: in other words we are being warned to beware of the traps in metaphorical language, or, in a common Oriental phrase, of confusing the moon with the finger pointing to it. But as we read on we find that the Tao can, after all, be to some extent characterized: the way is specifically the "way of the valley," the direction taken by humility, self-effacement, and the kind of relaxation, or nonaction, that makes all action effective. Tao is said also to mean art, and every art or skill is founded on sequential repetition or practice. The Middle Ages used the word *habitus* to describe the "way" in which one acquired skills: one who could read Latin was said to have the "habit" of Latin. The metaphor of road or track here seems to have a counterpart with something in the objective world, or so we gather from modern studies of the way the nervous system operates in cultivating such "habits."

The figure in the Sermon on the Mount, contrasting the straight and narrow way to salvation with the broad highway to destruction, has been the basis of a number of sustained allegories, the best known being Bunyan's *Pilgrim's Progress.* To keep the figure of a "way" going for a whole book, the course pursued has to be a very laborious one: this is theologically defensible for Bunyan, even though we can see that the difficulty of the journey is a technical as well as a religious requirement. Towards the end of the second book Bunyan says: "Some also have wished, that the next way to their Father's house were here, that they might be troubled no more with either hills or mountains to go over; but the way is the way, and there is an end." One wonders if there is not a suppressed voice also in Bunyan's mind asking: Why do we have to be stuck with a malicious and spiteful God who puts so incredibly difficult an obstacle course between ourselves and himself? In the great *danse macabre* with which the second book concludes the dying Valiant-for-Truth says: "Though with great difficulty I am got hither, yet now I do not repent me of all the trouble I have been at to arrive where I am," where the suppressed voice is almost audible.

Whatever the dissenting voices, the spatial aspects of the journey metaphor, the movement from here to there, is obviously essential to Bunyan. The City of Destruction and the City of God must be thought of as different places: there must be an explicit repudiation of the attitude that regards "the next way to their Father's house" as "here," though many equally religious poets, such as Blake, would adopt that attitude. We are here in a curious limbo of language where the metaphor seems to be something "more" than a metaphor. My own view is that every form of speech can be reduced to metaphor, but metaphor is primary language, and metaphor cannot be reduced to another kind of language: as long as we use words at all we can never escape metaphors, but only change them. I want to return to this point later.

Less dogmatic writers than Bunyan adopt more flexible forms of journeys. Even Bunyan's figure is Y-shaped, that is, there is a choice to be made between the right way and the wrong way. A similar figure turns up in Greek mythology in the story of the choice of Hercules, who chooses between pleasure and virtue in the form of a forking road. But, of course, the doctrine of original sin, and parallel doctrines in other religions, indicate that every man is on the wrong path to begin with. Hence the frequency of such themes as that of Robert Frost's "The Road Not Taken," which is based on the fact that every choice excludes every other choice, and that every life is full of roads not taken that continue to haunt us with a sense of possible missed opportunities. Eliot's *Quartets* begin by saying that some rigorously fatalistic cause-effect philosophies may tell us that the phrase "it might have been" is entirely futile, but, as soon as it has told us that, we instantly begin again with "it might have been" fantasies. The reason is ultimately that mankind took the wrong way at the fall, and all such fantasies are connected with nostalgia for the unfallen state. Here again, of course, the same theme can be treated ironically: Borges's story "The Garden of Forking Paths" encloses a number of paths within a cycle of unvarying identity.

So far we have been speaking of journeys over the surface of the earth. But in mythology our world has always been a middle earth, with different forms of experience above and below it. Once again the "above" and "below" are spatial metaphors, but metaphors that are very difficult to confine to the purely hypothetical area of the literary metaphor. Mircea Eliade tells us of the shamanism centered in Siberia, where a major part of the shaman's arduous spiritual training consists of journeys to heights and depths. The symbol of ascent may be a tree, a mountain, or a ladder. The ladder, or staircase, appears in the Book of Genesis with Jacob's vision, and the same figure of a ladder recurs in Plato's *Symposium* as the image of the progress in love from fascination with a physically beautiful object to union with the ideal form of beauty. The Greek word for ladder, *klimax,* and the Latin word, *scala,* will give us some notion of the immense proliferation of this image. Scale, or marks of degree, represents the indispensable instrument of all physical science, and nature seems to lend itself to such measurement, as in the electromagnetic ladder that runs up through the colors to gamma rays. The dependence of the art of music on the scale needs no elaboration, and it was a common view not many centuries ago that scale and degree were essential to the form of human society as well.

Very frequently the image of ascent takes the form of a spiral path going around a mountain or tower. Such towers or ziggurats were common in the ancient Near East, and the story of the Tower of Babel, which was designed to reach heaven from earth, is the demonic parody of the vision of Jacob in Genesis. According to Herodotus some of these towers had seven turnings, each colored differently to represent the seven planets. The greatest literary development of this image is of course the *Purgatorio* of Dante, where purgatory is represented as a vast mountain on the other side of the world, with seven turnings, at each of which one of the seven deadly sins is removed. At the top is the Garden of Eden, where Dante recovers his freedom of will and the original innocence that he possessed as a child of Adam before the fall. The garden at the top of the mountain descends symbolically from the chamber at the top of the ziggurat, where, according to Herodotus, the body of the god's bride was laid to await the descent of the god. The connecting symbolic link in the Bible is the identity of the Garden of Eden with the body of the bride described in the Song of Songs as "a garden enclosed, a fountain sealed." Dante passes over this identification, but two female figures, first Matilda and then Beatrice, appear at the top of the mountain, and the latter conducts Dante through another journey past the seven planets into the presence of God.

The assumption underlying such journeys is the same as the assumption underlying the chain of being, namely the assumption that every created thing has its "natural place" in the chain of being. Medieval physics even held that anything in its natural place had no weight. And yet the whole conception of a natural place ("kindly stead" is Chaucer's phrase for it) is disturbed by the fact that every creature has impelled within it a desire to return to its creator, and so until everything is in God and God is all in all, in Paul's phrase, there will still be a motive for a journey of some kind. God being above nature, there is strictly speaking no such thing as a natural place at all, at least in this eschatological context.

The immense suggestiveness of the spiral climb up the mountain may be connected with the fact that each revolution on the spiral is circumferential: that is, one acquires a complete vision or understanding of what one is doing at each stage. It has been suggested that some actual mountains may have been equipped with spiral paths for ritual purposes. One writer claims to have found such an ancient spiral climb on the Glastonbury Tor, and it is possible that some of the Psalms in the Bible, especially those marked "a song of degrees," were connected not merely with ritual pilgrimages to Jerusalem but more specifically with a climb up one of its hills, whether spirally or not. The figure itself retains its power in literature until our own time. In the seventeenth century John Donne says of Truth:

> on a huge hill
> Cragg'd, and steep, Truth stands, and he that will
> Reach her, about must, and about must go;
> And what the hill's suddenness resists, win so.

The disciples of the Renaissance grammarian in Browning's poem are not necessarily going up a spiral, but the symbolic appropriateness of ascent is as strong as ever:

> Leave we the unlettered plain its herd and crop;
> Seek we sepulture
> On a tall mountain, citied to the top,
> Crowded with culture!

In our century T. S. Eliot, in *Ash-Wednesday*, builds his poem around the figure of a staircase, modeling his metaphor explicitly on Dante's *Purgatorio*, although his earlier poetry also shows a constant fascination with the image. Contemporary with *Ash-Wednesday*, Yeats was producing books of poems with such titles as *The Tower* and *The Winding Stair*, even buying himself a round tower, of a type frequent in Ireland, to live in. James Joyce

218

was also writing at the same time the epic of *Finnegans Wake*, founded on the story of the Irish hod carrier who fell off a ladder, an event he associates on the first page of his book with the fall of man. Ezra Pound in the *Cantos* was, according to his own statement, erecting a verbal tower corresponding to those in Herodotus, whose terraces were the color of the stars.

There are, naturally enough, variant patterns of this metaphorical journey: there is the journey to the sea or the bank of a sacred river like the Ganges or Jordan, where sins are metaphorically washed off. The pilgrimage of the initiates at Eleusis, where the greatest of the Greek mysteries was held, was to the sea, and perhaps the great resonance of the cry of "the sea!" in Xenophon's *Anabasis* is connected with it. Again, Jacob saw the angels going up and down on his "ladder," and, as Donne remarks, it is interesting that the angels, who presumably can fly, are portrayed as going up and down the ladder one step at a time. In fact that dreary and totally unauthenticated story that one of the subjects discussed in the Middle Ages was the number of angels that could stand on the point of a pin probably owes what basis it has to the question of whether angels occupied space or not when they moved or simply manifested themselves in different places. The answer to the question would therefore be either none or an infinite number, depending on whether the metaphor of a journey was appropriate to angels.

In any case, angels are often invoked to account for one recurring feature of mystical experience, the involuntary journey, where a seer or visionary suddenly finds himself in a quite different place. Ezekiel in the Old Testament represents himself as being physically in Babylon with other Jewish captives, but transported to Jerusalem to see visions of its present desolation and future glory. Mohammed also had an experience, alluded to in the Koran, of a journey from Mecca to Jerusalem at night: accounts of this introduce a magic flying horse and add a further journey through the seven heavens like that of Dante. In the seventeenth century the poet Henry Vaughan, describing his conversion in his poem "Regeneration," tells us that he first climbed the mountain of morality to no purpose, and was then suddenly transported to the earthly paradise alluded to earlier:

> *With that, some cried "Away!"; straight I*
> *Obey'd, and led*

Full East, a fair, fresh field could spy
Some call'd it, Jacob's bed.

Such involuntary journeys are, of course, usually associated with a dream state, and were a common feature of shamanism, referred to earlier. We remember that in *King Lear* Edgar assumes the role of Tom o'Bedlam, and Tom o'Bedlam is associated in a ballad, first collected in the eighteenth century but quite possibly going back to something very similar in Shakespeare's day, with a shamanic vision of this kind:

With an host of furious fancies
Whereof I am commander,
With a burning spear, and a horse of air,
To the wilderness I wander.
By a knight of ghosts and shadows
I summoned am to tourney
Ten leagues beyond the wide world's end,
Methinks it is no journey.

But of course the central involuntary journey is death, where the metaphor of travelling seems inescapable. We can find an example without leaving *King Lear,* in Kent's dying speech: "I have a journey, sir, shortly to go: / My master calls me: I must not say no." Many initiate and mystery cults were founded on a practice of giving instruction to their members about what they would meet after death and how to deal with it. This aspect of journeying forms the theme of the various sacred books written for the guidance of the dying, of which the Egyptian and Tibetan Books of the Dead are the best known. The Egyptian journey was to a world very like this one, where anything dangerous or sinister could be warded off by spells or by a proclamation of one's virtue during life. This conception of a postdeath "better land" is ignored in the Old Testament, though it seems to have been well known in Greece, judging from Plato's attacks on it, and even in popular Jewish belief. But it was in Christianity that it made its most energetic revival, and a quasi-material heaven very like the ancient Egyptian one was central to most forms of Christianity as late as the nineteenth century—still is, of course, in some quarters. The Tibetan Book of the Dead, on the other hand, is set in the framework of the Buddhist belief in reincarnation. Here the recently dead soul is informed, by the reading of the book to him, that he will see a series, first of benevolent, then of wrathful, deities, and that as all these are hallucinations projected from his own mind, he should not commit himself to any belief in their substantial existence. In practically all cases the discarnate soul is assumed to wander in an intermediate world between death and birth known as "Bardo," until he is finally attracted to a female womb and enters it. Here again there is a continuing cycle within which all journeys take place.

In the majority of these journey metaphors, the journey is seldom regarded as a good thing in itself. It is undertaken because it must be: if the journey is a metaphor for life, life has to be followed to the end, but the end is the point of the journey, or at least the quality of the end is. It is conceivable, however, that a journey might have a value in itself. If so, obviously there would have to be something inside the traveller to resonate against the experience, so the theme of journeying for the sake of the experience of journeying would often be at the same time a journey into oneself. Such a journey implies not a progress along a straight path leading to a destination, as in Bunyan, but a meandering journey. Instead of going from point A to point B, the journey might have a moving series of point B's, a further B appearing in the distance as soon as one reaches the nearest one. Thus Tennyson's "Ulysses":

> I am a part of all that I have met;
> Yet all experience is an arch wherethro'
> Gleams that untravell'd world, whose margin fades
> For ever and for ever when I move.

We may contrast this with Homer's Odysseus, with his consuming passion to return home, turning down the offer of immortality itself from Calypso in order to be with his Penelope, and with Dante's Ulysses, whose restless curiosity is regarded as a kind of blasphemy, and leads him eventually to hell. Tennyson's type of journey, which is frequent in the Romantic period, is a continuous discovery, and any final destination can be only stagnation. We find such meandering journeys in the knight-errant romances of the Middle Ages, where the journey takes the form of a continuous series of adventures in a world that is never likely to run out of a sufficient supply of giants and dragons and suppliant heroines in a fix. The wrong kind of meandering journey is the labyrinth or maze. In the meander the route may be indirect or unexpected, but there is no danger of getting lost because the traveller is always where he is. In the labyrinth there are many false turnings, so that the journey may end nowhere, in a state of total confusion and loss of direction, unless a guide appears, as Ariadne with her clue appeared to Theseus.

Archaeologists have discovered many designs, going back to very ancient and primitive times, for both meander and labyrinth patterns. The meander, which seems to form part of the Avebury construction near Stonehenge, was associated by eighteenth-century antiquarians with serpent worship. Troy also seems to have been linked with similar ritual journeys, and even the word *Troy* has been derived by some scholars from Western European Celtic or Teutonic origins. In the *Aeneid* we are told of a "game of Troy," the concluding act in the war games of the fifth book, which sounds like a military tattoo or series of cavalry maneuvres, and which had a tradition passing through ancient Troy to contemporary Rome (contemporary with Virgil, that is). In the sixth book we have Aeneas' journey to the lower world, through the cave of the Sibyl, the structure of which is associated by Virgil with Daedalus, the builder of the Cretan labyrinth. Even in Romantic times, where the journey with value in itself is so frequent, we may get a labyrinthine parody, as in Shelley's *Alastor,* where the journey is a pursuit of a mocking illusion.

Throughout the Christian centuries journeys downward tended to be demonized: in the metaphorical cosmos of the Middle Ages hell was what was "down," and only the prestige of Virgil kept the convention of the downward journey going at all. It is Virgil, of course, who guides Dante through hell, hell being a descending spiral, a parody of the upward-tending spirals of purgatory and paradise. The symbolic ambiguity of the spiral meets us all through the history of symbolism: on one side there is the cornucopia, on the other the whirlpool of death. Again, journeys into the interior of the self were not common in earlier ages, because according to Christian doctrine the self was in possession of demonic forces, and one should search rather for the source of grace, such as the "cloud of unknowing" of a fourteenth-century mystical treatise.

But with the Romantic movement in particular, the sense of levels of the self below consciousness, which might be evil but might also be connected with the creative powers, or with more neutral and ambiguous phenomena, notably dreams, began to complicate the journey metaphor. Such a poem as Browning's "Childe Roland to the Dark Tower Came" describes what is clearly a journey into the self, a perilous and sinister journey towards what may very well be evil, but a journey that must be undertaken nonetheless. Perhaps the definitive modern form of this type of journey is Conrad's *Heart of Darkness,* where there is a quite credible journey into the interior of Africa, almost traceable on a map, which is at the same time a journey into the darkness of the human heart as represented by the figure of Kurtz. What is remarkable about this story is that there is really nothing strictly allegorical in it: that is, the journey to the interior of the human self and the journey to the interior of Africa are simultaneous, independent, and equally significant.

The contrast we drew earlier between the meandering and the labyrinthine journey, the journey where one keeps finding things and the journey where one gets lost, often meets us in contemporary poetry. The American poet Theodore Roethke has a poem called "Journey to the Interior," which begins: "In the long journey out of the self / There are many detours" but the journey is into the self as well, as the title suggests. We begin with the figure of a speeding car, and this suddenly stops as the self becomes motionless but the world around it continues speeding. The poem ends with an extraordinary mystical vision where all the powers of death come to life in the soul and burst into song. It is interesting to contrast the poem with another of the same title by Margaret Atwood, which tells us rather of the dangers of interior journeys, the absence of signposts and the ease of getting permanently lost. It seems to me that a significant number of contemporary Canadian poets seem to be following up the nineteenth-century theme of fascination with a huge, threatening, largely unexplored environment with a theme of exploring this environment and the poet's self at the same time. In an article on the subject I gave examples from A. M. Klein, Gwendolyn McEwen, Jay Macpherson, and others. The moral ambiguity of meeting both good and evil in the depths of the self comes out vividly in a little poem by Alden Nowlan who ascribes the same journey to St. Francis of Assisi and to Bluebeard.

T. S. Eliot tells us, on the authority of Heraclitus, that "the way up and the way down are one and the same," but Heraclitus seems to have had some conception of the journey of life as travelling in opposite directions at once, so that we are continually dying one another's lives and living one another's deaths. The meandering journey recurs in Yeats's "winding path," called in his occult cosmos the *Hodos Chameliontos,* the way that continually changes color. But there seems to be in him also a continuous unwinding of the winding path which he speaks of in his poem "Byzantium." He often associates this unwinding process with a purgatorial afterlife, but clearly this way of expressing it is not a doctrine for him, only one of several possible metaphors. The ancestry of this image goes back to the ancient theme of the cosmic dance, where movement and countermovement are of equal importance. In the great Elizabethan poem of Sir John Davies on the cosmic dance, *Orchestra,* the contradictory movements are associated also with the story of Penelope, winding and unwinding her web.

In another poem of Robert Frost, "West-Running Brook," there is a dialogue between a male and female speaker taking place on a mountain watershed where all the brooks are flowing toward the east except one that has decided to go in the opposite direction. As they continue to examine this contrary motion, the man notices an eddying movement in its current that punctuates the sequential movement toward the west with a stasis where the water seems to be standing still. He says:

> It is this backward motion toward the source,
> Against the stream, that most we see ourselves in,
> The tribute of the current to the source.
> It is from this in nature we are from.
> It is most us.

One thinks also of the journey to the source of the river at the end of Yeats's "The Tower." A modulation of this arrested movement in the journey is the interrupted journey, of which perhaps the greatest example in literature in Shakespeare's *Tempest,* the arresting of the Court Party returning from Africa to Italy and the rearranging of their lives in consequence. *The Tempest* owes a good deal to the *Aeneid,* where the midway interruption of Aeneas' journey in the visit to the lower world is also what enables him to see the point of his quest. The corresponding theme in the Bible, I should think, is the interruption of the Exodus by the death of Moses, who climbs a mountain to see the Promised Land in the distance, leaving younger successors to complete the quest. It has not been sufficiently remarked, I think, that Moses was the only man in history ever to see the Promised Land. Those who went further merely entered Canaan, and started another cycle of history.

We have seen that many of these journey metaphors come from the teaching of Jesus in the Gospels. They occur mainly in the more exoteric part of his doctrine, the Sermon on the Mount and other addresses to a public still immersed in a time-world, where it seems appropriate to suggest extensions of time, in such conceptions as "the next world" or "the afterlife," to unknown forms of existence, and to keep the metaphor of the completed journey for this life. But in the dialogues between Jesus and his disciples in the Gospel of John we seem to be in a more esoteric area. The discussion in John 14 is so familiar that it tends to slide in and out of the mind without leaving much impression, and the paralyzing paradox of what is being said misses us entirely. Jesus tells his disciples that he is going to prepare a place for them, that they know where he is going, and consequently they know the way. They protest that they don't at all know where he is going, and therefore they can't possibly know the way. Jesus' answer, "I am the way," explodes, or, as some would now say, deconstructs, the whole metaphor of journey, of the effort to go there in order to arrive here. Philip asks to be shown the Father, and gets the same type of answer: there is nothing there; everything you need is here. In the synoptics Jesus makes the same point in telling his disciples that the kingdom of heaven, the core of his teaching, is among them or within them. Nothing in Jesus' teaching seems to have been more difficult for his followers to grasp than his principle of the hereness of here.

Gertrude Stein remarked of the United States: "There is no there there," meaning, I suppose, that the beckoning call to the horizon, which had expanded the country from one ocean to the other in the nineteenth century, had now settled into a cultural uniformity in which every place was like every other place, and so equally "here." This is a kind of parody of Jesus' conception of his kingdom as here, but nevertheless it forms a useful starting point. Several religions, notably Zen Buddhism, emphasize first of all the fact that "there is nowhere to go," attempting to drive us into an intolerable claustrophobia from which there is no escape except by a kind of explosion of the ego-self into the spiritual body that is the real form of itself. Similarly with Jesus' "I am the way." Once we form part of the body of the Word which is both ourselves and infinitely larger than ourselves, the distinction between movement and rest vanishes: there is no need for a "way," because the conception "away" is no longer functional.

Metaphor, I said earlier, is primary language: every type of language can be reduced to metaphor, but when we are speaking in metaphorical language itself there can be no further reduction: we can only exchange one metaphor for another. But metaphor is normally a statement of identity, of the type "A is B." In literature metaphor is asserted only: we say that A is B, but we know quite well that A is not B and that no one is confused enough in his mental processes to think that it is. The essential point here is that literary metaphor, which is purely hypothetical, grows out of an existential type of metaphor, as we might call it, where a subject does identify himself with something not himself, in an experience that has no further need for language, although it has also fulfilled the entire function of language. As long as we say, for example, "I believe that," we are caught in a verbal trap, because we don't know who "I" is or what "that" is: all we know is that the barrier between subject and object is still there, so that we can't distinguish between what we believe and what we believe we believe, or might believe if we knew more, like Philip. But when we pass from the language of metaphor into the identities that metaphor asserts, we have reached the kind of faith the New Testament is talking about: the *hypostasis* of the hoped-for, the *elenchos* of the unseen.

IV

✧

The Double
Mirror

✧

W HAT I want mainly to talk about is my present preoccupation with the Bible, which I am trying to study in
relation to secular literature and criticism. This involves relating
it to issues in critical theory, so far as I understand them. I get a
strong impression that many contemporary critics are talking
about the Bible even when they avoid mentioning it. Many critical issues originated in the hermeneutic study of the Bible; many
critical theories are obscurely motivated by a God-is-dead syndrome that also arose from biblical criticism; many of the principles advanced by such theorists often seem to me more
defensible when applied to the Bible than they are when applied
elsewhere.

The traditional view of the Bible, as we all know, has been
that it must be regarded as "literally" true. This view of "literal"
meaning assumes that the Bible is a transparent medium of
words conveying a "true" picture of historical events and conceptual doctrines. It is a vehicle of "revelation," and revelation
means that something objective, behind the words, is being conveyed directly to the reader. It is also an "inspired" book, and
inspiration means that its authors were, so to speak, holy tape
recorders, writing at the dictation of an external spiritual power.

This view is based on an assumption about verbal truth that
needs examining. Whenever we read anything our minds are
moving in two directions at once. One direction is centripetal,
where we establish a context out of the words read; the other is
centrifugal, where we try to remember what the words mean in
the world outside. Sometimes the external meanings take on a

structure parallel to the verbal structure, and when this happens we call the verbal structure descriptive or nonliterary. Here the question of truth arises: the structure is true if it is a satisfactory counterpart to the external structure it is parallel to. If there is no external counterpart, the structure is said to be literary or imaginative, existing for its own sake, and hence often considered a form of permissible lying. If the Bible is true, tradition says, it must be a nonliterary counterpart of something outside it. It is, as Derrida would say, an absence invoking a presence, the "word of God" as book pointing to the "word of God" as speaking presence in history. It is curious that although this view of biblical meaning was intended to exalt the Bible as a uniquely sacrosanct book, it in fact turned it into a servomechanism, its words conveying truths or events that by definition were more important than the words were. The written Bible, this view is really saying, is a concession to time: as Socrates says of writing in the *Phaedrus,* it is intended only to call to mind something that has passed away from presence. The real basis of the Bible, for all theologians down to Karl Barth at least, is the presence represented by the phrase "God speaks."

We have next to try to understand how this view arose. In a primitive society (whatever we mean by primitive), there is a largely undifferentiated body of verbal material, held together by the sense of its importance to that society. This material tells the society what the society needs to know about its history, religion, class structure, and law. As society becomes more complex, these elements become more distinct and autonomous. Legend and saga develop into history; stories, sacred or secular, develop into literature; a mixture of practical knowledge and magic develops into science. Society struggles to contain these elements within its overriding concerns, and tries to impose on them a structure of authority that will keep them unified, as Christianity did in medieval times. About two generations ago there was a fashion for crying up the Middle Ages as a golden age in which all aspects of culture were unified by common sentiments and beliefs. Similar developments, with a similar appeal, are taking place today in Marxist countries.

However, artists, historians, scientists, theologians find increasingly that they make discoveries within the growing structure of their discipline, and that they owe a loyalty to that structure as well as to the concerns of society. Thus astronomers had to advance a heliocentric view of the solar system even when social anxieties demanded a geocentric one; historians of Britain had to reject the Arthurian story although popular feeling clung to it. Social authority gives ground in some areas more willingly than others. The presence pointed to by the Bible was, in practice, identified with a theological interpretation which was the right interpretation, to be understood before the Bible itself could be understood. These interpretations took different linguistic forms before and after the Reformation, but were always primarily structures of authority, intended to impose a unity on believers that was really uniformity, in public expression at least.

Such interpretations grew up partly because the verbal texture of the Bible is very different from that of descriptive writing, as a glance at it shows. A descriptive writer who aims at conveying some truth beyond his verbal structure avoids figures of speech, because all figuration emphasizes the centripetal aspect of words, and belongs either to the poetic or to the rhetorical categories. The Bible is full of explicit metaphors, hyperboles, popular etymologies, puns, in fact every figurative device possible, many of which are defined in dictionaries simply as errors of grammar or logic. But the vices of grammar and logic are often the virtues of poetry, and while no one would call the Bible a poetic structure, it has all the characteristics of poetry, which accounts for most of its very specific literary influence. Its narratives range from legend to partisan history, but historical fact as fact is nowhere marked off in it.

In short, the Bible is explicitly antireferential in structure, and deliberately blocks off any world of presence behind itself. In Christianity, everything in the Old Testament is a "type" of which the "antitype" or existential reality is in the New Testament. This turns the Bible into a double mirror reflecting only itself to itself. How do we know that the Gospel is true? Because it fulfills the prophecies of the Old Testament. But how do we know that the Old Testament prophecies are true? Because they are fulfilled by the Gospel. Is there any evidence for the existence of Jesus as a major historical figure outside the New Testament? None really, and the writers of the New Testament obviously preferred it that way. As long as we assume a historical presence behind the Bible to which it points, the phrase "word of God," as applied both to the Bible and the person of Christ, is only a dubious syllepsis. In proportion as the presence behind disappears, it becomes identified with the book, and the phrase begins to make sense. As we continue to study the significance of the fact that the Bible is a book, the sense of presence shifts from what is behind the book to what is in front of it.

As for "inspiration," if there is one thing that biblical scholarship has established beyond reasonable doubt, it is that authorship, inspired or not, counts for very little in the Bible. The third Gospel is traditionally supposed to have Luke for its author, but the gospel itself is an edited and composite document, with nothing, beyond perhaps the first four verses, of which Luke is likely to be in any real sense the author. Editing and compiling are highly self-conscious activities, and the word *inspiration* cannot add much to a study of them. If the Bible is inspired in any sense, all the glossing and editing and splicing and conflating activities must be inspired too. There is no way of distinguishing the voice of God from the voice of the Deuteronomic redactor. This suggests a qualification of the view that biblical language is poetic, however, as the poetic and the inspired are often popularly supposed to be related.

Poetic language is closely associated with rhetorical language, as both make extensive use of figures of speech. The Bible uses a language that is as poetic as it can be without actually becoming a poem. But it is not a poem; it is written in a mode of rhetoric, though it is rhetoric of a special kind, called by the theologian Bultmann, among others, *kerygma* or "proclamation." In a last effort to evoke the ghost of the referential, Bultmann says that to see this *kerygma* in the Gospels we must get rid of myth, which he regards as an obstacle to it. To a critic, however, myth means primarily *mythos* or narrative, more particularly the kind of self-contained narrative which is meant by the English word *story* in contrast to history. Such myth is the only possible vehicle of *kerygma,* and as every syllable of the Gospels is written in the language of myth, efforts to demythologize the Gospels would soon end by obliterating them.

The literal meaning of the Bible, then, if we are right, must be a mythical and metaphorical meaning. It is only when we are reading as we read poetry that we can take the word *literal* seriously, accepting everything given us without question. There may be meanings beyond the literal, but that is where we start. In teaching the Bible I stress the unity and consistency of its narrative and imagery, and at some point a student will ask:

"Why can't we have it both ways? Why not a body of narrative and imagery that is also a definitive replica of truths beyond itself?" The answer is that description is a subordinate function of words. Even one word is a sign and not a thing: two or three words begin to form grammatical fictions like those of subject and predicate. What words do with greatest power and accuracy is hang together. Of course there are verbal structures that are based on description and reference, but the Bible is too deeply rooted in the nature of words to be one of them. At a certain point of intensity a choice must be made between figurative and descriptive language, and the Bible's choice of the figurative is written on every page of it.

Questions of biblical criticism, we see, are models for many critical questions about secular literature. When I began the study of literature as a student, it was generally assumed that the critic's duty was to work out an "interpretation" of the poem before him, and that when all the really expert critics compared their interpretations a consensus would emerge that would be, more or less, the right way to look at the poem. The fact that no such consensus ever emerged was a problem to faith, but nothing more. I now feel that the word *interpretation* is a red herring: to be given a poem and look round for an interpretation of it is like being given the kernel of a nut and looking round for a shell, which seems to me as perverse an approach to poems as it is to nuts. What I do think is that the text before us is something other than ourselves, that we have to struggle with it as Jacob did with the angel, but that there is nothing to come up from behind, like the Prussian army at Waterloo, to assist us. The otherness is the text itself. However, we are not quite as much on our own as Jacob was: there are other critics, and we do become increasingly aware that a text is the focus of a community.

This does not mean that all critics are going to agree any better than before, but that in their disagreements an element that we may call the egocentric can get gradually diminished. It was Oscar Wilde who defined, in two almost unreasonably brilliant essays, the situation of criticism today. One was called "The Decay of Lying," which attacked the view that literature gains dignity and validity from its reference to something beyond itself. The word *lying* calls attention to the fact that literature turns its back on all such reference. The other was called "The Critic as Artist," which promoted the reader to a co-creator with the poet, completing the operation that the poet is compelled to leave half done. By a *critic* Wilde meant, I think, a serious and representative reader, who knows that his response is socially and culturally conditioned, but is nonetheless capable of weeding out of that response an egocentric element, such as: "I don't like the way this poem ends because if I were writing it I wouldn't end it that way." I have always connected this egocentric element with the conception of the critic as judge or evaluator. It is a commonplace now that observation is affected by the observer, even in the most quantitative sciences, and the necessity for observing the observer is now fairly acute in literary criticism. What I think happens is a struggle for identity in the course of which the false subject or ego and the false object or the referential signified get thrown out together.

In ordinary experience we think of ourselves as subjective, and of everything else as objective. We also tend to think of the objective as the center of reality and the subjective as the center of illusion. But then we enter a theater and find that an illusion is presented to us on the stage objectively, as a sense datum. We could search the wings and dressing rooms forever without finding reality behind it: whatever is there that is not the play is in front of it, in the mood created in the audience. What reality there is seems to be emerging from the coinciding of two illusions. Thus in *The Tempest*, Prospero takes a group of people living in a reality so low as to be a form of illusion, soaks them in a different kind of illusion featuring hallucinations and elemental spirits, and sends them back home on a much higher level of reality.

We referred to Socrates' remark in the *Phaedrus* that the inventor of writing was told by his critics that his was not an art of memory (*mneme*) but of reminding (*hypomnomena*). What his critics did not realize was that the act of recalling is a far more vivid and intense experience than memory itself. When Elizabethan critics used Horace's phrase about poetry as a "speaking picture," they implied that poetry gives us, not the familiar remembered thing, but the glittering intensity of the summoned-up hallucination. On this basis we can perhaps understand the long-standing association between written books and the art of magic, another theme of *The Tempest*. Without his books, says Caliban, Prospero would be as much of a sot as I am. Magic establishes a charmed circle where spirits can be invoked, held, and commanded by words, and in this unity of word and spirit we have perhaps the most genuine form of an altered state of consciousness. It has often been noted that the question of human freedom cannot be worked out on the basis of the relation of man and nature alone. As our view of the world becomes more objective, the question arises of what is not objective. For everything we see in ourselves is objective also. What is left can only be, as I think, our participation in a community of language, whether the language is that of words, mathematics, or one of the other arts. This is all that can really be distinguished from the objective world. As Nietzsche said, nature has no laws, only necessities; and just as we find our conception of necessity in the physical world, so we find in the languages of words and numbers and arts the charter of our freedom.

We notice that while the Bible ends with a vision of the end of time and of history as we have known it, it is a remarkably open ending. It ends with an invitation to "come" or approach, under the image of drinking the water of life. The implication is that its reality starts in the reader's mind as soon as he finishes reading. Milton speaks of the Word of God in the heart, the possession of the Word by the reader, as having an authority higher than that of the Bible itself. Milton was not concerned about the chaos of "private judgment," the individual setting himself up as the measure of all things, because in his view the real reader was not the ego but the Holy Spirit, who would unite all readers without forcing them into uniformity.

Once again the biblical principle is an analogy to procedures in secular criticism. If we say that authorship, inspiration, historical accuracy and the like are not important in the Bible, what is important? One thing that seems to me to be so is the conception of canon, the idea of a collection of books unified, not by consistency of argument or doctrine—there are no true rational arguments in the Bible—but of vision and imagery. There are no definable boundaries between canonical and uncanonical, but there are different areas or contexts, where some things are closer to us than others. Culture begins, we said, in a largely undifferentiated mixture of religious, historical, legal, and literary material which is important to the concerns of its society. It seems to be ending today in a vast chaos of *écriture* where there are no

235

boundary lines between literature and anything else in words. Of course there are no boundary lines; but I think that when the present plague of darkness has lifted we shall start making discriminations again. We shall, I think, even reestablish the referential for the verbal structures that clearly require it, which would still exclude literature and the Bible. But our new discriminations will be contexts and not delimited areas. Such a word as *comedy* means something intelligible, and has conveyed an intelligible meaning for thousands of years. But there is no such "thing" as comedy: it cannot be defined as an essence which excludes other essences. We can express only its general range and ambience, and our feeling that sometimes we are inside it and at other times on its periphery or outside it.

Similarly, there is a canon in secular as in sacred literature, though there is no way of establishing such a canon on a basis of value judgments. In those passages in the New Testament where the Bible has become self-conscious enough to comment on itself, we are told that the word of God is a two-edged sword, dividing things and not reconciling things. But this can hardly mean a dialectical instrument of the Hegelian kind, where every statement is a half-truth implying its own opposite. The real division is rather between the two worlds of spiritual life and spiritual death, and this division is made by a use of language that bypasses the argumentative and the aggressive. Much the same thing is true of secular literature. The word *classic* as applied to a work of literature means primarily a work that refuses to go away, that remains confronting us until we do something about it, which means also doing something about ourselves.

The main difference is one of initiative. The rhetoric of proclamation is a welcoming and approaching rhetoric, in contrast to rhetoric where the aim is victory in argument or drawing an audience together into a more exclusive unit. It speaks, according to Paul, the language of love, which he says is likely to last longer than most forms of communication. Wherever there is love there is sexual symbolism, and the rhetoric of the Bible, which seeks out its reader, is traditionally a male rhetoric, all its readers, whether men or women, being symbolically female. In secular literature, where the category is purely poetic, the sexual symbolism is reversed: there it is the poetic artifact that is symbolically female, the daughter of a Muse. These are metaphors, and of course any metaphor can be misleading or confusing. But metaphor was made for man and not man for metaphor; or, as my late and much beloved colleague Marshall McLuhan used to say, man's reach should exceed his grasp, or what's a metaphor?

The Mythical
Approach
to Creation

✧

THE TITLE of this paper is slightly misleading. Creation is a myth, and there are no mythical "approaches" to it because there are no nonmythical ones. What I want to discuss is the progression of three phases in the social use of myth, the pre-literary, the literary, and the postliterary, as illustrated by the creation myths in Genesis.

To summarize first of all my general view of myth: a myth to me is primarily a *mythos,* a story, narrative, or plot, with a specific social function. Every human society has a verbal culture, and in the preliterary phase, when abstract thought has not developed, the bulk of this culture consists of stories. Usually there then arises a distinction between stories which explain to their hearers something that those hearers need to know about the religion, history, law, or social system of their society, and less serious stories told primarily for amusement. The more serious group are the myths: they grow out of a specific society and transmit a cultural heritage of shared allusion. We may call the myth a verbal *temenos,* a circle drawn around a sacred or numinous area. The less serious group become folktales, which travel freely over the world through all barriers of language. Myths travel too, but they tend to keep settling down: thus Sumerian myths eventually expanded into the Hittite area, and from there into archaic Greece.

Preliterary myth arises in a state of society in which there is not as yet a firm and consistent distinction between subject and

238

object. A statement that a subjective A is an objective B is a metaphor, and at the center of preliterary myths are the gods, who, being partly personalities and partly associated with some department of nature, are ready-made metaphors. It has been said that there are no metaphors in Homer, but in another sense Homer is all metaphor: what goes on inside the human heart, such as *thymos,* are events of the same entity as storms and the like in nature. The appearance of a god or goddess in the form of a well-known friend is unusual but quite in accord with the ways of gods. In Christianity a divine nature taking on a human form is a portentous miracle that can happen only once in history, but such a view is very remote from Homer. Again, the primary question about a preliterary myth is not Is it true?, because the linguistic problems in establishing verbal truth are not yet in the foreground. The primary question is something more like Do we have to know this?, and the affirmative answer characterizes the genuine preliterary myth.

As culture becomes more pluralistic and specialized, the conception of literature more or less as we know it comes into the foreground. The Homeric poems, for early Greek culture, were primarily writings that educated Greeks had to know, but for us they are safely within the category of literature. But as soon as that category is clearly recognized, the question arises that led Plato to attack not only Homer but all poets: What kind of verbal structure conveys truth?

In the popular mind there is only one way in which words can express truth, and that is the truth of correspondence, where a body of words describes a set of external facts or events or propositions, and is said to be true if we find the correspondence of the words and what they describe satisfactory. The basis of literature, of course, is hypothetical: we know, for example, that Jane Austen tells us a good deal of truth about Regency society, but the framework of her story is about people with no historical existence. The next step is the preposterous dilemma of an antithesis between truth of correspondence and all other uses of words. If truth of correspondence is the only form of verbal truth, then all literary or mythical structures are essentially untrue, and while nonliterary structures may be true or false, all true structures must be nonliterary.

This imaginary antithesis has been thrashed over so often, from Aristotle's *Poetics* on, that we may well feel that the question

is obsolete. I wish it were. As it is, the religious bodies maintaining that revelation must be either literally true or else untrue
are the ones that are most dramatically increasing their member-
ship, appeal to the most devoted followers, and take in the most
money, and we must either join or imitate them if we want that
kind of success. A newspaper controversy can still be stirred up
whenever a prominent churchman announces that he does not
"literally believe in" the Virgin Birth or whatever, the statement
being taken on all sides as heretical rather than as simply illiterate. The Bible is mythical rather than historical, because for its
purposes myth is the only vehicle for what has traditionally been
called revelation. But anyone who points this out is still likely
to be called antihistorical.

It is generally accepted that the opening words of the Gospel of John, "In the beginning was the Word," were intended to
form a Christian commentary on at least the first of the two
creation myths of the Bible. The verse in Genesis, "And God
said, Let there be light: and there was light," implies for Christian commentary that the Word was the creative power that
brought the thing it named into being. I have elsewhere called
attention to the curious passage in Goethe's *Faust,* where Faust is
confronted with the opening words of John, refuses to accept
them, and eventually produces the mistranslation "In the beginning was the deed [or act]." I should have added that this in fact
has been also the traditional Christian translation too, however
much a reversal of what is being said. The assumption is still
that in the beginning God did something, and the words are
servomechanisms telling us what he did. There can be no "literal" belief in the creation, or in anything else, without the inference that what God did was prior in significance to whatever
anyone, including God, said about it. In the cultural disputes of
the early years of the Bolshevist revolution in Russia, Trotsky
attacked the formalists of his day by saying that they were bourgeois idealists who believed that in the beginning was the Word,
whereas all good Marxists, being dialectical materialists, knew
that in the beginning was the deed. One can understand such a
view in Marxism, but for Christianity to use words to decry the
primacy of the Word seems very strange. If the Word is the beginning, it is the end too, the Omega as well as the Alpha, and
what this principle indicates is that to receive the revelation of
the Bible we must examine the total verbal structure of the

Bible. This implies a deliberate and conscious renouncing of what is called "literal" belief, which always means subordinating the Word to what the Word is alleged to describe.

Myths, I have often said, stick together to form a mythology, unlike folktales, which simply interchange themes and motifs so stereotyped that they can be counted and indexed. One reason why I have said it so often is that works of literature, which grow out of mythology, also stick together, but we have no word corresponding to *mythology* that expresses the unity that works of literature make up. However, a mythology nearly always begins with some form of creation myth, and all other myths unfold from it. A creation myth is in a sense the only myth we need, all other myths being implied in it. Some critics, notably Coleridge, also think that the only theory of literature we need is a theory of creativity, of how works of literature begin to be. Anyway, the Bible certainly begins with the theme of creation, and it is common knowledge that in the Book of Genesis there are two creation myths. The one in the first chapter, and the first three verses of the second, is usually called the Priestly account; the one that runs from Genesis 2:4 to the end of the second chapter is called the Jahwist account, from the name it uses for God. The Jahwist one is considerably earlier than the Priestly account, which is almost certainly postexilic, the textual order being the reverse of the chronological one.

The Priestly account, as we all know, is divided into seven stages, each being assigned a day of a week. First comes the creation of light, then of the "firmament" or sky separating upper and lower waters, then of vegetation, then of the sun, moon, and stars, then the creatures of water and air, then of the land animals, including human beings, and finally an archetypal Sabbath or day of rest. The Jahwist account may also be divided into seven stages. First, a "mist" or irrigating fountain is set up in the middle of a dry, parched earth. Second, the first human being is created, whom we may call "the being" or "the adam" with a lower-case *A*. Third comes the creation of the garden; fourth the creation of the four rivers, fifth the creation of living creatures other than humans, sixth, the creation of the first woman out of the body of the "adam," and finally the statement, a human Sabbath corresponding to that of the other account, that the two

241

human beings were in the state of innocence, naked and not ashamed.

In the Priestly narrative there is a strong emphasis on division and contrast: light is separated from darkness, land from sea, the "firmament" from chaos. The kinship of human beings to the land animals is clearly recognized, and men and women are created together. As in the Jahwist account, humanity forms the climactic work of creation, but in the Jahwist account human beings are in a totally different category from everything else that lives. The Priestly account is a vision of creation largely in terms of what was later to be called *natura naturata,* a cosmic structure or system reaching from chaos up through the human to the divine. The Jahwist account sees rather a *natura naturans,* a growing fertile nature with humanity at its center.

Neither creation myth is a serious attempt to tell us the history of how the order of nature came into being. If either had ever been intended to do so, one would have expected the Priestly account, for example, to be just a little cleverer, and not had the world of vegetation created before the sun was. God's phrase when he creates the sun and moon, "let them be for signs," indicates that in the context of creation the sun and moon are elements of a calendar. But here we have something rather more than the fussiness of a pedantic deity making sure that his festivals are going to be celebrated at the right time. What is actually coming into being is the human consciousness, and what is being presented to that consciousness is the sense of order and design in the universe that has prompted every creative effort in human arts and sciences. Similarly, the day of rest at the end is not merely an explanation of the origin of the Sabbath: it means among other things that the creation has become objective to its Creator, which implies that it must become objective to human consciousness also. The Priestly cosmos is something to be contemplated and admired, and the door is left open for the later conception of nature as a second book or Word of God for man to read, as well as for all the feelings of wonder and awe and beauty that are central to the conscious human heritage.

Similarly, in the Jahwist account the vision of two human beings naked and unashamed is the culmination of a vision of creation as a home for conscious beings, a world where nature is not simply the human environment but an extension of humanity itself, with nothing of the alienation that it now has. The fact that human consciousness is the mirror of creation is symbolized by the bringing of land and air animals to the adam to be named, the bestowing of names being clearly regarded as a necessary completion of the creative process. This seemed so important to the God of Milton's *Paradise Lost* that he is constrained to add, somewhat apologetically, "Understand the same of fishes." Both creation myths are structures of human concern, but the ascribing of the creative process to God indicates that what is opened to humanity in the vision of the cosmos is infinite, and that we shall never find ourselves permanently in the position of Narcissus, gazing into a verbal and mathematical mirror of our own divising.

The fact that in the Jahwist account woman is created out of the body of the adam led to later speculation, in the Cabala and elsewhere, that the original adam must have been androgynous, becoming male only after a female principle had been separated from it. The story of the fall is attached to the Jahwist narrative, and that story tells us that the woman took the initiative in breaking the divine prohibition regarding the tree of knowledge. This was of course a standard proof-text, for many centuries, rationalizing a patriarchal social system, and in fact the Jahwist account itself says that patriarchy would result from the fall. Commentary has been so anxious to make this point that it has overlooked the fact that the creation of woman is placed at the end of this creation account, as the climax of the whole procedure. Besides, the conception of fall is unintelligible without its complement of reconciliation. Humanity falls as woman, that is, as sexual being, and it is clear that the eating of forbidden fruit has a good deal to do with the loss of innocence and the developing of the sexual relation as we now know it, or what D. H. Lawrence calls sex in the head. In the Jahwist account, as in so many forms of social psychology today, morality, the knowledge of good and evil, is founded on the repressing or sublimating of the sexual instinct. But if humanity falls as woman, humanity must be redeemed as woman. In Christian typology the souls of all human creatures, whether they are biologically men or women, are symbolically female, forming the body of the bride Jerusalem or the people of God. The Virgin Mary in Catholic thought is placed at the head of all created human beings,

243

below only the Jesus who was begotten, and she is the second Eve in much the same sense that Jesus, in the Pauline phrase, is the second Adam.

There is no myth of fall attached to the Priestly account directly, but later legend and commentary filled up the blank with myths of a fall, not of human nature from a paradisal garden, but of demonic nature from a divine court. We have the story of Lilith, alleged to be the first wife of Adam, and the mother of all devils, and the story of the fall of Satan after a war in heaven. The two myths were of course combined later, when the serpent who initiated the fall of Adam and Eve, and who is nothing but a serpent in the Jahwist account, is assumed to be a mouthpiece for Satan. The fall of the rebel angels is referred to in the New Testament, but is most elaborately recounted in the Book of Enoch.

At this point I have to invoke a critical principle I have often mentioned before, a sequence of two acts in the critical operation. Once we "hear" a *mythos* or story being read, or read it ourselves in temporal sequence, we then make a *gestalt* or simultaneous apprehension of it which is usually described in a visual metaphor as an act of "seeing." Someone about to tell a joke may say, regrettably, "Have you heard this one?" After we have heard it, we then "see" the joke, grasp its simultaneous meaning, or what Aristotle would call its *dianoia*. But once we "see" the joke we do not want to hear it again. Similarly, we may read to the end of a detective story to "see" who the murderer is, but once we have discovered his identity we normally do not want to read the book again until we have forgotten it. Other *mythoi*, such as those used in religious rituals, show the same transition from hearing to metaphorical seeing. The reading of the Collect in the mass is followed by the elevation of the host; in the initiation rites at Eleusis, we are told, the initiates were shown a reaped ear of corn as the climax of the revelation involved; according to Zen Buddhism, after the Buddha had completed a sermon he held up a golden flower, the only listener who got the point being, of course, the founder of Zen. Every work of literature makes an appeal to us to grasp its total meaning in a single act of apprehension, and it is a common device for a novel, let us say, to bear the title of some visual emblem which symbolizes that total apprehension. Examples would include

Henry James's *The Golden Bowl,* D. H. Lawrence's *The Rainbow,* and Virginia Woolf's *To the Lighthouse.*

It is because of the importance of this attempt at simultaneous understanding that the word *structure,* a spatial metaphor derived from architecture, has become so prominent in literary criticism. What we call a "classic" in literature is often a literary work so complex that understanding the "structure" becomes an indefinite and tentative sequence of responses. If we are presented with something like *King Lear,* we hear or read the play, and make an effort to understand what it means as a whole. We are soon oppressed by the inadequacy of this effort; we must hear or read it again and make a better attempt, and a process is started that could conceivably go on all through one's life, at least if one is professionally concerned with literature. In my book *The Great Code* I made a tentative effort to outline the "structure" of the Christian Bible when we attempt to "see" it as a totality, and found, not to my surprise, that the Book of Revelation at the end of the New Testament provided the best guide to that structure. Here I shall attempt to suggest a rough outline of the "structure" of the two creation myths, although, remembering that the two narratives were read as one for practically their whole history, we cannot separate them, beyond noting a few degrees of difference in emphasis.

The visual "emblem" of the structure of the creative narratives, corresponding to the examples given from secular literature, Henry James's golden bowl or Lawrence's rainbow, would obviously be some form of *axis mundi* image, something that suggests the linking of all aspects of the creation in a single concept. For the Priestly account the most natural form of *axis mundi* image would be the ladder, or staircase, of Jacob's great vision at Bethel, an image of which mountains and towers are predictable modulations. For the Jahwist account the readiest image would be the world tree, or tree of life, that stretches from earth to heaven in so many mythologies—so many, in fact, that it does not appear in the Bible except in parody form, though it is implied frequently enough.

One of the most important facts in the history of religion is that in later thought the cosmological ladder is assumed to represent a structure of hierarchy, order, rank, and degree. God is at the top of the cosmos; his court of angels, who are apparently

245

being addressed in Genesis 3:22, would rank next. Then comes the paradisal home of man, taken from the Jahwist account, then the world of nature we see about us, also in ranks, with human beings at the top, then animals, plants, inorganic matter, and, at the bottom, the chaos or "face of the waters" mentioned at the beginning.

Two by-products of this ladder cosmos have been of particular importance in the history of thought: the great chain of being and the Ptolemaic universe. The first was a ladder of existence polarized by the conceptions of form and matter, and stretched from pure form without matter, or God, at the top to chaos at the bottom, chaos being as close as we can get to pure matter without form. Evil, the world of the devils, comes below this, but is not part of the order of nature. The Ptolemaic universe similarly stretched from a primum mobile, a circumference of a finite universe, down through the starry and planetary spheres to the "fallen" world of four elements. Every aspect of creation had its own stratified hierarchy. The metals, for example, were the aristocrats of the mineral world, and even they were subdivided into the noble metals, gold and silver, and the tin and lead that we still call the "base" metals.

A vision of the cosmos as essentially a structure of authority and degree naturally commended itself to all social establishments, and this view of creation lasted for so many centuries because it seemed to justify and rationalize a society similarly based. A society with a sovereign at the top, and aristocracy underneath, and stratified groups of commoners below that, was clearly the "natural" way for human beings to organize themselves, imitating as it did the originally created order. That is why the domain of evil, of the hell that Milton places below chaos, is not part of the order of nature: rebellion against God being totally unnatural, rebellion in human society is similarly unnatural. This hierarchical world consolidates into four main levels: the highest is that of heaven, in the sense of the presence of God, the next the paradisal home originally intended for man, the next the theologically "fallen" natural environment we live in now, and at the bottom is the demonic order. Man is born into the third of these worlds, and his essential quest is to try to raise himself, with the assistance of divine grace and such accredited human aids as institutional religion and social authority, as near as he can to the second level in the Garden of Eden which is his proper home. The Garden of Eden has disappeared as a place, but persists as an inner state of mind. However, the phrase I just used, "try to raise himself," is ungrammatical, because all initiative must come from above.

But whatever authority itself may say, nonetheless wherever there is authority there is also at least some conception of potential resistance to that authority, and, as we said, the later legends of the rebel angels tell us that there has even been resistance to the authority of God himself. We are told that close behind the Priestly account in Genesis lies a much older myth in which creation took the form of a victory over a dragon, out of whose body the cosmos was formed. Many biblical writers, including those in Isaiah, Ezekiel and the Psalms, are familiar with the dragon-killing myth as a poetic symbol for the creation, and for them the dragon-killing is associated not only with the original creation, but with the deliverance from Egypt and the final restoration of Israel. The Book of Job seems to have a particularly close relationship to the Priestly account, in the way that it sees the suffering of man as a battleground of divine and demonic cosmic forces. At the beginning we have a very puzzling dialogue between God and a Satan who is a tolerated guest in God's court; at the end we have a speaking God pointing out to Job the monstrous dragon from whom Job has apparently been delivered.

The Jahwist account, starting as it does with God as concerned with gardens, trees, and landscape rather than cosmic order, has bequeathed to later ages the sense of God as a benevolent designer who made all things for the convenience of man. It is largely this account that kept the criticism of the arts in so infantile a state for so many centuries, for here God himself is the supreme artist, and no human art can be more than the faintest of shadows of his workmanship. Man's primary destiny, we said, is to try to return to his original paradisal home in which nature and art are the same thing, nature being, as Sir Thomas Browne remarked, the art of God. Another remark of Browne, referring to arguments from design and the doctrine that God made all things in nature primarily for human use, shows how far we have come from thinking in these terms: "How America abounded with Beasts of prey and noxious Animals, yet contained not in it that necessary Creature, a Horse, is very strange."

More important even than the conception of divine design in the Jahwist narrative is the suggestion of a fall in sexual ex-

247

perience through eating of the tree of morality. Just as the Priestly narrative has a particularly close relation to the Book of Job, so the Jahwist one is symbolically close to the Song of Songs, that wonderful group of love poems in which a paradisal retreat, "a garden enclosed, a fountain sealed," is identified with the body of the bride. Here we meet another kind of ladder, the one that appeared in Plato's *Symposium* outside the biblical tradition entirely, but was later forced on an unwilling Christian bureaucracy by the poets. In the Middle Ages a quest of love, so closely approximating the regeneration of the soul in orthodox Christianity as to amount to a parody of it, was established as a central theme of literature. Such a quest of love may be sublimated and devoid of explicit sexuality, as it is in Dante, or it may retain the theme of sexual union, as it does in *The Romaunt of the Rose.* But we are never far from the sense that the ultimate quest is not so much the sexual union of a man and a woman as the union of all human beings with the nature that forms their environment, a nature usually mythologized as a mother, in which the primitive metaphorical identity of the subjective and the objective has been reestablished.

Every central image in the Bible has its ideal or apocalyptic form, the one suggested by God to his people, and its demonic or parodied form, the one worshipped by the heathen kingdoms without. The world-tree image, we said, appears chiefly in the parody form, notably in Ezekiel and Daniel; the ladder image finds its parody in the story of the Tower of Babel. In Mesopotamian cities the temple or home of the god normally stood in the center, and thus symbolically formed a link between heaven and earth. A common feature of such ziggurats, as they are called, was a spiral staircase, and according to Herodotus there were often seven of these staircases, each colored differently to represent the seven known planets. At the top of the building, Herodotus says, was the chamber in which the body of the bride was laid to await the descent of the god. Babel is not said to be spiral in shape, though portrayed as such in Brueghel's picture and elsewhere, but the figure of the spiral tower or mountain runs through Mithraic symbolism and reappears in a Christian setting in Dante's *Purgatorio,* where there are again seven complete turns, each one removing one of the seven deadly sins, and here again the original paradise of Eden, the enclosed garden and sealed fountain which is the body of redeemed humanity, the bride of God, appears at the top.

The cosmos of authority lingered until the eighteenth century, although of its two pillars, the chain of being and the Ptolemaic universe, the latter was in ruins by Isaac Newton's time. The chain of being was still in place for Pope early in the eighteenth century, but Voltaire was very doubtful about the *échelle de l'infini,* which he recognized to be a facade for the authority of the status quo. And under the hammer blows of the American Revolution, the French Revolution and the Industrial Revolution, the ladder as a spatial metaphor for the *axis mundi,* and as a cosmic vision guaranteeing the birthright of established authority, finally disappeared.

The effects of this in literature are what I am particularly concerned with, and they can be traced through the Romantic movement down to our own time. Let us look, as an example, at the imagery of four poets of the early part of this century, T. S. Eliot, W. B. Yeats, Ezra Pound, and James Joyce. In his early poetry Eliot seems fascinated by the staircase as an image of crisis: such a line as "Time to turn back and descend the stair" from *Prufrock* reminds us that our word *climax* comes from the Greek word for a ladder. In *Ash-Wednesday* we have a much more elaborate staircase, avowedly taken from Dante's *Purgatorio,* where the soul journeys from the seashore of experience and nostalgia to a garden at the top. Yeats, though he maintains that all ladders are planted in the human heart, is full of "tower" and "winding stair" images, where a "soul" ascends to the annihilating of its ego-center and a "self" descends to a new life. He even bought one of the round towers with spiral staircases that still exist in Ireland as a personal symbol.

Ezra Pound begins his *Cantos* with an adaptation of the descent to the lower world in the *Odyssey,* where Ulysses first meets Elpenor, one of his crew who had fallen off a ladder and broken his neck, and then goes on to the central image of the spiral tower of Herodotus with its seven turnings, each colored differently to represent the seven planets. Even the terrible experience of being locked in a cage during the Second World War did not prevent the Pisan Cantos from beginning defiantly with the resolve to "build the city of Dioce whose terraces are the color of stars." Joyce's *Finnegans Wake* is founded on a ballad about an Irish hod carrier who, like Elpenor, fell off a ladder and broke his neck, later coming to life at his funeral wake to demand a share of the whisky. In Joyce the fall of Finnegan is associated with the fall of Adam and the flood of Noah on the first page: Finnegan himself, however, is dissuaded by the other members of the wake from waking up, so he continues to sleep and dream, his dream being the turning cycle of human history.

The use of this ancient ladder or staircase image by the four leading poets of their generation does not mean that any of them, even Eliot, have any interest in trying to set up the old cosmic image of social authority once again. What they are producing is a series of what it is now fashionable to call "deconstructions" of that image. Deconstruction, however, is in itself, I think, a birdshot critical technique: it aims at a variety of targets and bags whatever it happens to hit accidentally. I think the "deconstructions" going on in regard to this image have a more restricted aim, and are not simply a series of Darwinian mutations thrown out at random.

I said that the Priestly account of creation suggests a hierarchical ladder stretching from the divine to the demonic. One of the central themes of Romanticism, and one that crystallizes mainly around the figure of Byron, is the annexing of the demonic to the human. It is man who works evil and creates hell, or, as the Romantic poet Beddoes remarked: "There's but one devil ever tempts a man, / And his name's Self." The next stage is the separating of the real evil that man does from the activity that is merely assumed to be evil by those devoted to the status quo: the revolutionary acts, including most of the genuinely creative ones, that threaten authority. In English literature the most powerful treatment of this distinction is Blake's *Marriage of Heaven and Hell,* which lays down the program that all Blake's later work follows. Humanity is ruled by inertia and terror: the expression of human energy threatens this; consequently human energy, which is rooted in the sexual instinct, is condemned as evil. There certainly is such a thing as real evil, but most of that comes from the defenders of established authority, who find cruelty essential to their ascendancy. This is a conception of human liberty that sees liberty as a birthright that man can and should lay claim to. It is a view of liberty similar to those of, say, Jefferson or Shelley, but very different from earlier theories. Even the revolutionary Milton did not think of liberty as anything that man wanted: man is terrified of the maturity and responsibility that liberty brings with it. Liberty is good for man because it is something that God wants man to have; but the initiative must come from the divine grace that is above man on the scale of being. After the Romantic movement, however, the ladder of being became a two-way staircase, with ascent as well as descent, just as Jacob originally saw it. For if the demonic is really an aspect of the human, the angelic is too: man has titanic powers for both construction and destruction that he has never consistently used, except in the service of the wrong kind of authority. The cosmic ladder reconstructed in this form is, mythologically, the liberation of Prometheus, and it is certainly no accident that Shelley's poetic masterpiece is called *Prometheus Unbound.*

The Jahwist myth of creation, where man falls out of the state of innocence into a state of sexual repression and alienation from nature, had always had its countermovement in the cult of Eros, which, as I observed, had been forced on European culture in the Christian period by the poets. Naturally the cult of Eros continued and expanded in the Romantic period: we may notice two aspects of this expansion here. In the first place, the traditional ladder goes down into the demonic world; consequently, in spite of the prestige of Virgil, who in the sixth book of the *Aeneid* gave so memorable a vision of a descent to a lower world, there are very few such quests in Christian literature, apart from descents to hell like Dante's *Inferno.* But after the Romantic period descent themes become much more frequent, and, above all, the lower world comes to be associated with the world of dreams, which are soon recognized to be closely linked to the creative powers. In the second place, Romantic love poetry often touches on the theme of regeneration of nature. In the "Introduction" to the *Songs of Experience* in Blake, the "lapsed Soul," or what falls at the beginning of time, is not Adam or Eve but a female "Earth" (the "adamah" of Genesis 3:7) who contains humanity as well as its paradisal environment. Similarly, the poet proposes to his beloved in Shelley's *Epipsychidion* a union that includes much more than the merging of two human bodies:

> *Let us become the overhanging day,*
> *The living soul of this Elysian isle,*

251

Conscious, inseparable, one.

The influence of the two creation myths as I have sketched it illustrates most of the major features of the social function of myth. First, a myth has two aspects: it is part of a vision of the cosmos, constructed from human concern, and it is also very likely to be seized on by whatever establishment or pressure group is in power and expounded in their interest. Thus both myths, the Priestly one in particular, were interpreted as justifying various structures of social authority, but it was precisely this aspect of the myths that proved to be mortal. Similarly, the upward-moving Romantic myths were also turned into rationalizations of authority as soon as the theory of Darwinian evolution began to filter into popular mythology. This view saw the whole evolutionary process as leading up to humanity as its climax, and as able to continue only through humanity. Such a view was already implied, in fact asserted, in the Genesis accounts, where man is also said to be given the domination over the whole natural order. But various problems with ecology and the natural environment have begun to indicate to us that there is a limit to the domination of man over nature, and that if the domination becomes too great a tyranny nature may simply push him off the planet. It seems better not to turn visionary myths into authoritarian blueprints.

I have briefly glanced at the role of preliterary myth in human culture, and in discussing the Genesis creation myths I have been concerned with the second stage, where the mythical tends to be identified with the literary, and excluded from the conveying of genuine information. I have no space or time to outline a postliterary theory of myth, but I conclude with a suggestion or two about the factors involved.

We do not talk about verbal truth as confidently as we used to do, but I think there are three contexts in which what has traditionally been called or associated with truth can be brought into alignment with words. First is the context of the integrity of a verbal structure. We may, for instance, read an aphorism in the Book of Proverbs or elsewhere, and reflect how profoundly true it is, or we may read a work of literature and feel that it conveys, within a fictional or hypothetical framework, essential truths about either its own cultural context or about the human situation generally. We know, for instance, that Jane Austen tells

us a good deal that is true about Regency society and that Wordsworth has a conception of nature that some of us find true to our
own experience. Such structures integrate a great mass of incidental experiences, as a powerful magnet picks up piles of scrap
iron. This is by far the most important association of words and
truth, and is much the closest to the conception of faith in the
New Testament as the *hypostasis* and *elenchos* of the unseen and
hoped for. But it demands an active response to the structure of
what is being presented, not a passive one to the content, and
hence is often not realized to be a form of truth at all.

Second, there is the kind of sequential verbal truth of the
type we call logic, but this is a highly specialized use of words,
however important in itself, and in our ordinary verbal experience we seldom encounter it. What we encounter is usually rhetoric in a logical disguise. Third, there is the verbal truth of
correspondence already discussed.

Truth of correspondence is of course essential, and we could
hardly get through an ordinary day of experience without it. But
it is also the most approximate and ambiguous form of the three,
and though incessantly useful it is never definitive. Truth of correspondence is really a technique of measurement, where the
standard or criterion of measurement is outside the verbal structure. And verbal structures have too many features peculiar to
themselves for any external truth to pass through them undis-
torted. There is figurative language, for instance: most of the
words we use contain a large and unacknowledged deposit of
metaphor and analogy in them. And there are the syntactic relations, such as those of subject, predicate, and object, which we
often assume to be built into the world around us, but are actually only built into the grammar of our language.

It is, I am convinced, through the criticism of mythology,
which unravels the implications of a myth from within and studies its context with other myths outside it, that we arrive most
closely to what we can learn through words, or the contact with
words that has traditionally been called revelation. To examine
the creation myth of the Bible, we said, we need to disentangle
it from the various kidnappings by authority that distorted it
into a justification of that authority. Doing this releases other
myths, whose relation to it may be then clearly seen: I gave the
example of the liberation of Prometheus and Eros myths. Marxism and Freudianism are two of the most powerful intellectual

forces in the world today: I think it is quite intelligible to say that Marxism grew out of the myth of Prometheus, as Freudianism did out of the myth of Eros. As Emily Dickinson says, sardonically but with some affection as well, of the Christian God: "He will refund us finally / Our confiscated gods," and he does so as soon as his own mythology is detached from the wrong kind of authority.

The subject can never meet the object, the Other, as the Other, but can only encounter it in the intermediate realm of language, to which both subject and object are assimilated. My interest in myth and in metaphor is based on the fact that the language of myth and metaphor is self-contained, not dependent on reference to something else. And wherever I turn in pursuit of my verbal interests, I come up against the fact that our ordinary experience rests on unreal and fuzzy experiences of time and space, and that myth and metaphor are among other things techniques of meditation, designed to focus our minds on a more real view of both.

For example, metaphor says, grammatically and syntactically, that A is B: at the same time it suggests that nobody could be fool enough to believe that A really is B. The statement "A is B" is therefore neither logical nor antilogical: it is counterlogical. The word *is* is really there to destroy the sense of an intervening space between the personal element A and the natural element B, and leads us into a world where subject and object can interpenetrate with one another, as freely as they did in Homer's day. What the metaphor does to space the myth does to time. The myth, also, asserts that something happened, and conveys also the sense that such a thing could not have happened in just that way. Myth does not, like history, present a past even as past: it presents it as present. But its present is not the unreal present of ordinary experience, chained to a dead past and an unborn future and never itself quite coming into existence at all. It is a present where, as Eliot says, past and future are gathered: the present of Jesus' aphorism "Before Abraham was, I am." When we are at the point of taking in a vision of time and space of the kind that myth and metaphor offer us, we are ready to meet the conception of a mythical and metaphorical creation that was there from the beginning, but is there again, reborn as soon as we look at it with fresh eyes.

✧

Crime and Sin
in the Bible

✧

THOSE WHO are listening to me know much better than I do
how difficult it is to define a crime, a misdemeanor, or any
form of antisocial behavior, apart from a violation of a specific
law already in existence. Some legislation may be empirical or
pragmatic in its basis, like traffic regulations, but there seems to
be a powerful deductive force in law that impels us to look for
principles and premises from which we derive our laws. A country with a written constitution, like the United States, has at
least that means of providing principles, though the amount of
amending and reinterpreting needed to keep it functioning so
often reminds us of the well-known old knife with its new blade
and new handle.

A written constitution is often the consequence of a successful revolution, and a country with a revolutionary tradition normally acquires a strongly deductive attitude to the social
contract, or at least the more doctrinaire of its citizens do. Thus
the American Revolution brought with it a popular involvement
in the conception of what should be considered genuinely American behavior and attitudes, a feature of American life that
Tocqueville discusses at length. Similarly, Marxist revolutions
may produce a climate of opinion in which undesirable behavior
can be characterized as remnants of bourgeois attitudes. Not all
of these ethical trends are incorporated into actual law, but they
can act as a powerful legal force nonetheless. The importance of
this factor in law is that it seems to point further back than the
major premises of a constitution, the rights of man, equality
before the courts, and the like, to something more primitive

255

embedded in human nature and destiny. Every constitution has to be thought of, in practice, as in some sense an inspired document. Defining the nature of its inspiration is another matter.

We may find it more relaxing to live in Canada, where nobody thinks about what a hundred percent Canadian is, and where a committee on un-Canadian activities would be faced with a totally unintelligible agenda. But even a system of law based on precedent has problems with the pressures exerted by the majority on individuals and minorities. In Canada we have had a series of ad hoc agreements and compromises like the Quebec Act, which made some effort, in fact a rather remarkable one for the eighteenth century, to keep the civic rights of both English- and French-speaking Canadians in mind. But the indigenous peoples, the Japanese Canadians during the Second World War, and other such groups, would tell a different story.

The theory of precedent, of course, as formulated by Burke and by what is called the Whig interpretation of history, is that it operates in a liberal direction, toward increasing freedom and equality. The barons who compelled King John to sign Magna Carta were, on this view, ultimately acting for the benefit of the common man. But this conception of precedent has had to be modified a good deal, the reason that concerns us just now being that it does not go back far enough. If we pursue the ancestry of precedent, we eventually move into a prehistoric period in which laws are rationalized by a myth telling society that they have been revealed by the gods. Once revealed, they are then enforced by an ascendent class, in whose interest the laws are interpreted. No conception of precedent can wholly shake off the influence of these mythical and prelegal origins. Let us listen to Blackstone, in the eighteenth century, commenting on the regulation about Sunday observance:

> Profanation of the Lord's Day, vulgarly (but improperly) called *sabbath-breaking,* is a ninth offense against God and religion, punished by the municipal law of England. For, besides the notorious indecency and scandal of permitting any secular business to be publicly transacted on that day, in a country professing Christianity, and the corruption of morals that usually follows its profanation, "the keeping of one day in seven holy, as a time of

relaxation and refreshment as well as for public worship, is of admirable service to a state, considered merely as a civil institution. It humanizes by the help of conversation and society the manners of the lower classes, which would otherwise degenerate into a sordid ferocity and savage selfishness of spirit: it enables the industrious workman to pursue his occupation in the ensuing week, with health and cheerfulness; it imprints on the minds of the people that sense of their duty to God, so necessary to make them good citizens, but which yet would be worn out and defaced by an unremitted continuance of labour, without any stated times of recalling them to the worship of their Maker."

The one secular principle involved here, that mandatory holidays create better working conditions, gets in by the back door. It is clear that the major premises from which Blackstone is deriving his argument are, first, the traditional rituals of Christianity, which go back to still earlier Jewish ones, and, second, the principle that the lower classes should be kept firmly in their lower place. Clearly, it would be profitable to look at some of the origins of these assumptions: in particular, the religious origin, which so often includes the myth already mentioned, that the original laws were handed down to a specific human society by divine beings.

The word *crime* is social and secular in context: murder and theft are crimes because they are disturbances of the social order. The word *sin* is religious in context, and has no meaning outside a religious framework. Sin is primarily man's effort to block or frustrate the will of God, and though, in a normal state of society, crimes are usually regarded also as sins, they are so only when and because God is assumed to disapprove of them. So any legal code that goes back to a divine revelation has the conception "sin" as its major premise from which the conception of "crime" is derived.

In primitive societies the conception of sin begins in such features as taboo, where, for example, certain things must not be touched, certain foods not eaten, certain ceremonies not witnessed by outsiders. There then develops the sense of certain ritual obligations owed to the gods, the neglect of which, even if unconscious, will bring disaster. In the Book of Exodus there is a list of prescriptions in chapter 31, described as "the ten commandments," which are concerned almost wholly with these ritual obligations, and consequently may be older than the better-known decalogue in Exodus 20 and Deuteronomy 5, which I shall return to in a moment. Central to these ritual obligations is the conception of sacrifice. At each of the three major festivals, sacrificial offerings are to be brought to God, "and none shall appear before me empty." Similarly, the period from Friday to Saturday sunsets is to be withdrawn from social and utilitarian pursuits, including the making of money. Every firstborn male animal, including the firstborn son of human beings, belongs to God as a sacrifice, though the son is to be redeemed by a lamb instead, or may be devoted to God in a more sublimated sense, like the infant Samuel.

The conception of sacrifice also enters warfare, and the most ferocious penalties are connected with disregarding the claims of God in war. If the Israelites are to conquer Canaan, all the loot they acquire belongs to God, which in practice means the priesthood. Joshua takes the city of Ai, then meets with a sharp repulse at the next town. He learns that an Israelite named Achan has kept some of the loot from Ai for himself, so not only is he stoned to death, but his entire family is wiped out and all his possessions confiscated. Similarly, prisoners captured in battle are to be killed as sacrifices to God. When King Saul captures the Amalekite king Agag he spares his life, as we should think, out of ordinary human decency, but the prophet Samuel, after denouncing Saul for having committed an utterly unforgivable sin against God, falls on Agag and hews him in pieces, and from then on King Saul never has any luck again.

No doubt in prebiblical times these sacrifices were thought of as actually feeding the gods, as they still seem to be in Homer. We can also see clearly enough a prebiblical cult of human sacrifice, which the Mosaic code is designed both to abolish and to reestablish on a more rational moral basis. But the prophets are emphatic that God has no need of the smoke of sacrifice and the like, and the rationale for these ritual obligations has to be looked for elsewhere.

The Hebrew word *torah* means the whole body of instruction necessary for the people of Israel, including the laws. The

New Testament writers relied mainly on the Septuagint (Greek) translation of the Old Testament, and as the Septuagint rendered *torah* as *nomos,* the King James and other translations speak simply of the "law." But if we look at the Book of Deuteronomy we see something far bigger than a legal code: it is a contract or treaty between God and Israel transmitted through Moses, and it gives us not merely a code but a theological and historical context for that code.

The details of this context are filled out in the other books of the Pentateuch. First comes the founding of the society of Israel on a revolutionary basis. Moses in Egypt is informed by the voice speaking from the burning bush that the God of Israel is about to give himself a name, enter history, and take a very partisan role in it, the role of delivering an enslaved people from the bondage of the Egyptian establishment. The revolutionary origin gives, as remarked earlier, a strongly deductive cast to the structure of laws, and we are constantly being referred back to the original contract. For example, one of the most attractive features of the Deuteronomic code is its relatively humane attitude to slavery, and the Israelite community is frequently reminded of the central reason for adopting such an attitude: that they themselves were once slaves in Egypt.

Most of us, I assume, would share the assumptions about liberty and equality as the basis of law that have been formulated at least since John Stuart Mill's time. We take for granted the principle of the equality of all citizens before the law and the principle of the greatest amount of individual autonomy consistent with the well-being of others. To the extent that the laws are bent in the interests of a privileged or aggressive group; to the extent that citizens live under arbitrary regulations enforced by terror, to that extent we are living in an illegal society. If we regard our own society as at least workably legal, we also take largely for granted that the real basis for the effectiveness of law in such a society is an invisible morale. The law in itself is compelled to deal only with overt actions, so that from the law's point of view an honest man is any man not yet convicted of stealing. But no society could hold together with so loose a conception of morality: there has to be a sufficient number of self-respecting citizens who are honest because they like it better that way.

The Pentateuch in general, and the Book of Deuteronomy

in particular, is an extraordinary tour de force of social thought in which certain obligations toward God are assumed to build up in each person an inner morale that, so to speak, insulates that person from becoming a disintegrating force in society. The *torah* is designed, among many other things, to provide a kind of vertical dimension to law. The relation of the individual Israelite to the God of Israel, built up by the habits of action and thought fostered by the laws of the Sabbath and the like, is the source of the inner moral energy that is needed to keep society together. Sin, thought of as primarily the neglect of ritual obligations, thus becomes the source of crime, so that one can never eradicate crime from society by secular legislation alone.

If we look at the familiar structure of the Decalogue, the ten commandments as we know them, we can see an illustration of this conception of secular crime being derived from ritual neglect. The first four commandments are concerned with the obligations of religion: Israel must be faithful to its God, not make images of him or of other gods, take the name of God seriously, and rest on the Sabbath. The fifth commandment, to honor one's parents, makes a transition to the moral sphere, but is connected with the ritual group by the promise that observing it will be rewarded by God with long life. The four commandments following the prohibitions against murder, adultery, theft, and slander, would, if they stood alone, be thought of as purely moral and secular. The final commandment against coveting brings us back to that inner state of mental integrity which is the real basis of all law.

This deductive construct, in which the commands of God, the neglect of which is sin, form the premises for social morality, or law in the context of "law and order," is not unmatched in the ancient world: the role of sacrifice and other ritual practices in Hinduism is very similar, and there are other religion-based legal codes, like that of Islam, that develop later partly under biblical influence. Still it is a rare achievement: the legal code of Hammurabi in Babylon, for instance, impressive as it is, does not seem to have acquired anything like the same prestige among its people. We note in passing that such codes enclose a specific society and mark it off from others. The Deuteronomic code implies that God is uniquely related to Israel, and that Israel's ritual obligations are not necessarily binding on other nations. But for most of its history Israel was not an independent nation, but a province subject to the authority of Egypt, Assyria, Babylonia, Persia, Greece, and Rome. These heathen nations were the source of the secular and moral law, not less so when they allowed the Israelites to keep their ritual obligations. So the question arises: What happens when sin and crime are violations of conflicting structures of authority?

We may take an example from perhaps the most haunting situation of the sort in human culture: the dilemma of Antigone in Sophocles. Here Antigone is forbidden by Creon, the ruler of Thebes and the source of its secular law, to bury her brother's body, and yet not to bury it would be a sin against one of the most solemn of Greek ritual obligations. Antigone does not hesitate: it is the sin that it is important to avoid, not the crime. She suffers accordingly, but the disaster that befalls Creon vindicates her in the eyes of the audience at least. Similar dilemmas rise to a climax in the persecution of the Jews under Antiochus of Syria, the persecution that provoked the Maccabean rebellion.

When the Christian religion began, a century or so after the Maccabees, this problem of a possible clash between religious and secular authority was very much in the foreground. Paul strongly advises submission to the secular authority of the Roman Empire, but what he says sounds a trifle hollow in view of the persecutions that started almost immediately, affecting Christians and Jews alike. Apart from this, there was also the question: How far is the Old Testament code binding on Christians? In what sense are Christians to be regarded as a new Israel? In this controversy Paul emerged as the leader who proclaimed that Christianity was to be brought to the Gentiles outside Israel, and that the ritual obligations of Judaism, such as circumcision, were no longer binding on Christians. The effect of the Christian reformulation of law was to drive a much wider breach into the two conceptions of sin and crime, and the consequences of doing so are still with us.

In the teaching of Jesus, especially in the Sermon on the Mount in Matthew, which includes commentaries on some of the ten commandments, the distinction between the inner integrity that resists sin and the overt action of a crime is pushed about as far as it will go. The overwhelming emphasis is on the inner state of mind. If A murders B, and C merely wishes with all his being

that D were dead, A is legally a murderer and C is wholly innocent of murder. From the point of view of the Sermon on the
Mount the chief difference between the A who murders and the
C who feels murderous is that A has more guts. Again, Jesus
interprets the prohibitions against murder and adultery and theft
as positive enthusiasms for human life, for the respect and self-
respect of women, for property. There is nothing here that cannot
be paralleled in contemporary Rabbinical teaching, perhaps, but
some of the inferences drawn in the New Testament, more particularly by Paul, forecast another revolution.

Paul sees in the story of the fall of Adam in Genesis the
existence in human life of what is called original sin. The beginning of sin for him is an inherent condition of the soul, which is
there before any act is. Consequently ritual obligations, while
they symbolize a desire to be rid of original sin, are still ineffective: it is the inner condition itself that has to be transformed.
This transformation sets one free from the law, according to Ga-
latians, which is perhaps the earliest of Paul's writings. But one
is not set free from the law by breaking the law, only more
tangled up with it than ever. Jesus said that he thought of his
teaching as fulfilling the law, not abolishing it: that means that
there is an aspect of the law, called by Paul the "spiritual" aspect,
which is reestablished, and another aspect that disappears.

This means that, for example, justice is the internal condition of the just man, and the external antagonist of the criminal.
But the just man, to maintain his justice, has to be far stricter
with himself than any law could provide penalties for. Justice as
conceived by the gospel cannot be legalized: if we tried to make
the transformed inner state spoken of by Paul and Jesus into a
new code of law, the most frightful and fantastic tyranny would
result. One can have a law against rape, but Jesus' conception of
adultery includes all the men who mentally rape every woman
who catches their eye, and this kind of "adultery" cannot become
a basis for legislation. If it did, we'd have the situation of black
farce in Gilbert's *Mikado:*

> *The youth who winked with roving eye,*
> *Or breathed a non-connubial sigh*
> *Was thereupon condemned to die.*

This was the basis on which Milton argued for divorce in the
seventeenth century. Divorce is permitted in the Mosaic code,

but is apparently prohibited by Jesus. Milton claimed that Jesus was talking about marriage in the spiritual or gospel sense, as a lifelong union that can be consummated, which means finished, only by the death of one of the partners. Its model is the relation of Adam and Eve before the fall, for each of whom there was, quite literally, no one else. But it is clearly nonsense, Milton says, to pretend that every sexual union in society is a spiritual marriage of this kind.

Of course the fact that Milton had to make such an argument, and was bitterly denounced for doing so, indicates that the original distinction between sin and crime was very largely ignored in practice. It was there in theory: in the Middle Ages the deadly sins were divided into seven groups, pride, wrath, sloth, envy, avarice, gluttony, and lechery. Preachers tended to leave lechery to the end as the most interesting. All crime is the result of one or more of these sins, but not one of them in itself necessarily results in crime. Still, the bulk of canon law was incorporated into secular law, and deviations from it were treated as crimes, whether the crime was eating meat in Lent or holding heretical doctrines. A new set of ritual obligations was set up, and it is clear that there is no change of principle when the day of rest is altered to Sunday from Saturday or the rite of circumcision replaced by the rite of baptism. Then, of course, there have always been the moralists, who want to turn as much sin, or what they consider sin, into crime as possible, and pass laws accordingly. In the seventeenth century there were also extreme Nonconformists who held that nothing was either sinful or criminal unless it was explicitly said to be so in the Bible. The Bible obligingly came through with denunciations of everything they disapproved of anyway except polygamy, which it nowhere condemns. So that one had to be chalked up to the law of nature, a frantically muddled area of thought which I shall have to glance at in a moment. During the prohibition era, the drys, most of whom had strong Protestant commitments, ran into a similar difficulty with a Bible which, while it condemns drunkenness, never conceives of the possibility of a human life totally deprived of fermented beverages.

The original Christian distinction between sin and crime was a part of the revolutionary aspect of Christianity, and the progressive blurring of the distinction was the result of the revolutionary impulse being smothered under new forms of entrenched privilege. The significance of the revolution which appears at the beginning of so many legal codes, of Israel in Egypt, of the American, French, and Russian revolutions of our times, is that a revolution repudiates an existing structure of law and authority. Christianity holds that Jesus was without sin, yet he was put to death as a criminal. This means that crime represents a social judgment, and society is never wholly capable of making such a judgment. It has no standards, in itself, for distinguishing what is below the law from what is above it: it cannot tell a prophet from a blasphemer, a saint from a witch, a philosopher from a teacher of subversive doctrines. Hence the martyred careers of Jesus, Joan of Arc, and Socrates.

This issue can hardly be called obsolete today, when Nazi Germany and similar dictatorships have made us familiar with the conception of a criminal society. Many liberal-minded Canadians, highly respected people who never come within sight of arrest or imprisonment, would, if they were living in South Africa, find their consciences nagging them because they were *not* in jail. Antisocial behavior may result from motives that are considered good in other societies, or by the same society in a different phase of its history. Whether the relativity of crime could also apply to sin or not is a more difficult question. I think of a sardonic story by Marcel Aymé, in which a simple and saintly man in a French provincial town wakes up one morning to discover that he has acquired a halo, clearly visible except when he wears a hat. His wife is furious: nobody in *her* family ever had halos, and how was she to explain this to the neighbors or to the concierge? As he couldn't wear his hat all the time, he would have to choose between her and the halo. So he conscientiously sets out to commit all the seven deadly sins, loses his reputation, his friends and his job, and finally ends as a pimp in a brothel. But his motive in doing all this was so fundamentally innocent that the halo stayed firmly in place.

The story, farcical as it is, indicates a genuine dilemma about the criteria for sin and crime. In a normally functioning society a crime is a breach of the legal code. But a society may pass laws so grotesquely unjust that obeying the laws of such a society may be the real crime. This at least, I assume, was the principle the Nuremberg trials after the Second World War attempted to establish. What criteria come into focus then? Many of the liberal-minded people I just spoke of, who would be dissidents in a racist or dictatorial country, have strong religious commitments, and for them a criminal society derives its criminal nature from sin, from being under the judgment of God. But the experience of our century indicates that any religious ideology, Christian or Jewish or Islamic or Hindu or whatever, is a most insecure basis for a modern state. In fact, as in South Africa or Iran, a religious ideology is often a major contributing factor to an intolerable legal code.

Conceptions derived from natural law or the law of nations concern me here only insofar as they have been traditionally a part of the relation of crime to sin in the Bible. The notion of natural law is really not in the Bible: in the Bible the same God is in charge of both the moral and the natural orders, and nature is thought of as a fellow creature of man, who, like man, has an order imposed on it by divine will. In the biblical view there cannot be such a thing, strictly speaking, as a miracle, because God does as he likes in both human and physical worlds. Natural law grew out of the sort of questions asked by the pre-Socratic philosophers. What is the world made of? Is there a primary substance? What really are the stars? Are there such things as atoms? These are questions that move in the direction of science, and from them came the observation that some things in nature behaved regularly enough to be predictable. It was a considerable setback to science that this emerging view of natural law should have been associated, by a violent and foolish pun, with law in its human and social context. Natural laws are not "broken"; if we fall out of a tree we do not break the law of gravitation: we merely illustrate it. But the confusions engendered by the pun still persist, even when the conception of God is replaced by a mother-goddess figure of Nature. We have it still in Einstein's unwillingness to accept the element of chance in quantum mechanics, and in the frequent assertion that evolution did not arise by "blind chance," but chance operating within a framework of law. As long as law in nature means simply the human observation of the predictable element in it, this amounts to saying that things happened as they did because they happened as they did.

The law of nations, the *ius gentium* of Grotius and others, which is often associated or identified with natural law, arose, according to Sir Henry Maine, in Roman efforts to define the legal status of non-Romans. It is thus extrabiblical in origin, but it became attached to the central myth of the Bible in a way that persisted down to at least the eighteenth century. According to this myth, which derives from Paul's emphasis on the fall of Adam and the original sin that resulted, there are two levels of nature. The upper or human level is the one God created with the Garden of Eden and the original Adam and Eve. The lower or physical level is the one that Adam fell into, which all of us, being his descendants, are now born in. Man is not adjusted to this lower level of nature, as the animals and plants appear to be. Many things are "natural" to man, such as wearing clothes, being conscious, and using reason, which are natural to nothing else in the environment. Edmund Burke was insisting as late as the French Revolution that "art is man's nature," not something man has imposed on nature.

It follows that we cannot appeal to anything in physical nature to determine the answer to the question What is natural to man? In Milton's *Comus* a chaste Lady is imprisoned by Comus, who tries to seduce her with arguments drawn from the animal world and its lack of self-consciousness about sexual intercourse. The Lady's answer is too virtuous to be altogether coherent, but the general line of her argument is that on the human level of nature it is her chastity that is natural, not promiscuity. On the other hand, "nature" is often invoked as a standard against which socially disapproved behavior, such as homosexuality or incest, may be measured. The hero of the late Greek romance *Daphnis and Chloe* is tempted to a homosexual relationship, but refuses because, though a simple and untutored country boy, he has never seen such relationships among animals. Being only the hero of a pastoral story, he does not do the research into animal behavior that might have qualified his position. But we can already see what the general conclusion is. The humanly natural is what is natural on the human level of nature, that is, the form of human society sanctioned by custom and tradition and authority. What is natural to man, then, is a question with a completely circular answer: it is whatever constituted authority says is natural, and you will accept this or else.

If we are trying to arrive at criteria by which to judge an unjust society, then, I see nothing in any of the traditional conceptions of natural law that will help. Let us go back to where we started, the biblical view that crime is a by-product of sin, sin being rooted in one's obligations, ritual or moral, to God. These obligations, however universal the religion aims at being, are essentially tribal: they enclose the group of believers, even if they can be numbered in millions, and separate them from others with different obligations or with no traditions. Some of these excluding obligations are very potent: dietary laws, for instance, which separate different groups on a basis of what can become something like physical nausea. The nausea may work negatively also: a Moslem woman in Pakistan, for example, once remarked to me about Hindus: "I hate those people; they don't eat beef." An American senator of some years back similarly opposed any aid to the starving people of India on the ground that India had plenty of cows wandering around, which the Indians were too perverse to eat.

Those of you who know more law than I do will know better than I how such mutually exclusive bodies can be absorbed into a secular state. All I can contribute is the social vision I have picked up from the study of literature. The sense of obligations to God of course makes the God objective to man, and his revelation of them equally so. It would not be difficult, however, to see behind every religion an expression of human concern, a word so broad that I hope it is self-explanatory. I think there are primary and secondary concerns. Primary concerns rest on platitudes so bald and obvious that one hesitates to list them: it is better to be fed than starving, better to be happy than miserable, better to be free than a slave, better to be healthy than sick. Secondary concerns arise through the consciousness of a social contract: loyalty to one's religion or country or community, commitment to faith, sacrifice of cherished elements in life for the sake of what is regarded as a higher cause. All through history primary concerns have had to give way to secondary ones. It is better to live than die; nevertheless we go to war. Freedom is better than bondage, but we accept an immense amount of exploitation, both of ourselves and of others. Perhaps, with our nuclear weapons and our pollution of air and water, we have reached the first stage in history in which primary concerns will have to become primary.

The reason why this interests me is that I think primary concern expresses itself in mythology, in the stories and rituals surrounding the food supply, the sexual relation, the work which is a socially creative act and not an alienated drudgery, the play which is the expression of energy and not a mere distraction. It is this mythology that develops into literature. Secondary concerns produce ideology, and the normal language of ideology is the dialectical language of argument and thesis, which is invariably aggressive, because every thesis contains its own opposite. I am not suggesting an original Golden Age of pure myth: every myth, in the most primitive society, has also an ideological social function. Every work of literature, therefore, which descends from mythology, is an ideological product, an expression of the culture of its age. But some literary works show the capacity to make contact with an audience far removed in space, time, and culture, and it is the task of the critic to reveal in such works the primary myth underlying the ideological surface. In an age of ideological deadlock like ours, with so many foolish and irresponsible people saying "Let's go to war to smash somebody else's ideology," I feel that this critical task has taken on a renewed social importance.

As long as we are talking of categories, the Bible is a mythological sacred book, but not a work of literature, though it is full of literary qualities. What keeps it from being literature is the objective nature assumed about its God and his revelation. This objectivity restricts its appeal, or much of it, to the special response of belief, which includes belonging to one definite community and not another. But we may also think of the Bible as coming to us through the power of the creative human imagination, which it clearly does whatever we believe about its ultimate source. In that context, we can make the same critical operation we make with literary works, trying to isolate the original myth under all the accretions of ideology, which for the Bible extend over several millennia.

Central to that original and underlying myth within the Bible is the legal metaphor of the trial, with prosecutors, defendants, and, of course, a supreme judge. We find this most explicitly in the Book of Job, in some parables of Jesus, and in the Book of Revelation that concludes the New Testament, but it is there all through in some form. The role of accuser is typically that of the devil, the Satan or adversary of mankind; the role of the defendant is identified with that of Jesus in the New Testament, with that of the restorer of Israel in the Old. Accuser and defendant represent the aspects of our lives that relate to past and future: the accuser says, "This is what you have done," the defendant says, "This is what you still may do." In history, a revolution, which so often results in a new legal code, may sweep away the accumulated crime and sin of the past and usher in a new social order looking to the future. As time goes on, the future vision fades out and the record of the past resumes its continuity. I think it is possible to see, in the central myth of the Bible, a vision that rises above the progression from past to future into a higher form of the present, a vision of human creative power continually making the new by reshaping the old. On this level we pass beyond the specific religious revelation into a more comprehensive view of human destiny. In such a view there would be included, I should think, an understanding of what has been called sin that does not have the arbitrary quality of the objectified revelation. This would include a fuller perspective of the crime that traditionally derives from sin. That would give us a saner and less anxious vision of the origins of human evil and of the methods of encountering it.

Blake's Bible

I T IS obvious that Blake is, even by English standards, an intensely biblical poet. His approach to it is wholly that of a poet and painter: he has little of Milton's or Herbert's doctrinal content. As we all know, Blake developed a cosmic vision of a universe inhabited by dramatis personae of his own invention. His treatment of that vision remains remarkably consistent throughout his life, though it was not static: many vague and undeveloped areas of it become clearer and more detailed as he goes on. But at no time does he stray very far away from the Bible as his main source.

Blake never believed, strictly speaking, either in God or in man: the beginning and end of all his work was what he calls the "Divine Humanity." He accepted the Christian position because Christianity holds to the union of divine and human in the figure of Christ, and, in its conception of resurrection, to the infinite self-surpassing of human limitations. But any God Blake would accept would have to be not simply a personal God but an anthropomorphic one. A God who is not at least human is in practice only a scarecrow of superstition and cowardice scraped up from a subhuman nature and stuffed full of the malice and cruelty that man derives from nature. As for human societies in themselves, Blake regards them, or came to do so, as mostly aggregates of psychotic animals. A human being comes equipped with a potentially divine power centered in his ability to create, to love, to destroy his own grasping and clutching ego, and only such things make him human. In any case a divine being could communicate with a human being only in human language, and at the point of communication the difference between God and man would become an identity. Blake often has to speak for convenience of God *and* man, but either word separated from the other represents a sterile and sinister illusion. Traditionally, the Bible opens with an account of a creation by God followed by a fall of man, and man is responsible only for the consequences of his own fall. For Blake, the fall of man was a part of a badly bungled job of creation for which man is equally responsible; hence the primary duty of man at present is to recreate his world into something that makes more sense, human and divine.

We may take as our guide to Blake's development the famous passage from a poem in a letter written in 1803, where he speaks of having attained a "fourfold" vision:

> 'Tis fourfold in my supreme delight,
> And threefold in soft Beulah's night,
> And twofold always. May God us keep
> From single vision and Newton's sleep.

Anyone trying to follow Blake biographically is bound to feel that he is on several time clocks at once: this statement is about six years later than the discovery at the beginning of the poem called *The Four Zoas:* that "Four Mighty Ones are in every Man." Blake was one of a minority of visionaries in the West to think in fours and eights rather than the traditional constructs derived from the Trinity. His chief biblical sources here are the four rivers of Eden, the fourth figure who appears along with the three in Nebuchadnezzar's furnace, and the "fourfold Gospel," which is connected with his four "Zoas." Let us begin with what Blake meant by a "single vision," omitting the reference to Newton for the moment.

According to the Book of Genesis, Adam and Eve were placed in a garden with instructions to eat of every tree except one, which of course was the one that most attracted them. The tree was called the knowledge of good and evil, and in eating of it they became self-conscious about their sexual differences, which had not bothered them before. In short, what human beings acquired, at the dawn of history, was a repressive morality founded on a sexual neurosis. Such a knowledge had been forbidden because it is not a genuine knowledge of anything, even of good and evil.

When we look at the Bible as a sacred book, then, the worst way of misreading it is to take this neurotic repressiveness as the form of divine revelation, making moral taboos and sexual prudery the basis for behavior acceptable to God. Such an attitude is really a form of devil-worship, as it enforces the exact opposite of what the same Genesis story presents as the original ideal. There is, it is true, some evidence that the Bible considers submission to arbitrary authority to be the best procedure for man. But there is better evidence that struggling against such authority is really what is required. The major pattern for this is the Exodus from Egypt, where revolution against a social establishment is the first and primary event in the history of Israel. All through the Old Testament the historians and prophets keep returning to this Egyptian revolution as the essential factor in the relation, or what Blake would call the identity, of God and man. In the New Testament the death and resurrection of a socially rejected Christ forms the counterpart to the Exodus, and completes the overcoming of the gap between the divine and the human. Clearly, one needs a countervision of the Bible, setting a gospel of freedom against the imbecile manifesto of moral inertia, social conformity, and sexual shame. Milton before Blake had spoken of the Bible as the charter of human liberty, and regarded all efforts to make it seem to endorse tyranny as perverse.

Blake speaks of the American Revolution as having a profound effect on his political and social thinking: with the fall of the Bastille in 1789 this expanded into a temporary conviction that after centuries of tyranny the world was coming into a new age of liberty. *The Marriage of Heaven and Hell* is a satire, partly political and partly religious, concerned with what we should now call left- and right-wing points of view. The left-wingers are called "Devils," the conservatives "Angels." The tone is light and good-natured throughout: the "Devils" are lively and amusing, and the "Angels," if sometimes stupid, are not really evil. At the end of this work Blake describes how he, taking the role of a "Devil," demonstrates to an "Angel" the true nature of Jesus. For the "Angel" what is unique about the life of Jesus was its conformity to moral virtue: he was the only man to have achieved the utterly futile goal of a life without sin. The "Devil" shows him that in fact Jesus broke all the ten commandments he is supposed to have endorsed, and that what was really significant about his life was that established moral authority found him intolerable. The "Angel" is converted, and the episode ends:

> Note: this Angel, who is now become a Devil, is
> now my particular friend: we often read the Bible

together in its infernal or diabolical sense, which the world shall have if they behave well.

I have also the Bible of Hell, which the world shall have whether they will or no.

We get a hint here of two levels of seriousness, one of good-humored satire, and another that is more aware of the real depths of the conflict opening up in Blake's day between the forces of liberty and those of repression. The *Marriage* was engraved in 1793, but the text suggests that it was written around 1790. In a very short time Britain had gone to war with France and installed a repressive government, and the tone adopted by Blake becomes more bitter and denunciatory. What he thinks of the "single vision" of the Bible he puts into fairly explicit language in a couplet scribbled in the Rossetti Notebook: "The Hebrew nation did not write it, / Avarice and Chastity did shite it." Chastity, because the notion that sexual abstinence is a good thing in itself, is a neurosis that is a fruitful breeder of further neuroses. Avarice, because this kind of perversion can be made only in the interests of some established authority, religious or secular. At this period of his life, Blake regarded such radical figures as Voltaire, Rousseau, and Paine as fighters in the vanguard of freedom. Some of the most significant statements he made at this time occur in a series of marginalia he wrote on a book by Bishop Watson, a series of letters addressed to Tom Paine and denouncing Paine's *Age of Reason.* This was in 1798, at the height of the antirevolutionary hysteria in England. All through his annotations Blake sees Paine and his iconoclastic attacks on the historical validity of the books of the Bible as the authentic voice of the Holy Spirit, fighting for rudimentary common sense against superstition. One of his first comments runs: "Paine has not attacked Christianity. Watson has defended Antichrist."

When Blake speaks of his fourfold vision as "twofold always," he means among other things that he is constantly aware of the contrast between a physical and a spiritual world. This could be translated into a Platonic construct, but it would be wrong to regard Blake as Platonic. The New Testament speaks of visible and invisible worlds, but for Blake the function of the invisible world is to make the genuine form of the world visible—the function that is carried out by poets and painters. It is called the spiritual world because spirit means air or breath, and the spiritual enables the invisible to become visible in the same way that the invisible air makes it possible to see the physical world. Hence Blake's countervision of the Bible makes it possible also to see what is really happening in the world at the end of the eighteenth century. In the Watson notes Blake opposes the notion of an exclusive or peculiar Word of God, addressed only to whatever group, Jewish or Christian or what not, lays claim to it, with what he calls the "everlasting gospel" (Revelation 14:6), the proclamation of peace and liberty for man which, even if originally centered in Christianity, becomes the proclamation that, as he says, "all religions are one." One of Blake's latest verbal works is the doggerel poem called "The Everlasting Gospel" (c. 1818), which indicates in its opening lines how little Blake's attitudes on this subject had changed over the years:

> *The Vision of Christ that thou dost see*
> *Is my Vision's greatest enemy;*
> *Thine is the friend of all mankind,*
> *Mine speaks in parables to the blind.*
> *Both read the Bible day and night,*
> *But thou read'st black where I read white.*

Blake is the kind of writer who constantly seems to be anticipating later writers, and in this opposition of genuine Christianity to the infantile bourgeois morality that calls itself Christianity he may remind us of both Kierkegaard and Nietzsche. But one should be aware of differences as well as resemblances. Kierkegaard's *Attack upon Christendom* has little of Blake's awareness of the worldwide political and social implications of a revolutionary view of the Bible: he thinks of his area of attack as primarily psychological. Again, in Nietzsche's ridiculing of the moral blinkers that man puts on to prevent himself from seeing what is there, there is no acceptance of resurrection as the symbol of man's self-transcendence into an enlarged framework of existence. So although Zarathustra tells us that man is something to be surpassed, he has to settle for conceptions of renewal and rebirth and cyclical return. Renewal and rebirth, for Blake, are only parodies of resurrection. Eventually Nietzsche came to contrast a life-denying Christ with a life-affirming Antichrist figure whom he identifies with Dionysus. As Dionysus was the most hypochondriac of all dying gods, and, even more strangely for Nietzsche, the most obsessed with the sexual impulses of females, it seems that Nietzsche had, from Blake's point of view, either lost control of his vision or gone over to what Blake would have considered the real Antichrist, namely Caesar or the authority of the "all too human" world.

Once Christianity had come to power in both spiritual and temporal areas, the Bible became the basis for a cosmology that helped to rationalize the existing structures of authority. The reason why the Bible became such a basis is that it is written mainly in poetic and metaphorical language, and cosmologies are essentially metaphorical structures. The language of logic and dialectic always suggests the possibility that the opposite of what it affirms may also be true, but the language of metaphor is far subtler and more pervasive. A metaphor will be "believed," that is, assumed as part of the framework of one's thinking, as long as it seems emotionally convincing, and is irrefutable until it ceases to be so.

According to the traditional cosmology, the universe is a hierarchy of authority stretching from God down through spiritual and human beings to animals, plants, the mineral world, and finally chaos. Creation was the establishing of an ordered hierarchy above chaos, and it contains four main levels. At the top is heaven in the sense of the place of the presence of God. Next comes the earthly paradise, the home God intended man to live in. Third is the present "fallen" world, which humanity has inhabited since the fall of Adam, and fourth is the demonic world. The ups and downs of this cosmos may sometimes be acknowledged to be metaphorical ups and downs, but until about Newton's time most people took the "up" of heaven and the "down" of hell to be more or less descriptive.

According to this construct, God is above nature, the demonic world below it, and in the middle are two levels of nature or creation itself. They are the levels of human and of subhuman or physical nature. Since Adam's fall, all of us are born in the lower world of subhuman nature, but we do not belong there. Our real place is on the upper level or human world. This was originally the Garden of Eden, which no longer exists as a place, but up to a point can be recovered as a state of mind. Many things are natural to man that are not natural to any other members of his environment, such as wearing clothes, using reason and consciousness, and being under social discipline. Man can do nothing by himself: all initiative has to come from above: however, the instruments of grace transmitted by a thoughtful establishment are all in place: obedience to law, the practice of moral virtue, and the sacraments of religion will bring him as close as he can get to his real level in the cosmos.

This cosmos had two by-products that for a long time were taken seriously as scientific concepts. One was the structure of the Ptolemaic universe. Heaven was somewhere outside this universe, and then we have the series of spheres, from the primum mobile down through the planets to the moon, and from the moon to the "sublunar" world of the four elements that since the fall are subject to decay. After Newton's time, these conceptions ceased to carry much conviction. For Dante, the planetary spheres could be guided in their courses by companies of angels, but the Newtonian laws of gravitation and motion suggested a gigantic mechanism without personality of any kind, regardless of Newton's own efforts to struggle against such a suggestion. That is why, in Blake's poem *Europe,* which covers the historical sequence from the birth of Christ to the coming of the French Revolution, it is Newton who blows the trumpet of the Last Judgment or the coming of a new age.

The other by-product was the chain of being, the ladder that was formed out of the two principles of form and matter, and stretched from God, who was pure form, through spiritual and human existence into the subhuman world until it reached chaos, which is as close as we can come to pure matter without form. The chain of being was firmly in place as late as the eighteenth century, in Pope's *Essay on Man,* but Voltaire was beginning to feel very doubtful about the *échelle de l'infini,* which he saw clearly to be a disguise for arbitrary authority. For, of course, although in theory the authority it manifested was that of God, in practice the church and state reproduced that authority on earth, and demanded the same unquestioning obedience. The metaphorical kernel of the chain of being was the natural place, the "kindly stead," as Chaucer calls it, which all the elements seek by instinct and which man should seek in his own society. It was, of course, only because it was a structure of authority that this construct had lasted so long, and the factor that was destroying it in Blake's day was the sequence of revolutions,

American, French, Industrial, that exposed its skeleton of secular power.

One can find revolutionary ideas in many eighteenth-century writers; but there was one aspect of the situation that Blake was the first poet in English literature, and so far as I know the first person in the modern world, to understand. This was the fact that all the assumptions of the last eighteen centuries at least had been enclosed by a metaphorical framework, that this framework was obsolete, and that another was taking its place.

Blake's early works include the *Songs of Innocence,* where the symbol of innocence is the child. The child is innocent not because he is morally virtuous, but because he is instinctively civilized: he assumes that the world makes some kind of human sense, and was probably made for his own benefit. He grows up into the world of experience, and discovers that this is not true. What then happens to his childhood vision? The answer is easy enough now, but I know of no one before Blake who gives it. The childhood vision is driven into the metaphorical underworld that we call the subconscious, where it keeps seething and boiling with frustration, the frustration becoming increasingly sexual with puberty. The vision is of a world of objective experience sitting on top of a subjective furnace of frustrated desire.

The objective world, with which we all have to come to terms, is the source of the power of conservatism in human life that Blake calls Urizen. The subjective world squirming and writhing beneath it, a titan under a volcano, Blake calls Orc. In *The Marriage of Heaven and Hell,* "heaven" and "hell" are called that because they are the polemical terms used by the conservatives, or "Angels," who are terrified at the thought of human energies, especially sexual energies, getting loose. The "marriage" Blake speaks of is an explosion of revolutionary energy coming from Orc, the titan under the volcano, that will burn up the present world and restore to man his lost paradise.

This is the kernel, or middle division, of a metaphorical cosmos that grew more elaborate in Blake's later work, and finally became roughly the old authoritarian construct turned upside down into a revolutionary form. Instead of a heaven above, symbolized by the stars in their courses, the world up there becomes a world of outer space, held together only by the mechanism of gravitation: shapeless masses hanging on nothing, as

277

Thomas Hardy says. Below this comes the world of ordinary experience; below that a world of "nature" that seems to include human desire and energy, and yet, because of man's present alienation, excludes them as well. The true world corresponding to heaven can therefore only be metaphorically still further down. It is sometimes symbolized by Atlantis, the country that ought to be uniting America and England, but is now sunk underneath what Blake calls the "Sea of Time and Space."

Looking again at the center of this inverted cosmic metaphor, we get something that looks like a Noah's ark of traditional human values tossing precariously on a sea of nature. It is a proto-Freudian vision of an ego threatened by suppressed desires, a proto-Marxist vision of an ascendant class threatened by an alienated one; a proto-Darwinian vision of moral values threatened by natural aggression; a proto-Schopenhauerian vision of a world as representation threatened by a world as will. To have turned a metaphorical cosmos eighteen centuries old upside down in a few poems, and provided the basis for a structure that practically every major thinker for the next century would build on, was one of the most colossal imaginative feats in the history of human culture. The only drawback, of course, was that no one knew Blake had done it: in fact Blake hardly realized he had done it either. One thing that is remarkable about Blake's construct, in any case, is that it is at least as solidly biblical as its predecessor, something not true of later developments of it.

Around 1794 Blake began producing what were evidently intended to be parts of the "Bible of Hell" he had promised. They include *The Book of Urizen* and *The Book of Los,* both apparently parts of a Blakean version of the creation, and also *The Book of Ahania,* which is clearly a "deconstruction," as it might be called now, of the Exodus story. There are also the four "continent" poems, *America, Europe,* and the two parts of *The Song of Los* called "Africa" and "Asia." These may bear some analogy, although they are called prophecies, to what we call the historical books of the Bible. The somewhat pedantic scheme of biblical parody was soon abandoned for the more comprehensive designs of *The Four Zoas* and its successors, but remained a part of Blake's total vision. The central parody theme in *The Book of Urizen,* where the seven days of biblical creation become seven long ages of "dismal woe," recurs in *The Four Zoas,* and, more perfunctorily, in the still later *Milton.*

As Blake knew, there are two accounts of creation in Genesis: the first or Priestly account, which covers the first chapter, and the second or Jahwist account, which starts in Genesis 2:4. The Priestly account, though placed first, is historically later, and the two accounts are distinguished by the different names employed for God. The Priestly account, as everyone knows, shows God creating the world in a sequence of six acts or "days," with a concluding comment that the seventh "day" was a day of rest. The Jahwist account also consists of six acts, though they are not so often counted. First, God creates a "mist," out of what is apparently dry ground; second comes the creation of the adam (he is not "Adam" until later); then the creating of the Garden of Eden, then the irrigating of the garden with four rivers, then the creation of all the nonhuman living creatures, and finally the creation of woman. The seventh episode is again not an act, but the comment that Adam and Eve were in the state of innocence, naked and unashamed.

The two accounts of creation emphasize two aspects of nature, the nature that is a structure or system and the nature that is the totality of life. They are sometimes distinguished as *natura naturata* and *natura naturans:* physical nature and biological nature. At the same time having two such different accounts caused trouble for some commentators. In the first account, men and women are created on the sixth day along with the other land animals, whereas in the second the creation of human beings is quite separate from the other acts of creation and man and woman are created at different times. The difficulty bred the later legend of Lilith, Adam's first wife and mother of demons, a legend that failed to interest Blake. The story of the fall of man is attached to the Jahwist account, as such a story would have to be. God must have created a perfect or model world, and the alienation myth of a fall is needed to explain the contrast between such a model world and the chaotic mess we are in now. But no fall legend seems to be directly attached to the Priestly story of creation.

It emerges later, however, in the story of the fall of the rebel angels, whose leader is alluded to in Isaiah as Lucifer, or light-bearer. Of course traditionally this revolt is simply a revolt of evil against goodness, and if one accepts an omnipotent God, the war in heaven can be only some kind of practical joke on God's part, as it essentially is in *Paradise Lost.* But classical legends tell us of a revolt of titans which the titans very nearly won, and they also strongly suggest that the supreme god of the skies is a usurper, holding power by tyranny in the Greek sense of the word. Blake had already suggested, in *The Marriage of Heaven and Hell,* that there might be a devil's account of what happened as well as an angelic one, and that one might get some notion of such an account even from the Bible. For Blake, in any case, the first chapter of Genesis conceals a story of warring titanic beings, equally divine and human, whose struggles for power produced the world we are now in. It is from these wars that we got such things as the splendid ferocity of the tiger, who was created "When the stars threw down their spears," stars meaning spiritual beings.

In Blake the word *reason* means the exact opposite of what the words *mental* and *intellectual* mean. The mind creates out of the world something with a human shape and sense, and thereby forms a model of the kind of world man should be living in, and was living in before reason started mucking it about. Reason makes nothing out of the world: it merely stares at it, and then forms a squirrel cage of logic to revolve in. In *The Book of Urizen* we meet the titan of that name who should be, and once was, the mind or intellect of divine humanity, but who has transformed himself into reason, or passive consciousness. This immediately brings into the world what genuine imaginative work tries to abolish: the "cloven fiction," as Blake calls it, of subject and object. The subject is reduced to a "soul-shudd'ring vacuum," like the tabula rasa of Locke, the nothingness of a consciousness that cannot act, but can only be acted upon. The objective counterpart of this is a "world of solid obstruction," or objectivity at its deadest. Urizen no longer understands the conception of unity, which he also turns into its opposite, or uniformity: "One King, One God, One Law," he says. Naturally this is not done all at once: one of the remarkable features of the poem is the emphasis Blake gives to the immense length of time in the prehistorical world.

Urizen is thus not so much a creator as the condition of creation: he is the world we have now, the ruin out of which we have to try to rebuild the original form. His great antagonist is the fire-demon Los, a Lucifer figure who retains a higher kind of energy. Consciousness alone can see the world in any sort of human shape, and after seven ages of "dismal woe" Los does get some kind of intelligible human shape on Urizen. Some myths tell us how the world was made by the dismembering of a giant: here something of the same process in reverse seems to be going on as Urizen gradually becomes something of an objective counterpart to the humanity still present in Los. Both the creation books emphasize the separation of the two figures of Los and Urizen. What separates with them are the more organic and the more mechanical aspects of both human and natural worlds. Urizen gives birth to the four elements, and, in the interests of trying to keep everything uniform, inspires man with a fascination for the quantitative and measurable, the "starry floor," Blake calls it, the bedrock of recreation. Los creates the archetypal human family, a nuclear Freudian family of jealous father (Los himself), rebellious son (Orc), and anxious mother (Enitharmon). Both creation poems tell us of "many ages of groans," where nothing very cheerful appears to be happening.

The Book of Ahania is Blake's version of the Exodus, which he sees as a betrayed revolution. Fuzon, the son of Urizen and a fire-demon like Los, leads a revolt against his father and leaves Egypt. Urizen does not care whether his tyranny is Egyptian or Israelite in locale as long as it is tyranny, and very soon Fuzon's pillar of fire has given place to the sky-god Urizen's pillar of cloud, the twelve tribes of Israel (actually thirteen, because of the division of the tribe of Joseph) fall into the cyclical rhythms of the zodiac, and the moral law is reimposed. Urizen acquires a poisonous serpent, the same serpent that introduced the tree of morality to Adam and Eve, and Fuzon is crucified on the Tree of Mystery (metaphorically the same tree) as a sacrifice to the serpent. This is what Blake reads into the story of the brazen serpent on the pole in Numbers 21.

The incident thus recalls the fall of Adam and Eve and anticipates the death of the rebellious son Absalom and the crucifixion of Christ, all of these being symbols of the completing of the triumph of tyranny and the martyrdom of the rebel against it. It remains the central image of human society for 1800 years until the red Orc appears in America, announces that he is the Orc who has been throughout history "wreathed round the accursed tree," and is ready to do battle with the white reactionary terror of Albion. We may recall that American flags at that period featured trees, serpents, stars, an alternation of red and white, and a preoccupation with the number thirteen.

The Oedipal trio of father, mother, and son reappears in *The Book of Ahania,* along with a very unusual fantasy of a primal scene. Fuzon throws his "pillar of fire" at Urizen, which divides Urizen's loins and separates from his body the female figure of Ahania, who is, in a manner of speaking, Fuzon's mother. The poem concludes with a beautiful lament of this Ahania, an Earth Mother weeping for a dying god. Ahania has, of course, no counterpart in the Mosaic account of the Exodus, and her prominence here means that Blake is losing interest in the twofold stage of his biblical vision and is moving into the threefold one of "soft Beulah's night." Beulah means married, and is the word applied by Isaiah to the land of Israel reunited with its God as bride to bridegroom.

Up to about 1795 Blake had apparently assumed that the revolution of human liberty, after spreading from America to France, would then spread over the rest of the world: in that year he engraved the remarkable little poem "Asia," describing its penetration into that traditionally benighted continent. But it soon became clear to him that the reactionary powers would not disappear, but simply form an adversary relation with the revolutionary ones. This had happened before, Blake says, with the sixteenth-century Reformation, just as it was to happen again after 1917. An adversary situation, even if there is no war, impoverishes both sides, as both have to consolidate power on a basis of repression. This means that the apocalyptic contest of freedom and tyranny vanishes into dreamland, and the tactics of holding and gaining power emerge as the common ideology of both parties.

For Blake this common ideology was to be found in what he calls Deism or natural religion, and his opposition to it led him to denounce Voltaire and Rousseau on the same basis that he had already denounced the empiricism of Newton and Locke in England. Trying to explain why he hated "n.r." takes us into one of the most treacherous areas of symbolism, the male and female symbolism that recalls, but should not be confused with, the relations of men and women. It is also the most difficult area of Blake to explore, partly because Blake never shows much pictorial or verbal interest in what ought to have been his main bib-

lical source, the Song of Songs. Some personal anxieties may also
have obscured the clarity of this part of his vision.

In traditional Christian symbolism, all Christian souls,
whether of men or of women, are symbolically female, and make
up the Bride of Christ, Christ being symbolically the only male.
In Blake all human beings, both men and women, are symbolically male, and what is symbolically female is nature or the objective world. In Blake's myth of the creation-fall, one very
unexpected event was the forming of two sexes among human
beings. One of the "Eternals" in *The Four Zoas* says, "Humanity
knows naught of sex: wherefore are sexes in Beulah?" In *The Book
of Urizen* we learn that the same Eternals shuddered at the appearance of the first separate female form. Blake seems to be
taking quite seriously the hint dropped so lightly in Andrew
Marvell's poem "The Garden," that the real fall was the creation
of Eve. Originally, in the second creation account, there was an
androgynous "adam" and a garden which was itself the female
principle. This symbolism recurs in the Song of Songs, where in
the fourth chapter there is a male, that is a human, spirit or wind
in the garden, and where the garden itself, "a garden enclosed, a
fountain sealed," is what is female. A character in *The Four Zoas*
recalls the happy days of eternity "Where thou & I in undivided
Essence walk'd about / Imbodied, thou my garden of delight & I
the spirit in the garden." Elsewhere the symbolism becomes urban and focuses on the relation between a male God-Man and a
female Jerusalem, "a city, yet a Woman," as Blake says. This
suggests that the individual is the sexual male and the social the
sexual female. However, the present sexual relation within humanity provides the central imaginative focus for the kind of
energy that rebuilds the creation. In any case, Blake does not
mean that there is no sexual activity in his spiritual world, but
that there is a tremendous heightening of it, a total merging of
the creating and the responding aspects of the imagination.

There are two kinds of human subject, a positive subject
that recreates the world and a negative one that just stares at it.
The positive subject is the human imagination, which is constantly concerned with creation and love. The total body of what
a human being loves is that being's "emanation," and emanations
are symbolically female. The negative human subject is the ego
or "selfhood," who withdraws from creative effort and, because
full of desires and energies that have no outlet, is "in every man

insane and most deformed," and "a ravening devouring lust continually." Blake calls this ego figure the "Spectre," and all Spectres, like all imaginations, are symbolically male. Confronting the Spectre is the negative aspect of the symbolically female, or what Blake calls the Female Will, the elusive, evasive, mysterious outside world as it appears to the ego, who keeps trying to grasp and hold what is actually inside him, waiting to be born from his body as Eve was from Adam's. All Spectres are symbolically dead, unless provided with "counterparts" or "concentering visions" that bring them to life.

We express one aspect of this symbolism, very misleadingly, when we speak of a Father God and a Mother Nature. In the actual relation that emanation is more like a daughter: we may remember the prominence of daughters in the restoration of Job. Thus the theme of Blake's poem *Jerusalem* is the union of Albion, the imagination of the human race, with his emanation or daughter Jerusalem, the totality of what Albion constructs, loves, and surrounds. The opposite relation, of Spectre and Female Will, is almost exactly what was later to be called the "ghost in the machine." There being no God apart from humanity, nature apart from humanity is the subhuman; hence "natural religion" is simply a worship of the machinery which is all that the Spectre can see in nature. The Spectre can respond to this vision of machinery, most of which is in the stars, only by building more machinery of its own, and so "natural religion" takes the form of an industrialism that builds a system of exploiting other men on the basis of exploiting nature.

This threefold Beulah vision of the world is full of fairies and elemental spirits, which are not featured in the Bible but represent for Blake the original forms of what were later perverted into the heathen gods, nature spirits turned monstrous and tyrannical. Blake's fairies appear in the most unexpected places: in the middle of the intensely political poem *The Song of Los* in an exquisite picture of Oberon and Titania resting upon lilies. The conventionally mocking, teasing, mischievous qualities of these creatures indicate that they are part of a genuine but still incomplete vision of nature where all natural objects are human entities "seen afar," and where "All the Wisdom which was hidden in caves & dens from ancient / Time is now sought out from Animal & Vegetable & Mineral."

In the fourfold vision nature expands into the infinite worlds traditionally called heaven and hell, except that we have to remember that "Death & Hell / Teem with Life." This is the apocalyptic vision at the end of *Jerusalem* in which "All Human Forms [are] identified," as the entire universe turns inside out, going through the vortex of time and space to become the city and garden where man and nature are sexually at one. In the Bible the image for the fallen creation is the sea or watery deep that meets us at the beginning of Genesis and returns in the story of Noah's flood, a flood that has never really subsided. As the Atlantis story reminds us, the present world is symbolically submarine as well as subterranean. In Blake this watery chaos is the last of the four "Zoas" to become clear in his mind, the Tharmas who represents, Blake says, human strength and sublimity, and in the final vision turns from the water of death into the water of life. The Priestly account of creation also distinguishes the fire of life, the primordial light, from the sun created on the fourth day, and when man resumes his proper intelligence he can live in this fire as well as in the water of life.

With the fourfold vision we are in the world of full humanity: "The Sexual is Threefold, the Human is Fourfold," Blake says. Hence if I go on talking about mankind and of what "man" does, it is because the English language, in its infinite and illogical unwisdom, compels me to do so. Blake's reading of the Bible from his "fourfold" point of view is not simply a reversal of traditional readings. What he reverses is the directional emphasis: he reads forward to the end instead of constantly looking back to the beginning. We start with a waste and void chaos, a fall, a flood, a descent to Egypt, and other images of being thrown into an alien world, constantly subject to disaster, and with nothing but an invisible God to depend on and a vague hope for a better world in some kind of future, in or out of time.

Blake's Bible tells us, as its essential revelation, not that man fell into chaos, but that he can climb out of it if he uses all his creative capacities to do so. This means using everything he has that is imaginative, and the imagination, Blake says, is the human existence itself. In our day Ezra Pound, by no means either a biblical or a Blakean poet, also spoke near the end of his life of having tried to build a terrestrial paradise, and of urging humanity to be men and not destroyers. Blake, being both a biblical and an English poet, speaks of the central task of man as building Jerusalem in England, of remaking the world into its genuinely human form.

We think we fall asleep at night into the illusions of dream, and wake up in our bedrooms in the morning facing reality again. But of course everything in the bedroom is a human construct, and whatever humanity has made it can remake. We gradually discover that this principle applies to everything: what is real is what we have made, and what we have not yet made: *verum factum,* as Vico says. When Blake says that a man who is not a painter or poet is not a Christian, he is putting into paradox his principle that the release of the imagination, in any human sphere whatever, creates human form, and cannot destroy anything except unreality. Blake also says that the notion that before the creation all was solitude and chaos is the most pernicious idea that can enter the mind. In spite of the word *before,* he is not talking about time but about a spiritual reality that has always been here, and that the imagination is constantly struggling to make more and more visible. The apocalypse at the end of the Bible is not simply a new heaven and earth, but the old heaven and earth restored in their original forms. Visions of what humanity could accomplish if the destructive side of man did not get in its way are common enough: in Blake, however, God and creative man being the same thing, his apocalypse is neither a humanistic vision of a better future or a show of fireworks put on by God for an applauding or terrified human audience. It is the attaining of a divine and human identity whose creative powers are entirely without limits. Limits are in the forms of what is made, but the powers of making are infinite.

V

✧

Natural and
Revealed
Communities

✧

I AM using the connection of this lectureship with Thomas
More to reconsider his *Utopia,* a work I shall always associate
with butterflies in the stomach. In my first year as a junior in-
structor fifty years ago, I was assigned a course in sixteenth-
century literature, and *Utopia,* in the Elizabethan Robinson
translation, was practically the first text I taught to undergrad-
uates. Despite this, the lectures went very well: that is to say,
they disappeared. I asked the two stock questions about the book
and got the two stock answers. How many would rather live in
Utopia than in Henry VIII's England? Everyone. How many
would rather live in Utopia than in twentieth-century Canada?
Not one. That established the essential points about the book,
first, that *Utopia* made more sense than England then did, and
second, that no normal human being wants to live in anyone
else's Utopia. Then I sat back and let the students argue about
the book according to their own socialist, liberal, or laissez-faire
biases. *Utopia* was a most contemporary text for the nineteen-
thirties.

There had been a great awakening of interest in Communism during the depression, and some Communist critics, notably Karl Kautsky, had called attention to the proto-Marxist
features of Utopia's abolition of private property, of exploited
labor, and of a leisure class. Most striking of all, from this point
of view, was the climax of the narration of Hythlodaye, the character who has been to Utopia and whose account of it constitutes

289

the second book. He sums up his experience by contrasting the Utopian commonwealth with the "conspiracy of rich men" (*conspiratio divitum*) in Europe promoting their own interests and pretending that the conspiracy *was* the commonwealth. More conservative critics were horrified by the placing of More among the prophets of Stalin in a kind of Communist Old Testament, and many of them insisted that *Utopia* was a jeu d'esprit, an in-joke for a small elite of humanists, on no account to be taken seriously as a social blueprint of any kind. There is, it is true, a fair amount of in-joke apparatus about *Utopia,* such as the elaborate pretence that a real voyage has been made to a real place, a pretence neutralized by the meanings of the Greek words suggested in the proper names. Utopia itself means "nowhere"; its chief river, the Anydrus, is a river "without water"; its capital Amaurote suggests "cloud town," and so on. But humanists on the level of More and Erasmus did not think of themselves as a private elite: they were deeply committed and public-spirited men, and there is no real question that *Utopia,* in its intention as well as its reputation, was a very serious book. At the same time we do have the paradox of an idealized state whose religion is not only non-Christian, but seems to be, for most modern readers, so much more humane than anything produced under a Christian label in sixteenth-century Europe. This does constitute a genuine critical problem, even if we leave out the contrast with More's personal attitude and the things he says in his other writings.

The transition from medieval to modern England, from the medieval Warwick to the modern Wolsey, from Malory to More, had come with a rush in a generation or two, after being delayed so long by the Wars of the Roses. The feudal economy of medieval England lay dead with Richard III on Bosworth field, and England soon fell into something like the Italian city-state pattern, on a far larger scale, where the main secular figures were the prince, who now held supreme power instead of being the nominee of a baronial house, and the courtier, the servant and adviser of the prince. The main advance on the cultural front was of course the movement we call humanism. Medieval culture had been a Latin and vernacular culture: humanism promised an immense expansion of knowledge and wisdom when the Greek antecedents of this culture began to come into view. In the Middle Ages the greater number of highly educated people were clerics of one sort or another: the humanists, while deeply interested in biblical and patristic scholarship, brought in also a conception of secular education that could be fitted to the new facts of society.

For that society, the most important person to be educated was the prince, so a program for educating the prince or magistrate could serve as a model for education generally. Hence such works as Erasmus's *Institute of a Christian Prince,* which had many epigones, including Elyot's *The Governour* in England. The great classical precedent for this educational model was Xenophon's *Cyropaedia* (*The Education of Cyrus*), a fictional biography of the great Persian conqueror that places him within the context of a Persian society based on certain moral principles, including the supremacy of law. As one man, even a prince, cannot do everything, Castiglione provided, in his very influential *Cortegiano,* a similar model for the courtier, who was to place his accomplishments at the service of the prince. Had not Plato said that society was best off when philosophers were kings or kings took up philosophy? True, if the Seventh Epistle is anything to go by, Plato had pretty well given up on the princes of his time. But the goal of providing the prince, or those directly responsible to the prince, with an all-round education covering every aspect of the social life he was to give leadership to, would, if attained, practically make the scholar the architect of his society. In every age intellectuals are attracted to the idea of putting their expertise to a political use, and never seem to learn that the impulse is usually a mistake, and one well-known book of this century, Julien Benda's *Trahison des clercs* (*The Betrayal of the Intellectuals*), reminds us that this impulse is normally a mistaken one.

Thus Castiglione starts out full of enthusiasm for an education that trains the courtier for both peace and war, though as an amateur in both. He should know enough about literature and the pictorial arts to know how to patronize their practitioners, but should not engage too deeply in them himself. The implication, that the amateur, at least when he is a possible patron, is superior in social rank and status to the professional, remained a stereotype for centuries in England, where Castiglione, in the Elizabethan period, had a good deal of prestige. As late as Henry James's *Tragic Muse* the hero, torn between politics and painting as a career, remarks that the social establishment in England approves of the artist only if he is a gentlemanly bungler: if he takes his art seriously he becomes declassed. But as Castiglione goes on to consider the courtier's actual social function, he runs into a paradox that makes the end of his book rather sad and quixotic. The courtier should be young to acquire all his graceful skills, but if he is to advise the prince he needs to be considerably older. And why should any prince listen to his advice? Princes are out for fame and glory, not for the virtues of a local justice of the peace.

Further, if we look back at Xenophon's *Cyropaedia,* we wonder if this really is a book on education at all. Cyrus has high intelligence, and the sort of charm and magnetism that marks the born leader. But Cyrus is the first, and the only one available to Xenophon, of the series of world conquerors that later included Alexander and Caesar and the book is concerned almost entirely with his military enterprises. Machiavelli, who wrote a very different kind of treatise on the prince, praises the *Cyropaedia,* but the context in which he does so is significant: it is in the fourteenth chapter, which begins with the statement "A prince ought to have no other aim or thought, nor select anything else for his study, than war and its rules and discipline." The ideal prince is not the ruler who has had a model education, but the ruler who is always fighting or thinking about fighting. Castiglione's courtier becomes increasingly individualized and isolated as the book goes on, and the climax of his education is love, the ideal of Plato's *Symposium* rather than Plato's *Republic.* Xenophon's Cyrus is taught to love and be just to his own countrymen, but when he comes of age his father explains that he will now be concerned mainly with enemies, and for them he needs a morality the exact reverse of everything he has so far been taught.

When we turn from the humanist movement and its educational ideals to More's book, we note that there are no courtiers in Utopia, and no prince. It is true that More's Elizabethan translator rendered More's word *princeps,* which in its Utopian context means something like mayor, as prince, and thereby caused some misunderstanding. But the model of Utopia is republican, and is closer to the monastic orders, with their combination of authority and election, although the monastic structure is of course secularized, with the nuclear family as its unit. The Utopians detest war, and attach no glory to conquerors, but when they do go to war it is total and all-out war: no deals are made with the other side to keep it going for their mutual profit. Hence More avoids the paradoxes inherent in the "arts of peace and war" construct. But while he avoids them he is certainly well aware of them. Hythlodaye points out at considerable length that it is no use for him to try to put what he has learned about social organization from his sojourn in Utopia at the service of a European prince. He would be promptly and constantly ignored, while the prince and his real counsellors went on with the planning of further wars. More represents himself in the book as urging that Hythlodaye should still continue to try to advise in spite of all rebuffs and setbacks. The fact that More himself is supposed to be urging this points, very obviously, to the tragic irony of More's own life, spent in the service of a prince who betrayed him and finally ordered him to the scaffold. But it also points to the fact that Utopia, even though it means "nowhere," is being accepted as some kind of social reality. We have next to ask, what kind?

As a revolution in education, humanism polarized the two elements in educational theory that educators are still wrangling about: the elements of content and of lifestyle. In the Middle Ages the student was thought of as being confronted by an objective body of knowledge: hence the popularity, in that period, of the encyclopedic treatise, covering the whole spectrum of medieval knowledge from God downward. For the humanists education was thought of as an individual acquirement, enabling one to become a personal force in society. This is the reality behind the cult of the amateur, already mentioned. No knowledge should get out of proportion to its social function: the pedant, however great his learning, has missed the central point of his education. Good style, specifically in the writing of Latin, thus becomes primary on the basis of the principle later formulated as *le style, c'est l'homme même.*

Philosophy, for example, becomes an aspect of social cultivation, as it is in the dialogues of Socrates with the young gentlemen of Athens. It is no longer to be a specialized profession with its own technical language, as in scholastic philosophy. Glancing back again to my first days of teaching: Thomist realism was then dominant in Catholic universities, and the Pontifical Institute of Medieval Studies had been set up by Gilson and Maritain on my own campus. It was thus puzzling to many of my students of that period that More should present his Utopians as not merely indifferent to abstract and generalized concepts ("second intentions"), but as quite unable to take in the notion of a real universal, even the universal "Man." The Utopians live in a very concrete world: they are keenly interested in, for example, astronomy, but they are postnominalist humanists, like More himself.

It is obvious that More was influenced by Plato's *Republic,* not so much in detail as in the general idea of constructing a social model. Plato, it appears, presents his Republic (which incidentally is not a republic, though Utopia is) primarily to answer the question What is justice? We have justice, Plato thinks, when everyone works at what he is best fitted to work at. In designing the form or idea of a just society, Plato looks at the actual society of his own day to see if he can find an intelligible structure in it. The French philologist Georges Dumézil says that the Indo-European peoples of the ancient world show in their mythologies a conception of human society as divided among three major classes: the red men or warriors, the white men or priests, the blue men or artisans. In India this conception was actually embodied in the three castes of Indian society, and it seems to be also the intelligible principle that Plato discovers in his. Plato's state has a philosopher-king and his counsellors, a warrior caste not involved in marriage or family life, and a caste of producers.

At the end of book 9, it is agreed that such a state could probably not exist, but that the wise man should live according to its principles whatever his actual society is like. It looks as though the real point of Plato's *Republic* was to construct an allegory of the wise man's mind, the philosopher-king, warriors, and artisans symbolizing respectively his reason, his will, and his desires and appetites. Similarly *Utopia* is in part an allegory of a humanist's education, an education that acquires the shape, when completed, of a model vision of society that constantly informs him and gives direction to his social life. Everyone who has a responsible social function at all works with some such model, however unconscious, in his mind: a world of greater health for the physician, greater equity for the social worker, and the like. That is why, when Hythlodaye comes back from Utopia a convinced Communist revolutionary, whose only remedy for Europe is to scrap the whole setup and start over on a Utopian basis, More himself urges a more practical and gradualist attitude, using the Utopian vision as a basis for ad hoc reforms.

According to Erasmus, Utopia is much closer to England than the fiction in the book about a voyage to a new world would suggest. If one of its aspects, *Utopia* is an educational treatise setting England beside an imaginary yet real form of England, an England making the kind of moral sense that an educated humanist tries to make of whatever society he lives in. It has much in common with another educational treatise written later in the century, Spenser's *Faerie Queene*. Here the whole apparatus of chivalric romance is consolidated into a world called "Faerie," which is a moral model of England itself, and is therefore, as Spenser indicates in his introduction to the second book, "nowhere," that is, not in space. Both More's Utopia and Spenser's Faerie have affinities with Dante's *Purgatorio,* another construct that brings out the moral shape of the life on Dante's side of the world.

It remains to ask what corresponds in More's vision to the three classes of Plato. Utopian society is not Christian, and Utopians do not have the full or revealed forms of the theological virtues, faith, hope, and love. But no human society, Christian or not, can function without at least a modicum of the four natural virtues, fortitude, prudence, temperance, and justice. Utopia is a society in which these virtues are set free to function properly on a basis of nature and reason. In theory, all societies are equipped with stage one, the natural virtues, and Christian societies with stage two, the revealed virtues. If Utopia can get so far with stage one only, why cannot Europe get infinitely further with both stages? The answer, of course, is that Europe has practically nothing of either stage. Thus, unlike Plato, More's book contains a strong element of satire: this comes out most explicitly in the first book, which although written later certainly belongs to the total vision.

We may think, vaguely and with much hindsight, of the age of More's *Utopia* as one of great exhilaration. A new Atlantis had sprung out of the west: Athens and Jerusalem were now only Turkish towns; the center of power was moving from the Mediterranean to the Atlantic seaboard countries: new worlds, new wealth, new learning, were there for the taking. More, being a practical man, took shorter views. He saw the terrible human dislocations in great social changes: he saw the misery brought about by the enclosure movement, the futility of the hideous penal laws, and the prospect of more and more wars. As he looked more deeply, he saw the roots of these evils in social inequality with its inevitable consequence, the overproduction of the superfluous and the underproduction of the necessary. At this point we may realize that the satirist Lucian, four of whose dialogues were translated by More into Latin, was perhaps a more specific influence on More than Plato was.

In Lucian's dialogue *Zeus Trageodus* a conference of gods is called, who are to come represented by their statues. Zeus tells Hermes, who is arranging the conference, to put the gold statues in the front row, silver ones next, and so on. Hermes objects that some attention should be paid to quality of workmanship, because only barbarians can afford gold statues, and all the Greek gods will be out in the bleachers. Zeus agrees that quality of workmanship should come first (Lucian himself began as a sculptor's apprentice), but still preference must be given to gold, or the whole human economy that keeps the gods going will fall to pieces. It is not a very long step from here to the Utopian use of gold for chamber pots and children's toys, although, of course, More is also building on the insight, very rare for his time, that gold is only the symbol of wealth, not its reality.

When we look at the literary genres belonging to or closely related to *Utopia,* we notice a form that recurs frequently: the form of the mirror satire, the depiction of a society that is essentially just like ours, but looks silly because we are seeing it objectively. A century later than More, Joseph Hall, an Anglican bishop who collided with Milton, wrote such a satire, *Mundus Alter et Idem* (*Another World, yet the Same World*). The form is still going strong in the Victorian Samuel Butler's *Erewhon.* In More's own day this kind of satire is represented by Erasmus's *Encomium Moriae* (*Praise of Folly*), where the narrator reminds us of the professional fools that were a feature of Renaissance courts, and in fact of More's own household. As a literary archetype—*King Lear* is the obvious example—the Fool, with a capital *F,* is by no means a fool in himself, but sees folly all around him, and cannot help saying so. As a result his social situation would be intolerable if he were not in a position where no one takes him seriously. "I would fain learn to lie," the Fool says to King Lear, and may well mean it.

Lucian's *Dialogues of the Dead* portray scenes of the newly dead gathered on the shore of the Styx, to be ferried across by Charon into the land of shades. This is a classical form of what was still popular in More's day as the *danse macabre*, the vision of death as striking down people in every walk of life, the only visible form of social equality. The irony in Lucian is naturally based on the formula "You can't take it with you." The more one has, the more one has to leave behind, and the more noise one is apt to make about leaving it, especially if it has been stolen in acts of tyranny. The Fool figure here is Menippus the Cynic, Lucian's hero, who has possessed nothing during his life, and has therefore been greatly despised. But by having nothing, he is infinitely better adjusted to whatever awaits him after death. I suspect that the name Hythlodaye, which seems to suggest something like "babbler" or "speaker of trifles," is connected with the character type who is considered a fool but is not one, and whose vision or picture (imago) of Utopian life enables him to see the folly around him in Europe. Like Menippus, the Utopians live with a simplicity and economy that their neighbors consider perverse or stupid, but makes them look proportionately more sensible from an outside perspective. We shall come back to this "outside perspective" later.

Utopia is a society based on nature and reason, though both of these terms need qualifying. The ready acceptance of discipline by the Utopians, the deliberate emphasis on the monotony and uniformity of their clothes, houses, and cities, implies that they think of nature as primarily a system or order, the aspect of nature sometimes called *natura naturata*. This order of nature transcends reason but not itself. The Utopians are reasonable, but they are not rationalists: reason is for them a servant for man to use, not a mental tyranny that uses him. They even have saints who devote themselves to the most unpleasant and irksome work: their motivation is not rational, but is still natural within this conception of nature. The secular monastic features of Utopia remind us a little of Rabelais, who knew *Utopia* and admired it. Rabelais gives us a secular send-up of monastic communities in the Abbey of Thélème, whose members reverse the traditional monastic vows of poverty, chastity, and obedience by being all well-off, married, and doing as they like. This also is a "natural" society, but the immense emphasis on eating and drinking and excreting and copulating in Rabelais provides at least as much evidence as we need that Rabelais's "nature" is *natura naturans*, the nature of biology rather than physics or mathematics.

Thus *Utopia* introduces to modern literature the problem of the "natural society," and begins the arguments about whether such a thing is possible or not. The element in More's satire that contrasts a sensible non-Christian Utopia with a silly and vicious Europe that is technically Christian reappears in Montaigne's essay on the cannibals. In many respects, says Montaigne, moral as well as physical, the cannibals live more sensibly than we do. A simple outdoor life keeps them healthy; they have a government of sorts, but not one that systematically robs and starves the helpless; they may eat their enemies, but do not burn them alive or torture them to death over doctrinal trivia. What really can be said against them as compared with us? Well, of course, Montaigne says in his last sentence, *ils ne portent point de hault de chausses:* they don't wear breeches. Montaigne's tone is light but his point is serious. Twenty years ago, in attending the Montreal Expo, I dropped in to the Canadian Indian exhibit, where the walls were covered with printed statements expressing the exhibitors' opinion of their white visitors. I remember nothing of the actual wording, but what was said in effect was: You conquered us, not fairly in battle but by infecting us with your foul diseases; you stole our land and shut us up into open-air cages; you trapped the animals and burnt the forests we depended on for food and shelter; worst of all, you robbed us of our Great Spirit and put your own horrible scarecrow in its place. The question of a natural society is clearly not dead.

In the eighteenth century the natural society debate came into the foreground with the political revolutions that brought in the second phase of the modern world. The conservatives, Swift at the beginning of that century and Burke at the end of it, clung to the traditional view. Man lives in a different order of nature from the nature of animals and plants. Many things are natural to man that are not natural to anything else living in his environment. It is natural to man to wear clothes, to be under social discipline, to be aware of moral obligations: man's nature, as Burke explicitly says, is a nature which is also art. The last book of *Gulliver's Travels* provides some fine print for this thesis: a natural society might be achieved by exceptionally gifted animals like the Houyhnhmns, but man is not really an animal, and Swift creates the Yahoo to remind us of what man would be like if he were one. He would not, for example, be an attractive animal: he would be more like rats and weasels than like baby pandas or koala bears.

On the other side we have Rousseau, who suggests that the

traditions of human civilization are based on what ought to be a society of nature and reason, but have lost touch with it. Civilization produces a grotesque inequality in society, symbolized, as in More, by an immense overproduction of superfluous things. The real human community of nature and reason lies groaning underneath this. Rousseau, like Rabelais and Montaigne, is thinking primarily of nature in the context of *natura naturans*. What is new and different is the revolutionary shape of his construct. The natural society for him is an immense fettered energy that would transform the world if it were liberated.

The debate is still with us, and so far as our present tentative solutions go, each side has scored a point. On the conservative side, it is generally agreed that there are not and cannot be any noble savages; no human society can be fully natural in the sense of doing away with an envelope of culture and custom that insulates it from the physical world. On the other, the traditional belief that human nature should dominate over physical nature has been expressed in a relentless exploitation of natural resources, and this exploitation is now running into diminishing returns. Hence the importance of ecological movements insisting that humanity is as wrong in enslaving and exploiting nature as it is in enslaving and exploiting other men, and that no improvement in human conditions of any importance is possible unless this is taken into account. I am at present, however, concerned with the aspect of the question that comes into literature.

We notice first that the conception of a human society which is natural in the sense of being primarily related to physical nature is a constant theme in literature, and is much older than More. It produced the pastoral, a convention of Greek origin; it produced the bucolic poetry of Virgil; it produced even the shepherd symbolism of the Bible, though otherwise it is outside the mainstream of the Christian tradition, Christianity being a big-city religion with a strongly urban basis in its organization and symbolism. This by-form of Utopian fiction we may call the Arcadia. More's Utopia is not an Arcadia, even though there is a constant interchange between country and city life, the absence of which in the nineteenth century is emphasized in the *Communist Manifesto*. One romance not often mentioned in discussions of Utopias is Pater's *Marius the Epicurean*, which gives us an idealized picture of the half-pastoral religion of the late pagan

299

world, stressing its quiet serenity and slightly overripe beauty, and then brings it into collision with the new force of Christianity.

The Arcadian or pastoral tradition has produced much that is very lovely, in painting and music as well as literature, but in literature it seldom gets very far away from what is called escape reading. The reason is that the pastoral assumes a stabilized human population. The disciples of Darwin in the nineteenth century, in renewing the study of the relation of human to physical nature, inherited a theory of unstable population from Malthus and gave it a good deal of prominence. Huxley's essay on *Evolution and Ethics* starts with the Darwinian conception of evolution as a competition for the means of subsistence, in which the mutations that promote survival are conserved, and those that do not are wiped out. Then a human society is established, say on an island, and sets up a counterevolutionary or ethical movement. It educates children, takes care of the weak and helpless, aids the handicapped, and tries to rehabilitate misfits. The result is that the population increases until there is hardly room to breathe, and the old ruthless evolutionary pattern with its ferocious struggle to survive gradually returns. Again we notice how many things in his brief sketch More does *not* overlook. The population of Utopia does increase, and from time to time the Utopians occupy land that their neighbors regard as useless and proceed to make its desert blossom like the rose. If the neighbors prove unreasonable in giving up such territory, the Utopians will settle in it by force—a growing point of a very different social development that More does not pursue.

Ever since *Utopia* was published, there has been in literature a steady production of imaginary communities. In the nineteenth century, largely as a reaction to the excesses of laissez-faire, there were a large number of romances describing eutopias, "good places," seriously intended social models. We have seen how simplistic it would be to classify More's book with these even though that does not detract from More's essential seriousness. Along with the eutopia goes the vision of what has been called the dystopia, the society that has allowed itself to follow certain tendencies until it freezes into a claustrophobic nightmare, as in Orwell's *1984*. One reason for this development is that one man's eutopia is likely to be another's man's dystopia. Thus *Looking Backward*, Edward Bellamy's description of the Boston of the twenty-first century, published in 1889, impressed many people in its day as a great manifesto of human emancipation, but it horrified William Morris, who wrote *News from Nowhere* to set up a contrasting picture of the good life.

Even in More there are strict limitations on freedom of movement from one city to another, even sharper limitations on freedom of speech and on public assemblies, and a relentless, all-pervasive discipline in family life as well as in the public at large. There is also the omnipresent appearance of bondmen to remind the virtuous of the consequences of straying too far out of line. Although I imagine many of More's contemporaries would be impressed with the humanity of Utopian discipline (one does not at any rate see gibbets with twenty men hanging from them as in England), still many of us would see in the features just mentioned cracks in the facade indicating a latent hysteria under all the parade of order.

The imaginary society is a central theme in our century of what is so inaccurately called science fiction. There are two main forms of science fiction: a software philosophical fantasy descending from More's *Utopia,* and a hardware technological one of which the ancestor is Bacon's *New Atlantis.* The *New Atlantis* has no time for such subtleties as a non-Christian ideal state: Bacon simply sends a Bible floating on the sea to the shores of Atlantis before the story begins, so that they have already been converted to Christianity. Bacon is concerned almost entirely to describe the project he tried to interest King James in, an institute of scientific research and technological innovation.

We notice that Bacon's slight and amusing sketch, like practically all the hardware romance that has descended from it, is future oriented. As long as technology is continuously being improved, society is in a constant state of revolutionary ferment. But there is always the possibility that those obsessed with power will see in a certain phase of technology a chance for seizing and holding power, arresting further developments and establishing a permanent tyranny. This is what happened with the invention of the "telescreen" in *1984.*

More important, a eutopia, or social model presented as a straightforward ideal, attempts to present a human life without self-conflict. But in our ordinary experience life without self-conflict is possible only for machinery or for social insects like ants and bees. In insect states the individual hardly exists except as a social functionary. In Samuel Butler's *Erewhon,* the inhabitants, long before the narrator arrives, have abolished machinery in obedience to the arguments of a scripture called "The Book of the Machines," which tells them that human beings have already been reduced to "affectionate machine-tickling aphids," and that after machines have finally learned to reproduce themselves they will take over human society. Butler himself regards this fear as ludicrous: in fact, the pseudoargument is part of his attack on Darwinism as a view of life that confuses the organic with the mechanical. But it is not wholly ludicrous: we may think (to use an example I have often given) of the way in which the primary technological invention, the wheel, immediately became a symbol of fate and fortune, of what dominates and tyrannizes over human life instead of serving it as a machine should do.

In any case, the great majority of social constructs in science fiction today are dystopias. I may single out one for an obvious reason: R. M. Lafferty's *Past Master,* published in 1968. In this story we have a Utopian society in the future which has turned into a dystopia. The rulers, who have acquired the power to travel in time, reach back into the past and lift Thomas More out of the sixteenth century to serve as a rallying point for this moribund Utopia of the future. More at first is exhilarated to see a working model of the society he dreamed of, but before long it is obvious that he is regarded as only a stooge by his employers, and by the end of the story he has been sentenced to be beheaded.

The use of More in this story reminds us that More's Utopia, unlike its hardware counterparts, is not future oriented. Utopian technology is of the simplest kind: they do not even have gunpowder, nor, fortunately, do their neighbors. They want no progress except a progress in expanding from where they are into a fuller life. In speaking of Lucian's *Dialogues of the Dead* earlier, I said that his hero, Menippus the Cynic, who has possessed nothing during his life, is for that very reason far better adjusted to whatever awaits him on the other shore of the Styx. Lucian offers no suggestions about what that "whatever" might be, and it is unlikely that he had any ideas on the subject. More had, and the fact opens up a new dimension in his argument.

I suppose that a Marxist reading *Utopia* would feel that once alienation and exploitation were abolished, the projecting of a hope for immortality, for a next life compensating those who have been cheated out of this one, would disappear also. For

More, on the contrary, the Utopian way of life greatly intensifies the desire for immortality. Belief in the immortality of the soul is a doctrine that Utopians are as fanatical about as Utopians can get: anyone who denies the doctrine instantly becomes isolated from Utopian society and is degraded to a second-class citizenship. Here again we may glance at some of his precedents. Plato's *Republic* ends with a vision of reincarnation, immortality, and the universe turning on the spindle of necessity. Cicero imitated Plato in his *De Republica,* fragments of which were discovered only in the nineteenth century: his sixth book, however, had been preserved by a later writer, Macrobius, who wrote a commentary on it. That book, the famous *Somnium Scipionis (Dream of Scipio)*, a favorite book of Chaucer, gives us a vision of later history in the context of a description of the structure of the universe. It looks as though there is some impetus in the Utopia form that tends to carry it through to a perspective beyond that of social life in this world.

Such a perspective is hinted at in the final pages of More's *Utopia,* when Hythlodaye and his companions bring Christianity, in a humanistic setting, to the commonwealth. The Utopians welcome Christianity, partly because of the communistic elements in the life of the early postpentecostal church. One convert, however, who shows too much zeal in propounding his faith and denouncing all others, is quietly restrained, though on secular and not religious grounds. The tactics necessary to keep Christianity going in the late Roman empire are not necessary in Utopia, where there is no divine Caesar and no state worship. We are left with a Utopia which will accept Christianity, but without persecuting non-Christians or compelling them to profess belief in Christian doctrines. It is left to the inner strength of Christianity to make itself the keystone of the Utopian arch, fulfilling the natural and reasonable elements in that society and providing a clear vision of the belief in immortality that the Utopians already hold.

The year after *Utopia* was published, Luther nailed his ninety-five theses to the door at Wittenburg, and the humanist liberal found himself again confronted with a revolutionary situation, not the imaginary revolution of Hythlodaye, but an actual one. More instantly took the anti-Lutheran point of view: he never seems to have considered the merits of the Reformers' case to the extent that Erasmus did. I am concerned here only with some discrepancies in the relation of *Utopia* to More's life. It should be remembered that my own commitment is to the other side, but I am not suggesting that there was anything in More's own life that he could or should have done differently.

When a liberal is caught in a revolutionary situation, the revolutionary can always say to him: your liberal dreams of improvements within the existing order are just that—dreams. It is the revolutionary who reshapes history, and if you want to get anywhere in history you must join us. We can see from *Utopia* that this argument would have little force with More. Once their eponymous ancestor Utopus had transformed them from barbarians to a civilized people, the Utopians have no further interest in history, in fact do not believe in a history that is going anywhere, and do not share the modern conviction that the static is inherently bad. For them, if the static is the stable, what is wrong with it?

And yet, for example, among the Utopian priests there are some women. True, they are elderly, widowed, and few in numbers, and one wonders how, in so rigidly patriarchal a society as Utopia (one of its least attractive features) women could develop enough self-confidence to be anything at all. Still, they are there, and within a year or two More was ridiculing Luther and Tyndale for advocating the ordaining of women in the Reformed church. More important, the Utopian toleration for the different sects who all believe in a single God certainly does not enter into the judicial decisions of More' life. The usual answer to such difficulties is that revelation, which for More would come through the church, may often contradict nature and reason by being stricter and less flexible. This pattern was established in Old Testament times, when detailed and precise dietary laws were imposed on Israel but not on other nations. But if the intolerance of revelation comes from a wiser source than the tolerance of reason, it seems strange that it not only looks more stupid but causes more human misery. Is it really revelation, or just one more example of the human resistance to it?

To revert for the last time to my teaching *Utopia* in the thirties: it was widely believed then that capitalism, with or without a revolution, would evolve into socialism, socialism being assumed to be not only more efficient but morally superior. That did not happen: the two economies simply froze into an adversary situation, with democracies resisting reforms that sounded like Communism, the Communist countries resisting reforms that sounded like bourgeois revisionism. This deadlock repeated the religious polarizing of the sixteenth century. An adversary situation, it seems clear, impoverishes both sides. A revolution, once it reaches the point of establishing contact with what has preceded it, has no resources for anything but repression; those outside the revolution are similarly forced into a reactionary repression. The liberal may get clobbered from both ends, but an impartial view would say that he is the one who has been right all along.

I think of *Utopia* as belonging to the first great wave of humanism, a reforming movement that envisaged a far profounder reform of both church and society than either Reformation or Counter-Reformation achieved. This is more obvious in Erasmus than in More, but a good deal of the same reforming vision is in *Utopia*. All human communities, real or imaginary, are aggregates. We use the word *body* in two senses: it means the physical structure of the individual, and it means, metaphorically, the unity of a community, the body politic. The revealed community, as we get it in the apocalyptic parts of the New Testament, is a spiritual existence in which the metaphor has become a reality, and where, in Christian terms, there is only the body of Christ, which is both individual and social.

But in our present mode of existence social bodies will always be aggregates, and tolerance and flexibility are the best conditions for them. Even the individual body is a community of billions of cells and bacteria, with specialized functions and yet, presumably, with no "knowledge," whatever knowledge may be in such a context, that they are forming a larger body. But they too can make mistakes about their relation to that body, as we see in the intolerant anarchist revolution we call cancer. I myself have allergic ailments that, I am told, are caused by a panic-stricken xenophobia among the blood cells, their inability to distinguish a harmless from a dangerous intruder. Good health, in both bodies, depends on a sense of unity that also rejects a hysterical insistence on uniformity. Plato remarked that the most frightful tyrannies were very like his ideal pattern entrusted to the wrong people. In a world where no people can be exactly the right people, Utopia can exist only where More put it, in the "nowhereness" of the consciousness within the individual mind. There it can do much to inform and reform the society around it, as long as we neither abandon its vision or try to deduce an actual society from it.

Castiglione's
Il Cortegiano

✧

CASTIGLIONE'S *Il Cortegiano* purports to describe a conversation among a number of people gathered at the court of the duke and duchess of Urbino in the spring of 1507. They had proposed, as one of their after-supper "games," the ideal courtier as a theme for a discussion extending over four nights. Some kind of actual discussion seems to have been the basis for the book, and Castiglione himself was no doubt present at it, though he follows the modest precedent of Plato in the *Phaedo* and represents himself as absent in England. He was not able to get down to completing the book, however, until some years later, and a good deal happened in that time. The duke of Urbino, Guidobaldo da Montefeltro, was a childless invalid who had adopted his young nephew Francesco della Rovere as his heir. Francesco, who makes an attractive appearance at the end of book 1 as a boy of seventeen, succeeded his uncle, and retained Castiglione in his service. He also committed two murders, and was expelled from Urbino by Pope Leo X, who replaced him with his own nephew. Castiglione was forced into temporary retirement by this, and thereby gained the leisure to finish his book. Several of those who figure in the dialogue were at that time refugees from other courts and cities—Giuliano de Medici from Florence, the Fregoso brothers from Genoa, Castiglione himself from Mantua— but many of them were senior statesmen by the time the book was finished. Giuliano de Medici, though he died in 1516, lived long enough to see his family restored to power in Florence and his brother elected to the Papacy.

It was part of Castiglione's code that gentlemen who wrote

should be in no hurry to entrust what they wrote to the printing press. The press was useful for scholarly editions of the classics, and, in the more revolutionary England, for religious and political polemic, but poets, even prose writers, who belonged to the gentry tended to keep their work in manuscript and pass it around to friends. The final release to the printer was often accompanied by protests about the forcing of the author's hand by importunate readers of the manuscript. In Castiglione's case the importunate reader was the famous Vittoria della Colonna, and Castiglione's disclaimer seems to have been genuine enough. *Il Cortegiano* was not in fact published until 1528, fourteen years after completion, and Castiglione died in the next year. Although Castiglione of course wrote other things, *Il Cortegiano* was not so much a book by him as his book, his legacy to posterity, and the longer he postponed its publication, the more it receded into a distant past, as an increasing number of those featured in it died. The retrospective feeling about the book, the sense of its celebration of an ideal already left behind by history, was as obvious to Castiglione himself as it is to us, and forms part of the book's intention.

Many of those who belonged to Castiglione's original group are still well known, partly because they had the sense to get their portraits painted by Raphael or Titian. Castiglione alludes to himself also as a kind of verbal painter, and speaks in his preface of the skill of "making, by perspective art, that which is not seem to be." The remark suggests an interesting link between portrait painting and the ideology of an ascendent class. In English history, for example, we derive much of our sense of Henry VIII's character from Holbein's portrait of him standing stockily with his feet wide apart, his cruel little eyes glittering out of his terrifying face. And most of our feeling for the glamour and romance of the cause of the seventeenth-century Cavaliers comes from Van Dyck's portraits of Charles I and Queen Henrietta Maria, and from the haunting melancholy and charm with which he invested those two rather commonplace people. Similarly, it is Raphael who preserves for us the sly wit of Bibbiena, the imperturable calm of Emilia Pia, and the melancholy sensitivity of Castiglione himself.

However, other aspects of culture were developing besides painting which were much less tender to the sensibilities of a declining ruling class. Two Genoese whose names are familiar to us if not to Castiglione, Christopher Columbus and John Cabot, had begun the exploration of America that eventually shifted power from the Mediterranean city-states to the Atlantic nations, England, France, Spain, Portugal. In many respects *Il Cortegiano* was the testament of a disappearing culture to the emergent seaboard countries. It was Francis I of France who urged Castiglione to complete his book for the sake of posterity, Charles V who described its author as one of the finest gentlemen in the world, and Elizabethan England which responded eagerly to the book (in the translation of Sir Thomas Hoby published in 1561), and found in Sir Philip Sidney the embodiment of Castiglione's ideal.

The two essential facts of Renaissance society were the prince and the courtier, and it is not surprising that two of the most influential Renaissance books should be Machiavelli's *Il Principe* and Castiglione's *Il Cortegiano,* which were written at much the same time. But the city-states of Italy, with their intense local loyalties and lack of national feeling, could not provide a broad enough economic base to compete with the courts of France and England, where the destruction of the feudal system had replaced the rebellious barons of the Middle Ages with the servants of a highly centralized monarchy. In England, the rise of a wealthy middle class limited the power of the prince— Henry VIII was the only king of England to have the kind of absolute power that was common on the Continent for many centuries later—and the courtier ideal did not last long after the death of Elizabeth I. But it was a very intense ideal while it lasted, and its incorporation into Elizabethan literature, including some of Shakespeare's plays, has helped to preserve it for the English-speaking world.

We have noted something wistful and nostalgic in Castiglione's tribute to what was even then a vanishing ideal, even though he deprecates such an attitude in his introduction to the second book. At the time of the discussion the glory of Urbino itself was in decline: its greatness had been due to Guidobaldo's illustrious father Federico, but Guidobaldo was prevented by ill health from achieving much in either war or peace, and the court was held together by the duchess. The importance of this fact for Castiglione's argument will meet us later. In the next decade it became increasingly obvious that the real powers in Italy were France, Spain, and the Empire (at that time linked to Spain), and that what they did would determine Italian history, regardless of how many princes and courtiers modeled themselves on Italian handbooks. Castiglione died two years after the sack of Rome: in that brutal context, an idealized courtier looks rather woebegone and Castiglione himself a quixotic figure, without the schizophrenic mental armor that kept the original Quixote serenely believing in his fantastic code. But the great beauty and power of the book clearly derive from something other than the historical context, and we must try to see what this is.

Castiglione defines both his genre and his literary tradition when he says in his introduction: "I am content to have erred with Plato, Xenophon, and Marcius Tullius; and just as, according to these authors, there is the Idea of the perfect Republic, the perfect King, and the perfect Orator, so likewise there is that of the perfect Courtier." Central to Italian humanism was the admiration of Plato not merely as a philosopher but as a literary artist. A century earlier the humanist Berni (Leonardo Aretino) had spoken of the urbanity of the Platonic dialogue, of how well people kept their temper in the discussions, of the pleasantness and fluency of the style, and of the pervasiveness of the quality called in Greek *charis,* of which Castiglione's "grace" is a fair translation. Castiglione's genre is essentially that of the Platonic symposium (along with its Latin developments in Cicero's *Tusculan Disputations* and the like), in which a discussion is maintained on a topic which has a Platonic form or idea behind all its manifestations, with the hope that eventually something of that form or idea could be glimpsed by those taking part. Thus something of the Platonic form of love, also one of Castiglione's main themes, is glimpsed at the end of the dialogue which is explicitly called the *Symposium.*

Plato's dialogues are often concerned with issues in education, but do not envisage a curriculum or organized program for education much beyond conversations with Socrates. The question of what an educated man ought to know and what his social responsibilities are arises later, and focuses, with Cicero and later Quintilian, on the figure of the orator. In Cicero's *De Oratore,* one of the books most influential for Renaissance culture, the orator becomes the type of the educated man (*doctus vir*), with a scope and range of extraordinary versatility, making up in brilliance what it might lack in depth. For Quintilian at least the orator's training was moral as well as intellectual. The oratorical ideal retained a good deal of prestige through the Middle Ages, when most educated people were trained either for the church or the law, and in either case would need to know how to speak. Hence a central place was given to rhetoric, and as rhetoric is a study of the figuration of language as well as of verbal persuasion, it was an excellent training for poets as well.

With the Renaissance the prince emerged as both the head and the center of his society, and with him came the revival of the form we may call the cyropedia, the treatise on the education of an ideal prince, whose training would be an educational model because he would be the most important person in his society to educate. The original *Cyropaedia* of Xenophon, to which Castiglione refers, dealt with the training of Cyrus, one of the authentically great men of the ancient world, and a legendary figure in both classical and biblical literature. Erasmus's *Institute of a Christian Prince,* published in 1615 when Castiglione was working on *Il Cortegiano,* established the cyropedia as a central Renaissance genre. In England, the great epic of Elizabethan literature, Spenser's *Faerie Queene,* is in one of its aspects a cyropedia, an educational treatise on the qualities of the ideal prince, identified with the romantic hero Prince Arthur.

The sixteenth century was one of the world's greatest ages in educational theory, and in choosing the courtier for his theme, Castiglione must have felt that he had a more up-to-date model than the orator and a more practicable one than the prince. Much of the medieval oratorical ideal remained in the Renaissance, because nonmilitary professional careers were still mainly concerned with the church and the law. The immense prestige of the Church as an employing institution is visible all through Castiglione's book, despite his efforts to keep everything explicitly religious out of the discussion, and to construct an essentially secular ideal of education. We may note that three of those who take part in his symposium were later made cardinals. But shifting the model from orator to courtier gave it a more concrete social reference. As for the cyropedia form, it would have been difficult to discuss the perfect prince in such a genre without sinking into flattery of the prince nearest at hand, and as this was the invalid duke of Urbino, who retired to bed after supper and took no part in the conversations, such flattery would have been largely wasted in any case.

As for Plato's *Republic,* we can hardly ascribe much direct influence from it, or from Plato generally, on Castiglione, although he had a profoundly Platonic cast of mind, and Platonic idealism appealed to him deeply. "There is a perfection for everything, even though it be hidden," he says. But he is clearly anxious to avoid the Utopian theme itself, which would mean bypassing the education of the individual in favor of a theoretical regulating of society. Two major English writers, Spenser and Milton, expressed a preference for Xenophon's *Cyropaedia* over Plato's *Republic* as the more practical and concrete of the two books, and Castiglione also concerns himself only with what from his point of view were more or less practical possibilities.

Still, when we come to the fourth book, where the courtier's social function as an adviser to the prince is discussed, it seems clear that the courtier must have some vision of the form of society too, if he is to perform his duties intelligently. The subject of a cyropedia may be the ideal prince, but the author of a cyropedia could only be an ideal courtier, as Castiglione describes him, and his theory of education would have to derive itself from a social vision. It is, I think, the latent Utopian tone of Castiglione's dialogue, its implicit reference to a hidden perfection in society itself, that makes it still relevant to us. Among the great educational books of that very fertile period, we have to place Sir Thomas More's *Utopia* (1516) in the first rank. In More's book there is a collision of views between Hythlodaye, the traveller who has been to Utopia and has returned a convinced Communist, and More himself, who listens to his narration. Hythlodaye is now a revolutionary who feels that nothing can be done for Europe until private property is abolished and the various principalities replaced with something more like the Utopian republic. More represents himself, in contrast, as feeling rather that Hythlodaye should use his knowledge of Utopia to act as a counsellor to European princes, trying to inform their policies with something of the Utopian spirit. Castiglione's courtier has no Utopia to go to, but he has a similar informing vision to communicate.

The first book of *Il Cortegiano* opens the discussion, sets out the kind of person the courtier is to be, outlines the general range of what he should know, and sketches in the cultural context of his society. The main line of discussion is sustained first by Ludovico da Canossa, a reasonable and open-minded speaker, who expresses the general consensus (with some disagreement) that the courtier should be of noble birth, though as a matter of convenience more than as a feeling of propriety. It is not that one kind of man is inherently better than another, but that one of the most essential qualities of the courtier, as we shall see more fully in a moment, is spontaneity, doing things with the effortless ease of one accustomed to doing them from birth, which is simpler if in fact he has been accustomed to them from birth. If he is not nobly born, in other words, all his courtly qualities will be acquired, and the strain of acquiring them is likely to show through at some point.

The primary profession of the courtier is said to be military, but everything he does in war as well as peace is done as an amateur, leaving strategy to the professionals. One would expect him to know enough to be a commissioned officer: this is no doubt assumed, but all the emphasis is on his bearing and deportment, on manifesting his courage to the right people, on his ability to ride well (Castiglione had a special interest in horsemanship), and the like. Castiglione is not temperamentally much of a warrior, however, and he takes more pleasure in describing the courtier at peace and at play. Here again, one would expect that one reason for his being an amateur would be administrative: that is, he need not be a great painter himself, but he should know who the best painters are, know why they are the best, and see to it that they are fully employed. One gets the impression, though, that Castiglione's prince does not delegate much authority to his courtiers, no doubt mainly because of the limited area of the Italian city-states. The English treatises in the same general genre, from Elyot's *Governour* (1531) to Milton in the next century, lay more stress on the educated man's responsibilities as a magistrate or deputy officer. Castiglione's courtier, in contrast, seems to be almost entirely a court functionary.

The scope of the courtier's peacetime activities covers mainly sports and the fine arts, including literature. The courtier should be an amateur poet, writing gracefully and wittily within a convention; he should understand something of music, painting, and sculpture. Many fine and eloquent things are said of these arts, especially music, where the musical amateur's preference for the single melodic line with an instrumental accompaniment—normally the lute—over elaborate contrapuntal structures like the madrigal is made clear. Some of the issues discussed seem rather barren in themselves: for instance, is sculpture superior to painting because it has one more dimension, or inferior because of its more restricted subject matter? The issue is raised apparently only to make it clear that both arts belong in a civilized environment.

In the verbal arts, scholarly erudition is not stressed to the degree that it is in the orator's training: what the courtier knows is far less important than how he displays his knowledge, as in the apt placing of quotations. The strong humanist prejudice against using words not generally employed in conversation is felt throughout: in the third book, discussions of Aristotelian philosophy are sharply broken off by the two chief women, the duchess and Emilia Pia, who tell the speakers that they must speak so as to be understood. We are obviously in an age when the technical language of scholastic philosophy is giving way to the more colloquial idiom used by most of the major philosophers between Bacon and Leibnitz, who tended to be socially amateurs rather than school philosophers. We notice too that while Tuscan has, among Italian dialects, the immense prestige conferred by Dante, Petrarch, and Boccaccio, no center dominates the whole country in the way that London dominated England and Paris France, making its own dialect the standard form of the language and reducing all others to rustic or clowns' speech.

But whatever the courtier does, he must do it with "grace": everything leads up to that as the final manifestation of courtliness. Grace is almost impossible to define: it eludes verbal formulation, because "he who has grace finds grace," and those who do not have it are unlikely to know what it is. Grace is manifested, however, in two ways. One is by *sprezzatura,* another untranslatable word conveying the sense of masterly ease, spontaneity, the tossed-off quality that shows nothing of the long practice that has led up to it. The other is by *disinvoltura,* the grace of bodily movements, the repose of the trained athlete. The courtier must demonstrate these qualities in athletics, in riding (in almost all European languages the words for members of the aristocracy are derived from horseback riding), and whenever he attempts poetry or music. "We may call that art true art which does not seem to be art; nor must one be more careful of anything than of concealing it." This is of course a very ancient principle, and is also reinforced by the tradition of the orator, who tries to conceal the fact that he is persuading. Even so one wonders why there is so heavy an emphasis on these qualities. I think there are two answers, one relatively superficial, the other more profound.

The superficial answer is that the courtier is a member of the aristocracy, and it is the social function of the aristocracy to put on a show. To use a criterion that Castiglione does not, the aristocracy illustrates for the rest of the community the level of civilized, leisurely, privileged living that their taxes are supporting. The association of aristocracy with showmanship runs through all human history: the Americans, with no hereditary aristocracy, have, with a fine sense of fitness, made one out of their entertainers. Castiglione thinks of the courtiers as primarily under the eyes of other courtiers: "Gentlemen are seen in public spectacles before the people and before ladies and great lords," he says. But, especially in the second book, the sense of the courtier as under the eyes of the rest of the community is also present. In any case, what Thorstein Veblen calls "conspicuous consumption" is essential not only to the morale of the gentry themselves but to that of the rest of society, which sees in its aristocracy the visible models and embodiments of the flower and fruit of civilization.

We have derived two words from the metaphor of the masked actor: *hypocrite* and *person.* The former contains a moral value judgment, the latter does not. If we compare Castiglione on the courtier with Machiavelli on the prince, we see a remarkable parallel: both are constantly on view: what they are seen to do is, socially speaking, what they are; their reputations are the most important part of their identity, and their functional reality is their appearance. The difference is that Machiavelli's prince, being the man who must make the decisions, must accept the large element of hypocrisy involved; must understand how and why the reputation for virtue is more important for him than the hidden reality of virtue. It is essential for the prince to be reputed liberal, Machiavelli says, though he is probably better off if in reality he saves his money. For the courtier, whose social function is ornamental rather than operative, the goal is an appearance which has entirely absorbed the reality, a persona or mask which is never removed even when asleep. In regard to women, we are told that men are fearful of being deceived by art, that is, of being manipulated. For the prince manipulation is essential; for the courtier it is not.

This really means that, considered as an educational ideal, the courtier's training goes in the direction, not of concealing a reality under a bravura performance, as the actor conceals his private identity on the stage, but of total candor and openness. To do things with "grace" is possible only if they are done with the practiced skill that has descended from the consciousness to what we should now call the unconscious mind, and this in turn means that "grace" marks the total absorption of the courtier's education into the courtier's personality.

The second book, much the longest of the four, carries on from the first, and the main speaker, Federico Fregoso, adds little to what Ludovico had already said, except that Ludovico is a liberal-minded person and Fregoso is a stilted, not to say stupid, snob. Here the sense of being constantly under social inspection extends to a feeling of stage fright. The courtier should avoid such sports as wrestling (recommended in the first book), not merely because the straining and heaving involved makes *sprezzatura* impossible, but because the courtier might be defeated by someone of inferior rank, which would be unseemly. We catch a glimpse of the extent to which in practice an aristocracy is really a kind of army of occupation. We also notice an increasing influence as we go on of Aristotle's ideal of the "magnanimous man," and of the principle that "the safest thing is to govern ourselves according to a certain decorous mean." Aristotle, of course, had no notion of making his "middle way" into a cult of mediocrity, but Fregoso, with his emphasis on such matters as dressing in dark clothes and making a good impression even without speech, seems to be subsiding into the view that being inconspicuous is an essential part of grace.

Finally Bibbiena takes over, and, from an obviously immense repertoire, gives a large number of examples of the kind of jokes, smart repartee, and stinging epigrams (*arguzie*) that the courtier may use. Jokes are very hard to translate, because of their reliance on accidents of language; more important, anecdotes quickly lose the flavor of the specific occasion of which they form part. Some of the stories turn on exaggeration, of the type known as "tall stories" in American folklore, and among them are some hardy perennials. The story of the people whose speech froze to ice on a cold day and could be heard only when it thawed out again is still going strong in a Victorian farce called *Handy Andy* (1845).

But although the anecdotes themselves often lack freshness, the principles behind them are of great educational importance. First, the emphasis put on them indicates the humanist principle of making conversation and ordinary speech the basis of all verbal communication. Second, the element of satire is heavily involved: the courtier is apparently intended to score off other people a good part of the time, and satire implies a moral principle. If a pompous and overdignified person slips on a banana peeling, we find it funny: if a blind man does so we do not. What is involved, then, is the educational principle of making something that is naturally aggressive into something that is socially acceptable, or rather functional. Education is largely a matter of channeling energies, and energy without education tends to be anarchic, even brutal—modern taste does not find Bibbiena's examples invariably urbane, especially the practical jokes and hoaxes at the end. Then again, the success of a joke or epigram depends entirely on time and place, and the practice of such things imbues the courtier with that sense of distributing the rhythm of life which is the inner secret of grace.

The third book purports to describe a "Court Lady" as the complement of the male courtier. The main speaker is Giuliano de Medici, again a sensible and good-humored person, and a young man named Gasparo Pallavicino, with the omniscience of twenty-one, casts himself in the role of an extremely tedious misogynist. In this attempt to provide a mate for "a courtier that never existed and perhaps never can exist," there is a good deal of delicate humor. There is irony in the fact that although this group is said to have a heavy predominance of males, nevertheless it is held together by two women, and hence the crucial importance of women in the courtier's life is being demonstrated all through the disagreements in the discussion. An extraordinary amount of sexual hostility is expressed in this book, and again the reason is the same: sexuality is normally aggressive and domineering, and education is largely a matter of channeling its energy into something more in keeping with civilized life.

There is also a delicate humor in the way that Castiglione represents his courtiers as plunging away from the main theme into other areas, such as the distinctions of Aristotelian philosophy. In fact the main subject is so frequently torpedoed that it is hardly defined at all with any clarity. As Pallavicino says: "To wish to give her knowledge of everything in the world, and allow

317

her those virtues that have so rarely been seen in men during the past centuries, is something one cannot endure or listen to at all." Anything rather than face the fact that courtiership means nothing whatever without women, and that the courtier has no real social function at all unless his society admits women on the same level.

Giuliano de Medici does his best: he points out to Palla-vicino, with great courtesy, that "mankind" means men and women, not males, and that Pallavicino's attempt to align men and women respectively with Aristotle's form and matter is illiterate nonsense. He says that if women often desire to be men, it is not because men are better "but in order to gain freedom and to escape that rule over them which man has arrogated to himself by his own authority." And yet even he can hardly discuss the subject without giving a long series of stories, mainly from Plutarch's essay on the virtues of women, about all the admirable females who commit suicide after rape—in other words, conform to male codes. The discussion also revolves around what is in the context a quite genuine problem: society and the Church insist that monogamous marriage is the only possible love-relation between a man and a woman, yet a far more promiscuous kind of lovemaking is obviously built in to the courtier's code. It is one of many issues which are too complex to be resolved in the argument.

In the fourth book the argument draws toward its climax, and focuses on the courtier's social function as the adviser of the prince. Some feel that he is to be not an adviser but a teacher, and this raises a problem. If he knows enough to teach the prince, he is presumably a person of considerable age and experience; if he is to be that, what becomes of all his graceful accomplishments in riding, playing tennis, singing to a lute, and the rest, which are normally best performed by a young man? The group, and perhaps Castiglione as well, never quite come to terms with the fact that they are really talking about two different ideals here, one courtly and the other humanistic, one active and the other contemplative. Trying to combine the two merely brings us up against the old paradox: "Si la jeunesse savait, si la vieillesse pouvait."

There is a prevailing sentiment in this fourth book that the courtier is there to know and see the truth, and tell the truth to the prince; that he is to instill the principles of virtue, little by little, into the prince's mind; that he is to promote justice and *vergogna* wherever he can. *Vergogna* combines the ideas of a sense of honor, of reverence for the fitness of things, and of guilt if honor is betrayed: it is an almost perfect translation of the Homeric term *aidos,* and like it expresses something very central in the heroic code. Half a century after his death, Castiglione's book was banned by the Inquisition and placed on the Index: this of course was silly, and reflects a time when the Catholic Church was frightened by everything. But it is true that the heroic code underlying the ideal of the courtier is committed to the world and the world's educational values. Castiglione's code has much in common, not only with the classical heroic code, but with similar codes across the world, like the samurai code in Japan. Every aristocracy contains within it a tendency to make an autonomous religion out of its social status. A strong attraction in W. B. Yeats toward this element in Japanese culture is combined with an equally strong admiration for Castiglione.

There are objections by some in the group to this new program for the courtier: is he to become simply a schoolmaster, and even if he were to succeed in his aim of educating the prince, would he not make him a mere justice of the peace rather than a great monarch? Ottaviano Fregoso stresses the extroverted and historical side of a ruler's greatness, his glory and wealth and splendid buildings, as against the philosophical and contemplative. But there is also a feeling that the pattern of what is being talked about derives from Aristotle's relation to Alexander and Plato's to Dionysius, and whatever has Aristotle and Plato for its exemplars can hardly be an ignoble ideal. But the tone of melancholy that recurs throughout the book is very marked here. It is generally agreed that monarchy is the best form of government because it is the most "natural," and because God is thought of as a sovereign monarch, and it is also urged that some promising young men, Francis I in France, Henry VIII in England, will make very good princes. But we get glimpses of futility, of a sense that the courtier is to make these great cultural efforts merely to help a prince who probably won't listen—and, according to Machiavelli, shouldn't listen, except for reasons of publicity.

In the third book we ran into an impasse: the courtier

should be a lover, but religion and society will only tolerate marriage. In the fourth book we find a contrasting impasse: the courtier is to inform the prince's mind with justice and virtue, and yet, as Machiavelli demonstrates, ethical scruples merely hamper and inhibit a prince. His subjects are half men and half vicious animals, and the prince must not forget the animal qualities, the lion's courage and the fox's cunning, if he is to remain a prince. Castiglione does not admit this kind of argument, but he has lived through the same age as Machiavelli and has seen much the same kind of history. The hopelessness of the prospect of the prince's will and the courtier's wisdom forming a unity remains in the background, however justified the efforts towards such a union may be.

The book concludes with Bembo's panegyric on love, which has the function of suggesting that the courtier's training does have a goal which is of value in itself, and leads far beyond his duty as the prince's adviser. Bembo climbs the Neoplatonic ladder of love, postulating three levels in man, with an impelling power attached to each. These are sense and appetite; reason and choice; intellect and will. By will is meant the emancipated and purified will that, in a more religious context, Virgil leaves Dante with near the end of the *Purgatorio.* It is a power, Bembo says, of conversing with angels. Each level is a form of what Plato calls Eros, and in the course of climbing the ladder Eros discovers his identity with beauty. Beauty is of divine origin, and has goodness for its center, which means that we have first of all to pass through the tiresome argument that all beautiful people are good, except those who regrettably are not. The lover begins in the physical world of sense, admiring beautiful bodies; the soul in him then awakens and sees the form of beauty within bodies, and finally, as reason gives way to intellect or universal reason, beautiful forms become the universal form of beauty and love passes from the contemplation of it to union with it. Pallavicino puts up his customary protest against including women in so high an ideal, but is silenced for the moment with a reference to the role of Diotima in Plato's *Symposium.* A far more effective and beautiful answer is the final vision of the dawn breaking outside the windows as the courtiers have talked through the night, with all the stars scattered except for Venus, the focus of all beauty, who guards the confines of night and day.

Bembo's vision reflects the Platonism of Ficino, but is not

confined to its age: the Eros ladder has been climbed many times since, its last major appearance in our culture being, perhaps, Hegel's *Phenomenology of the Spirit*. Similarly, Machiavelli's conception of the prince belongs to a tradition of absolutizing the will that reaches its culmination in Nietzsche. But the real "relevance" of such books to our own time rests on a different basis. In the course of time, prince and courtier become metaphors for elements that are in all of us. Each of us, that is, has a prince and a courtier within himself, a principle of will and a principle of "grace" which in the last analysis turns out to be love. (The love, we said, is that of Eros, not the Christian *agape*, but *agape* by definition is a "grace" that does not come from man, and there are no rules for educating it.) The will is developed by our vision of society and of our place in that society; grace and love come from our vision of culture. The life of will is the life of work; the life of grace and love is the life of leisure, of play, of the "games" of which Castiglione's dialogue is one. In Castiglione's day the courtier was the servant of the prince; in our day the life of leisure is subordinate to the life of work. But we are slowly coming around to think that perhaps the life of leisure is the real life, and that play is that for the sake of which work is done. Similarly, no one in Castiglione's book questions the social superiority of the prince, yet in Bembo's vision we are carried up to a world which has left all princes behind, and far below.

Such a conception of leisure cannot, of course, remain associated with an elite and privileged minority, but has to spread through the whole of society. In the French Revolution the revolutionary ideals of modern man were defined as liberty, equality, and fraternity. The first two have been vigorously pursued in different parts of the world: they are both impersonal, and depend on mass movements. The third, fraternity, has been practically ignored as an ideal: it is the ideal of personal respect, and is infinitely more difficult to maintain and promote than the others. But it must become increasingly the chief preoccupation of our time, and as it does so, the kind of educational ideal associated with it will come more clearly into focus. Castiglione is one of the very few educators who have grasped the importance of this ideal, and that is why his book is not only a beautiful handbook of grace but a profound vision of human destiny.

✦

The Meeting of
Past and Future
in William Morris

✦

THERE IS no one in English literature who raises more fascinating and complex questions connected with the relation of art to society than William Morris. Part of the complexity, of course, comes from his bewildering versatility. In the intervals of running a business, designing furniture and wallpaper patterns, studying medieval recipes for dyeing textiles, setting up a press for printing fine editions, and agitating both for socialism and for stopping the "restoring" of medieval buildings, he produced a great mass of poetry and fiction, enough in its sheer range and bulk to have made half a dozen quite respectable reputations. Many people would not consider him a major poet or storyteller or translator, but even they would have to admit that he was a major figure, in literature as in many other areas.

The difficulties in understanding Morris are not in his writing as such but in his motives for writing what and as he did. His total work may be divided into five main divisions, which overlap a good deal but are still in a roughly chronological order. First, the early poetry, including "The Defence of Guinevere," and the early stories, appearing mainly in the *Oxford and Cambridge Magazine,* where he attained an intensity and vividness of emotion not often equaled in his later work. Second, the period of verse romance, including *Jason,* the collection of tales in *The Earthly Paradise,* and the remarkable masque *Love Is Enough.* Third, his epic and romance translations, which include the *Volsunga Saga,* the *Aeneid,* the *Odyssey, Beowulf,* and various Northern and Old French romances, an activity that spread over all his later life. Fourth, essays and lectures on socialism, more particularly on its relation to the place of the so-called lesser arts in society. Fifth, a period of long prose romance and fantasy: *The Wood beyond the World, The Well at the World's End, The Story of the Glittering Plain, The Sundering Flood,* and others. There is also a genre in this period which combines romance with is political vision: *News from Nowhere,* probably his best-known book, *The Dream of John Ball, The King's Lesson,* and the narrative poem *Pilgrims of Hope.*

All this work has had very mixed reception. In Mackail's biography of Morris there is, for all his imagination and sympathy, a tendency to dismiss the whole socialist side of Morris as a perversion of his talents, a typical example of a creative person becoming ensnared in the siren's toils of a political movement he never understood. For the final romances Mackail has a very limited admiration: one would have expected, for example, some mention of *The Sundering Flood,* if only because it was Morris's last work. Those of Morris's contemporaries who better understood and shared his political sympathies had even less use for the prose romances. Bernard Shaw spoke of them as the resuscitation of Don Quixote's library. A hasty reader of some criticism on Morris might easily get an impression of a dithering kook, too overcome by his own restless versatility to focus his mind properly in any one direction.

With the hindsight of another century, we may perhaps still say that Morris's political sympathies were naive, but we can hardly say that they were peripheral, or showed any unawareness of where history was going in his time. History has vindicated his interest in Marxism, not by showing that any of it was right—certainly anything in it connected with predicting the future has turned out to be rather grotesquely wrong—but by showing that it was profoundly relevant to the concerns of England in the 1880s. And yet, what of these dreamy romances, with their archaic language, hazy characterization, and meandering plots? Are they at least not a retreat from Morris's extroverted world of business and design and political activity into some kind of childhood fixation: the eight-year-old dressed in a toy suit of armor whom Mackail speaks of, and whom so many of Morris's critics invoke?

Here again the cycles of history have qualified our certainties. Marxism was a minority movement in England in Morris's day, but it has expanded now to the point where Morris's interest in it shows a good deal of prescience. Similarly, the late romances fell stillborn from his press and were destined apparently to remain so indefinitely. But within the last quarter-century or so there has been a quite unexpected development in the area often (and very inaccurately) called science fiction. Some of the bestselling works in this area are Frank Herbert's *Dune* trilogy, Ursula LeGuin's *Earthsea* trilogy, Zelazny's *Amber* trilogy, Asimov's *Foundation* trilogy. The frequency of the trilogy form is doubtless due to the sensational success of Tolkien's *Lord of the Rings,* and these works are routinely compared to Tolkien in the blurbs, although Eddison's trilogy of *Memison* books was in the field earlier than Tolkien. Morris wrote no romance that was formally a trilogy, but some of them are long enough to have been arranged in that form. In any case, the genre itself seems clearly to have begun with Morris, apart from the fact that Morris was at least one significant influence on Tolkien.

What is noticeable about the contemporary books is that they are romances that deliberately revert from science fiction hardware, however much of it they incidentally incorporate, back to hand-to-hand dueling with the equivalent of swords, back to plots and intrigues of a kind that would hardly be out of place in Jacobean drama. The political situations are regularly drawn from models of the past: corrupt empires holding on to power but being threatened by revolts, younger sons of aristocratic families forging reputations for themselves through heroic achievement like destroying monsters. Bernard Shaw's comment is not far off the mark, either for Morris himself or for his successors. Works in this genre are historical romances in which both the history and the geography have been invented, and the settings are as arbitrary as those indicated in Morris's "world's end" titles. In this same so-called science fiction area are other romances that are retellings of traditional tales and myths, like the Mabinogion stories in Evangeline Walton, which remind us of Morris's other interest in collecting and retelling so many of the great stories of the past. Once again Morris has proved to be profoundly prescient, whatever our opinion of the books themselves. Many commentators on Morris assume that his preoccupation with romance and his socialist interests formed a schizophrenic contradiction in his mind. But when both have turned out to be so central in our own cultural environment, we cannot help wondering about this assumption, even if we draw the inference that our world is schizophrenic too.

Morris himself has left very few comments on his late romances, beyond a letter to a paper explaining that a review of his *Wood beyond the World* was mistaken in thinking that the story was an allegory of capital and labor. Doubtless it was, but before archetypal criticism many pseudoissues clustered around the word *allegory,* and the fact that an allegorical reading of a story may be forced and unconvincing does not mean that it has no external relations at all. Certainly the twentieth-century romances mentioned above are not intended simply as escape reading, but have connections, however oblique, with other twentieth-century preoccupations. Similarly there are political overtones in the struggle of a free state against a slave state in the early story "Gertha's Lovers," and these recur in the late romance *The Roots of the Mountains.* Another early story, "Svend and His Brethren," tells of the hero Svend, who leads an exodus out of a war-crazed community to more peaceful surroundings along with his six brothers, who represent the arts and crafts of a civilized society. A similar theme recurs in the very late *Sundering Flood,* where there is a battle in which the hero is supported by the apprentices of the "lesser crafts."

Morris abandoned his one attempt at a novel with a contemporary setting, remarking that he would never try such a thing again "unless the world turns topsides under some day." Yet he also remarked of Swinburne's *Tristram of Lyonesse* that it was founded on literature, not on nature, which is not good enough in these days when "the issue between art, that is, the godlike part of man, and mere bestiality, is so momentous." The reflection that a poet ought not to turn to past literature for inspiration when culture is locked in a St. George-and-dragon social struggle is precisely the one that might be—and was—applied to Morris himself. We are forced to conclude that there was a quite clear connection in Morris's mind between romance and the state of society, and that that connection was the reverse of the usual one.

As for the verse romances, we can understand their comparative eclipse if we approach them negatively and by contrast with another Victorian poet who is Morris's direct antithesis in almost every respect, Gerard Manley Hopkins. In one of his sketches for a unified critical theory, Hopkins says that the mind has two kinds of energy, a transitional kind, where one thought or sensation follows another, and an "abiding" kind, which he says may be called contemplation. There seems to me at least an analogy, and perhaps a real connection, between this distinction and several others that Hopkins makes. There is the distinction between "overthought," the superficial meaning conveyed by the syntax, and "underthought," the deeper meaning conveyed by the imagery and metaphors, which in some Shakespeare plays, for example, may be telling us something quite different from the syntactical sense. There is also the better-known distinction between "running" rhythm and the more syncopated "sprung" rhythm, with its greater variety of stresses and beats against the established meter. There is the distinction between the "Parnassian" level of writing which any genuine poet may achieve by habit and practice, and the totally unpredictable flashes that occasionally sweep across it. The general pattern is that of a middle level, and something else that may be called metaphorically either above and higher, or below and deeper.

It is clear that Morris devoted himself to the "Parnassian" level of writing, as in *The Earthly Paradise,* where the writing is invariably competent but seldom startling or haunting. He also devotes himself to the "transitional" kind of mental energy that emphasizes movement and continuity. He is lost without some kind of story to tell, and is the least contemplative of poets: the level of meaning is fairly uniform, and the kind of romances read in *Il Penseroso,* "where more is meant than meets the ear," are on the whole not his kind, even though we may find many phrases with a surprisingly complex resonance. Again, he sticks closely to the "running" forms of meter and rhyme and stanza that English imported from French and Italian sources, and (apart from his translation of *Beowulf*) he shows little interest in the native accentual and alliterative rhythms that Hopkins explored so powerfully. In terms of the value judgments that half a century ago were practically unquestioned, all this suggests that Morris is the worst example in English literature of what Eliot meant by the dissociation of sensibility. But even these value judgments are no more immortal than any others, and it may be significant that the greater part of critical theory today gives its main attention to narrative and "transitional" poetic techniques. Without trying to create a new set of value judgments, it might be rewarding to inquire into Morris's motives for his obviously deliberate choice of what seems, or has seemed, the more commonplace path.

If we look at *News from Nowhere,* the most accessible of Morris's books, we can see at once how completely Morris has recreated the future of his country in his own personal image. Himself a tireless producer of so much practical and manual work, without a lazy bone in his body, he shows us an England where everyone, from earliest childhood on, is incessantly working, and where the most serious social problem is a shortage of things to do. The nineteenth-century visitor inquires about the system of educating children, and is told that there isn't any: children quickly pick up the skills of carpentering and cooking and thatching and shopkeeping. Asked about the cultivating of the mind, his informant says "we don't encourage early bookishness," but that children also pick up languages easily enough, and some of them even read books. Disregarding the deliberately polemical tone, we can see that what Morris is talking about is what he calls, in his lecture on "The Lesser Arts" (1877: the earliest of his important lectures on art and society), "the art of unconscious intelligence." He wants to build on such an art, in the future, a new art of conscious intelligence; but the practical education of young children in his Utopia is the foundation of an activity on which all Morris's social values depend.

Morris was strongly influenced, as he says, by Carlyle and Ruskin, and was converted to socialism by reading Mill's hostile discussion of it. His reading of Marx and other socialists came much later. Naturally Morris had no use for the reactionary drift of Carlyle's thought or his hero cult, but one feature of that thought strongly attracted him. Carlyle generally talks about work in the abstract rather than the condition of the worker, and sometimes gives the impression that any sort of work is good for the moral fiber. But in *Sartor Resartus* he makes it fairly clear that drudgery, that is, servile, exploited, and alienated work, is not what he means by work. Drudgery in this sense is an aspect of a society of which the other aspect is "Dandyism," where some people do nothing at all, and where other people are consequently forced into excessive work in order to support them.

Ruskin carried this principle much further in Morris's direction in *Stones of Venice*. Here, especially in the section called "The Nature of Gothic," he found that the ugliness of much of Victorian civilization was an aesthetic fact pointing to a moral principle. Mass production means machine production, which in Ruskin's day meant turning human beings into machines, and obliterating everything creative or pleasurable from their work. He gives as an example men who sit in a factory all day chopping glass rods into beads, "their hands vibrating with a perpetual and exquisitely timed palsy." Such pseudowork illustrates two interrelated social facts: that the process of mechanizing human labor is a form of penal servitude, and that its product is therefore bound to be both ugly and unnecessary. Ruskin, like Carlyle, did not follow up the revolutionary implications of this principle, but he comes close to supplying Morris with what Marxist literature would hardly have supplied him: a definition of work as creative act.

Ruskin's documentation was aesthetic, drawing mainly from the history of architecture, painting, and sculpture; but he seldom made a purely disinterested aesthetic judgment, as he was so constantly aware of the social and moral principles involved. Morris took over Ruskin's method and reversed it. He began with purely aesthetic judgments about the hideousness of most Victorian industrial products, and in attempting to replace at least some of them with better-designed work he saw increasingly the social, then the moral, and finally the political significance of what he was doing. This is perhaps one reason why, with all his devotion to medieval craftsmanship, he so seldom expressed any interest in, or even awareness of, the religious aspect of medieval culture, which is not on the direct line from aesthetic reaction to political conviction. His social interest in the Middle Ages focuses on John Ball and the Peasants' Revolt, the only time in English history, perhaps, when something like a proletariat appeared in the foreground of events.

Morris regarded his "lesser" or minor arts, the arts of design, essentially as aspects of architecture: never a practicing architect himself, he nevertheless felt that architecture was the context for them all. Architecture in its turn cannot be separated from its own larger social context in, say, town planning, and so, eventually, of social planning as a whole. It is this sense of social context that links Morris to such later developments as the Bauhaus movement in Germany, and at the same time separates him from what Mackail calls the "multiplying of amateurism," the handicraft art that produces individually designed objects in a social vacuum, or what may be called the ashtray syndrome. But by the time we have expanded the social context of the "minor arts" of design into social planning, we have also, perhaps, begun to develop a certain distrust for the word *planning,* which seems to suggest a small group of know-it-alls imposing their views on the rest of society. Morris asks rather: "What signs are there of collective skill, the skill of the school, which nurses moderate talent and sets genius free?" It is this collective skill that the vision of *News from Nowhere* is based on. The inhabitants of that world are careful about preserving the monuments of the past, but are not superstitious about them. If they did have to destroy one, it would not be an act of vandalism, because they would be capable of rebuilding with an equal sense of authority.

The real context of social planning, then, is a society in which work has been defined as creative act, and thereby becomes the energy by which an intelligent being expresses his intelligence. Work in this sense cannot be separated from leisure, and can exist only in a society in which there is no longer a "leisure class" with another class of exploited workers supporting them, but in which the working class *is* the leisure class, and vice versa. Such a society would reconstitute the word *manufacture* by bringing it back to its original meaning of something made by a brain-directed hand. The natural emotional response to producing anything attractive by one's own hands is pleasure, and what Morris emphasizes more than anything else is the continuous happiness of the people in his Utopia.

If we say of *News from Nowhere* "but this system would never work," we are expressing the kind of panic that Morris was attempting to counteract. A society is not a "system": human beings have no business trying to identify their community with a machine of any kind. And of course "it" would never work: it is only people who work. Morris often says that he is not opposed to machinery as such (though the inhabitants of his future England seem to get along with astonishingly little of it), but that the purpose of machinery is to absorb slavery. When exploitation and alienation are removed from people their natural energies are set free. The real question Morris is asking is rather: "I have given you a picture of a happy and healthy community. Do you like the picture? If not, what's wrong with it, as a picture?" On that basis, objections to it would soon start taking the form of expressions of distrust in human freedom itself.

Morris's examples of unconscious intelligence, in "The Lesser Arts," are the Paleolithic artifacts that were beginning to be discovered in his day. Such an unconscious intelligence, as he clearly recognized, is very close to consciousness. Similarly, we admire, for example, Shaker furniture, but if Shakers themselves had applied the kind of self-conscious aesthetic canons to their work that we do, they could probably not have produced it at all. It would be a surprising inference that the people who produced such work were less intelligent than the people who collect it: the Shaker craftsmen merely possessed a kind of intelligence that did not get in the way of their "unconscious" skill. Morris's poetry, in particular, is similarly an attempt to let an acquired skill flow through the consciousness without being disturbed by that consciousness. Morris says that anyone should be able to compose poetry while his mind is partly on something else, such as weaving or dyeing. It is clear that there is an analogy in his mind between the kind of hierarchy that separates the "major" from the "minor" arts and the social hierarchy that puts a leisure, or do-nothing, class on top of an exploited working class. His determination to treat poetry as though it were a "minor" or "useful" art has a political reference: he wants to see the major arts democratized, made the possession of everyone like the arts of design. Though usually classed as a late Romantic, Morris has nothing of the Romantic elitism that regards the creative person or "genius" as a special form of humanity, almost a biological mutation of it.

There are several reasons why Morris thinks that the art of design could become the focus of revolutionary social developments. For one thing, people are often willing to put up with badly designed furniture, textiles, and ceramics because they are "merely material" things that ought not to take up the time and energy we devote to the "higher" aspects of life. This phony idealism is an exact counterpart of a class structure in which the ascendant class withdraws from work. On the contrary, being dissatisfied with our "merely material" surroundings soon leads to a vivid perception of, not merely the shoddiness and ugliness of the designs presented to us, but the social conditions that find shoddiness and ugliness cheaper to produce and easier to sell. If we find the attack on the cultivating of the mind in *News from*

Nowhere rather hard to take, it is worth remembering that society enforces compulsory education of the young because it wants docile and obedient citizens. One must read to obey the traffic signals; one must learn arithmetic to make out one's income tax. If we assume that the mind is naturally active, education becomes that activity of the mind and not an externally imposed and alien structure standing for what some anonymous authority wants us to do.

Morris's original associates in his socialist activities were Anarchists, and the journal *Commonweal,* which he edited, was an Anarchist publication. After he left that position and broke with most of the group, he remarked in a letter that his experience had taught him that "Anarchism is impossible." That sounds like a shift to a more orthodox Marxist position: it has even been suggested that he may have been in closer touch with Engels, who had inherited Marx's manuscripts, than is generally thought. But Morris was all his life a pure anarchist, with a lower-case *a.* His *News from Nowhere* was written partly as a protest against Bellamy's socialist Utopia *Looking Backward,* a vision of Boston in the year 2000 where everyone is drafted to serve in an "industrial army," and where recreation consists largely of listening to government propaganda over the "telephone," or what we now call the radio. Communist movements since Morris's time have followed Bellamy and not Morris, and have also followed the course that Morris most hated: economic centralization, concentrating on mass production and distribution, setting up a rigid chain of command throughout the whole of society. Even the curious Janus-faced attitude to violence that gives Anarchism both a terrorist side and a peaceful side recurs in Morris: he says he has a religious hatred of war and violence, yet *News from Nowhere* predicts the rise of the counterideology of fascism much more clearly than most socialist writing of his day did.

What the later Morris was, perhaps, was that very rare bird, a Marxist uncorrupted by Leninism. Marx thought of Communism as a natural evolution out of capitalism: when capitalism had reached a certain stage of deadlock through its inherent contradictions, a guided revolutionary movement could shift the control of production from a few exploiters to the workers. This evolutionary development did not occur: Communism was established in an essentially preindustrial country, and became simply the adversary of capitalism, not its successor. What attracted Morris to Marx were such things as the comments on the impoverishing of the rural by the urban parts of society in the *Manifesto,* the vision of capitalism as a dehumanizing relationship, in contrast to earlier social connections which, though still based on exploitation, were at least personal ones, and, above all, the anarchist ultimate goal that Marx envisioned, when all states have withered away and imposed controls are no longer needed.

And so, the informant of the narrator in *News from Nowhere* says, "We discourage centralization all we can." Not only has the British Empire vanished in Morris's ideal world, but England itself has broken down into small local units and local councils. The House of Parliament has been turned from a verbal dungheap into a literal one, and in its place has come a decentralizing of control that the most extreme Jeffersonian might consider chimerical. It was later than his remark about the impossibility of Anarchism that Morris said: "It will be necessary for the unit of administration to be small enough for every citizen to feel himself responsible for its details." He also says that the goal of State Socialism is one that sickens him. When he goes on to say that "variety of life is as much an aim of true Communism as equality of condition," we realize that Morris is talking about something quite different from what left-wing movements of his time—and since—have been primarily concerned with.

That concern has been, of course, with political control and economic development, both of which are normally centralizing movements. Most of the effective social entities today are the huge Continental powers which, whether capitalist or socialist in organization, keep expanding from that basis through various forms of political and economic imperialism. Morris is interested in cultural development, and cultural tendencies seem to go in the reverse direction. The more mature a culture is, the more it tends to circumscribe itself in smaller units. If we wish to study "American literature," for example, and discover what the creative literary imagination tells us about America, we find that "American literature" is mainly an aggregate of Mississippi authors, New England authors, Middle Western authors, California authors, expatriate authors, and so on over the whole area. Canadian literature has followed the same tendency more recently, and even the much smaller area of Great Britain shows us

332

a Hardy confined to "Wessex," a Lawrence from the Midland region, a Dylan Thomas from South Wales, and the like.

When the reading population of Great Britain was so much smaller, before Wordsworth's time, English literature was essentially a London literature, but with the Industrial Revolution and the rise of the great Midland cities the picture quickly changed. We have Shelley remarking, in the preface to *Prometheus Unbound,* that a great cultural advance would result from breaking England up into many smaller units like those of Renaissance Italy. It was abundantly clear in Morris's day that cultural developments had to be distinguished from political and economic ones if the total social picture were to be a healthy one. To attach culture to the centralizing movements of politics and economics produces a cultural totalitarianism, an empty, pompous, officially certified pseudoart. To attach a political and economic movement to a decentralizing cultural one produces a kind of neofascist separatism. Nothing could be more remote from anything Morris wanted than totalitarianism or fascism, and it is understandable that so many political and economic questions are simply waved away in *News from Nowhere.* The book in fact often reads as though it were being deliberately confined to the cultural aspect of social vision.

To the laissez-faire capitalism that emphasized liberty to the point of forgetting about equality, and the State Socialism that emphasized equality to the point of forgetting about liberty, Morris opposed the third and very neglected revolutionary element of fraternity. If Matthew Arnold is right, liberty is the specifically middle-class contribution to the classless society of genuine culture that Arnold envisaged, and equality the specifically working-class one. It should follow that it is the aristocracy that dramatizes for society as a whole the conception of fraternity, and perhaps this is one reason why there are so many stories about heroic warriors linked in some kind of chivalric brotherhood in Morris's romances. The curiously childlike quality of the people in *News from Nowhere,* who sometimes seem to be living in a gigantic kindergarten, is not inconsistent with this, because the genuine aristocracy or privileged class of every society are the children. But in Victorian times the aristocracy is too unfunctional to be invoked. With his usual insouciance in such matters, Morris dismisses the whole "class-conscious" compulsiveness of revolution with the remark "What we of the middle class have

333

to do, if we can, is to show by our lives what is the proper type of a useful citizen, the type into which all classes should melt at last." Not many left-wingers in Morris's day would have foreseen that the bourgeoisie would eventually become the standard of maturity for Communist societies.

Even fraternity, of course, can become socially oppressive, and in the background of *News from Nowhere* there looms the specter of interminable picnics and similar forms of extroverted cheer, in a society where the more contemplative aspects of leisure are so disregarded. As in so many Utopias, the inhabitants are so preoccupied with reciting the litany of benefits that their system gives them as to have, quite simply, no time to think. Towards the end of the story, however, Morris shows his awareness of this, and shows too that this society of young people who have torn themselves loose from the fetters of history has still to face the question of historical continuity. The heroine remarks to the narrator that she wonders whether they are really right in paying so little attention to their past history: an old fallacy might seem to the uninstructed a glittering novelty. She goes on to say that while she would not force anything on her children, she would hope to impress on them an essential part of herself: "that part which was not mere moods, created by the matters and events round about me." One gets a strong impression that the next generation of this exuberant society might see the children back in school.

The negative side of Morris's attitude appears in occasional melancholy remarks to the effect that perhaps in the immediate revolutionary future the arts may have to go underground or disappear for a time. The question raised here by implication is a very searching one, and I know of no statement by Morris indicating that he fully understood it himself, but some attempt to understand it seems essential to understanding Morris.

We said that culture seems to develop spatially in the opposite direction from political and economic movements. The latter centralize and the former decentralize. The process is obscured by two factors: one is the constant itch by expanding empires to kidnap their cultures and force them into a kind of advertising for themselves. The other is the fact that cultural products have to be marketed, and to that extent follow the rhythms of economics. The curiously anomalous economic position of Morris himself, whose patrons certainly did not come from a quarter of society sympathetic to his social views, is too obvious to need more than a mention. But apart from the complications of the spatial contrast between culture and economy, is there a corresponding contrast in their movement in time?

It is clear that political and economic movements follow the ordinary rhythm of clock time, moving toward the future and away from the past. When a country has gone through a revolutionary experience, many aspects of its past are neglected or suppressed. The arts it formerly produced are often regarded as the debris of exploitation. And yet tourists and visitors to the country may keep asking to see these arts, not out of reactionary fervor, but simply because any cultural product that is genuine in its own terms retains a quality of social innocence, whatever the conditions pervading its original environment. On the other hand, even without a revolutionary experience, there is a cycle of taste that keeps burying the cultural products of the past, especially the more recent past. It is normal for the culture of every age to look grotesquely out of date and old-fashioned to its immediate successor: as time goes on, the old-hat gradually turns into the "quaint," and eventually the quaint acquires the dignity of the "primitive," and comes back into fashion.

Thus at the end of the Middle Ages the two movements of Renaissance and Reformation, in very different ways, reacted against medieval culture in favor of cultural developments much earlier in time: the Augustan age and the age of primitive Christianity. The Renaissance movement in particular consolidated a view of history that is perhaps at its clearest in Gibbon. The Augustan age was the highest cultural pinnacle of European civilization, and was the golden age of Latin. It was succeeded by the silver age of Nero, and then, as monkishness and barbarism increased, it reached a nadir during the "dark" ages until the Renaissance rediscovered the essential facts about human civilization. Gibbon presents us with a typically humanist version of history, a U-shaped movement going through the decline and fall of Rome and the subsequent rise of rational values to his own time. Obviously a good deal of confidence about his own time was incorporated into this view.

The nineteenth century produced many people who did not like most of its culture, and Gibbon's view of history is exactly reversed by Ruskin, who in *Stones of Venice* plotted a chart of history that rises from the "servile" art of the pre-Gothic to its culmination in the decorated phase of Gothic, then declines into overelaboration until we reach the Renaissance, which Ruskin explicitly calls a "fall." After that everything gets worse until Ruskin's own time, when the painting of Turner and the Pre-Raphaelites suggests some upturn. Ruskin provides an almost mathematical proof of the superiority of the middle phase of Gothic architecture to every other form of human building. This thesis was taken up by various Catholic apologists, such as Belloc and Chesterton, who applied it to other aspects of medieval life. Morris, however, like Ezra Pound later, was a disciple of Ruskin who adopted the view that medieval culture preserved an integrity steadily corrupted later by what Pound calls "usura" and sloppy workmanship produced by illegitimate social demands, but ignored the religious dimension of the argument.

What we notice about all these conflicting phases of taste is that in cultural movements there seems to be a strong tendency to move backwards in time, to seek out a congenial period in the past, very frequently the distant past. Thus while political and economic movements go forward into the future, which in the twentieth century means carrying an increasing amount of technological baggage with them, cultural movements tend to rediscover neglected or forgotten earlier times in our tradition.

The admiration for medieval culture which Morris shares with many others of his time and later seems to have some unconscious connection with the view of Western civilization developed by Vico in the eighteenth century and expanded by Spengler in the twentieth. For Spengler, history takes the form of a series of "cultures" which behave like organisms, starting in a "spring" of heroic aristocracy, organized priesthood, and a peasantry bound to the land. Thence it develops towards a "summer" of city-states like those of the Renaissance, then an "autumn" when, as in the eighteenth century, the potentialities of the culture are exhausted, then a "winter" of annihilation wars, dictatorships, technology in place of creative arts, and rootless masses of people crowding into huge and bloated cities. This has been the shape of Western culture: it was preceded by a classical one which had its spring in the time of Homer, its summer and autumn in the city-states of Greece, and its winter with Macedonian and Roman imperialism. Morris betrays no awareness of any

such view of history, but *News from Nowhere* does present a somewhat childlike society with a strong temperamental affinity for
the medieval, as though a future and a past childhood spoke to
each other. There is an implied contrast with, say, the senile
second childhood of the complex gadgetry of the 1851 Exhibition. In such romances as *The House of Wolfings,* again, there seems
to be something of a contrast in Morris's mind between a young
and healthy, if barbaric, civilization, and an older and crueler
one in his account of the struggle between a northern tribe and
the Romans.

In our day every society must go through some kind of revolutionary upheaval because of the technological changes taking
place over the world. The revolutions do not all have to be Marxist or anarchist, and even if they were there would still be many
different varieties of them; but the revolutionary element is built
into contemporary society everywhere. A technological revolution makes the world more uniform: one cannot take off in a jet
plane and expect a radically different way of life in the place
where the plane lands. The uniformity in its turn is enforced by
the new class that comes to power with the social change, because they invariably discover that their own prerogatives are
bound up with resistance to any further change.

What was defined by Julien Benda, much later than Morris,
as the *trahison des clercs* may be seen from this point of view as the
nervous itch on the part of intellectuals to try to help turn the
wheel of history into the future, to prove to themselves and others that they are of some historical use after all. But when the
wheel of history turns it is precisely they who seem most expendable. This process is dramatized, for example, in Plato, who concentrates on the figure of Socrates, martyred for being a gadfly in
the Athens of his time. But then, being after all a revolutionary
thinker, Plato goes on to the *Laws,* which preaches the absolute
control by society of its teachers, a vision of society where Socrates does not appear and where he certainly could not function.
It is dramatized too in the development of early Christianity,
when the generation of martyrs is succeeded by a generation of
persecutors. It is dramatized also, in different ways, in the careers of Milton, of Victor Hugo, of Gorky, and countless others.

It looks as though it were the distinctive social function of
the creative mind to move in the opposite direction from the
politico-economic one. This means that he may have to face the

charge of being a reactionary, but cultural developments in time, as in space, seem to go in opposition to the political and economic currents. The creative tendency is toward the prerevolutionary, back to a time when, so to speak, Socrates and Jesus are still alive, when ideas are still disturbing and unpredictable and when society is less vainglorious about the solidity of its structure and the permanence of its historical situation. Morris's "medievalism" has precisely this quality about it of moving backward from the present to a vantage point at which the real future can be more clearly seen. I have noticed from my study of the Bible how these backward-moving pastoral myths seem to be the other side of a genuinely prophetic vision, looking beyond the captivities of Egypt and Babylon to a recovery of long lost innocence. The fact that innocence may not have been lost but simply never possessed does not impair the validity of the vision; in fact it strengthens it.

Thus what seems the self-pitying nostalgia of the "Apology" of *The Earthly Paradise,* where "the idle singer of an empty day" calls himself a "dreamer of dreams, born out of my due time," can also be read in another light. Perhaps the singer is idle only because the day is empty. The reference cannot be a self-identifying one, "idle" being the last epithet that anyone, even Morris himself, could apply to the author of *The Earthly Paradise.* It is rather an expression of something in nineteenth-century culture that has become helpless and powerless, something now crooked which perhaps only a dreamer of dreams can set straight.

Yeats, with his unusual readiness to take off in helicopters that Morris is not sure have been invented yet, remarks in his essay in *The Celtic Twilight* called "Enchanted Woods":

> They [the fairies of the Irish countryside] live out their passionate lives not far off, as I think, and we shall be among them when we die if we but keep our natures simple and passionate. May it not even be that death shall unite us to all romance, and that some day we shall fight dragons among blue hills, or come to that whereof all romance is but
>
> *Foreshadowings mingled with the images*
> *Of Man's misdeeds in greater days than these,*

> as the old men thought in *The Earthly Paradise*
> when they were in good spirits?

The quotation is from the epilogue to the story of Acrisius, the classical tale told for the month of April. Morris does not think in categories like living after death in fairyland, and the total scheme set up in *The Earthly Paradise,* though a deeply haunting one, has a different reference. The "Wanderers" of the Prologue are old men, half from the Mediterranean and the other half from the North, who after their wandering, in the course of which they have been welcomed as kings and worshipped as gods, have met together on a lonely island to interchange their traditional stories. Nothing happens except that they tell them.

Yet these impotent old men are clearly being identified with the stories they tell; and the stories themselves, it seems to me, are conceived as latent powers, imaginative projections of life that humanity at present can see no use for, and yet are the sources of all the styles of living, past, present, and future, that it has set up. They are myths that form a mythology, and a mythology is the world man builds as distinct from the world that surrounds him, so far as the former world can be presented in words. In his curious mania, as it sometimes seems, for telling and translating all the world's great stories he can get his hands on, Morris seems to be collecting the swords and spears of traditional heroism, of chivalry and romance and warfare and magic and mystery, so that they can be beaten into the plowshares and pruning hooks of a new world where man had made his peace with himself and with nature.

The World
as Music
and Idea in
Wagner's *Parsifal*

✧

ON THE subject of Wagner I have to speak as a pure outsider. I am interested in Wagner as a creative figure with an immense cultural influence, but I have never been to Bayreuth: I have seen very few Wagner operas, and the whole spectacular side of Wagner, the spears that freeze over the heads of the virtuous, the swans and doves and dragons and other ambulatory fauna, has always been of minor interest to me. In fact I have reservations about the genre itself. I once saw a work of Monteverdi in which the singers performed offstage while the action on the stage—an episode from Tasso—was mimed, and I have never quite lost the feeling that that was the direction in which opera should have developed.

Considering the time and place of my youth, it was inevitable that there should be a long interval between my first music lessons and my first opera (which was *Lohengrin*). Hence my early musical experiences crystallized around the great keyboard composers, who produced the music I feel I really possess. Then I went through a period, during the Second World War, when I loathed Wagner's music to the point of physical nausea. That meant, of course, that I was accepting the Nazi identification with Wagner, and such paranoid elements in Wagner's character as his anti-Semitism seemed to me at that time very central. So

I can understand even Nietzsche's hysteria on the subject of Wagner in general and of *Parsifal* in particular, although the source of my own hysteria was anti-Nazi and not anti-Christian. I learned from this negative experience not to trust value judgments too much, even when they come from the pit of the stomach, which is where the sixteenth-century alchemist Helmont located the soul. Nevertheless, it is sometimes an advantage to have come to such a controversial figure as Wagner the hard way, so that the stock prejudices against him have already been made conscious.

One of the most extraordinary features of Wagner's mind, which is familiar but still needs emphasizing, is the way in which all his mythological themes seemed to be present to him at once, aspects of a single colossal vision that he turned to one at a time. If the operas were all alike, this would not be remarkable: it is their individuality that makes it so. We remember that Lohengrin was Parsifal's son, that the central and obvious source for the Parsifal story was the *Parzival* of the medieval poet Wolfram von Eschenbach, who appears in his own right as a character in *Tannhäuser,* and that Wagner had originally thought of introducing Parsifal as a minor character into the later part of *Tristan.* So we are not surprised to find that he had been reading Wolfram and pondering an opera on his hero quite early in his career, around 1845. But by the time he was able to give his full time and energy to the subject, he was aware that it would probably be his last opera, and in a letter to King Ludwig, after making his regulation plea that *this* time he must have complete freedom, he adds that, like William Tell, if his arrow fails he has no other to send after it. A touch of genuine pathos here is given by the fact that "Parsifal" was Wagner's private name for King Ludwig, and that Wagner was dead within a few months of *Parsifal's* first performance.

The story of Parsifal comes from one of the Grail romances. There are so many Grail romances, and they interlock in such curious ways, that one feels at first that there must have been some archetypal poem which contained all the essential Grail themes, of which the poet we happen to be reading has picked up only bits and pieces. But we soon realize that criticism needs another conception when dealing with legends like this, something closer to "total tradition" than to "lost first poem." A great myth like that of the Grail means everything essential that it has ever been made to mean in the history of its development, and the complete story is the one that emerges gradually in the course of time, which in English literature takes us down through Malory to Tennyson, Swinburne, Charles Williams, and many others still to come.

Wagner will always be slightly peripheral to the total Grail story, I think, because in *Parsifal*, as in *Tristan*, he obliterates the Arthurian context of the cycle. To adapt a phrase of Vinaver about Malory, he has no Camelot to balance his Corbenic [Malory's name for the Grail castle], and so we have no contrasting base of social operations and no roots in a specific body of legend. The *Ring* is solidly entrenched in the Siegfried story, but a Grail story without an Arthurian court is as disembodied as an *Odyssey* without Ithaca. A work of art derives its identity from its context within the art, including the context of its tradition, and anything that has to be called a *Bühnenweihfestspiel* clearly has problems with identity. I am not speaking of anything that Wagner should have done and did not do: I am trying to indicate the context of what he did. *Parsifal* belongs to a genre of drama that I have elsewhere called the *auto* (taking the word from Calderón): a musical and spectacular drama that is neither tragic nor comic, but presents an audience with a central myth in its cultural tradition, like the biblical plays of the Middle Ages. The latter were associated with the Feast of Corpus Christi, and the symbol of communication so prominent in *Parsifal* is appropriate to its tradition.

For most of us the Holy Grail is part of a Christian legend. It was, according to tradition, the cup used by Jesus at the Last Supper, when he identified the wine in it with his own blood. It was later used to catch the actual blood and water that flowed from his side when it was pierced, on the cross, with a lance of a Roman soldier, traditionally named Longinus. Bleeding lance, or spear, and chalice of divine blood thus form together an unauthorized but very haunting pair of Christian symbols. When Wagner read Wolfram, he was, according to his letters to Mathilde Wesendonk, disappointed in him, and seems to have got more, at least at first, from Wolfram's main source Chrétien de Troyes and from the poets who continued Chrétien's unfinished story. One reason, it seems clear, was that Wolfram has no notion of a Christian context for his imagery. Wolfram's Parzival comes to the castle of the Grail, and sees borne in procession there a number of mysterious objects. They include a bleeding lance, but it is not said to be the lance of Longinus; they include a Grail, but the Grail in Wolfram is not a chalice: it is apparently a stone, though a stone with miraculous healing powers, able to raise the phoenix from its ashes. The manuscripts, which clearly reflect confusion in the minds of their scribes, usually call it *lapsit exillis*. If *lapsit* is a scribal error for *lapis*, then it could be *lapis exilis*, slender stone, whatever that means, or *lapis elixir*, the philosopher's stone of alchemy, or *lapis exilii* or *exsulis*, stone of exile, which suggests a meteorite fallen from the sky.

The conception of the Grail as the chalice of the passion of Christ is associated with another cycle of stories connected with Joseph of Arimathea, who is said to have brought the Grail to Glastonbury in England. As we push further into the stories, there seem to be hints of Celtic and pre-Christian sources, where the lance and grail were sexual and fertility symbols, emblematic of love and war, as Yeats would say. Sometimes the Grail is not a cup but a flat dish, a platter or salver, which seems to be the original meaning of the word *grail*. Sometimes a sword replaces the spear or lance, and in the Welsh version of the Percival story, *Peredur*, there is a procession bearing a bleeding lance and a severed head. As lance and grail become more fixed in the Christian legend, the alternative images, the sword, the dish, the severed head, began to cluster around the passion of John the Baptist, whose birth is traditionally at the summer solstice, at the opposite end of the calendar from the birth of Christ. The John the Baptist parallels, whatever their actual importance, were emphasized by the Grail scholar Karl Simrock, who was one of Wagner's sources. Nineteenth-century poets tended to be more interested in the John the Baptist passion than in that of Christ, because the women connected with it, traditionally named Salome and Herodias, could be so easily assimilated to their cherished theme of the femme fatale. We notice that "Herodias" is one of the names that Klingsor applies to Kundry. Herodias also appears in nineteenth-century fiction as the name of a female counterpart of the Wandering Jew: this is clearly one of the roles associated with Kundry, who says that she laughed at the passion of Christ, and has been looking for the release of death ever since. Other commentators have connected the four main images of the two legends, lance, chalice, sword, dish, with the four suits of the Tarot pack of cards, but Wagner does not follow them, though a number of other writers did so, notably Yeats.

In any case the Christian associations of the imagery seem to go back to fertility images, caldrons of plenty and the like, which are older than Christianity. We may compare the growth of the story best known to us as that of St. George and the dragon, which also evolved from a pre-Christian into a Christian legend. Here a young knight comes over the sea to a wasteland ruled by an aged and impotent king, whose land is laid waste by a dragon. He kills the dragon, rescues and marries the king's daughter (who has just been chosen by lot to be fed to the dragon), and becomes the new king. The overtones of a nature myth where winter, sterility, age, and death give place to their opposites is clear enough. But the same story becomes absorbed into Christian symbolism, where Christ, the new or second Adam, kills the dragon of death and hell, rescues his bride the church, and redeems the old and impotent king who is the first Adam. The close relationship of this myth to that of the Grail story needs no laboring.

An enthusiastic Wagnerian, Jessie Weston, who also translated Wolfram's *Parzival* into English verse, was an Arthurian scholar whose book *From Ritual to Romance* attempted, on the basis of Frazer and similar writers of his generation, to trace the Grail stories back to a pre-Christian mythology. Her book was a definite and acknowledged influence on Eliot's *Waste Land,* but *The Waste Land,* while it uses a good deal of Frazerian and pre-Christian imagery, is again a Christian poem, in which an aged and impotent king seems to be identified both with Wolfram's "Fisher King" and with the first Adam. There are several Wagnerian echoes in Eliot's poem, though the only one linked to *Parsifal* is a quotation of the last line of Verlaine's sonnet on *Parsifal,* which refers to the boys' choir singing in the dome ("coupole") at the end of act 1, and propheysing the coming of a compassionate fool. Eliot puts this, as we should expect, in a grimly ironic context.

Verlaine treats *Parsifal* as simply Christian in its imagery, but Wagner also gives us a powerful sense, especially in the Good Friday music of the third act, of an immemorial revival of nature pushing its way through winter to spring. He has not eliminated the pre-Christian fertility and nature-myth basis of the story, nor

344

has he tried to do so. The Christian setting of the opera, there-fore, needs to be approached with some caution. Amfortas in Wolfram is wounded in the testicles, which makes him a quite explicit symbol of sterility, and brings him closer to Attis and other dying fertility gods than to Christ. Wagner's Amfortas is wounded in the side like Christ, and by the same spear or lance, though, unlike Christ, he acquires his wound as a result of sin and weakness, and can only be healed by the same spear. Parsifal is the agent of Amfortas's redemption, but he is not a duplicate of Christ, even though Kundry does seem to address him once as though he were. For one thing, as Wagner remarked, Parsifal is a tenor, which in our musical tradition will not do for Christ. He is a figure of a post-Christian legend, much more in the po-sition of, say, the Knight of Holiness identified with St. George in the first book of Spenser's *Faerie Queene,* a human figure anxious to follow Christ in his dragon-killing quest, but subject to hu-man limitations and frailties on the way. Redemption must come to the redeemer, as the text says. Parsifal, it is emphasized, is primarily a *reiner Tor,* a pure fool, a phrase which makes no sense when applied to Christ. What sense does it make when applied to Parsifal?

We can get two clues to this, one from the greatest fool in literature, the Fool in *King Lear,* the other from Wolfram. The Fool in *King Lear* does not lack intelligence: while he is on the stage he is generally the shrewdest person there. But he is a "natural": he cannot help telling the truth, and is tolerated as an entertainer because, as Freud explained centuries later, the sud-den and disconcerting emergence of the truth is the basis of most wit and humor. In Shakespeare, as in every poet of his day, there are two levels of nature, the higher nature that God originally created for man and the lower nature that man entered with his fall, the level of nature that Edmund accepts when he says, "Thou, Nature, art my goddess." The Fool is a survival from the higher nature of truth and loyalty, who can exist in a lower world only through the very limited privileges that a licensed fool has. Goneril, we note, does not believe that the Fool is really a fool, because he is a "natural" on a level of nature that she does not know exists. Parsifal is not born with the ability to see things as clearly as the Fool does, but he has the same instinctive sympathy with Amfortas that the Fool has with Lear, a sympathy symbol-ized by his feeling the same pain that Amfortas feels. Such sympathy is a quality of innocence, and enables Parsifal to destroy the illusions of Klingsor, as innocence and illusion cannot ultimately inhabit the same world.

In Wolfram, Parzival comes, by accident, to the castle of the Grail, meets the keeper of the Grail there, called also the Fisher King, who is impotent and suffering, and sees the great procession with the bleeding lance and the holy stone. The latter, it appears, can cure everything except what ails the Fisher King. Parzival, whose father had died in his infancy, has been taught by his mother and by an old knight named Gornemans to behave respectfully when with strangers, and above all not to ask too many questions. So he watches the mysterious procession without comment or inquiry, or expressing the curiosity he feels. The next day he discovers that his silence was not only a grave discourtesy but something like a mortal sin. If he had asked the question, the king's agony would have ended, and the wasteland transformed into a garden. As he did not, he is reviled and cursed as the greatest disaster that ever came to the land.

At first this sounds like one of those irrational situations that occur in romance simply because they occur, included by Wolfram because it was in his source. The question of why it was in his source, even if we could answer it, would take us too far from Wagner. Almost always, in romance as elsewhere, the hero succeeds by doing what his elders have told him to do, minding his manners and keeping his mouth shut. A male-centered literature has tended to associate curiosity with the disasters caused by the inherent weakness of females. Yet Parzival's is a most eerily suggestive one nonetheless. Perhaps this is partly because we have all had dreams in which we accepted mysterious and portentous imagery without question, and may have felt on waking that if we had only been sufficiently conscious to ask ourselves about the meaning of what we saw, we might have made a major breakthrough to another dimension of experience altogether. We have mentioned Eliot, and we may remember how as early as "Prufrock" Eliot is haunted by the theme of "some overwhelming question," which he associates with the return of Lazarus from the dead.

In Wolfram, Parzival eventually gets back to the Grail castle near the end of the story and asks the healing question, which appears to be something like "Dear uncle, why do you have this terrible pain in the testicles?" Even Wagner quailed before the prospect of putting this in the recitativo, although he had, as we saw, already moved the area of pain to a more respectable address. In Chrétien de Troyes the question is rather Whom does the Grail serve?—a much more profound question, but superfluous one for Wagner, for whom the Grail obviously serves the knights of the Grail. Wagner has redistributed the traditional themes of his sources in a most ingenious way. The theme of sexual impotence is transferred to Klingsor, who has castrated himself in order to achieve purity through an act of self-will. Klingsor therefore really is the life-denying spirit that Nietzsche thought he saw in the whole opera. The equivalent of Parzival's failure to ask the crucial question comes when Gurnemanz decides that, prophecy or no prophecy, Parsifal is nothing but a fool.

This happens at the end of the first act, in symmetrical contrast to Parsifal's succession to Amfortas as leader of the Grail knights at the end of the third. It is a rejection by a father figure, more or less: at least Gurnemanz has previously addressed Parsifal as "my son." In the second act Parsifal descends into a world of illusion which Wagner obviously associated, as we should do, with Parsifal's own unconscious. Naturally he meets in that world the ghost of his mother Herzeleide, whom he has, unknown to himself, violated, that is, killed, as he has broken her heart by leaving her. Herzeleide is personated by Kundry, the one female figure of the opera, who represents all the ambivalence of traditional Christianity to female figures. In the Bible the symbolic maleness of God seems to represent the fact that nature, which is usually female in mythology, is morally alien to man and keeps him imprisoned in an endless round of death and rebirth. The flower maidens Parsifal meets are spirits of nature: they are not evil, but they are creatures of a morally irresponsible and nonhuman world. The redeeming God has to be male, but man, who is to be redeemed, is in that context symbolically woman, the forgiven harlot who appears in Old Testament prophecy and as the Magdalen figure of the Gospels.

Kundry is neither wholly a siren of nature nor a Magdalen, but is torn between the two, an Ariel who desperately longs to be a Caliban, the servant of human society, but cannot live in that world either. In Klingsor's world she feels that Parsifal could be her savior if she could get into sexual contact with him, and Parsifal has to explain to her that she cannot be redeemed by her own desire. In the Grail world she becomes, in the third act, a forgiven and released Magdalen figure. Wagner is said to have been annoyed by those who pointed to the Kundry-Magdalen parallels, but he could hardly have put her through the routine of washing Parsifal's feet and wiping them with her hair without feeling that there was an echo in the room somewhere.

We have been speaking of Christian redemption in *Parsifal,* but Wagner has also been developing an interest in Buddhism, running parallel to his interest in Christianity though not, as he saw it, inconsistent with it. This had come largely from his reading of Schopenhauer, and before he wrote *Parsifal* Wagner had meditated dramas on both Jesus and Buddha. In Buddhism the great enemy is illusion, and illusion is caused by the ego-centered nature of our perception. Here again we have two levels of nature, though metaphorically the better one is usually thought of as deeper rather than higher. In this context Parsifal's confrontation with the memory of his mother represents the deepest hold that the habit-energy of his ego still has on him, and the only way to break from it is through compassion, the sudden sense of identity with Amfortas that cuts him loose from Kundry. Buddhism also puts a high valuation on the stillness and the calmness of mind that comes from emptying it of self-conscious thoughts, and the "pure fool" aspect of Parsifal, which sometimes leaves him unable to articulate the simplest sentence, is connected with that.

In the *Ring* cycle the disturbances set in motion by Alberich's theft of the gold cause a crisis among the gods. The gods, or at least Wotan, find that they have become an establishment, and get caught up in all the casuistry and false decisions of an establishment mentality. At the end of *Götterdämmerung* the gods have had it, and the new reign of man is prophesied. There were contemporary and later German writers, some of them insane, who were or tried to be polytheists with a genuine belief in the old gods, classical or Nordic. But Wagner was not one of them, and no other conclusion for the *Ring* was conceivable except a humanistic one. What kind of man would genuinely deserve to succeed the gods? This, I think, is the question that *Parsifal* is mainly concerned with. *Parsifal* assumes that the coming of Christ, symbolized by the Grail, has been essential to the answer, so the question takes the form of what the model of human action is that Christianity provides. The answer is still complex, but its principle is that true human action is antiheroic, not in the sense of lacking courage, but in regarding patience and endurance as still greater virtues. In the *Ring* all the heroic quests are essentially ways of feeding the gods, keeping them supplied with the youth and energy essential to their supremacy. The Valkyries, the choosers of those slain in battle, symbolize this conception of the heroic life as a continuous sacrifice by man to nourish the gods. In *Parsifal* the Grail does the feeding, because the essential sacrifice, of God for man, which is what keeps man alive, has already taken place, and reversed the direction of the cult of heroic warfare.

The theme of the renunciation of a heroic quest, which runs all through *Parsifal*, had already appeared in the *Ring*, because the whole titanic struggle started by Alberich's theft can only end when the stolen gold is put back where it was. The effectiveness of this theme for romance was demonstrated in the next century by the sensational success of Tolkien, who retells the story of a ring that must not be won but lost, the Nibelung story interpenetrated with the spirit of redeeming simplicity in *Parsifal*, symbolized by his "hobbits." The *Parsifal* is much more explicitly the drama of a renounced quest, to the point of being something of an antidrama. This is because the central theme of the spiritual growth of Parsifal himself is so closely connected with the theme of temptation.

When Milton wanted to show the nature of genuine Christian heroism in *Paradise Regained*, he chose the theme of the temptation of Christ in the wilderness by Satan. That meant an epic of four books in which Satan thinks up one enticing illusion after another, while Christ merely stands in the center and rejects them. An epic based on the central episode of Buddha's life, his enlightenment under the Bo tree, rejecting one after another of the illusions of Mara, would not be very different. In this kind of theme the dramatic situation is the reverse of the moral one: our sympathies are dramatically with Satan, with Mara, with Klingsor, because they do the dramatic work. To make heroes of Jesus and Buddha and Parsifal because they refuse to do it makes moral sense but a dramatic paradox. One feels that while there is a lot going on in *Parsifal*, what is not going on, to any great extent, is the kind of dramatic action that would be needed (at least up to Wagner's time) to keep a purely verbal play on the stage.

And yet in all major drama a neutralizing balancing power,

which the Greeks called nemesis in its tragic aspect, can be seen
at work. In Shakespeare's romances, while the surface action
moves towards the marriage of young and happy people, the major action is a setting right of something wrong in the past. The
theme of *The Tempest* looks as though it were going to be Prospero's revenge on his enemies by his power of magic. But Prospero renounces both his revenge and his magic, and regains his
dukedom, as W. H. Auden makes him say, at the moment when
he no longer wants it. The "rarer action," as Prospero calls it, is
a neutralizing of the expected revenge action. Wagner remarked
that the Grail was the spiritualized version of the Nibelung
hoard. But Parsifal does not acquire the Grail by a dragon-killing
quest: he merely gets his head clear of the kind of illusion that
such dragons represent, and the Grail thereby acquires him.

Going by the text alone, the characters of *Parsifal* do seem
to be a life-denying lot, crippled or half dead, and resembling
characters in a play of Beckett more closely than they do those in
any earlier work of Wagner's. Amfortas is in mortal agony, longing for death, until almost the last moment of the drama; Titurel
speaks from a tomb in the first act and is buried in the third;
Kundry, who practically has to be dug out of the ground at the
beginning of the third act, also longs for the death she finally
gets; Gurnemanz seems old and tired even at the beginning, and
proportionately more so at the end. Parsifal himself makes his
entrance as a stupid oaf shooting a swan, an oaf's idea of fun, and
then proves to be unable even to answer any questions, much less
ask them. He finally, as we saw, becomes such an encumbrance
to what action there is that Gurnemanz pushes him irritably off
the stage. Whatever one thinks of the phrase "music of the future" applied to Wagner, *Parsifal* at least is the drama of the
future, pointing the way to the kind of dramatic struggle with,
and within, stagnation that we have later in Strindberg, Chek-
hov, Beckett, and Sartre.

All through Wagner's work runs the theme of *comitatus*, the
brotherhood united by some form of distinctive heroism or
skill—even the *Meistersinger* make up such a group. But the
knights of the Grail move toward exhaustion in the third act,
where much of the dominant music is very like a funeral march.
In the course of the action Gurnemanz remarks that in the world
of the Grail castle time has given place to space. I don't know
what this meant altogether, but certainly the atmosphere is one

of suspended time, like the life-in-death of the Ancient Mariner, or the world between incarnations in a Japanese No play. Another parallel would be Ezekiel's vision of a valley of dry bones, transformed into "an exceeding great army" by a power that Christian readers of Ezekiel would identify with the Resurrection, the ultimate transforming power that immediately follows Good Friday.

It seems to me significant, however, that Wagner kept the traditional Good Friday as the setting for his third act, instead of changing it to Easter Sunday. For the main action of the opera is less a resurrection than a harrowing of hell. There are, as always, two levels of hell. The deeper level, the world of the self-castrated Klingsor in which Kundry is unable to die, is the real hell: it will always be there as long as man insists on living in egocentric illusion, but it is still illusion and is unredeemable. Above it is the limbo of the moribund Grail knights: this world can be redeemed and its inhabitants set free.

What the verbal action of *Parsifal* really dramatizes, I think, is not primarily anything Christian or Buddhist or pagan, but Schopenhauer's two worlds of will and idea. The world of will, for Schopenhauer, is a subhuman and a submoral world, out of which we have come, and which involves far more suffering than happiness for human beings. The flower maidens are relatively well adjusted to such a world, because they have very little consciousness and next to no memory. A conscious being in this world can only do evil, whether willingly like Klingsor or unwillingly like Kundry, but in either case possessed by desire without fulfillment, the spear without the Grail. Amfortas is in a conscious, sensitive, peaceful world of representation or idea, but suffers horribly because he is still caught in the toils of the desiring world as will: he has the Grail without the spear. If Klingsor were to acquire the Grail, the world of conscious moral values would be flooded over by the will and would disappear: if the Grail knights were to regain the spear, they would acquire the creative power which is desire with fulfillment. One reason why Schopenhauer is so central to *Parsifal* is that, in speaking of music as the primary language of the will, he provided a genuine social and intelligible human context for music. Most philosophers who talk about music, such as Plato, are of no use to a practical composer.

The libretto of *Parsifal* was very hard on Nietzsche, who had talked of a Superman to surpass present mankind, a new master of morality to replace the old slave moralities of Buddhism and Christianity, and of a gospel affirming life in place of the life-denying programs of the great religions. I suspect that the elements derived from Schopenhauer infuriated him even more than the Christian ones, as Schopenhauer was probably another Oedipal father whom Nietzsche wanted to kill. But it should be kept in mind, in reading Nietzsche's shrieking abuse of the ideology of *Parsifal,* that Nietzsche had heard none of the music of the opera except the overture, and he talks very differently about that—in a private letter, it is true. We may concede to Nietzsche that *Parsifal* is a story of a group of sick and dying puppets, although they are awaiting a colossal transfiguring power that will hurl them into a new life. If we ask what kind of dramatic device could conceivably represent such a power, we have, for Wagner, an immediate and obvious answer: the music.

Parsifal being a very late work, it is not a "number" opera, with detached arias like Senta's ballad in *The Flying Dutchman* or Wolfram's song to the evening star in *Tannhäuser.* Some Wagner criticism gives the impression that Wagner wrote a libretto, then composed a number of leitmotifs, each one with an allegorical relationship to some character or image in the story, then mixed these up in a musical pastiche where they appear at appropriate moments. How anything resembling a structure could emerge from such a procedure is an unanswered question. The opposite extreme is represented by Lorenz's four-volume study attempting to demonstrate, not simply that the music has a structure, but that the musical structure in fact *is* the structure of the opera. This tends to suggest that Wagner's music dramas are simply overgrown symphonies with vocal obbligato. But even the longest symphony has to have some basis in symphonic form, and the structural principles of Wagner's music seem to be quite different from those of symphonic form.

This statement, however, is less true of *Parsifal* than of any other Wagner opera. *Parsifal* begins and ends in the same key (A-flat major), and the second act also begins and ends in the same key (B-minor). We may call this pure accident, but accidents in Wagner are seldom if ever pure. It looks as though tonality has a function for this opera which is unusual for operas in general, even for Wagner's. All through the work, again, there is a contrast of diatonic and chromatic textures. The diatonic ones are associated with the Grail and the ideas and virtues it inspires. The chromatic passages predominate in the world of Klingsor in the second act, and are also associated with the agony of Amfortas and with the more screaming and scampering aspects of Kundry.

The overture presents the three main Grail themes: we may follow tradition, for the most part, and associate them respectively with the Christian virtues of love, hope, and faith. We begin with what is called the Love Feast motif, an eerie, plaintive, isolated melody followed by arpeggios on the chord of A-flat. We are not, of course, in the world of preconscious innocence represented by the open E-flat chords at the beginning of *Rheingold:* the function of these arpeggios is to establish the underlying rhythm of the very syncopated first theme. The second theme is a well-known liturgical cadence called the "Dresden Amen," which would have been familiar to many in Wagner's audience. A third theme, with four descending notes prominent in it, follows and provides a rhythmical contrast to the gentle and wavering opening. A quite sudden modulation of this theme from A-flat to D-major was associated by Wagner, apparently, with the spreading of the Grail faith throughout the world. The opening theme recurs, wistful and elusive as ever, and the overture ends on a dominant seventh of almost intolerable insistence, lingering even in the first recitativos after the curtain rises.

All three themes are strongly diatonic and seem to set the pattern for three modes of feeling. The Love Feast theme, in spite of its gentle subsidence at its close, is mainly a rising melody with a dotted rhythm in its rise that recurs, in different forms, through various moods of aspiration and yearning, including even the central theme of the Good Friday music. All three acts of *Parsifal* begin with a summons to wake up, the second and third being both addressed, for different reasons, to the harassed Kundry, and Klingsor has a demonic parody of rising rhythm associated with him as the curtain goes up on the second act.

The Dresden Amen is one of a group of themes that seem to express a mood of waiting, with calmness and patience, for some kind of deliverance from the prison-paradise of the Grail world. The most important of these themes of hope, as we might call them, is the hymn that prophesies the coming of the compassionate fool. The more vigorous theme called Faith reminds us that the Grail knighthood is still a band of heroes, even though

353

their heroism has outgrown the fighting stage, and it is linked with the marching rhythm of the procession in the first act, which moves with a somewhat plodding stateliness towards the unveiling of the Grail. The march in the third act, where the burial of Titurel is involved, has a slightly different rhythm, closer, as said, to a funeral march, in contrast to the more spirited martial theme that accompanies the entrances of Parsifal. In the chromatic tumult of Klingsor's world in the second act we hear two themes in particular associated with temptation and illusion. One is the waltzing rhythm of the flower maidens' chatter, the other the pastoral six-eight (later nine-eight) rhythm of Kundry's account to Parsifal of his childhood with his mother. Both have curious recalls of the formulas of popular nineteenth-century music: they are equal in attractiveness and technical skill to anything else in the opera, but manage to suggest something a bit bogus, or at least commonplace, at the same time.

The opening of the third act, depicting the exhaustion and low morale of the Grail knights and Parsifal's inability to find them, wanders uncertainly around the key of B-flat minor: so uncertainly that one critic has suggested that the real tonic chord is a diminished seventh rather than the chord of B-flat minor. Wagner is never atonal, and when he seems to move away from tonality it generally means that chaos is coming again. The third act then alternates between hope and fear, rising to a dissonant climax when the knights insist that the suffering Amfortas, who is at the end of his endurance, uncover the Grail once more, and we wonder if a demonic parody of the sacrifice of Christ is about to be enacted on this Good Friday. However, Parsifal is present this time with his healing spear, and the opera ends with the motif of Faith having it all its own way, in a limpidly diatonic conclusion.

Even an amateur with no training in musical analysis, like myself, could follow the evolving, intertwining, and metamorphosing play of the various themes throughout the opera for a long time; but we do not have a long time (changed to space, like the Grail world, in the context of an essay), and I wish to make one point only about the music. The verbal framework of *Parsifal*, we suggested, was derived from Schopenhauer's construct of the world as will and idea, or representation of the world in a conscious mind. This construct, though it has a popular reputation for pessimism, is nevertheless one within which

354

the redemptive efforts of Christianity and Buddhism become at least intelligible. But the music expands from here into a much larger vision of humanity led by its own inner nature to rise toward some infinite power which is both itself and the opposite of itself, an effort neither quixotic nor hopeless because the infinite power has already descended to meet it. I hear this perhaps most clearly at the moment of Parsifal's prayer before the spear, but its overtones and resonances are on every page of the opera, and make me wonder whether music, which defines nothing and expresses everything, may not be the primary language of the spirit, and not merely, as Schopenhauer said, of the suffering and enduring will.

Cycle and
Apocalypse in
Finnegans Wake

SINCE THE fourteenth century, there has never been a time when English literature has not been influenced, often to the point of domination, by either French or Italian literary traditions, usually both at once. For Chaucer, the major foreign influence was Boccaccio, whose *Teseide* and *Filostrato* form the basis for *The Knight's Tale* and *Troilus and Criseyde* respectively. In Tudor times the Petrarchan sonnet was the central model, both in technique and theme, for lyric poetry, and Ariosto at least contributed very heavily to the major epic of the period, Spenser's *Faerie Queene*. After the Restoration, French influence, of the neoclassical type, rose to dominance, headed by the critical theories of Boileau, whose slighting reference to "leclinquant de Tasse" marked the ascendancy of French satire over Italian romance. Romanticism, however, found Britain at war with France, when it was a patriotic duty to prove that French literature was second-rate, as we can see in Coleridge. The second generation of Romantics brought back Italian as the dominant foreign influence: Byron translated a canto of Pulci; Boiardo is a presence in Peacock's last story, *Gryll Grange;* Shelley (and Keats in translation) owed much to Dante, who had previously had, for religious reasons, relatively little influence. Romantic Italianism reached its climax in Browning, although Browning reflects the pictorial and visual culture of Italy more than its literature.

In the generation of Joyce, Eliot, and Pound, which came to maturity around the First World War, Eliot's main debts are to the French: the Italian influences are, again, confined largely to Dante, whom he imitates with great skill in an episode in *Little Gidding*. Ezra Pound's contacts with Italian literature, history, and art are of vast range and erudition, though they also include a good many red herrings. Joyce's Italianism is more centrally in the Romantic tradition. Stephen Dedalus in *Ulysses* complains, using the title of an Italian play, that he is the servant of two masters, one English and one Italian, but there he is talking about the political ascendancy of Great Britain and the Roman Catholic domination in religion. As literary masters, the Italians predominate in Joyce over all other non-English influences. Joyce's great debt to Dante, at every stage of his career, has been fully documented in a book-length study, and he owed much to other Italian writers, including Gabriele D'Annunzio, who cannot be considered here. But *Finnegans Wake* is dominated by two Italians not previously represented to any extent in English literature before. One is Giambattista Vico, whom Joyce did much to make a major influence in our intellectual traditions ever since. The other is Giordano Bruno of Nola, in whom no previous writer in English except Coleridge seems to have been much interested, although he lived in England for a time and dedicated his two best-known books to Sir Philip Sidney.

During the years when Joyce was working on *Finnegans Wake,* publishing fragments of it from time to time under the heading of *Work in Progress,* a group of his disciples brought out a volume of essays with the eminently off-putting title of *Our Exagmination round his Factification for Incamination of Work in Progress.* The first of these essays, by the disciple whose name is by far the best known today, Samuel Beckett, was on Joyce's debt to Italian writers, more especially Vico. Despite Beckett's expertise in Italian—all his major work reflects a masterly command of Dante—the essay is very inconclusive, mainly, I imagine, because the entire structure of *Finnegans Wake* was not yet visible, and the essays were designed to point to something about to emerge and not to expound on something already there. However, since then every commentary has been largely based on Joyce's use of Vico's cyclical conception of history.

Vico thinks of history as the repetition of a cycle that passes through four main phases, a mythical or poetic period, an age of the gods; then an aristocratic period dominated by heroes and heraldic crests; then a demotic period; and finally a *ricorso,* or return to chaos followed by the beginning of another cycle. Vico traces these four periods through the classical age to the fall of the Roman Empire, and speaks of a new cycle beginning in the medieval period. In the twentieth century Spengler worked out a similar vision of history, although he uses the metaphor of organisms rather than cycles. Spengler influenced Yeats to some degree, but not Joyce. The first section of *Finnegans Wake,* covering the first eight chapters, deals with the mythical or poetic period of legend and myths of gods; the second section, in four chapters, with the aristocratic phase; the third, also in four chapters, with the demotic phase, and the final or seventeenth chapter with the *ricorso.* The book ends in the middle of a sentence which is completed by the opening words of the first page, thus dramatizing the cycle as vividly as words can well do.

In contrast, there seems relatively little concrete documentation for the influence of Bruno of Nola, and one of the most useful commentaries, which has Vico all over the place, does not even list Bruno in the index. Yet Bruno was an early influence, coming to Joyce's attention before his growing trouble with his eyesight forced him to become increasingly dependent on the help of others for his reading. In his early pamphlet "The Day of the Rabblement," he alludes to Bruno as "the Nolan," clearly with some pleasure in concealing the name of a dangerous heretic under a common Irish one. What the Nolan said, according to Joyce, was that no one can be a lover of the true and good without abhorring the multitude, which suggests that the immature Joyce, looking for security in a world where his genius was not yet recognized, found some reassurance in Bruno's habitual arrogance of tone. Bruno's "heresy," evidently, seemed to Joyce less an attack on or repudiation of Catholic doctrines than the isolating of himself from the Church through a justified spiritual pride—the same heresy he ascribes to Stephen in the *Portrait.* As far as Bruno's ideas were concerned, Joyce was less interested in the plurality of worlds, which so horrified Bruno's contemporaries, and concentrates on a principle largely derived by Bruno from Nicholas of Cusa, who was not only orthodox but a cardinal, the principle of polarity. Joyce tells Harriet Shaw Weaver in a letter that Bruno's philosophy "is a kind of dualism—every power in nature must evolve an opposite in order to realize itself and opposition brings reunion." Most writers would be more likely to speak of Hegel in such a connection, but that is not the kind of source one looks for in Joyce. In the compulsory period of his education Joyce acquired some knowledge of the Aristotelian philosophical tradition, and learned very early the numbing effect of an allusion to St. Thomas Aquinas. But there is little evidence that the mature Joyce read technical philosophy with any patience or persistence—not even Heraclitus, who could have given him most of what he needed of the philosophy of polarity in a couple of aphorisms.

In a later letter to Harriet Weaver, Joyce says, referring to both Vico and Bruno: "I would not pay overmuch attention to these theories, beyond using them for all they are worth." That is, cyclical theories of history and philosophies of polarity were not doctrines he wished to expound, the language of *Finnegans Wake* being clearly useless for expounding anything, but structural principles for the book. It is this question of structural principles that I should like to look into at the moment, rather than simple allusion. Many of Joyce's allusions, especially to run-of-the-mill fiction and poetry written in nineteenth-century Ireland, are there primarily because the setting is Irish; many of his structural principles derive from sources he seldom refers to. He owed a great deal more to Blake, for example, than one would realize from the number of references to him—more than he himself realized, probably. Again, if *Finnegans Wake* is a dream, the researches of Freud and Jung on dreams must be relevant to it, as both of these were prominent names in Joyce's milieu. Joyce's references to Freud and Jung are rare and usually in somewhat hostile contexts, but the hostility may be partly protective. When some of Freud was read to him he remarked that Vico had anticipated Freud, but in view of his use of Freud's Oedipal and censorship conceptions, his theory of wit, and his analysis of the condensation and displacement of the dreamwork, the remark seems to be something of a boutade. Again, Joyce had personal reasons for not wanting to come too close to Jung, but Jung's "collective unconscious" may also be a structural principle in the book.

Finnegans Wake was published in the year that I began continuous teaching, and within a few months I bought the copy that I still have, for ninety-eight cents on a remainder counter in Toronto. I was fascinated by the book, but was preoccupied at the time with the Blake prophecies, and was in no position to go into orbit around it. When the Blake book was off my hands and I started working on the *Anatomy of Criticism*, I had to account, so to speak, for the existence of *Finnegans Wake*. True, there was a popular fallacy at the time, which I kept hearing for the next twenty years, that all works of literature were "unique," and that the critic should not try to detract from that uniqueness. The notion rested on a confusion between criticism as a body of knowledge about literature and the experience of reading, which is central to criticism but not part of it. Every experience is in some sense unique, but the unique as such cannot be an object of knowledge. So the task remained, as did, of course, the confusion. It seemed to me that there was an epic form that tended to expand into a kind of imaginative encyclopedia, and that the limit of this encyclopedic form was the sacred book, the kind of scriptural myth that we find in the Bible, the Prose Edda and in Hindu literature. The affinities of *Finnegans Wake*, for all its pervasive irony, appeared to be closest to that form, and I could see that the Bible (along with missals and prayer books, both Catholic and Anglican), the Koran, and the Egyptian Book of the Dead were much in Joyce's mind. Otherwise there seemed to be no critical theory that really illuminated what Joyce was doing. Joyce himself certainly did not provide one: his critical abilities were limited, and he seems to have been content to go along with the generally accepted statement that the language of *Finnegans Wake* is "dream language." But while it is true that the dream condenses and displaces and superimposes and puns and plays every kind of verbal trick, it hardly produces the linguistic Niagara that Joyce's seventeen years of work on *Finnegans Wake* accumulated. One cannot blame his contemporaries for insisting that he was wasting his genius on something that fell outside literature: one can only marvel at his persistence and inner confidence. But at his death, however extraordinary his achievement, it still seemed to be completely sui generis, and Eliot's remark that one *Finnegans Wake* was probably enough sounded like the most unassailable common sense. It was perhaps not until Jacques Derrida and his "deconstruction" techniques that the theory implied by *Finnegans Wake* really came into focus. The deconstructing critic tends to approach every text in the spirit in which Joyce approached the first drafts of his *Work in Progress* fragments. *Finnegans Wake* is a book in which practically every word provides, in addition to a surface meaning that may or may not be there, a great variety of "supplements" providing a number of further aspects to the meaning. Deconstruction implies a concept not far removed from Freud's concept of the censor, the process of achieving meaning by excluding unacceptable meanings; and Joyce's dream language, while the activity of censorship is certainly recorded in it, escapes, to a very unusual degree, from the kind of psychological gaps that mental censorship leaves in narrative-directed writing.

Then again, *Finnegans Wake* is a book of "traces." The central character, Finnegan himself, is effaced by his "death," or falling asleep—the two things seem to be much the same thing at the opening of the book—and what follows is a "differential" pursuit of echoes and reverberations into a world of words rather than a "logocentric" invoking of a presence. It is natural that commentators influenced by Derridean theories should be doubtful about the presence in the book of any continuous "story line" and regard the identity of the dreamer as an irrelevant question in a book where nothing has any consistent identity at all. I think, however, that Joyce, belonging to an older generation, was old-fashioned enough to prefer a set of narrative canons, however distinctively handled.

We begin with the figure of Finnegan, who is both Finn, the great legendary hero of Ireland, and the subject of a ballad about a hod carrier who fell off a ladder, broke his neck, had a funeral wake in his honor, and woke up in the middle of it demanding a share of the whiskey. In Joyce the twelve mourners at the wake persuade Finn to go back to sleep, and tell him that he is about to be superseded by another character, whose full name, we eventually learn, is Humphrey Chimpden Earwicker, but who is most commonly to be recognized by his initials HCE. Finn and HCE are frequently identified in the book, and both are married to the central female figure, whose full name is Anna Livia Plurabelle, with the initials ALP. Nevertheless we are told, as explicitly as we are told anything in the book, that Finn and HCE are distinguishable aspects of the same identity, like persons of the Trinity.

Finn seems to be Joyce's equivalent of the giant man out of whose body the world is made that we find in so many creation myths, although in *Finnegans Wake* his body seems to extend only from the Head of Howth on the northeast to Phoenix Park on the southwest. But this Dublin area is a world that mirrors and epitomizes the world, and in this sense Finn belongs to the family of the Indian Purusha, the Norse Ymir, the Cabalistic Adam Kadmon or Qodmon, and Blake's Albion. HCE, then, is Finn-again, Finn asleep and dreaming, whose dream is the recurring cycle of history. A dream ends by waking up, but although there are various intimations of an awakening throughout the book, especially in the final chapter, the dream of human history is an unending dream in which all attempts to wake up continue to be baffled as Finn was at the beginning. Stephen Dedalus in *Ulysses* speaks of history as a nightmare from which he is trying to awake, but it is clear that he never does wake up in that sense anywhere in the book. Similarly, the narrative of *Finnegans Wake* goes around in a circle to form the book of "Doublends Jined" (Dublin's Giant and double-ends joined), and the *ricorso* at the end is not a resurrection but only a return. All the dreamers in *Finnegans Wake,* so far as they are individual people, may wake up and go about their business in the morning, but even so they are still contained within the larger dream of time.

HCE has two sons, Shem and Shaun, who represent the conflict that is the pervading characteristic of history, although they are both essentially aspects of HCE, according to the principle of polarity. Near the beginning of the book we enter a "museyroom" with mementos of Napoleon and Wellington: this episode was evidently suggested by an illustration in Freud's treatise on wit and the unconscious. Wellington is or could be considered an Irish hero: one thinks of Bernard Shaw's remark that the only match for a French army led by an Italian would be a British army led by an Irishman. Apart from that, however, the result of the battle of Waterloo was not of great importance to Ireland, and in fact there are suggestions that Napoleon actually won the battle, as no doubt he did in his dreams on St. Helena. The essential point is that Napoleon and Wellington are both products of the same historical force of European imperialism, and in that context their opposition is illusory.

This is the simplest form of a conflict of polarities: in a slightly more complex one a defender of something in Ireland is fighting an invader who threatens it. Early in the book there is an encounter of two giants, Mutt and Jute: Jute seems to be connected with Danish invaders and Mutt with the Irish under Brian Boru, who stopped them at the Battle of Clontarf. A century later there was the twelfth-century English conquest under Henry II, along with which came the absorption of the native Irish church by the Roman Catholic organization. The link between the two is afforded by the fact that the pope at the time of Henry II's invasion was Adrian IV, Nicholas Brakespear, the only pope of English origin. But even here the polarities merge. In the colloquy between Mutt and Jute, Mutt says of the tide coming in and going out of Dublin Bay: "Hither, craching eastuards, they are in surgence; hence, cool at ebb, they requiesce" (17: 25). We note the prominence of the initial letters HCE at the beginning of each clause, indicating that invasion, resistance, withdrawal, and absorption, like the flow and ebb of the tide, are all aspects of the same force appearing as opposites.

In later historical periods the opposition can take a form like that of the "Devils" and "Angels" of Blake's *Marriage of Heaven and Hell,* where creative radicals struggle against established conservatives. As a rule the "Micks," the partisans of the "Angels" represented by St. Michael, are much more popular and highly regarded, especially by women, than the "Nicks," partisans of the opposite side, identified as that of "Old Nick" or the Devil by their opponents. In this aspect of the conflict "Shem," the writer and social misfit, becomes an exile and "Shaun" his brother assumes a great variety of social roles, including that of a highly indecorous priest. Joyce identifies himself to a great extent with Shem, and there is a good deal—many readers, including the present one, would say far too much—about Joyce's poverty and the neglect of his genius. Still, there is a good deal about Dante in Dante and even more about Bruno in Bruno. Vico also wrote an *Autobiography,* and, as Hugh Kenner reminds us, tells us that he fell off a ladder in the library and was for a time thought to be dead. There are other writer-heroes, notably Swift, and even a political one, Parnell.

The rivalry of brothers comes mainly from the Book of Genesis, where the chief archetypes are, first, Cain and Abel, and then Esau and Jacob. Often the two brothers expand into three. The line of succession runs through neither Cain nor Abel but through a third brother, Seth, and Noah also had three sons, of whom one was called Shem and another Ham, Ham being cursed and made subordinate to the others. Similarly the two "sons of thunder" (the significance of this word will meet us in a moment) among Jesus' disciples, James and John, whose names remind us of Shem and Shaun, are usually joined by a third, Peter. The theme of three brothers comes into such popular phrases as "Tom, Dick, and Harry," often echoed in the book, and into Swift's *Tale of a Tub,* where three brothers, Peter, Jack, and Martin, each think up their own way of perverting the teachings of the New Testament.

In any case the sons, or more generally the younger generation, whether two or three, may direct their rivalries not only against one another but against their father. This may take the regular Oedipus form of trying to replace him in the affections of the mother (ALP), or simply of cuckolding an older man, as notably in the Irish story of Tristram and King Mark. This situation expands into the usual conflict of generations: the antagonism of Parnell to his predecessor Isaac Butt, of Joyce himself to Yeats, and above all of an interminable shaggy dog story (said to be originally a story in the repertoire of Joyce's father) of how a certain "Buckley" shot (or didn't shoot) a "Russian General."

The female characters in *Finnegans Wake* reflect the ambiguity between the elusive, tantalizing siren whose indifference is deplored in so much poetry and the cherishing wife and mother whose constant care is the fostering of life. This is the usual relation of the daughter-figure Issy or Isabel, who is linked to Isolde, and who is eloquently described by the Joyce scholar Adeline Glasheen as "a perfect triumph of female imbecility," to her mother ALP. Issy is usually portrayed as a narcissistic figure gazing into her own mirror reflection, recalling Alice before her adventures or the two women, Stella and her shadowy companion Rebecca Dingley, who were the recipients of Swift's Journal with its disguising "little language." Here, naturally, the second or shadow girl readily turns into the younger woman in Swift's life, Vanessa. Like HCE and his sons, ALP and her daughter often merge into the same identity, but again they are polar opposites: we may call them, borrowing from both Robert Graves and the Song of Songs, the white goddess and the black bride. The former is what Blake would call the "Female Will," the retreating figure who fascinates, beckons, or betrays, but always eludes. The latter, who is consistently associated with the Liffey river flowing through Dublin, is the power of renewal that flows out into the sea on the last page of the book, just before returning to the headwaters of the "riverrun" on the first page.

Most commentators believe that there is an individual

dreamer at the core of the book, a tavernkeeper in Chapelizod, just up the Liffey river from Dublin. His name is generally assumed to be the filled-out form of HCE, but it is also possible that his name is Porter (there are other candidates), though his wife's name seems to be, in all of her contexts, consistently Anna Livia. This Earwicker, or Porter, seems to be of English, Protestant, and ultimately Scandinavian origin, his dream expressing some alienation about finding himself in Ireland (as he sinks into sleep we hear a voice saying "So This Is Dyoublong?"). Thus there is a latent conflict with the other aspect of himself, Finn, though the reality masked by that opposition appears to lie outside the book. The individual dreamer, if he is there, has two sons, usually called Jerry and Kevin, a daughter Isabel, at least two servants, a potboy and a cleaning woman; twelve customers in his pub (the mourners at Finn's wake), and a number of shadowy neighbors, including a mysterious "Magrath" and the "Maggies," who are evidently schoolmates of Issy or Isabel.

We seem to have, then, three major concentric circles of dream. The innermost is the individual dream of the tavernkeeper, the outermost the dream of mankind which is history, while in between there is the constant metamorphosis of the relations of Shem to Shaun, the universalized forms of Jerry and Kevin. The individual story assimilates the intensely studied scenes of Dublin life in *Dubliners* into the book; the Shem-Shaun rivalries incorporate *Portrait of the Artist as a Young Man* and *Stephen Hero*, with their focus on the social and cultural situation of Joyce himself; the dream of the many-sided Everyman whose *periplus* voyage covers the whole of the known world incorporates *Ulysses*. In *Ulysses* Stephen is an ex-Catholic intellectual and the figure who eventually becomes a symbolic father is Jewish; in *Finnegans Wake*, which was completed during the rise of Nazism in Europe, these affinities are reversed, Shem being "Semitic" and Shaun mainly parody Catholic. The activities of the tavernkeeper and his family during the previous day form the "manifest content" of the dream, the things on which the mind has not yet slept, as Freud says; the archetypal expansion of those activities to cover all human history forms the latent content. One would also expect the universal, autobiographical, and local imagery to predominate in turn through the three phases of Vico's cycle, and to some degree they do.

However expanded, the Dublin setting, or the Irish setting

generally, remains constant throughout the book. One reason, not impossibly the decisive reason, why Vico and Bruno of Nola are so important in the dream is that there is a Vico Road just outside Dublin and a Dublin bookshop called Nowlan and Browne. It is clear that the *coincidentia oppositorum*, the real unity of apparent opposites, is only one small aspect of an epic quest in which the dragon to be slain, the enemy of the quest, is co-incidence itself. A coincidence is a piece of design that one cannot find a use for, and in that sense there is no such thing as a coincidence in *Finnegans Wake*. If we ask who the hero is that is to achieve such a quest, the answer is, clearly, the reader of the book, "the ideal reader suffering from an ideal insomnia," as Joyce says. The reader is not only the hero of *Finnegans Wake;* he is also the only character involved with it who is never allowed to sleep or dream.

The merging of the individual dream with the total dream of mankind appears to be the central postulate on which Joyce's book is based. In one extraordinary interview, Joyce spoke of himself as a kind of psychopomp summoning the spirits of the dead. Naturally he would be most attracted to highly speculative thinkers who try to break out of the rigid Cartesian dualism in which so much of our intellectual attitude is still confined. One such thinker is Samuel Butler: Butler is not a major influence on *Finnegans Wake,* but there are several references to *Erewhon* and *The Way of All Flesh*. The latter is a bildungsroman in which the author examines a younger version of himself in order to objectify the younger self and break something of its hold on him, as Joyce's *Portrait* does with Stephen Dedalus.

In his biological writings, Butler deals with the conception of personality in such a way as to show that the personality has no clear circumference or center. All life interpenetrates with all other life, and all life constitutes a single being. In *The Way of All Flesh* he draws the inference that eventually we shall have to abolish the distinction of subject and object, internal and external, and live and work within a purely metaphorical universe. A few pages further on Butler quotes his hero as saying that no incontrovertible first premise for a philosophical system can ever be found, because "no one could get behind Bishop Berkeley." Joyce's references to the story of Buckley and the Russian General, already mentioned, often refer to Buckley as "Berkeley," which would associate the "Russian General" with, perhaps,

Lenin, who made Berkeley the cockshy for the bourgeois idealism he was out to destroy. In itself this is probably overzealous
commentary, but it is not inherently impossible that Berkeley
should be for Joyce, as for Yeats, the Irish philosopher who had
effectively removed the barriers between waking and dreaming
life.

Butler and Berkeley lead us to an idealistic tradition from
which Bruno also derived. In his book *God the Known and Unknown*, Butler equates his conception of the unity of all life with
a "known" aspect of God. Such a foray into natural theology may
seem unusual for a post-Darwinian writer, but it brings us close
to Bruno's doctrine *natura est deus in rebus*, that nature is an incarnation of God in whom "all is in all." We referred earlier to
Joyce's remark that Vico had anticipated Freud: perhaps, similarly, Bruno for him had anticipated something of Jung's "collective unconscious."

Like other scriptures, *Finnegans Wake* begins with the standard
mythical themes of beginning: creation, fall (or some other myth
about how man became mortal), and a universal deluge. In *Finnegans Wake* these are all essentially the same event: when man
fell, the world he fell into was this one, and this world is symbolically submarine as well as subterranean. The assimilation of
the three events is identical with Blake's myth of the fall when,
as he says in *Europe:* "the five senses whelm'd / In deluge o'er the
earth-born man." In Blake's *Jerusalem* Albion lies asleep in Atlantis at the bottom of the "Sea of Time and Space" for most of the
poem, the archetypal leviathan or sea monster of the indefinite.
Joyce's Finn is a land monster or "behemoth" whose "bronto-
ichthyian form" (7: 14, 20) can be dimly discerned in the landscape.

Freud's analysis of dreams gives us little sense of the real
nature and importance of the anxiety dream, the deep uneasy
guilt feelings that can hardly be explained as a mere blocking of
desire. There is, however, an extraordinary flash of insight in De
Quincey's mail-coach essay, where De Quincey speaks of a sudden
crisis in his own experience passing into his dreams and merging
there with a sense of original sin, of the kind which no doubt
prompted the fall myth itself, and which, he suggests, perhaps
everybody dreams over again every night. Nobody in *Finnegans*

Wake seems to have heard of De Quincey except the least likely character, Isabel (285, n. 6), but the individual dream of the tavernkeeper at least is constantly losing or finding its identity in some myth of the fall of man.

Mysterious things are hinted at about the dreamer's sons, who have expanded into three soldiers and remind us of the sons of Noah, of whom one saw his drunken father as he should not have been seen. The daughter has become two girls, whose bladders begin the running of water that flows through the book, where the voyeurism goes in the opposite direction. There is also an encounter in Phoenix Park, a place associated with death (the Phoenix Park murders) and treachery (the attempt to involve Parnell in them which was frustrated by one conspirator's misspelling of "hesitancy"). HCE is accosted by a "cad" (cadet or younger son) with a "pipe" (French slang for penis) and asked for the time. He gives a stuttering answer and his "hesitancy" starts rumors spreading around the world. In a larger context the stutter marks the mechanical repetition of moments that is our experience of time, which according to St. Augustine began with the fall. The time when the question is asked appears to be 11:32, which is also twenty-eight to twelve, those being numbers prominent in human efforts to work out a calendar with the solar and lunar cycles. Both have associations in the book. Isabel's schoolmates, called the "Maggies," number twenty-eight, and the twelve mourners who persuade Finnegan to go back to sleep suggest a zodiacal cycle, just as, according to Blake, the twelve tribes of Israel in the desert were hypnotized by the zodiac ("sons of Albion") into giving up their revolution for a deified robot's legal code.

We are accustomed nowadays to hear that the unconscious, however defined, is linguistically structured as well as the consciousness. Here again is something that Joyce might have absorbed from earlier writers: Butler, for example, tells us that all genuine and achieved knowledge is unconscious knowledge, the consciousness being concerned only with exploring the new and as yet unassimilated. In the conscious world verbal exchange, though the chief means of communication, is also used quite as much to conceal or disguise communication. We build up ironic, self-enclosed verbal structures that others can penetrate only obliquely, or else we stylize what we say in dramatic attitudes conditioned by the characters of those we talk to. Meanwhile,

the verbal currents boiling and swirling around in our unconscious keep up a constant jockeying for power, each trying to get
to a place where it can dominate the ego. This gives a particular
importance to the message from the outside that bypasses the
conscious mind and strikes directly into the unconscious. According to Vico, the cycle of history begins with the thunderclap,
interpreted by men (then giants) as the voice of God. Later, we
have oracles purporting to carry the voice of divine authority, and
eventually (to move outside Vico), the sacred scripture develops
a codified body of such messages.

In *Finnegans Wake* the inner babble of the individual mind
expands into a vision of mankind as dreaming a communal dream
of conflicting voices, with occasionally a voice of command or
exceptional authority penetrating and for an instant silencing the
tumult. The series of thunderclaps, of a hundred letters each,
that mark the beginning of a new phase of history begins on the
opening page, and HCE is associated with the "earwig" or *perce-
oreille* ("Persse O'Reilly"), the insect that traditionally penetrates
the ear of a sleeper. We may compare a line from the close of
Blake's *Jerusalem,* just as the final apocalypse begins: "Her voice
pierc'd Albions clay cold ear." It is only the voice of the poet, the
successor in society of the oracle and scripture, that carries this
authority now, though the voice is constantly neglected. "Hear
the voice of the Bard," Blake pleaded, and went on to say that
the Bard's message is outside time and descends directly from the
voice of God in Eden. It was also Blake who applied to himself
the motto of John the Baptist, "The voice of one crying in the
wilderness."

For a century after Blake's death poets were fascinated by
the figure of John the Baptist, the herald and announcer of a new
age, whose passion, unlike that of Jesus, involved their cherished
theme of the femme fatale. Yeats, we remember, devoted much
of his energy to proclaiming a new age and seeing signs of it in
contemporary Ireland, even though, according to the most reli-
able of his clocks, the Christian era still has another thousand
years to go. At the end of *Portrait of the Artist as a Young Man,*
Stephen identifies his friend Cranly with John the Baptist,
clearly reserving a greater role for himself, which in *Ulysses* it
seems obvious he is not going to attain. *Finnegans Wake* seems to
me largely based on the theme of annunciation, with Vico and
Bruno standing guard over it partly because their first names,

Giambattista and Giordano, suggest John the Baptist at the Jordan.

The struggles of Shem and Shaun, with their metamorphoses, form the main action of the book. Shem is the "penman" or "punman" who carries on the poetic and oracular tradition, and two elements in his technique are important for understanding his oracular role. One is the incessant use of the thematic phrase. Such phrases as "the same anew," "up guards, and at them," "Honi soit qui mal y pense," and dozens of others appear in astonishing variations throughout. This device is often linked to Wagner's leitmotif technique, although Joyce was not really a Wagnerian. In a preliterary age such thematic phrases would be magical formulas. The other technical element, which also harks back to preliterary magic, shows the poet as preeminently the knower of names, and, in the unconscious, calling a name can command an appearance. For all the distortion, there is a continuous orgy of naming in *Finnegans Wake:* books of the Bible, suras of the Koran, lyrics of Tom Moore, catalogues of rivers and cities, just for a start.

I have elsewhere spoken of two aspects of poetry deeply involved with the unconscious as charm and riddle. Charm in particular is linked to the oracular, to the sense of magical compulsion in its tradition, to an appeal to the past that takes the form "as that was, so may this be." Riddle is rather a perplexing of the conscious intelligence that prompts one to "guess" or identify the object it presents without naming. The riddle is the home of the pun, the metaphor, the verbal clusters formed in the unconscious and rising to the conscious surface. The charm is the home of incantation, of the mystery hidden in sound. Charm and riddle are a psychological contrast, and if we stayed entirely within either area we should get a bad case of what Eliot calls dissociated sensibility. If we stayed with the oracular world of charm, everything would seem solemn, awful, portentous, and the least breath of humor or irreverence would destroy the mood. If we stayed with the world of riddle, we should be subjected to an endless stream of irresponsible wisecracks. To walk the razor's edge between the two, to achieve an oracular charm that is witty and a wit that evokes profound and haunting depths of linguistic experience, is a considerable tour de force, not to speak of keeping it up for over six hundred pages.

In the first chapter we are told a strange tale of a certain Jarl

van Hoother, the earl of Howth in a Dutch or Scandinavian disguise, who is another context of HCE and who has two sons,
named, in this tale, Tristopher and Hilary. A female figure
known as a "prankquean" kidnaps first one son and then the
other, keeping each in the wilderness for forty years and convert-
ing them to something else. Trisopher is converted to being a
"luderman," presumably some form of playboy; Hilary is converted to a "tristian," a sorrowful Christian or Tristram. As we
read this we are reminded of Bruno's personal motto, used at the
beginning of his play *Il Candelaio* and elsewhere: *In tristitia hi-
laris, in hilaritate tristis.* The solemn and the gay are interchangeable aspects of the same thing, and this may well be the essence,
for Joyce, of Bruno's theory of polarity.

Shem is the writer; Shaun is ultimately the product of what
is written. Shaun is, first, the public that receives the poet's message, ridicules and belittles it when it cannot ignore it, and yet
unconsciously keeps transforming and often perverting it into
social institutions and codes of behavior. Shem works directly in
the stream of time that supplies the energy of history; Shaun
spatializes what Shem does, though he himself does not really
know this, and regards himself as the intermediary between authority, whatever its source, and the public. Shem fails to guess
the most important riddle with which he is confronted, the "he-
liotrope" riddle in the mime chapter, but Shaun answers a great
many riddles, his confidence undiminished by the number of answers that are either wrong or irrelevant. Finally, in the fifteenth
chapter near the end, Shaun is subjected to a close and sustained
inquiry which brings out the fact that he is really the sum total
of the book itself, as one of its characters after another emerges
from him. The last one to emerge is HCE, who speaks as the
builder of cities and civilizations throughout history.

Yet even HCE is not the fundamental force of history, for
the great cities of the past are ruins now, and the most impressive
erections disappear in a world where "Gricks may rise and Troy-
sirs fall." Below him is the river of time, the ALP who continually renews herself, and HCE along with herself. All through
the book we keep hearing about a "letter" written by ALP, lost
in a dungheap but representing a creative energy of communication that Shem is in much closer touch with than either Shaun
or HCE. Shaun supplies us with a greatly distorted version of
this letter, but a more authentic one emerges at the very end,

just before the final farewell speech by ALP as she flows out and merges with the sea. ALP herself can only die and renew: as she sinks into her father the sea we catch a glimpse of the conjunction of a bird and woman that marks the starting point of a new cycle of time, like those of Leda and the swan and the dove and the Virgin in Yeats: "If I seen him bearing down on me now under whitespread wings like he'd come from Arkangels, I sink I'd die down over his feet, humbly dumbly, only to washup" (628: 9). But unlike the Magdalen whom she echoes, she is not present at a resurrection, only at a renewal. The book goes around in the circle of the *ricorso*. But there is another kind of vision hinted at in the very end of her letter: "Hence we've lived in two worlds. He is another he what stays under the himp of holth" (619: 11).

Of the two worlds, the higher one is the world of the turning cycle of life, death, and renewal; below it is the still sleeping Finn who is all mankind. When we are told at the beginning of the book that Finn is about to be superseded by HCE, we can see an analogy with the relation of Ireland to the constant stream of Irish invaders, Danish, Roman, British, and the rest. At the end we get a glimpse of an apocalypse opening up from below that will swallow the cycle: this does not happen, but the last line of *Finnegans Wake* contains the little noticed phrase "till thousends thee." What looks like the primary meaning of this is "till thou sends thee" or thyself, a second coming or reunion of HCE and ALP with a permanently awakened Finn. We are left with the sense that the imagery of the cycle, with its death followed by renewal and return, is the only imagery that human language, conscious or unconscious, can draw on to express whatever is beyond the cycle. Also that there is one polarity in which the opposed forces can never unite: the apocalyptic separation of the states of life and death.

We are left, finally, with the ultimate categories of time and space. Time is the inner energy of life, flowing in a relatively undisturbed form during sleep; our waking consciousness constructs a spatialized world, HCE's world of buildings and mountains. Joyce, who identifies with Shem, was told during his lifetime by various Shaun figures, such as Wyndham Lewis, that he ought to pay more attention to the spatial and objective world. Of Joyce's two mentors, Vico was particularly the theorist of time and history; Bruno, with his doctrine of an infinite universe, explored a new conception of space, pointing out that Aristotle, for example, who was so constantly quoted against him, had no word for space. Such words as *chora* and *topos* mean not space but place, space *there*. And yet Vico's cyclical conception of historical process is really a vision of time within a spatial metaphor, and Bruno's conception of the identity of polarized opposites a vision of the spatial subject-object confrontation dissolving back into a temporal flux. All our experience collapses in on a deadlock of categories, and there is nothing in human language, the expanded language of *Finnegans Wake* to get us out. Nothing, that is, except its confrontation with an insomniac reader who is still outside the book, struggling to make a sense of it that cannot ultimately be limited even to Joyce's sense. Such a reader is the closest we can come to Lewis Carroll's Humpty Dumpty, HCE before he fell off his wall, who could explain all the poems that had ever been written, along with a number that hadn't been written yet.

When *Finnegans Wake* was published and the responses confused and disappointing, Joyce stressed the wit of the book as its more obvious appeal, and asked why nobody could see that it was funny. But we should not overlook its seriousness as well, or the fact that he apparently read, for instance, Blavatsky's *Isis Unveiled* with close attention, was genuinely interested in Yeats's *Vision*, except that he regretted, as do other readers of Yeats, its being imprisoned in a system disconnected from the poetry, and even spoke of minor and less seminal books on comparative mythology, such as Allen Upward's *Divine Mystery*, as coming close to doing what he was trying to do in his way. The merits of these books are not significant: what they indicate is the existence of a motive in Joyce's compulsively careful organization very different from what the puns and so-called obscenities indicate by themselves. One can match the charm-and-riddle language of the book with much of the Old Testament and the Vedic Hymns, but one can also find a good deal of it in both Vico and Bruno. Vico's "new science" opened up a whole new field of scholarly endeavor, yet his central myth, which begins with giants terrified of a thunderclap, running into caves dragging their wives behind them, and so instituting private property, reads almost like parody. Bruno is a writer whose satire and scatology almost matches Joyce's own, who wrote a great deal of self-obsessed braggadocio, abuse of contemporaries, long meaningless catalogues, and heavy-handed humor, but who nonetheless died a martyr to his vision. Both writers are full of the contradictions of creative power itself, and both find their tradition continued in the epic of a drunken Irishman's mock funeral wake that expands into the sleep of Eve and Adam under the circling stars.

Index

375